HONDA

400-450 TWINS 1978-1987
SERVICE • REPAIR • MAINTENANCE

By

ED SCOTT

ALAN AHLSTRAND

Editor

CLYMER PUBLICATIONS

*World's largest publisher of books devoted exclusively
to automobiles and motorcycles*

**A division of INTERTEC PUBLISHING CORPORATION
P.O. Box 12901, Overland Park, Kansas 66212**

Copyright ©1989 Intertec Publishing Corporation

FIRST EDITION
First Printing November, 1978
Second Printing November, 1979
Third Printing June, 1979

SECOND EDITION
Revised by Ed Scott to include 1979 models
First Printing September, 1979

THIRD EDITION
Revised by Ed Scott to include 1980 models
First Printing December, 1980

FOURTH EDITION
Revised by Ed Scott to include 1981-1982 models
First Prnting March, 1983
Second Printing September, 1983
Third Printing June, 1984
Fourth Printing March, 1985
Fifth Printing March, 1986
Sixth Printing April, 1987
Seventh Printing November, 1987

FIFTH EDITION
Revised by Ed Scott to include 1983-1987 models
First Printing May, 1989

Printed in U.S.A.

ISBN: 0-89287-234-9

MOTORCYCLE INDUSTRY COUNCIL

COVER: Photographed by Mark Clifford.

Chapter One
General Information
1

Chapter Two
Troubleshooting
2

Chapter Three
Lubrication, Maintenance and Tune-up
3

Chapter Four
Engine
4

Chapter Five
Clutch and Manual Transmission
5

Chapter Six
Torque Converter and Automatic Transmission
6

Chapter Seven
Fuel and Exhaust Systems
7

Chapter Eight
Electrical System
8

Chapter Nine
Front Suspension and Steering
9

Chapter Ten
Rear Suspension
10

Chapter Eleven
Brakes
11

Chapter Twelve
Frame and Repainting
12

Index
13

CONTENTS

QUICK REFERENCE DATA IX

CHAPTER ONE
GENERAL INFORMATION 1

Manual organization
Notes, cautions and warnings
Safety first
Service hints
Special tips
Torque specifications
Fasteners

Lubricants
Expendable supplies
Parts replacement
Serial numbers
Basic hand tools
Tune-up and troubleshooting tools
Riding safety

CHAPTER TWO
TROUBLESHOOTING 19

Operating requirements
Emergency troubleshooting
Engine starting
Engine performance
Engine noises
Excessive vibration

Lubrication troubles
Manual and automatic
    tramsmission
Front suspension and steering
Brake problems

CHAPTER THREE
LUBRICATION, MAINTENANCE AND TUNE-UP 25

Pre-checks
Routine checks
Service intervals
Tires and wheels

Battery
Periodic lubrication
Periodic maintenance
Tune-up

CHAPTER FOUR
ENGINE 68

Engine principles
Servicing engine in frame
Engine
Cylinder head, camshaft and rocker
  arm assemblies (1978-1981)
Cylinder head, camshaft and rocker
  arm assemblies (1982-on)
Valves and valve components
Camshaft chain tensioner
Cylinder
Piston, piston pins and piston rings

Alternator
Oil pump
Oil cooler (1982-on except Rebel 450)
Oil pressure relief valve
Crankcase and balancer system
Crankshaft and connecting rods
Electric starter gears
Kickstarter (manual transmission)
Kickstarter (automatic transission)
Break-in

CHAPTER FIVE
CLUTCH AND MANUAL TRANSMISSION 147

Clutch
Clutch cable
External gearshift mechanism
Manual transmission and
  internal shift mechanism
Manual transmission

5-Speed manual transmission
  (CB400T I, CB400T II, CM400T,
  CM400C, CM400E)
6-Speed manual transmission
Internal shift mechanism

CHAPTER SIX
TORQUE CONVERTER AND AUTOMATIC TRANSMISSION 180

Torque converter
Automatic transmission
Internal shift mechanism

Gearshift drum and fork
Oil cooler

CHAPTER SEVEN
FUEL AND EXHAUST SYSTEMS 198

Carburetors
Carburetor operation
Carburetor service
Carburetor adjustments
Throttle cable replacement
Choke cable replacement
Fuel cable replacement
Fuel shutoff valve
Fuel tank

Fuel filter
Gasoline/alcohol blend test
Crankcase breather system
  (1986-on U.S. only)
Evaporative emission control system
  (1985-on California models only)
Exhaust emission control system
  (1986 CB450SC California models only)
Exhaust system

CHAPTER EIGHT
ELECTRICAL SYSTEM 233

Charging system
Alternator
Voltage regulator/rectifier
Ignition system
Ignition coil
Starting system
Starter solenoid

Lighting system
Clutch switch
Sidestand switch
Horn
Instrument cluster
Speedometer and indicator panel
Fuses

CHAPTER NINE
FRONT SUSPENSION AND STEERING 270

Front wheel (1980-1983 drum brake)
Front wheel (single piston
   caliper disc brake)
Front wheel (dual-piston caliper
   model except Rebel 450)
Front wheel (Rebel 450)
Front hub
Wheels
Tire changing
Handlebars
Steering head and stem
   (loose ball bearings)

Steering head and stem
   (assembled ball bearings)
Steering head bearing races
   (all models)
Front forks
Non-air assist front forks
   (Rebel 450)
Non-air assist front forks
   (all models except Rebel 450)
Air-assist front forks
Fork inspection (all models)

CHAPTER TEN
REAR SUSPENSION 319

Rear wheel
Rear hub
Rear hub (1978-1981 spoke wheel)
Rear hub (Rebel 450 spoke wheel,
   Comstar and Comcast wheel)

Driven sprocket assembly
Drive chain
Rear shock absorbers
Swing arm

CHAPTER ELEVEN
BRAKES 346

Front drum brake
Rear drum brake
Drum brake inspection,
   front and rear
Front disc brake
Front disc brake pad
   replacement
Front master cylinder (1978-1983)

Front master cylinder (1985-on)
Front caliper
Front caliper rebuilding
Brake disc
Front brake hose replacement
Draining the system
Bleeding the system

CHAPTER TWELVE
FRAME AND REPAINTING 404

Centerstand
Kickstand

Footpegs
Frame

INDEX 408

WIRING DIAGRAMS .... end of book

QUICK REFERENCE DATA

TIRE PRESSURES *

Model	Up to 206 lbs. (90 kg) psi	kg/cm²	Up to vehicle load limit psi	kg/cm²
CB400T, CB400A				
Front	24	1.75	24	1.75
Rear	32	2.25	36	2.50
1979-1980 CM400T, 1979-1980 CM400A, CM400E				
Front	24	1.75	24	1.75
Rear	28	2.0	36	2.50
1981 CM400A				
Front	28	2.0	28	2.0
Rear	28	2.0	36	2.50
1981 CM400E				
Front	24	1.75	28	2.0
Rear	28	2.0	36	2.50
1981 CB400T, 1981 CM400C, CM400T				
Front	28	2.0	28	2.0
Rear	28	2.0	36	2.50
CM450A, CM450C, CM450T				
Front	28	2.0	28	2.0
Rear	28	2.0	36	2.50
CM450E				
Front	24	1.75	28	2.0
Rear	24	1.75	36	2.50
CB450SC				
Front	28	2.0	28	2.0
Rear	28	2.0	36	2.50
Rebel 450				
Front	28	2.0	28	2.0
Rear	28	2.0	28	2.0

* Tire inflation pressure for factory equipped tires. Aftermarket tire inflation pressure may vary according to tire manufacturer's instructions.

REPLACEMENT BULBS

Item	Number
Headlight	
Rebel 450	12V 60/55W
All other models	12V 50/35W
Tail/brakelight	SAE 1157
Directional	
Front	
1978-1983	SAE 1034
1985-on	SAE 1073
Rear	SAE 1073
Instrument lights	SAE 57
Running light (models so equipped)	SAE 1034

MAINTENANCE AND TUNE-UP TORQUE SPECIFICATIONS

Item	N·m	ft.-lb.
Oil filter cover bolt	29-31	21-22
Oil drain bolt		
1978-1984	25-35	18-25
1985-on	32-38	23-27
Fork cap bolt	15-30	11-22
1982-1985 air-assist models		
and Rebel 450	15-30	11-22
1986 CM450SC	16-20	12-14
Fork bridge bolts		
Upper (1982-on)	9-13	7-9
Lower (1982-on)	18-25	13-18
Front fork interconnecting air hose (1982-on)		
Air connector-to-fork cap bolt	4-7	3-5
Air hose-to-fork cap bolt	4-7	3-5
Air hose-to-connector	15-20	11-14
Handlebar holder bolts	18-25	13-18
Rear axle nut		
Rebel 450	80-100	58-72
CB450SC	90-100	65-72
All other models	68-100	50-72
Fuel strainer cup	3-5	2-4
(models so equipped)		
Balancer chain		
8 mm adjust nut	20-24	15-18
Adjuster plate		
8 mm nut	20-24	15-18
10 mm nut	30-35	22-25
Cylinder head bolts	30-35	22-25

TUNE-UP SPECIFICATIONS

Valve clearance	
Intake	0.08-0.12 mm (0.003-0.005 in.)
Exhaust	0.12-0.16 mm (0.005-0.006 in.)
Compression pressure	
1979-1985	1,172-1,368 kPa (171-199 psi)
1986 CB450SC	1,000-1,400 kPa (145-205 psi)
Rebel 450	1,019-1,215 kPa (157-185 psi)
Spark plug type	
Standard heat range	
1978-1981	ND X24ES-U or NGK D8EA
1982	ND X24ESR-U or NGK DR8ES-L
1983-on	ND X24EPR-U9 NGK DPR8EA-9
Spark plug gap	
1978-1981	0.6-0.7 mm (0.024-0.028 in.)
1982-on	0.8-0.9 mm (0.032-0.036 in.)
Idle speed	
Manual transmission	1,200 ±100 rpm
Automatic transmission	1,250 ±100 rpm

ENGINE OIL CAPACITY

Engine size	Oil drain		Rebuild	
	U.S. qt.	Liter	U.S. qt.	Liter
Manual transmission	2.6	2.5	3.2	3.0
Automatic transmission	2.6	2.5	3.5	3.3

FRONT FORK OIL CAPACITY *

Model	cc	fl. oz.
CB400T	175	5.9
CM400A, CM400C, CM400T, CB45OT	172	5.8
CM400E	135	4.6
CM450A, CM450C	105	6.9
CM450SC	185	2.26
Rebel 450	114	4.5

* Capacity for each fork leg.

DRIVE CHAIN REPLACEMENT NUMBERS

Model	Number
CB400T, CB400A, CB450T, CM400E	DID 50DS-100L or RK 50KS-100L
CM400A, CM400C, CM400T	DID 50DS-102L or RK 50KS-102L
CM450A, CM450C, CM450E	DID 50DS-102L or RK 50KS-102L
CB450SC	DID 50H1-106LE or Takasago 520-106LE
Rebel 450	DID 525V or RK525 MO-21

HONDA

400-450 TWINS 1978-1987

SERVICE • REPAIR • MAINTENANCE

Introduction

This detailed comprehensive manual covers the Honda 400-450 series twins from 1978-1987. The expert text gives complete information on maintenance, tune-up, repair and overhaul. Hundreds of photos and drawings guide you through every step. Where differences occur among the models, they are clearly identified. The book includes all you will need to know to keep your Honda running right.

A shop manual is a reference. You want to be able to find information fast. As in all Clymer books, this one is designed with you in mind. All chapters are thumb tabbed. Important items are extensively indexed at the rear of the book. All procedures, tables, photos, etc., in this manual are for the reader who may be working on the bike for the first time or using this manual for the first time. All the most frequently used specifications and capacities are summarized in the *Quick Reference Data* pages at the front of the book.

Keep the book handy in your tool box. It will help you better understand how your bike runs, lower your repair costs and generally improve your satisfaction with the bike.

CHAPTER ONE

GENERAL INFORMATION

MANUAL ORGANIZATION

This chapter provides general information and discusses equipment and tools useful both for preventive maintenance and troubleshooting.

Chapter Two provides methods and suggestions for quick and accurate diagnosis and repair of problems. Troubleshooting procedures discuss typical symptoms and logical methods to pinpoint the trouble.

Chapter Three explains all periodic lubrication and routine maintenance necessary to keep the Honda running well. Chapter Three also includes recommended tune-up procedures, eliminating the need to constantly consult chapters on the various assemblies.

Subsequent chapters describe specific systems such as the engine, clutch, transmission (manual and automatic), fuel, exhaust, suspension and brakes. Each chapter provides disassembly, repair and assembly procedures in simple step-by-step form. If a repair is impractical for a home mechanic, it is so indicated. It is usually faster and less expensive to take such repairs to a dealer or competent repair shop. Specifications concerning a particular system are included at the end of the appropriate chapter.

Some of the procedures in this manual specify special tools. In most cases, the tool is illustrated either in actual use or alone. Well equipped mechanics may find they can substitute similar tools already on hand or can fabricate their own.

All dimensions and capacities are expressed in English units familiar to U.S. mechanics as well as in metric units. Refer to **Table 1** for Metric to U.S. conversions.

Tables 1-4 are at the end of this chapter.

NOTES, CAUTIONS AND WARNINGS

The terms NOTE, CAUTION and WARNING have specific meanings in this manual. A NOTE provides additional information to make a step or procedure easier or clearer. Disregarding a NOTE could cause inconvenience, but would not cause equipment damage or personal injury.

A CAUTION emphasizes areas where equipment damage could result. Disregarding a CAUTION could cause permanent mechanical damage; however, personal injury is unlikely.

A WARNING emphasizes areas where personal injury or even death could result from negligence. Mechanical damage may also occur. WARNINGS are to be taken *seriously*. In some cases, serious injury or death has resulted from disregarding similar warnings.

Throughout this manual keep in mind 2 conventions. "Front" refers to the front of the bike. The front of any component, such as the engine, is the end which faces toward the front of the bike. The "left-" and "right-hand" sides refer to the position of the parts as viewed by a rider sitting on the seat facing forward. For example, the throttle control is on the right-hand side and the clutch lever is on the left-hand side. These rules are simple, but even experienced mechanics occasionally become disoriented.

SAFETY FIRST

Professional mechanics can work for years and never sustain a serious injury. If you observe a few rules of common sense and safety, you can enjoy many hours servicing your own machine. If you ignore these rules you can hurt yourself or damage the bike.

1. *Never* use gasoline as a cleaning solvent.
2. Never smoke or use a torch in the vicinity of flammable liquids such as cleaning solvent in open containers.
3. If welding or brazing is required on the machine, remove the fuel tank to a safe distance, at least 50 feet away.
4. Use the proper sized wrenches to avoid damage to nuts and injury to yourself.
5. When loosening a tight or stuck nut, think about what would happen if the wrench should slip. Be careful; protect yourself accordingly.
6. Keep your work area clean and uncluttered.
7. Wear safety goggles during all operations involving drilling, grinding or the use of a cold chisel.
8. Never use worn tools.
9. Keep a fire extinguisher handy and be sure it is rated for gasoline and electrical fires.

SERVICE HINTS

Most of the service procedures covered are straightforward and can be performed by anyone reasonably handy with tools. It is suggested, however, that you consider your own capabilities carefully before attempting any operation involving major disassembly of the engine.

Take your time and do the job right. Do not forget that a newly rebuilt engine must be broken in the same as a new one. Keep the rpm within the limits given in your owner's manual when you get back on the road.

1. There are many items available that can be used on your hands before and after working on your bike. A little preparation before getting "all greased up" will help when cleaning up later. Before starting out, work Vaseline, soap or a product such as Invisible Glove (**Figure 1**) onto your forearms, into your hands and under your fingernails and cuticles. This will make cleanup a lot easier. For cleanup, use a waterless hand soap such as Sta-Lube and then finish up with powdered Boraxo and a fingernail brush.

2. Repairs go much faster and easier if the bike is clean before you begin work. There are special cleaners, such as Gunk or Bel-Ray Degreaser (**Figure 2**) for washing the engine and related parts. Just spray or brush on the cleaning solution, let it stand, then rinse it away with a garden hose. Clean all oily or greasy parts with cleaning solvent as you remove them.

> *WARNING*
> *Never use gasoline as a cleaning agent. It presents an extreme fire hazard. Be sure to work in a well-ventilated area when using cleaning solvent. Keep a fire extinguisher, rated for gasoline fires, handy in any case.*

3. Special tools are required for some repair procedures. These may be purchased from a dealer or motorcycle shop, rented from a tool rental dealer or fabricated by a mechanic or machinist—often at a considerable savings.

4. Much of the labor charged for by mechanics is to remove and disassemble other parts to reach the defective unit. It is usually possible to perform the

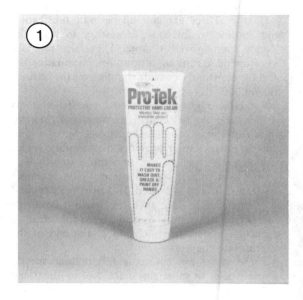

preliminary operations yourself and then take the defective unit in to the dealer for repair.

5. Once you have decided to tackle the job yourself, read the entire section *completely* while looking at the actual parts before starting the job. Making sure you have identified the proper one. Study the illustrations and text until you have a good idea of what is involved in completing the job satisfactorily. If special tools or replacement parts are required, make arrangements to get them before you start. It is frustrating and time-consuming to get partly into a job and then be unable to complete it.

6. Simple wiring checks can be easily made at home, but knowledge of electronics is almost a necessity for performing tests with complicated electronic testing gear.

7. Whenever servicing the engine or transmission, or when removing a suspension component, the bike should be secured in a safe manner. If the bike is to be parked on the sidestand or center stand, check the stand to make sure it is secure and not damaged. Block the front and rear wheels if they remain on the ground. A small hydraulic jack and a block of wood can be used to raise the chassis. If the transmission is not going to be worked on and the drive chain is connected to the rear wheel, shift the transmission into first gear.

8. Disconnect the negative battery cable when working on or near the electrical, clutch, or starter systems and before disconnecting any electrical wires. On most batteries, the negative terminal will be marked with a minus (-) sign and the positive terminal with a plus (+) sign.

9. During disassembly of parts, keep a few general cautions in mind. Force is rarely needed to get

things apart. If parts are a tight fit, such as a bearing in a case, there is usually a tool designed to separate them. Never use a screwdriver to pry parts with machined surfaces such as crankcase halves. You will mar the surfaces and end up with leaks.

10. Make diagrams or take a Polaroid picture wherever similar-appearing parts are found. For instance, crankcase bolts are often not the same length. You may think you can remember where everything came from, but mistakes are costly. There is also the possibility you may be sidetracked and not return to work for days or even weeks, in which interval carefully laid out parts may have become disturbed.

11. Tag all similar internal parts for location and mark all mating parts for position. Record number and thickness of any shims as they are removed. Small parts such as bolts can be identified by placing them in plastic sandwich bags. Seal and label them with masking tape.

12. Wiring should be tagged with masking tape and marked as each wire is removed. Again, do not rely on memory alone.

13. Protect finished surfaces from physical damage or corrosion. Keep gasoline and hydraulic brake fluid off plastic parts and painted and plated surfaces.

14. Frozen or very tight bolts and screws can often be loosened by soaking with penetrating oil, such as WD-40 or Liquid Wrench, then sharply striking the bolt head a few times with a hammer and punch (or screwdriver for screws). Avoid heat unless absolutely necessary, since it may melt, warp or remove the temper from many parts.

15. No parts, except those assembled with a press fit, require unusual force during assembly. If a part is hard to remove or install, find out why before proceeding.

16. Cover all openings after removing parts to keep dirt, small tools, etc., from falling in.

17. Wiring connections and brake components should be kept clean and free of grease and oil.

18. When assembling 2 parts, start all fasteners, then tighten evenly.

19. When assembling parts, be sure all shims and washers are installed exactly as they came out.

20. Whenever a rotating part butts against a stationary part, look for a shim or washer.

21. Use new gaskets if there is any doubt about the condition of the old ones. A thin coat of oil on gaskets may help them seal effectively.

22. Heavy grease can be used to hold small parts in place if they tend to fall out during assembly. However, keep grease and oil away from electrical and brake components.

23. High spots may be sanded off a piston with sandpaper, but fine emery cloth and oil will do a much more professional job.

24. Carbon can be removed from the head, the piston crown and the exhaust port with a dull screwdriver. Do *not* scratch machined surfaces. Wipe off the surface with a clean cloth when finished.

25. The carburetors are best cleaned by disassembling them and soaking the parts in a commercial carburetor cleaner. Never soak gaskets and rubber parts in these cleaners. Never use wire to clean out jets and air passages; they are easily damaged. Use compressed air to blow out the carburetor *after* the float has been removed.

26. A baby bottle makes a good measuring device for adding oil to the front forks. Get one that is graduated in fluid ounces and cubic centimeters. After it has been used for this purpose, do *not* let a small child drink out of it as there will always be an oil residue in it.

27. Some operations require the use of a press. It would be wiser to have these performed by a shop equipped for such work, rather than trying to do the job yourself with makeshift equipment. Other procedures require precise measurements. Unless you have the skills and equipment required, it would be better to have a qualified repair shop make the measurements for you.

SPECIAL TIPS

Because of the extreme demands placed on a bike, several points should be kept in mind when performing service and repair. The following items are general suggestions that may improve the overall life of the machine and help avoid costly failures.

1. Use a locking compound such as Loctite Lock N' Seal No. 242 (blue Loctite) on all bolts and nuts, even if they are secured with lockwashers. This type of Loctite does not harden completely and allows easy removal of the bolt or nut. A screw or bolt lost from an engine cover or bearing retainer could easily cause serious and expensive damage before its loss is noticed. Make sure the threads are clean and free of grease and oil. Clean with contact cleaner before applying the Loctite. When applying Loctite, use a small amount. If too much is used, it can work its way down the threads and stick parts together not meant to be stuck. Keep a tube of Loctite in your tool box. When used properly it is cheap insurance.

2. Use a hammer-driven impact tool to remove and install all bolts, particularly engine cover

screws. These tools help prevent the rounding off of bolt heads and ensure a tight installation.

3. When replacing missing or broken fasteners (bolts, nuts and screws), especially on the engine or frame components, always use Honda replacement parts. They are specially hardened for each application. The wrong 50-cent bolt could easily cause serious and expensive damage, not to mention rider injury.

4. When installing gaskets in the engine, always use Honda replacement gaskets *without* sealer, unless designated. These gaskets are designed to swell when they come in contact with oil. Gasket sealer will prevent the gaskets from swelling as intended, which can result in oil leaks. These Honda gaskets are cut from material of the precise thickness needed. Installation of a too thick or too thin gasket in a critical area could cause engine damage.

TORQUE SPECIFICATIONS

Torque specifications throughout this manual are given in Newton-meters (N•m) and foot-pounds (ft.-lb.). Newton-meters have been adopted in place of meter-kilograms (mkg) in accordance with the International Modernized Metric System. Tool manufacturers offer torque wrenches calibrated in both Newton-meters and foot-pounds.

Existing torque wrenches calibrated in meter-kilograms can be used by performing a simple conversion. All you have to do is move the decimal point one place to the right; for example, 4.7 mkg = 47 N•m. This conversion is accurate

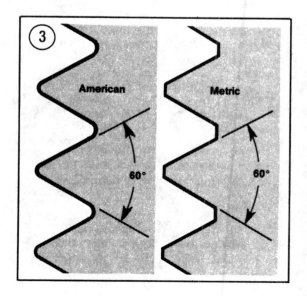

enough for mechanical work even though the exact mathematical conversion is 3.5 mkg = 34.3 N•m.

Refer to **Table 2** for standard torque specifications for various size screws, bolts and nuts that may not be listed in the respective chapters. To use the table, first determine the size of the bolt or nut. Use a vernier caliper and measure across the flats of the nut and across the threads for a bolt.

FASTENERS

The materials and designs of the various fasteners used on your Honda are not arrived at by chance or accident. Fastener design determines the type of tool required to work the fastener. Fastener material is carefully selected to decrease the possibility of physical failure.

Threads

Nuts, bolts and screws are manufactured in a wide range of thread patterns. To join a nut and bolt, the diameter of the bolt and the diameter of the hole in the nuts must be the same. It is just as important that the threads on both be properly matched.

The best way to tell if the threads on 2 fasteners are matched is to turn the nut on the bolt (or the bolt into the threaded hole in the piece of equipment), with your fingers only. Be sure both pieces are clean. If much force is required, check the thread condition on each fastener. If the thread condition is good but the fastener jams, the threads are not compatible. A thread pitch gauge can also be used to determine pitch. Honda motorcycles are manufactured with metric standard fasteners. The threads are cut differently than those of American fasteners (**Figure 3**).

Most threads are cut so that the fastener must be turned *clockwise* to tighten it. These are called right-hand threads. Some fasteners have left-hand threads; they must be turned *counterclockwise* to be tightened. Left-hand threads are used in locations where normal rotation of the equipment would tend to loosen a right-hand threaded fastener. When left-hand threads are used in this manual they are identified in the text.

Machine Screws

There are many different types of machine screws. **Figure 4** shows a number of screw heads requiring different types of turning tools. Heads are also designed to protrude above the metal (round or hex) or to be slight recessed in the metal (flat). See **Figure 5**.

Bolts

Commonly called bolts, the technical name for these fasteners is cap screws. Metric bolts are described by the diameter and pitch (or the distance between each thread). For example an M8×1.25 bolt is one that has a diameter of 8 millimeters and a distance of 1.25 millimeters between each thread. The measurement across 2 flats on the head of the bolt indicates the proper wrench size to be used. Use a vernier caliper and measure across the threads to determine the bolt diameter.

Nuts

Nuts are manufactured in a variety of type and sizes. Most are hexagonal (6-sided) and fit on bolts, screws and studs with the same diameter and pitch.

Figure 6 shows several types of nuts. The common nut is generally used with a lockwasher.

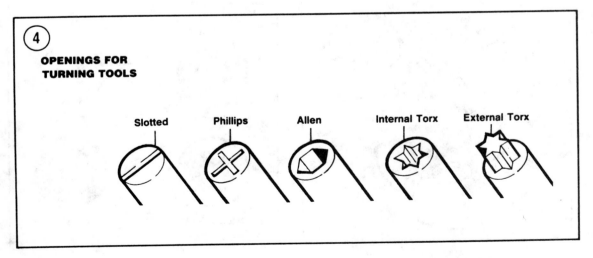

(4)

OPENINGS FOR TURNING TOOLS

Slotted Phillips Allen Internal Torx External Torx

Self-locking nuts have a nylon insert which prevents the nut from loosening; no lockwasher is required. Wing nuts are designed for fast removal by hand. Wing nuts are used for convenience in non-critical locations.

To indicate the size of a nut, manufacturers specify the diameter of the opening and the threads per inch. This is similar to bolt specifications, but without the length dimension. The measurement across 2 flats on the nut indicates the proper wrench size to be used.

Prevailing Torque Fasteners

Several types of bolts, screws and nuts incorporate a system that develops and interference between the bolt, screw nut or tapped hole threads. Interference is achieved in various ways: by distorting threads, coating threads with dry adhesive or nylon, distorting the top of an all-metal nut, using a nylon insert in the center or at the top of a nut, etc.

Prevailing torque fasteners offer greater holding strength and better vibration resistance. Some prevailing torque fasteners can be reused if in good condition. Others, like the nylon insert nut, form an initial locking condition when the nut is first installed; the nylon forms closely to the bolt thread pattern, thus reducing any tendency for the nut to loosen. When the nut is removed, its locking efficiency is greatly reduced. For greatest safety it is recommended that you install new prevailing torque fasteners whenever they are removed.

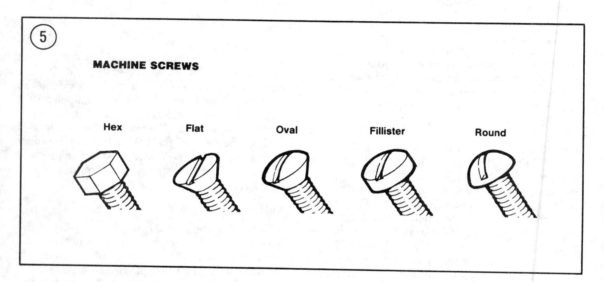

⑤

MACHINE SCREWS

Hex   Flat   Oval   Fillister   Round

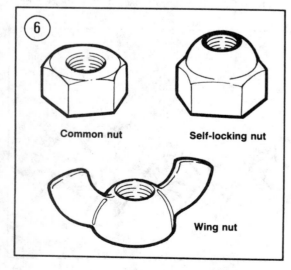

⑥

Common nut   Self-locking nut

Wing nut

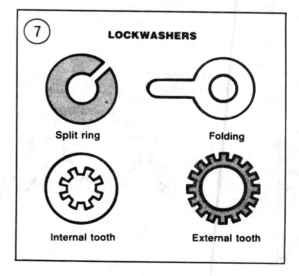

⑦   **LOCKWASHERS**

Split ring   Folding

Internal tooth   External tooth

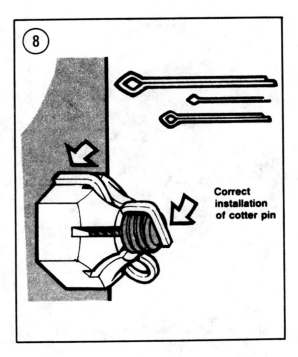

Correct installation of cotter pin

Washers

There are 2 basic types of washers: flat washers and lockwashers. Flat washers are simple discs with a hole to fit a screw or bolt. Lockwashers are designed to prevent a fastener from working loose due to vibration, expansion and contraction. **Figure 7** shows several types of washers. Washers are also used in the following functions:

a. As spacers.

b. To prevent galling or damage of the equipment by the fastener.

c. To help distribute fastener load during torquing.

d. As fluid seals (copper or laminated washers).

Note that flat washers are often used between a fastener to provide a smooth bearing surface. This allows the fastener to be turned easily with a tool.

Cotter Pins

Cotter pins (**Figure 8**) are used to secure special kinds of fasteners. The threaded stud must have a hole in it; the nut or nut lock piece has castellations around which the cotter pin ends wrap. Cotter pins should not be reused after removal as the ends may break and the cotter pin could then fall out.

Snap Rings

Snap rings can be internal or external design. They are used to retain items on shafts (external type) or within tubes (internal type). In some applications, snap rings of varying thickness are used to control the end play of parts assemblies. These are often called selective snap rings. Snap rings should be replaced during installation, as removal weakens and deforms them.

Two basic types of snap rings are available: machined and stamped snap rings. Machined snap rings (**Figure 9**) can be installed in either direction (shaft or housing) because both faces are machined, thus creating two sharp edges. Stamped snap rings (**Figure 10**) are manufactured with one sharp edge and one rounded edge. When installing stamped snap rings in a thrust situation (transmission shafts, fork tubes, etc.), the sharp edge must face away from the part producing the thrust. When installing snap rings, observe the following:

a. Compress or expand the snap rings only enough to install or remove them.

b. After the snap ring is installed, make sure it is completely seated in its groove.

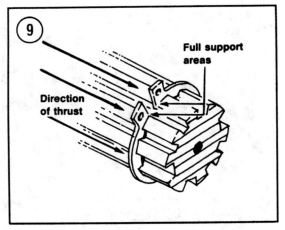

Full support areas

Direction of thrust

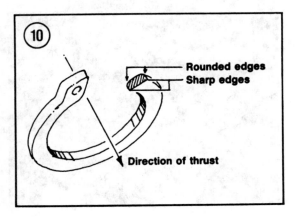

Rounded edges
Sharp edges

Direction of thrust

LUBRICANTS

Periodic lubrication ensures long life for any type of equipment. The *type* of lubricant used is just as important as the lubrication service itself. The following paragraphs describe the types of lubricants most often used on motorcycle equipment. Be sure to follow the motorcycle manufacturer's recommendations for lubricant types.

Generally, all liquid lubricants are called "oil." They may be mineral-based (including petroleum bases), natural-based (vegetable and animal bases), synthetic-based or emulsions (mixtures). "Grease" is an oil to which a thickening base has been added so that the end product is semi-solid. Grease is often classified by the type of thickener added; lithium soap is commonly used.

Engine Oil

Oil for motorcycle and automotive engines is graded by the American Petroleum Institute (API) and the Society of Automotive Engineers (SAE) in several categories. Oil containers display these ratings on the top of the can or on the bottle label (**Figure 11**).

API oil grade is indicated by letters; oils for gasoline engines are identified by an "S." The engines covered in this manual require SE or SF graded oil.

Viscosity is an indication of the oil's thickness. The SAE uses numbers to indicate viscosity; thin oils have low numbers while thick oils have high numbers. A "W" after the number indicates that the viscosity testing was done at low temperature to simulate cold-weather operation. Engine oils fall into the 5W-30 and 20W-50 range.

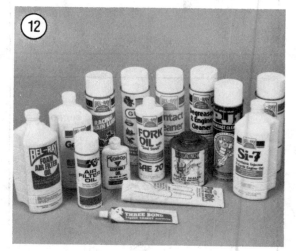

Multi-grade oils (for example 10W-40) have a constant viscosity. This allows the oil to perform efficiently across a wide range of engine operating conditions. The lower the number, the better the engine will start in cold climates. Higher numbers are usually recommended for engine running in hot weather conditions.

Grease

Greases are graded by the National Lubricating Grease Institute (NLGI). Greases are graded by number according to the consistency of the grease; these range from No. 000 to No. 6, with No. 6 being the most solid. A typical multipurpose grease is NLGI No. 2. For specific applications, equipment manufacturers may require grease with an additive such as molybdenum disulfide (MoS_2).

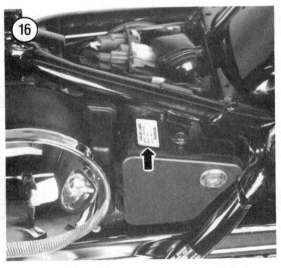

EXPENDABLE SUPPLIES

Certain expendable supplies are required during maintenance and repair work. These include grease, oil, gasket cement, wiping rags and cleaning solvent. Ask your dealer for the special locking compounds, silicone lubricants and other products (**Figure 12**) which make vehicle maintenance simpler and easier. Cleaning solvent or kerosene is available at some service stations or hardware stores.

PARTS REPLACEMENT

Honda makes frequent changes during a model year—some minor, some relatively major. When you order parts from the dealer or other parts distributor, always order by engine and frame number. Write the numbers down and carry them with you. Compare new parts to old before purchasing them. If they are not alike, have the parts manager explain the difference to you.

SERIAL NUMBERS

You must know the model serial number and VIN number for registration purposes and when ordering replacement parts.

The frame serial number is stamped on the right-hand side of the steering head (A, **Figure 13**). The vehicle identification number (VIN) is on the left-hand side of the steering head (B, **Figure 13**).

The engine serial number is located on the top right-hand surface of the crankcase (**Figure 14**). The carburetor identification number is located on the carburetor body above the float bowl (**Figure 15**). On models so equipped, the color label is attached either to the air filter air box or on the storage compartment under the seat (**Figure 16**). When ordering color-coded parts always specify the color indicated on this label.

BASIC HAND TOOLS

A number of tools are required to maintain a bike in top riding condition. You may already have some of these tools for home or car repairs. There are also tools made especially for bike repairs; these you will have to purchase. In any case, a wide variety of quality tools will make bike repairs easier and more effective.

Top quality tools are essential; they are also more economical in the long run. If you are now starting to build your tool collection, stay away from the "advertised specials" featured at some parts houses, discount stores and chain drug stores. These are usually a poor grade tool that can be sold cheaply and that is exactly what they are—*cheap*.

They are usually made of inferior material and are thick, heavy and clumsy. Their rough finish makes them difficult to clean and they usually don't last very long.

Quality tools are made of alloy steel and are heat treated for greater strength. They are lighter and better balanced than cheap ones. Their surface is smooth, making them a pleasure to work with and easy to clean. The initial cost of good quality tools may be more, but it is cheaper in the long run.

Don't try to buy everything in all sizes in the beginning; do it a little at a time until you have the necessary tools. The Stanley line, available from most hardware stores, is a good all-around line of tools and will last you a lifetime if you take care of them.

Keep your tools clean and in a tool box. Keep them organized with the sockets and related drives together and the open-end and box wrenches together, etc. After using a tool, wipe off dirt and grease with a clean cloth and place the tool in its correct place. Doing this will save a lot of time you would have spent trying to find a socket buried in a bunch of clutch parts.

The following tools are required to perform virtually any repair job on a bike. Each tool is described and the recommended size given for starting a tool collection. **Table 3** includes the tools that should be on hand for simple home repairs and/or major overhaul as shown in **Figure 17**. Additional tools and some duplicates may be added as you become more familiar with the bike. Almost all motorcycles and bikes (with the exception of the U.S. built Harley and some English bikes) use metric size bolts and nuts. If you are starting your collection now, buy metric sizes.

Screwdrivers

The screwdriver is a very basic tool, but if used improperly it will do more damage than good. The slot on a screw has a definite dimension and shape. A screwdriver must be selected to conform with that shape. Use a small screwdriver for small screws and a large one for large screws or the screw head will be damaged.

Two basic types of screwdriver are required to repair the bike—common (flat blade) screwdrivers (**Figure 18**) and Phillips screwdrivers (**Figure 19**).

Screwdrivers are available in sets which often include an assortment of common and Phillips blades. If you buy them individually, buy at least the following:

   a. Common screwdriver—5/16×6 in. blade.
   b. Common screwdriver—3/8×12 in. blade.
   c. Phillips screwdriver—size 2 tip, 6 in. blade.

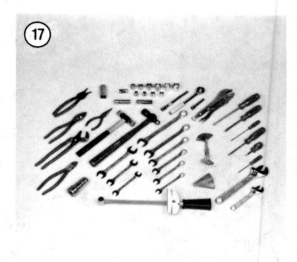

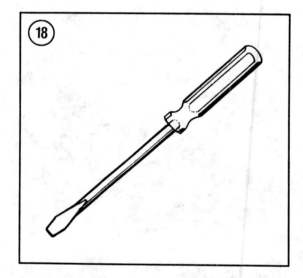

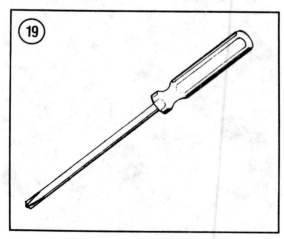

Use screwdrivers only for driving screws. Never use a screwdriver for prying or chiseling. Do not try to remove a Phillips or Allen head screw with a common screwdriver; you can damage the head so that the proper tool will be unable to remove it.

Keep screwdrivers in the proper condition and they will last longer and perform better. Always keep the tip of a common screwdriver in good condition. **Figure 20** shows how to grind the tip to the proper shape if it becomes damaged. Note the symmetrical sides of the tip.

Pliers

Pliers come in a wide range of types and sizes. Pliers are useful for cutting, bending and crimping. They should never be used to cut hardened objects or to turn bolts or nuts. **Figure 21** shows several pliers useful in bike repairs.

Each type of pliers has a specialized function. Gas pliers are general purpose pliers and are used mainly for holding things and for bending. Vise Grips are used as pliers or to hold objects very tight like a vise. Needlenose pliers are used to hold or bend small objects. Channel lock pliers can be adjusted to hold various sizes of objects; the jaws remain parallel to grip around objects such as pipe

or tubing. There are many more types of pliers. The ones described here are most suitable for bike repairs.

Box and Open-end Wrenches

Box and open-end wrenches are available in sets or separately in a variety of sizes. The size number stamped near the end refers to the distance between 2 parallel flats on the hex head bolt or nut.

Box wrenches are usually superior to open-end wrenches. Open-end wrenches grip the nut on only 2 flats. Unless it fits well, it may slip and round off the points on the nut. The box wrench grips all 6 flats. Both 6-point and 12-point openings on box wrenches are available. The 6-point gives superior holding power; the 12-point allows a shorter swing.

Combination wrenches (**Figure 22**) which are open on one side and boxed on the other are also available. Both ends are the same size.

Adjustable (Crescent) Wrenches

An adjustable wrench (also called crescent wrench) can be adjusted to fit nearly any nut or bolt head. See **Figure 23**. However, it can loosen and slip, causing damage to the nut and injury to

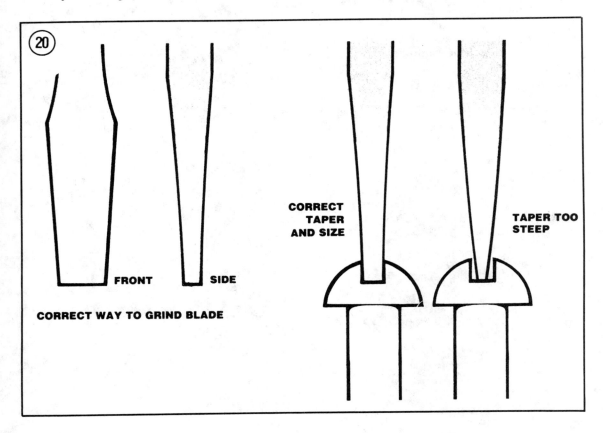

20

FRONT **SIDE**

CORRECT WAY TO GRIND BLADE

CORRECT TAPER AND SIZE

TAPER TOO STEEP

your knuckles. Use an adjustable wrench only when other wrenches are not available.

Adjustable wrenches come in sizes ranging from 4-18 in. overall. A 6 or 8 in. wrench is recommended as an all-purpose wrench.

Socket Wrenches

This type is undoubtedly the fastest, safest and most convenient to use. See **Figure 24**. Sockets which attach to a ratchet handle are available with 6-point or 12-point openings and 1/4, 3/8, 1/2 and 3/4 in. drives. The drive size indicates the size of the square hole which mates with the ratchet handle.

Torque Wrench

A torque wrench is used with a socket to measure how tightly a nut or bolt is installed. They come in a wide price range and with either 3/8 or 1/2 in. square drive. The drive size indicates the size of the square drive which mates with the socket. Purchase one that measures 0-140 N•m (0-100 ft.-lb.).

Impact Driver

This tool might have been designed with the bike in mind. See **Figure 25**. It makes removal of engine and clutch parts easy and eliminates damage to bolts and screw slots. Impact drivers are available at most large hardware, motorcycle or auto parts stores.

Circlip Pliers

Circlip pliers (sometimes referred to as snap-ring pliers) are necessary to remove the circlips used on the transmission shaft assemblies. See **Figure 26**.

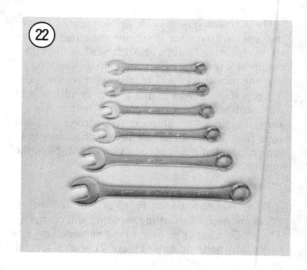

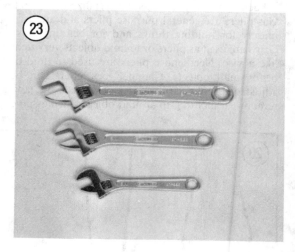

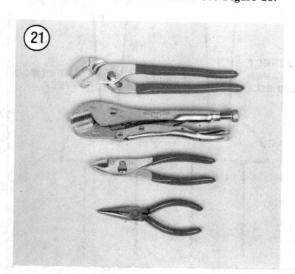

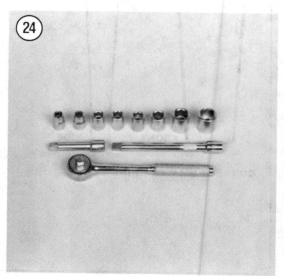

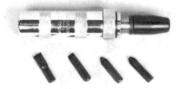

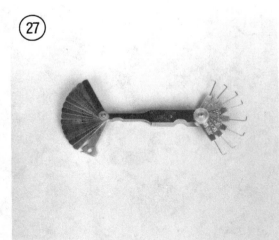

Hammers

The correct hammer is necessary for bike repairs. Use only a hammer with a face (or head) of rubber or plastic or the soft-faced type that is filled with buck shot. These are sometimes necessary in engine tear-downs. *Never* use a metal-faced hammer on the bike as severe damage will result in most cases. You can always produce the same amount of force with a soft-faced hammer.

Ignition Gauge

This tool (**Figure 27**) has both flat and wire measuring gauges and is used to measure spark plug gap. This device is available at most auto or motorcycle supply stores.

Other Special Tools

A few other special tools may be required for major service. These are described in the appropriate chapters and are available either from a Honda dealer or other manufacturers as indicated.

TUNE-UP AND TROUBLESHOOTING TOOLS

Multimeter or Volt-ohm Meter

This instrument (**Figure 28**) is invaluable for electrical system troubleshooting and service. A few of its functions may be duplicated by homemade test equipment, but for the serious mechanic it is a must. Its uses are described in the applicable sections of the book.

Strobe Timing Light

This instrument is necessary for tuning. By flashing a light at the precise instant the spark plug fires, the position of the timing mark can be seen. Marks on the alternator flywheel line up with the

stationary mark on the crankcase while the engine is running.

Suitable lights range from inexpensive neon bulb types to powerful xenon strobe lights (**Figure 29**). Neon timing lights are difficult to see and must be used in dimly lit areas. Xenon strobe timing lights can be used outside in bright sunlight. Both types work on the bike; use according to the manufacturer's instructions.

Portable Tachometer

A portable tachometer is necessary for tuning (**Figure 30**). Ignition timing and carburetor adjustments must be performed at the specified engine speed. The best instrument for this purpose is one with a low range of 0-1,000 or 0-2,000 rpm and a high range of 0-4,000 rpm. Extended range (0-6,000 or 0-8,000 rpm) instruments lack accuracy at lower speeds. The instrument should be capable of detecting changes of 25 rpm on the low range.

Compression Gauge

A compression gauge (**Figure 31**) measures the engine compression. The results, when properly interpreted, can indicate general ring and valve condition. They are available from motorcycle or auto supply stores and mail order outlets.

MECHANIC'S TIPS

Removing Frozen Nuts and Screws

When a fastener rusts and cannot be removed, several methods may be used to loosen it. First, apply penetrating oil such as Liquid Wrench or WD-40 (available at any hardware or auto supply store).

Apply it liberally and let it penetrate for 10-15 minutes. Rap the fastener several times with a small hammer; do not hit it hard enough to cause damage. Reapply the penetrating oil if necessary.

For frozen screws, apply penetrating oil as described, then insert a screwdriver in the slot and rap the top of the screwdriver with a hammer. This loosens the rust so the screw can be removed in the normal way. If the screw head is too chewed up to use a screwdriver, grip the head with Vise Grips and twist the screw out.

Remedying Stripped Threads

Occasionally, threads are stripped though carelessness or impact damage. Often the threads can be cleaned up with a tap (for internal threads on nuts) or die (for external threads on bolts). See **Figure 32**.

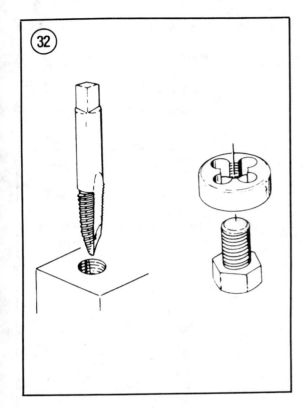

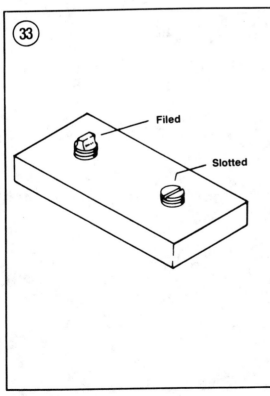

Filed

Slotted

Removing Broken Screws or Bolts

When the head breaks off a screw or bolt, several methods are available for removing the remaining portion.

If a large portion of the remainder projects out, try gripping it with Vise Grips. If the projecting portion is too small, file it to fit a wrench or cut a slot in it to fit a screwdriver. See **Figure 33**.

If the head breaks off flush, use a screw extractor. To do this, centerpunch the remaining portion of the screw or bolt. Drill a small hole in the screw and tap the extractor into the hole. Back the screw out with a wrench on the extractor. See **Figure 34**.

RIDING SAFETY

General Tips

1. Read your owner's manual and know your machine.
2. Check the throttle and brake controls before starting the engine.
3. Know how to make an emergency stop.
4. Never add fuel while anyone is smoking in the area or when the engine is running.
5. Never wear loose scarves, belts or boot laces that could catch on moving parts.
6. Always wear eye and head protection and protective clothing to protect your *entire* body. Today's riding apparel is very stylish and you will be ready for action as well as being well protected.
7. Riding in the winter months requires a good set of clothes to keep your body dry and warm, otherwise your entire trip may be miserable. If you dress properly, moisture will evaporate from your body. If you become too hot and if your clothes trap the moisture, you will become cold. Even mild temperatures can be very uncomfortable and dangerous when combined with a strong wind or traveling at high speed. See **Table 4** for wind chill factors. Always dress according to what the wind chill factor is, not the ambient temperature.
8. Never allow anyone to operate the bike without proper instruction. This is for their bodily protection and to keep your machine from damage or destruction.
9. Use the "buddy system" for long trips, just in case you have a problem or run out of gas.
10. Never attempt to repair your machine with the engine running except when necessary for certain tune-up procedures.
11. Check all of the machine components and hardware frequently, especially the wheels and the steering.

1. Avoid dangerous terrain.
2. Do not ride the bike on or near railroad tracks. The bike engine and exhaust noise can drown out the sound of an approaching train.
3. Keep the headlight, turn signal lights and taillight free of dirt and never ride at night without the headlight on.
4. Always steer with both hands.

5. Be aware of the terrain and avoid operating the bike at excessive speed.
6. Do not panic if the throttle sticks. Turn the engine stop switch to the OFF position.
7. Do not tailgate. Rear end collisions can cause injury and machine damage.
8. Do not mix alcoholic beverages or drugs with riding—*ride straight.*

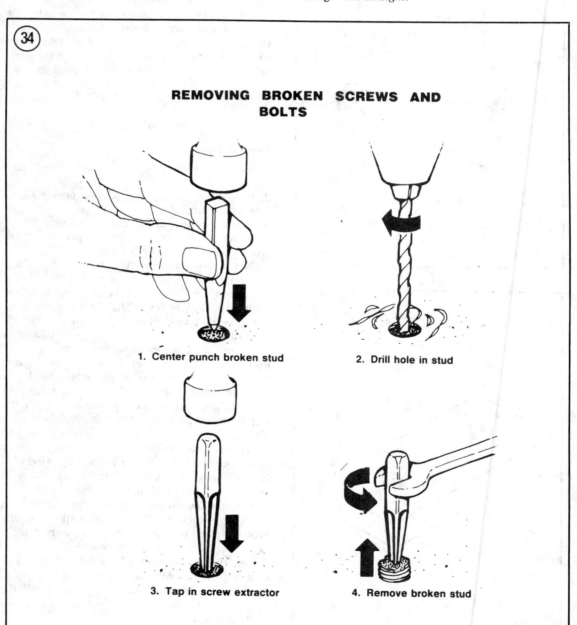

(34)

REMOVING BROKEN SCREWS AND BOLTS

1. Center punch broken stud

2. Drill hole in stud

3. Tap in screw extractor

4. Remove broken stud

Table 1 DECIMAL EQUIVALENTS

Fractions	Decimal in.	Metric mm	Fractions	Decimal in.	Metric mm
1/64	0.015625	0.39688	33/64	0.515625	13.09687
1/32	0.03125	0.79375	17/32	0.53125	13.49375
3/64	0.046875	1.19062	35/64	0.546875	13.89062
1/16	0.0625	1.58750	9/16	0.5625	14.28750
5/64	0.078125	1.98437	37/64	0.578125	14.68437
3/32	0.09375	2.38125	19/32	0.59375	15.08125
7/64	0.109375	2.77812	39/64	0.609375	15.47812
1/8	0.125	3.1750	5/8	0.625	15.87500
9/64	0.140625	3.57187	41/64	0.640625	16.27187
5/32	0.15625	3.96875	21/32	0.65625	16.66875
11/64	0.171875	4.36562	43/64	0.671875	17.06562
3/16	0.1875	4.76250	11/16	0.6875	17.46250
13/64	0.203125	5.15937	45/64	0.703125	17.85937
7/32	0.21875	5.55625	23/32	0.71875	18.25625
15/64	0.234375	5.95312	47/64	0.734375	18.65312
1/4	0.250	6.35000	3/4	0.750	19.05000
17/64	0.265625	6.74687	49/64	0.765625	19.44687
9/32	0.28125	7.14375	25/32	0.78125	19.84375
19/64	0.296875	7.54062	51/64	0.796875	20.24062
5/16	0.3125	7.93750	13/16	0.8125	20.63750
21/64	0.328125	8.33437	53/64	0.828125	21.03437
11/32	0.34375	8.73125	27/32	0.84375	21.43125
23/64	0.359375	9.12812	55/64	0.859375	21.82812
3/8	0.375	9.52500	7/8	0.875	22.22500
25/64	0.390625	9.92187	57/64	0.890625	22.62187
13/32	0.40625	10.31875	29/32	0.90625	23.01875
27/64	0.421875	10.71562	59/64	0.921875	23.41562
7/16	0.4375	11.11250	15/16	0.9375	23.81250
29/64	0.453125	11.50937	61/64	0.953125	24.20937
15/32	0.46875	11.90625	31/32	0.96875	24.60625
31/64	0.484375	12.30312	63/64	0.984375	25.00312
1/2	0.500	12.70000	1	1.00	25.40000

Table 2 STANDARD TORQUE SPECIFICATIONS

Item	N·m	Ft.-lb.
5 mm bolt and nut	4.5-6	3-4
6 mm bolt and nut	8-12	6-9
8 mm bolt and nut	18-25	13-18
10 mm bolt and nut	30-40	22-29
12 mm bolt and nut	50-60	36-43
5 mm screw	3.5-5	2-4
6 mm screw and 6 mm bolt with 8 mm head	7-11	5-8
6 mm flange bolt and nut	10-14	7-10
8 mm flange bolt and nut	24-30	17-22
10 mm flange bolt and nut	35-45	25-33

Table 3 WORKSHOP TOOLS

Tool	Size or Specifications
Screwdriver	
Common	5/16×8 in. blade
Common	3/8×12 in. blade
Phillips	Size 2 tip, 6 in. overall
Pliers	
Gas pliers	6 in. overall
Vise Grips	10 in. overall
Needlenose	6 in. overall
Channel lock	12 in. overall
Snap ring	–
Wrenches	
Box-end set	5-17 mm (24 and 28 mm)
Open-end set	5-17 mm (24 and 28 mm)
Crescent	6 in. and 12 in. overall
Socket set	1/2 in. drive ratchet with 5-17 mm sockets
Other special tools	
Strap wrench	–
Impact driver	1/2 in. drive with assorted bits
Torque wrench	1/2 in. drive 0-100 ft.-lb.
Ignition gauge	–

Table 4 WINDCHILL FACTOR

Estimated Wind Speed in MPH	Actual Thermometer Reading (° F)											
	50	40	30	20	10	0	—10	—20	—30	—40	—50	—60
	Equivalent Temperature (° F)											
Calm	50	40	30	20	10	0	—10	—20	—30	—40	—50	—60
5	48	37	27	16	6	—5	—15	—26	—36	—47	—57	—68
10	40	28	16	4	—9	—21	—33	—46	—58	—70	—83	—95
15	36	22	9	—5	—18	—36	—45	—58	—72	—85	—99	—112
20	32	18	4	—10	—25	—39	—53	—67	—82	—96	—110	—124
25	30	16	0	—15	—29	—44	—59	—74	—88	—104	—118	—133
30	28	13	—2	—18	—33	—48	—63	—79	—94	—109	—125	—140
35	27	11	—4	—20	—35	—49	—67	—82	—98	—113	—129	—145
40	26	10	—6	—21	—37	—53	—69	—85	—100	—116	—132	—148
*	**Little Danger** (for properly clothed person)				**Increasing Danger**			**Great Danger**				
					• Danger from freezing of exposed flesh •							

*Wind speeds greater than 40 mph have little additional effect.

CHAPTER TWO

TROUBLESHOOTING

Diagnosing mechanical problems is relatively simple if you use orderly procedures and keep a few basic principles in mind.

The troubleshooting procedures in this chapter analyze typical symptoms and show logical methods of isolating causes. These are not the only methods. There may be several ways to solve a problem, but only a systematic, methodical approach can guarantee success.

Never assume anything. Do not overlook the obvious. If you are riding along and the engine suddenly quits, check the easiest, most accessible problems first. Is there gasoline in the tank? Is the fuel shutoff valve in the ON position? Has a spark plug wire fallen off?

If nothing obvious turns up in a quick check, look a little further. Learning to recognize and describe symptoms will make repairs easier for you or a mechanic at the shop. Describe problems accurately and fully. Saying that "it won't run" isn't the same as saying "it quit at high speed and won't start" or that "it sat in my garage for 3 months and then wouldn't start."

Gather as many symptoms together as possible to aid in diagnosis. Note whether the engine lost power gradually or all at once. Remember that the more complicated a machine is, the easier it is to troubleshoot because symptoms point to specific problems.

After the symptoms are defined, areas which could cause the problems are tested and analyzed. Guessing at the cause of a problem may provide the solution, but it can easily lead to frustration, wasted time and a series of expensive, unnecessary parts replacements.

You do not need fancy equipment or complicated test gear to determine whether repairs can be attempted at home. A few simple checks could save a large repair bill and time lost while the bike sits in a dealer's service department. On the other hand, be realistic and don't attempt repairs beyond your abilities. Service departments tend to charge a lot for putting together a disassembled engine that may have been abused. Some dealers won't even take on such a job—so use common sense and don't get in over your head.

OPERATING REQUIREMENTS

An engine needs 3 basics to run properly: correct fuel/air mixture, compression and a spark at the correct time. If one or more are missing, the engine just won't run. The electrical system is the weakest link of the 3 basics. More problems result from electrical breakdowns than from any other source. Keep that in mind before you begin tampering with carburetor adjustments and the like.

If the bike has been sitting for any length of time and refuses to start, check and clean the spark plugs and then look to the gasoline delivery system. This includes the fuel tank, fuel shutoff valve and the fuel line to the carburetor. Gasoline deposits may have formed and gummed up the carburetor's jets and air passages. Gasoline tends to lose its potency after standing for long periods. Condensation may contaminate the fuel with water. Drain the old fuel and try starting with a fresh tankful.

EMERGENCY
TROUBLESHOOTING

When the bike is difficult to start or won't start at all, it does not help to wear out your leg on the kickstarter or run down the battery using the starter. Check for obvious problems even before getting out your tools. Go down the following list step by step. Do each one; you may be embarrassed to find your kill switch is stuck in the OFF position, but that is better than wearing down the battery. If it still will not start, refer to the appropriate troubleshooting procedure which follows in this chapter.

1. Is there fuel in the tank? Open the filler cap and rock the bike. Listen for fuel sloshing around.

> *WARNING*
> *Do not use an open flame to check in*
> *the tank. A serious explosion is certain*
> *to result.*

2. Is the fuel shutoff valve in the ON position?
3. Make sure the kill switch (**Figure 1**) is not stuck in the OFF position.
4. Are the spark plug wires (**Figure 2**) on tight? Push both of them on and slightly rotate them to clean the electrical connection between the plug and the connector.

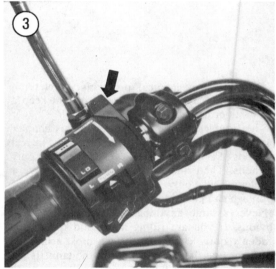

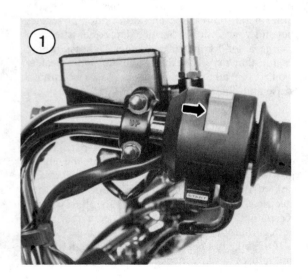

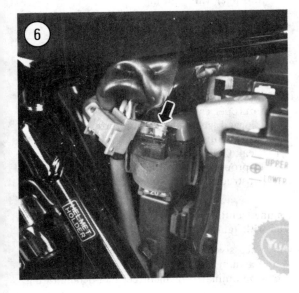

5. Is the choke in the correct position?
   a. Rebel 450 models: the choke lever (**Figure 3**) should be in the *raised* position for a cold engine.
   b. On all other models: the knob should be pulled *up* (**Figure 4**) for a cold engine and pushed *down* for a warm engine.
6. Is the transmission in neutral or the clutch lever pulled in? The bike will not start in gear without pulling in the clutch or having the automatic transmission in the NEUTRAL position.
7. On models so equipped, there is a special "kill switch" attached to the sidestand. This will shut off the engine if the sidestand is lowered when the transmission is in gear or if a gear is engaged while the stand is down.
8. Has the main fuse blown? Refer to **Figure 5** or **Figure 6**. Replace with a good one.

ENGINE STARTING

An engine that refuses to start or is difficult to start is very frustrating. More often than not, the problem is very minor and can be found with a simple and logical troubleshooting approach.

The following items show a beginning point from which to isolate engine starting problems.

Engine Fails to Start

Perform the following spark test to determine if the ignition system is operating properly.
1. Remove one of the spark plugs from the cylinder.
2. Connect the spark plug wire and connector to the spark plug and touch the spark plug's base to a good ground such as the engine cylinder head (**Figure 7**). Position the spark plug so you can see the electrodes.

> *WARNING*
> *If it is necessary to hold the high voltage lead in Step 3, do so with an insulated pair of pliers. The high voltage generated by the ignition pulse generator and CDI unit could produce serious or fatal shocks.*

3. Crank the engine over with the kickstarter or starter motor. A fat blue spark should be evident across the plug's electrodes.
4. If the spark is good, check for one or more of the following possible malfunctions:
   a. Obstructed fuel line.
   b. Low compression.
   c. Leaking head gasket.
   d. Choke not operating properly.
   e. Throttle not operating properly.

5. If spark is not good, check for one or more of the following:
   a. Weak ignition coil.
   b. Weak CDI pulse generator.
   c. Broken or shorted high tension lead to the spark plug(s).
   d. Loose electrical connections.
   e. Loose or broken ignition coil ground wires.

Engine Is Difficult to Start

Check for one or more of the following possible malfunctions:
   a. Fouled spark plug.
   b. Improperly adjusted choke.
   c. Contaminated fuel system.
   d. Improperly adjusted carburetor.
   e. Weak ignition coil.
   f. Weak CDI pulse generator.
   g. Incorrect type ignition coil.
   h. Poor compression.

Engine Will Not Crank

Check for one or more of the following possible malfunctions:
   a. Discharged battery.
   b. Defective or broken kickstarter mechanism (models so equipped).
   c. Seized piston.
   d. Seized crankshaft bearings.
   e. Broken connecting rod(s).
   f. Locked-up transmission or clutch assembly.

ENGINE PERFORMANCE

In the following checklist, it is assumed that the engine runs, but is not operating at peak performance. This will serve as a starting point from which to isolate a performance malfunction.

The possible causes for each malfunction are listed in a logical sequence and in order of probability.

Engine Will Not Start or is Hard to Start

   a. Fuel tank empty.
   b. Obstructed fuel line or fuel shutoff valve.
   c. Sticking float valve in carburetor(s).
   d. Carburetor incorrectly adjusted.
   e. Improper choke operation.
   f. Fouled or improperly gapped spark plug(s).
   g. Weak CDI pulse generator.
   h. Ignition timing incorrect (faulty component in system).
   i. Broken or shorted ignition coil.

   j. Weak or faulty CDI unit.
   k. Improper valve timing.
   l. Clogged air filter element.
   m. Contaminated fuel.

Engine Will Not Idle or Idles Erratically

   a. Carburetor(s) incorrectly adjusted.
   b. Fouled or improperly gapped spark plug(s).
   c. Leaking head gasket or vacuum leak.
   d. Weak CDI pulse generator.
   e. Ignition timing incorrect (faulty component in system).
   f. Improper valve timing.
   g. Obstructed fuel line or fuel shutoff valve.

Engine Misses at High Speed

   a. Fouled or improperly gapped spark plug(s).
   b. Improper ignition timing (faulty component in system).
   c. Improper carburetor main jet selection.
   d. Clogged jets in the carburetor(s).
   e. Weak ignition coil.
   f. Weak CDI pulse generator.
   g. Improper valve timing.
   h. Obstructed fuel line or fuel shutoff valve.

Engine Continues to Run with Ignition Off

   a. Excessive carbon build-up in engine.
   b. Vacuum leak in intake system.
   c. Contaminated or incorrect fuel octane rating.

Engine Overheating

   a. Obstructed cooling fins on the cylinder and cylinder head.
   b. Improper ignition timing (faulty component in system).
   c. Improper spark plug heat range.

Engine Misses at Idle

   a. Fouled or improperly gapped spark plug(s).
   b. Spark plug cap faulty.
   c. Ignition cable insulation deteriorated (shorting out).
   d. Dirty or clogged air filter element.
   e. Carburetor(s) incorrectly adjusted (too lean or too rich).
   f. Choke valve stuck.
   g. Clogged jet(s) in the carburetor(s).
   h. Carburetor float height incorrect.

Engine Backfires—
Explosions in Mufflers

a. Fouled or improperly gapped spark plug(s).
b. Spark plug cap(s) faulty.
c. Ignition cable insulation deteriorated (shorting out).
d. Ignition timing incorrect.
e. Improper valve timing.
f. Contaminated fuel.
g. Burned or damaged intake and/or exhaust valves.
h. Weak or broken intake and/or exhaust valve springs.

Pre-ignition (Fuel Mixture
Ignites Before Spark Plug Fires)

a. Hot spot in combustion chamber (piece of carbon).
b. Valve(s) stuck in guide.
c. Overheating engine.

Smoky Exhaust and Engine Runs Roughly

a. Carburetor mixture too rich.
b. Choke not operating correctly.
c. Water or other contaminants in fuel.
d. Clogged fuel line.
e. Clogged air filter element.

Engine Loses Power at
Normal Riding Speed

a. Carburetor incorrectly adjusted.
b. Engine overheating.
c. Improper ignition timing (faulty component in system).
d. Weak CDI pulse generator.
e. Incorrectly gapped spark plug.
f. Weak ignition coil.
g. Obstructed mufflers.
h. Dragging brake(s).

Engine Lacks Acceleration

a. Carburetor mixture too lean.
b. Clogged fuel line.
c. Improper ignition timing (faulty component in system).
d. Improper valve clearance.
e. Dragging brake(s).

ENGINE NOISES

1. *Knocking or pinging during acceleration—* Caused by using a lower octane fuel than recommended. May also be caused by poor fuel. Pinging can also be caused by spark plugs of the wrong heat range. Refer to *Spark Plug Selection* in Chapter Three.
2. *Slapping or rattling noises at low speed or during acceleration—* May be caused by piston slap (excessive piston to cylinder wall clearance).
3. *Knocking or rapping while decelerating—* Usually caused by excessive rod bearing clearance.
4. *Persistent knocking and vibration—* Usually caused by excessive main bearing clearance.
5. *Rapid on-off squeal—* Compression leak around cylinder head gasket or spark plug.

EXCESSIVE VIBRATION

Usually this is caused by loose engine mounting hardware or a faulty balancer system. Otherwise it can be difficult to find without disassembling the engine.

LUBRICATION TROUBLES

Excessive Oil Consumption

May be caused by worn piston rings and cylinder bores. Overhaul is necessary to correct this; see Chapter Four. May also be caused by worn valve guides or defective valve guide seals. Also check engine for external leaks.

Oil Pressure Lamp Does Not Light
When the Ignition Switch is Turned On

1. Remove the indicator bulb and make sure it is not burned out; replace the bulb if necessary.
2. Check to make sure the electrical wire to the switch is not broken. The wire from the oil pressure switch to the indicator bulb is blue/red on all models. Locate this blue/red wire connector and disconnect it. Ground the bulb side of this connector. If the light comes on, either the switch is faulty or the electrical wire from this point to the switch is faulty.
3. Perform this step before replacing a possible faulty switch. Reconnect the connector and remove the headlight bulb assembly as described in Chapter Eight. Again trace the blue/red wire. Disconnect this connector and ground the (blue/red wire) bulb side of this connector. If the light lights, either the switch is faulty or the

electrical wire from this point to the switch is
faulty. Reconnect the connector and install the
headlight assembly.

4. The final check is at the oil pressure sending
switch assembly. The oil pressure sending switch
on 400 cc manual transmission models is located
under the right-hand crankcase cover (**Figure 8**).
To gain access to the switch, perform Steps 1-8 of
Clutch Removal in Chapter Five. On automatic
transmission models and 450 cc models (except
Rebel 450), the oil pressure sending switch is
located on the oil cooler. Remove the bolts (**Figure
9**) securing the cover and remove the cover. On
Rebel 450 models, the oil pressure sending switch
is located at the front left-hand corner of the
crankcase. Remove the bolts securing the cover
and remove the cover (**Figure 10**).

5. Check that the electrical wire is connected to the
oil pressure sending switch and makes good
electrical contact. Pull the wire off and ground it to
the engine or frame. If the lamp lights, replace the
switch as described in Chapter Eight.

Oil Pressure Lamp Lights
or Flickers When the Engine is Running

This indicates low or complete loss of oil
pressure. Stop the engine immediately; coast to a
stop with the clutch disengaged or transmission out
of gear. This may simply be caused by a low oil
level or an overheated engine. Check the oil level.
If the oil level is correct, check for a shorted oil
pressure sending switch as described in Chapter
Eight. Listen for unusual noise indicating bad
bearings, etc. Do not restart the engine until you
know why the light came on and have corrected the
problem.

MANUAL AND AUTOMATIC TRANSMISSION

Transmission problems are usually indicated by
one or more of the following symptoms:
 a. Difficulty shifting gears.
 b. Gear clash when downshifting or from high
    to low.
 c. Slipping out of gear.
 d. Excessive noise in neutral.
 e. Excessive noise in gear.
Transmission symptoms are sometimes hard to
distinguish from clutch or torque converter
symptoms. Be sure that the clutch or torque
converter is not causing the trouble before working
on the transmission. Refer to Chapter Five or
Chapter Six.

FRONT SUSPENSION AND STEERING

Poor handling may be caused by improper tire
pressure, a damaged or bent frame or front steering
components, a worn front fork assembly, worn
wheel bearings or dragging brakes.

BRAKE PROBLEMS

Sticking disc brakes may be caused by a stuck
piston in a caliper assembly or warped pad shim.

A sticking drum brake may be caused by worn or
weak return springs, dry pivot and cam bushings or
improper adjustment. Grabbing brakes may be
caused by greasy linings which must be replaced.
Brake grab may also be due to an out-of-round
drum. Glazed linings will cause loss of stopping
power.

CHAPTER THREE

LUBRICATION, MAINTENANCE

AND TUNE-UP

If this is your first experience with a motorcycle, you should become acquainted with products that are available in auto or motorcycle parts and supply stores. Look into the tune-up tools and parts and check out the different fluids such as motor oil, locking compounds and greases. Also check engine degreasers, like Gunk or Bel-Ray Degreaser, for cleaning your engine before working on it.

The more you get involved in your bike the more you will want to work on it. Start out by doing simple tune-up, lubrication and maintenance. Tackle more involved jobs as you gain experience.

The Honda twin is a relatively simple machine but to gain the utmost in safety, performance and useful life from it, it is necessary to make periodic inspections and adjustments. Minor problems are often found during such inspections that are simple and inexpensive to correct at the time, but which could lead to major problems if not corrected.

This chapter explains lubrication, maintenance and tune-up procedures required for the Honda twins covered in this book. **Table 1** is a suggested factory maintenance schedule. **Tables 1-8** are at the end of this chapter.

PRE-CHECKS

The following checks should be performed before the first ride of the day.
1. Inspect the fuel line and fittings for wetness.

2. Check the fuel level.
3. Make sure the engine oil level is correct; add oil if necessary.
4. Check the operation of the clutch and adjust if necessary.
5. Check the throttle and the brake levers. Make sure they operate properly with no binding.
6. On disc brake models, check the brake fluid level in the master cylinder reservoir, add fluid if necessary.
7. Inspect the front and rear suspension; make sure they have a good solid feel with no looseness.
8. Inspect the drive chain for wear, correct tension and proper lubrication.
9. Check the drive chain roller and buffer for wear or damage; replace if necessary.
10. Check tire pressure as listed in **Table 2**.
11. Make sure the headlight, turn signals and taillight work.

ROUTINE CHECKS

The following simple checks should be performed at each stop at a service station for gas.

Engine Oil Level

Refer to *Checking Engine Oil Level* under *Periodic Lubrication* in this chapter.

General Inspection

1. Quickly examine the engine for signs of oil or fuel leakage.

2. Check the tires for embedded stones. Pry them out with your ignition key.

3. Make sure all lights work.

NOTE
At least check the brakelight. It can burn out anytime. Motorists cannot stop as quickly as you and need all the warning you can give.

Tire Pressure

Tire pressure must be checked with the tires cold. Correct tire pressure depends a lot on the load you are carrying. See **Table 2**.

Lights and Horn

With the engine running, check the following.

1. Pull the front brake lever and check that the brake light comes on.

2. Push the rear brake pedal down and check that the brake light comes on soon after you have begun depressing the brake pedal.

3. Check that the headlight and taillight are on.

4. Move the dimmer switch up and down between the high and low positions. Check to see that both headlight elements are working.

5. Push the turn signal switch to the left position and the right position and check that all 4 turn signal lights are working.

6. Push the horn button and note that the horn blows loudly.

7. If the horn or any light fails to work properly, refer to Chapter Eight.

Battery

The electrolyte level must be between the upper and lower level marks on the case (**Figure 1**). For complete details see *Battery Electrolyte Level Check* in this chapter.

Check the level more frequently in hot weather.

SERVICE INTERVALS

The service and intervals shown in **Table 1** are recommended by the factory. Strict adherence to these recommendations will go a long way toward ensuring long service from your Honda. However, if the bike is run in an area of high humidity, the lubrication and services must be done more frequently to prevent possible rust damage.

For convenience of maintaining your motorcycle, most of the services shown in the table are described in this chapter. However, some procedures which require more than minor disassembly or adjustment are covered elsewhere in the appropriate chapter.

TIRES AND WHEELS

Tire Pressure

Tire pressure should be checked and adjusted to accommodate rider and luggage weight. A simple, accurate gauge (**Figure 2**) can be purchased for a few dollars and should be carried in your motorcycle tool kit. The appropriate tire pressures are shown in **Table 2**.

NOTE
*After checking and adjusting the air pressure, make sure to install the air valve cap (**Figure 3**). The cap prevents small pebbles and dirt from collecting in the valve stem; this could allow air leakage or result in incorrect tire pressure readings.*

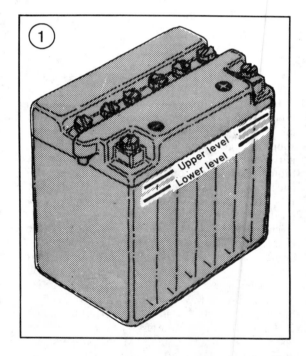

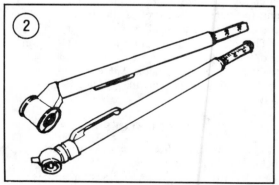

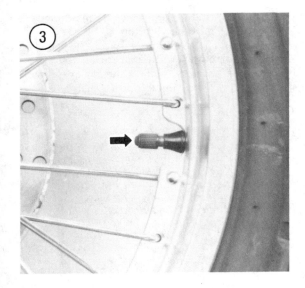

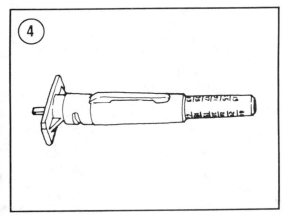

3

Tire Inspection

The likelihood of tire failure increases with tread wear. It is estimated that the majority of all tire failures occur during the last 10 percent of usable tread wear.

Check tread for excessive wear, deep cuts, embedded objects such as stone, nails, etc. Also check for high spots that indicate internal tire damage. Replace tires that show high spots or swelling. If you find a nail in a tire, mark its location with a light crayon before pulling it out. This will help locate the hole in the inner tube. Refer to *Tire Changing* in Chapter Nine.

Check local traffic regulations concerning minimum tread depth. Measure with a tread depth gauge (**Figure 4**) or small ruler. Because tires sometimes wear unevenly, measure the wear at several points. Tread wear indicators appear across the tire when tread reaches minimum safe depth. Replace the tire at this point.

Rim Inspection

Frequently inspect the condition of the wheel rims. If the rim has been damaged it might have been knocked out of alignment. Improper wheel alignment can cause severe vibration and result in an unsafe riding condition.

If the rim portion of the alloy wheel (models so equipped) is damaged, the wheel must be replaced as it cannot be repaired.

BATTERY

Removal/Installation and Electrolyte Level Check

The battery is the heart of the electrical system. It should be checked and serviced as indicated. The majority of electrical system troubles can be attributed to neglect of this vital component.

NOTE
The location and installation of the battery varies among the different models. It may be different from that shown in this procedure. Be sure to connect positive (+) lead to the positive (+) battery terminal and negative (-) lead to the negative (-) battery terminal when installing the battery.

The electrolyte level may be checked with the battery installed. However, it is necessary to remove the right-hand side panel on all models except the Rebel 450. The electrolyte level should be maintained between the two marks on the battery case (**Figure 5**). If the electrolyte level is low, it's a good idea to remove the battery so that it can be thoroughly serviced and checked.

1A. On Rebel 450 models, perform the following:

   a. Remove the bolt securing the battery outer cover (**Figure 6**) and hinge the cover down.

   b. Hinge the inner cover (**Figure 7**) down.

1B. On all models except Rebel 450, remove the right-hand side panel.

2. Remove the breather tube (A, **Figure 8**).

3. Remove the negative electrical cable then the positive cable from the battery (B, **Figure 8**).

4. On models so equipped, disconnect the battery hold-down strap from the battery carrier.

5. Lift up and pull the battery and tray out of the frame.

> *CAUTION*
> *Be careful not to spill battery electrolyte on painted or polished surfaces. The liquid is highly corrosive and will damage the finish. If it is spilled, wash it off immediately with soapy water and thoroughly rinse with clean water.*

6. Remove the caps from the battery cells and add distilled water to correct the level. Gently shake the battery for several minutes to mix the existing electrolyte with the new water. Never add electrolyte (acid) to correct the level.

7. After the level has been corrected and the battery allowed to stand for a few minutes, check the specific gravity of the electrolyte in each cell with a hydrometer as described in this chapter.

8. After the battery has been refilled, recharged or replaced, install it by reversing these steps.

Testing

Hydrometer testing is the best way to check battery condition. Use a hydrometer with numbered graduations from 1.100 to 1.300 rather than one with color-coded bands. To use the hydrometer, squeeze the rubber ball, insert the tip into the cell and release the ball. Draw enough electrolyte to float the weighted float inside the hydrometer. Note the number in line with surface of the electrolyte; this is the specific gravity for this cell. Return the electrolyte to the cell from which it came.

The specific gravity of the electrolyte in each battery cell is an excellent indication of that cell's condition. A fully charged cell will read 1.275-1.280, while a cell in good condition may read from 1.250-1.280. A cell in fair condition reads from 1.225-1.250 and anything below 1.225 is practically dead.

Specific gravity varies with temperature. For each 10° that electrolyte temperature exceeds 80 F,

add 0.004 to reading indicated on hydrometer. Subtract 0.004 for each 10 below 80 F.

If the cells test in the poor range, the battery requires recharging. The hydrometer is useful for checking the progress of the charging operation. **Table 3** shows approximate state of charge.

Charging

> *CAUTION*
> ***Never*** *connect a battery charger to the battery that is still connected to the bike's electrical system. Always* ***disconnect*** *the leads from the battery. During the charging procedure the charger may damage the diodes within the voltage regulator.*

> *CAUTION*
> *During charging, highly explosive hydrogen gas is released from the battery. The battery should be charged only in a well-ventilated area, and open flames and cigarettes should be kept away. Never check the charge of the battery by arcing across the terminals; the resulting spark can ignite the hydrogen gas.*

> *CAUTION*
> *Always remove the battery from the bike's frame before connecting the battery charger. Never recharge a battery in the bike's frame due to the corrosive mist that is emitted from the battery during the charging process. If this mist settles on the frame and surrounding area it will corrode the surface.*

1. Connect the positive (+) charger lead to the positive battery terminal and the negative (-) charger lead to the negative battery terminal.

2. Remove all vent caps from the battery, set the charger at 12 volts, and switch it on. If the output of the charger is variable, it is best to select a low setting—1-1/2 to 2 amps.

3. After the battery has been charged for about 8 hours, turn off the charger, disconnect the leads and check the specific gravity. It should be within the limits specified in **Table 3**. If it is, and remains stable after one hour, the battery is charged.

4. Clean the battery terminals, case, and tray and reinstall them in the motorcycle, reversing the removal steps. Coat the terminals with Vaseline or silicone spray to retard decomposition of the terminal material. Install the breather tube without any kinks or sharp bends. It must be clear in order to dissipate the gas normally given off by the battery.

New Battery Installation

When replacing the old battery with a new one, be sure to charge it completely before installing it in the bike. Failure to do so, or using the battery with a low electrolyte level, will permanently damage the new battery.

PERIODIC LUBRICATION

Checking Engine Oil Level

On models with an automatic transmission, the engine oil is also used in the torque converter. Engine oil level is checked with the dipstick, located on the top of the crankcase on the right-hand side. Refer to the following figures:

   a. **Figure 9** for automatic transmission models.
   b. **Figure 10** for Rebel 450 models.
   c. **Figure 11** for all other manual transmission models.

1. Start the engine and allow it to run for a couple of minutes.

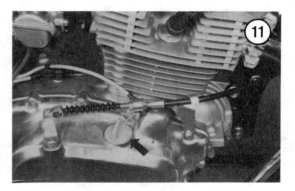

2. Shut off the engine and allow the oil to settle. Remove the dipstick, wipe it clean, and reinsert it; do not screw it in. Remove it and check level. The motorcycle must be level for a correct reading.

3. The level should be between the 2 lines, but not above the upper one (**Figure 12**). If necessary, add the recommended weight of oil (**Figure 13**) to correct the level. Install the dipstick and tighten it securely.

Changing Engine Oil and Filter

Regular oil changes will contribute more to engine longevity than any other maintenance performed. The factory-recommended oil change interval is listed in **Table 1**. The filter should be changed every other oil change. This assumes that the motorcycle is operated in moderate climates. In extremely cold climates, oil should be changed every 30 days. The time interval is more important than the mileage interval because acids formed by gasoline and water vapor from combustion will contaminate the oil even if the motorcycle is not run for several months. If the motorcycle is operated under dusty conditions, the oil will get dirty more quickly and should be changed more frequently than recommended.

Use only a high quality detergent oil with an API rating of SE or SF. The quality rating is stamped on the top of the can or label on plastic bottles (**Figure 14**). Try always to use the same brand of oil at each oil change. Refer to **Figure 13** for the correct weight of oil to use under different temperatures.

> *CAUTION*
> *On manual transmission models, do not add any friction reducing additives to the oil as they will cause clutch slippage. Also, do not use an engine oil with graphite added. The use of graphite oil will void any applicable Honda warranty. It is not established at this time if graphite will build up on the clutch friction plates and cause clutch problems. Until further testing is done by the oil and motorcycle industries, do not use this type of oil.*

To change the engine oil and filter you will need the following:

a. Drain pan.
b. Funnel.
c. Can opener or pour spout (canned oil only).
d. 17 mm wrench (drain plug).
e. 12 mm wrench (filter cover).
f. 3-4 quarts of oil depending on models.

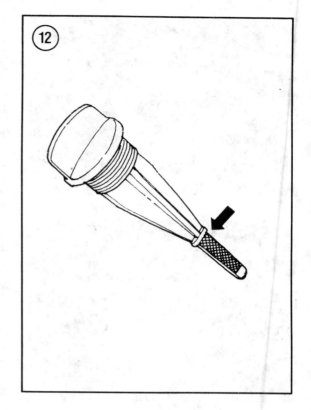

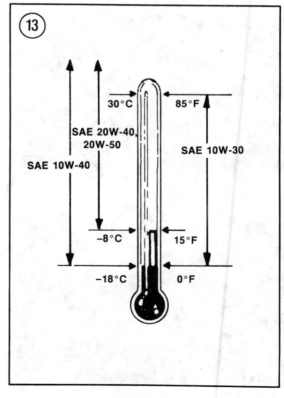

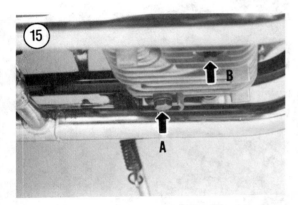

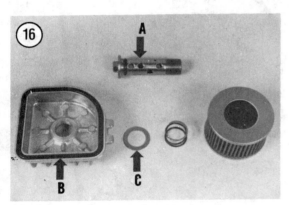

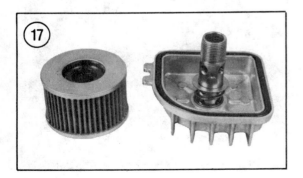

There are several ways to discard the old oil safely. Some service stations and oil retailers will accept your used oil for recycling; some may even give you money for it. Never drain the oil onto the ground.

1. Place the motorcycle on the center stand.
2. Start the engine and run it until it is at normal operating temperature, then turn it off.
3. Place a drip pan under the crankcase and remove the oil drain bolt (A, **Figure 15**). Remove the dipstick; this will speed up the flow of oil.

CAUTION
Do not let the engine start without oil in the crankcase. Make sure the ignition switch and engine kill switch are in the OFF position.

4. Let it drain for at least 15-20 minutes during which time kick the kick starter a couple of times to help drain any remaining oil.

NOTE
Before removing filter cover, thoroughly clean off all road dirt and oil around it.

5. To remove the oil filter, unscrew the bolt securing the filter cover (B, **Figure 15**) to the crankcase.
6. Remove the cover and the filter and discard the old filter. Clean out the cover and the bolt with cleaning solvent and dry them thoroughly. Remove all solvent residue.
7. Inspect the bolt O-ring (A, **Figure 16**) the cover seal (B, **Figure 16**) and the sealing washer (C, **Figure 16**). Replace these parts if damaged or deteriorated.

NOTE
Before installing the cover, clean off the mating surface of the crankcase—do not allow any road dirt to enter into the oil system.

8. Insert the bolt into the cover and install the spring and washer (**Figure 17**). Insert the filter and reinstall into the crankcase.
9. Tighten the filter cover bolt and the oil drain bolt to the torque specifications listed in **Table 4**.
10. Fill the crankcase with the correct weight and quantity of oil. Refer to **Table 5** for engine oil capacities.
11. Screw in the dipstick and start the engine. Let it idle at moderate speed and check for leaks.
12. Turn off the engine and check for correct oil level.

13. Remove the dipstick and wipe it clean. Reinsert it, but do not screw it in. Remove it and check level. Maintain the level between the upper and lower marks, but not above the upper one (**Figure 12**).

Front Fork Oil Change
(1982-1985 Air Assist Forks)

There is no factory recommended fork oil change interval but it's a good practice to change the oil at the interval listed in **Table 1**. If it becomes contaminated with dirt or water, change it immediately.

1. Place the bike on the center stand and place wood block(s) under the engine to support the bike so there is no weight on the front wheel.

> *WARNING*
> *In the next step, release air pressure gradually. If it is released too fast, oil will spurt out with the air. Protect your eyes and clothing accordingly.*

2. Unscrew the dust cap (**Figure 18**) and bleed off *all* fork air pressure by depressing the valve stem (**Figure 19**).

3A. On models so equipped, remove the trim plate (**Figure 20**) between the instrument cluster and the handlebars.

3B. On all models except the CB450SC cover the fuel tank with a heavy cloth or blanket to protect the surface from the handlebar. Remove the bolts securing the handlebar upper holders and remove the upper holders. Pull the handlebar assembly to the rear and rest it on the fuel tank.

4. Disconnect the air hose from the fittings on both the right- and left-hand fork top cap/air valve assemblies (**Figure 21**).

5. Unscrew the fitting from the fork top cap/air valve assembly (A, **Figure 22**). Unscrew the fork top cap/air valve assembly (B, **Figure 22**) slowly as it is under spring pressure from the fork spring.

6. Place a drain pan under the drain screw (**Figure 23**) and remove the drain screw. Allow the oil to drain for at least 5 minutes. *Never* reuse the oil.

> *CAUTION*
> *Do not allow the fork oil to come in contact with any of the brake components.*

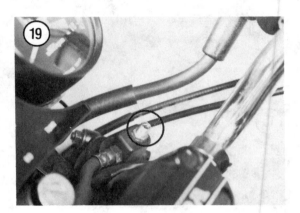

7. Inspect the gasket on the drain screw; replace it if necessary. Install the drain screw.

8. Repeat Steps 5-7 for the other fork.

9. Withdraw the upper short fork spring from each fork tube.

> *NOTE*
> *The spring spacer may stick to the bottom of the upper fork spring when the spring is removed; don't lose the spacer if it does come out with the spring.*

10. Refill each fork leg with the standard quantity of DEXRON automatic transmission fluid listed in **Table 6**.

> *NOTE*
> *In order to measure the correct amount of fluid, use a plastic baby bottle. These have measurements in fluid ounces (oz.) and cubic centimeters (cc) on the side.*

11. Inspect the O-ring seal (**Figure 24**) on the fork top cap bolt; replace if necessary.

12. If removed, install the fork spring spacer.

13. Install the upper short fork spring. Install the fork top cap bolt while pushing down on the spring. Start the fork cap bolt slowly; don't cross thread it.

14. Install both fork cap bolts and tighten each to the torque specifications listed in **Table 4**.

> *NOTE*
> *After both fork cap bolts are tightened they must be aligned to their original position to correctly accept the air hose. If necessary, loosen the upper and lower fork bridge bolts and rotate the fork tube until alignment is correct. Retighten the upper and lower fork bridge bolts to the torque specification listed in Table 4.*

15. Apply a light coat of grease to all new O-ring seals (**Figure 25**) on the air hose and fitting.

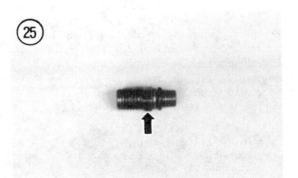

16. Install the air connector into the left-hand fork cap bolt and tighten to the torque specification listed in **Table 4**.

17. Install the air hose first to the right-hand fork top cap (without the connector) and tighten to the torque specification listed in **Table 4**.

NOTE
In the next step, hold onto the air hose connector (attached to the fork top cap bolt/air valve assembly) with a wrench while tightening the air hose fitting.

18. Install the air hose to the connector and tighten to the torque specification listed in **Table 4**.

19. If removed, install the handlebar assembly onto the lower holders. Align the punch mark on the handlebar with the top surface of the raised portion of the lower holders (**Figure 26**).

20. Install the upper holders and bolts. Tighten the forward bolts first and then the rear bolts. Tighten the bolts to the torque specification listed in **Table 4**.

WARNING
Never use any type of compressed gas as a lethal explosion may result. Never heat the fork assembly with a torch or place it near an open flame or extreme heat as this will also result in an explosion.

21. Inflate the forks to 60-100 kPa (8-14 psi). Do not use compressed air; use only a small hand-operated air pump as shown in **Figure 27**.

22. Apply the front brake and pump the front fork several times. Recheck the front fork air pressure; readjust if necessary.

22. Road test the bike and check for leaks.

Front Fork Oil Change
(1986 CB450SC Air Assist Forks and
Rebel 450 Models Non-air Assist)

There is no factory recommended fork oil change interval, but it's a good practice to change the oil at the interval listed in **Table 1**. If it becomes contaminated with dirt or water, change it immediately.

1. Place the bike on the center stand and place wood block(s) under the engine to support the bike so there is no weight on the front wheel.

CAUTION
In the next step, release air pressure gradually. If it is released too fast, oil will spurt out with the air. Protect your eyes and clothing accordingly.

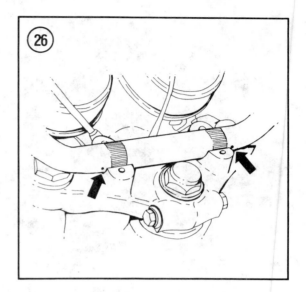

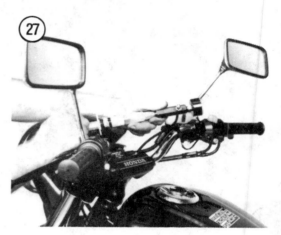

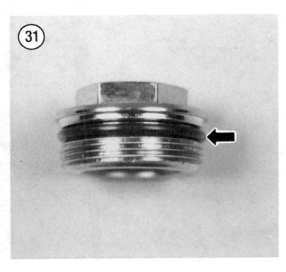

2A. On CB450SC models, perform the following:
   a. Unscrew the dust cap and bleed off *all* fork air pressure by depressing the valve stem.
   b. Unscrew the fork top cap/air valve assembly slowly as it is under spring pressure from the fork spring.

2B. On Rebel 450 models, unscrew the fork top cap (**Figure 28**) slowly as it is under spring pressure from the fork spring.

3. Place a drain pan under the drain screw (**Figure 29**) and remove the drain screw. Allow the oil to drain for at least 5 minutes. *Never* reuse the oil.

> *CAUTION*
> *Do not allow the fork oil to come in contact with any of the brake components.*

4. Inspect the gasket on the drain screw; replace it if necessary. Install the drain screw.

5. Repeat Steps 2-4 for the other fork.

> *NOTE*
> *On CB450SC models, the spring seat may stick to the bottom of the upper fork spring when the upper short spring or spacer is removed; don't lose the spring seat if it does come out with the upper fork spring.*

6A. On CB450SC models, withdraw the upper short fork spring from each fork tube.

6B. On Rebel 450 models, withdraw the spacer (**Figure 30**) from each fork tube.

7. Refill each fork leg with the following standard quantity of DEXRON automatic transmission fluid listed in **Table 6**.

> *NOTE*
> *In order to measure the correct amount of fluid, use a plastic baby bottle. These have measurements in fluid ounces (oz.) and cubic centimeters (cc) on the side.*

8. Inspect the O-ring seal (**Figure 31**) on the fork top cap bolt; replace if necessary.

9. If removed, install the fork spring seat.

10A. On CM450SC models, install the upper short fork spring into each fork tube.

10B. On Rebel 450 models, install the spacer into each fork tube.

11. Install the fork top cap bolt while pushing down on the spring. Start the fork cap bolt slowly; don't cross thread it.

12. Tighten each fork cap bolt to the torque specifications listed in **Table 4**.

13. On CB450SC models, inflate the forks to 60-100 kPa (8-14 psi). Do not use compressed air; use only a small hand-operated air pump.

14. Apply the front brake and pump the front fork several times. Recheck the front fork air pressure; readjust if necessary.

15. Road test the bike and check for leaks.

Front Fork Oil Change
(All Other Models)

The oil in the front fork should be changed at the interval listed in **Table 1** or at any time that excessive bouncing of the front end indicates a low oil level. There is no practical way of checking, draining and correcting the level with the forks installed in the fork bridges.

It is necessary to completely disassemble the forks to change the oil on these models. Remove and disassemble the front forks as described in Chapter Nine.

Control Cable Lubrication

The control cables should be lubricated at the interval indicated in **Table 1**. They should also be inspected at this time for fraying and the cable sheath should be checked for chafing. The cables are relatively inexpensive and should be replaced when found to be faulty.

The control cables can be lubricated either with oil or with any of the popular cable lubricants and a cable lubricator. The first method requires more time and the complete lubrication of the entire cable is less certain.

Examine the exposed end of the inner cable. If it is dirty or the cable feels gritty when moved up and down in its housing, first spray it with a lubricant/solvent such as LPS-25 or WD-40. Let this solvent drain out, then proceed with the following steps.

Oil method

1. Disconnect the cables from the front brake lever, the clutch lever and the throttle grip assembly.

NOTE
On the throttle cable, it is necessary to
remove the screws that clamp the

housing together to gain access to the cable end.

2. Make a cone of stiff paper and tape it to the end of the cable sheath (**Figure 32**).

3. Hold the cable upright and pour a small amount of light oil (SAE 10W-30) into the cone. Work the cable in and out of the sheath for several minutes to help the oil work its way down to the end of the cable.

NOTE
To avoid a mess, place a shop cloth at
the end of the cable to catch the oil as it
runs out.

4. Remove the cone, reconnect the cable and adjust the cable(s) as described in this chapter.

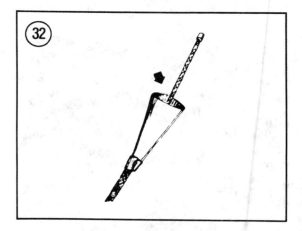

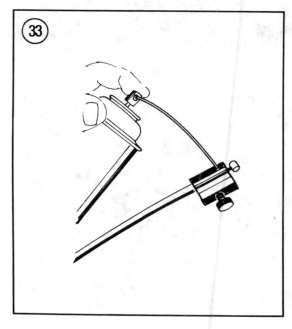

Lubricator method

1. Disconnect the cables from the front brake lever, the clutch lever and the throttle grip assembly.

> *NOTE*
> *On the throttle cable, it is necessary to remove the screws that clamp the housing together to gain access to the cable end.*

2. Attach a lubricator (**Figure 33**) to the cable following the manufacturer's instructions.

> *NOTE*
> *Place a shop cloth at the end of the cable(s) to catch all excess lubricant that will flow out.*

3. Insert the nozzle of the lubricant can in the lubricator, press the button on the can and hold it down until the lubricant begins to flow out of the other end of the cable.

4. Remove the lubricator, reconnect the cable(s) and adjust the cable(s) as described in this chapter.

Drive Chain Lubrication (CB450SC)

The CB450SC is equipped with an O-ring type drive chain. Oil the drive chain at the interval listed in **Table 1** or sooner if it becomes dry. A properly maintained drive chain will provide maximum service and reliability.

1. Place the bike on the center stand.

> *CAUTION*
> *The drive chain is an O-ring type. Do not use engine oil as a lubricant as it will damage the O-rings. Use a chain lubricant specifically formulated for use with this type of chain or the specified gear oil.*

2. Oil the bottom run of the drive chain with a commercial chain lubricant (formulated for O-ring chains) or SAE 80 or 90 gear oil. Concentrate on getting the lubricant down between the side plates of the chain links (**Figure 34**).

3. Rotate the rear wheel to bring the unoiled portion of the chain within reach. Continue until all of the chain is lubricated.

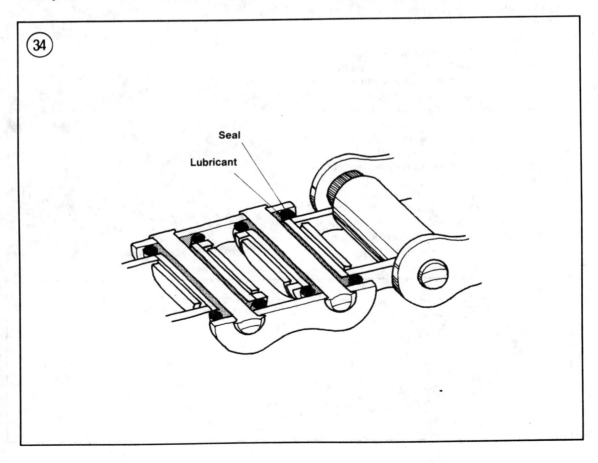

(34)

Seal

Lubricant

Swing Arm Grease Fittings
(Models so Equipped)

Lubricate the rear swing arm at the interval listed in **Table 1**, with multipurpose grease from a hand-type grease gun.

See **Figure 35** for the fitting on the right-hand side and **Figure 36** for the left-hand side.

Miscellaneous Lubrication Points

Lubricate the front brake lever, clutch lever and rear brake pedal pivot points.

PERIODIC MAINTENANCE

Drive Chain Adjustment

The drive chain should be checked and adjusted at the interval indicated in **Table 1**. A properly lubricated and adjusted drive chain will provide maximum service life and reliability.

The correct amount of drive chain free play, when pushed up midway on the lower chain run, is 15-25 mm (5/8-1 in.). See **Figure 37**.

1. Shift the transmission into NEUTRAL.
2A. On Rebel 450 models to adjust the tension, perform the following:
   a. Loosen the rear axle nut (**Figure 38**).
   b. Loosen the drive chain adjuster locknut (A, **Figure 39**) on each side of the swing arm.
   c. Turn the drive chain adjuster nut (B, **Figure 39**) on each side of the swing arm, in equal amounts, in either direction until the correct amount of free play is achieved.
2B. On all models except Rebel 450 to adjust the tension perform the following:
   a. On models so equipped, remove the rear axle nut cotter pin.
   b. Loosen the rear axle nut (A, **Figure 40**).
   c. Loosen the drive chain adjuster locknut (B, **Figure 40**) on each side of the swing arm.
   d. Turn the drive chain adjuster bolt (C, **Figure 40**) on each side of the swing arm, in equal

amounts, in either direction until the correct amount of free play is achieved.

> *NOTE*
> *On models so equipped, replace the drive chain when the red zone on the label aligns with the rear of the swing arm. Refer to Figure 41 or Figure 42.*

3. Rotate the rear wheel to move the drive chain to another position and recheck the adjustment. Chains rarely wear or stretch evenly. As a result, the free play will not remain constant over the

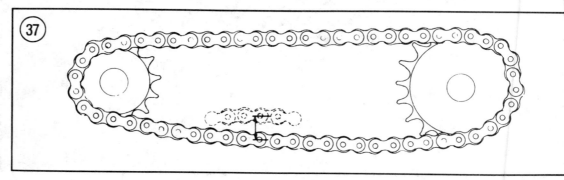

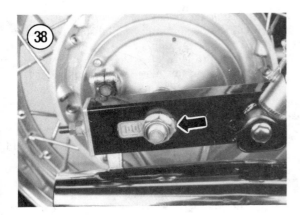

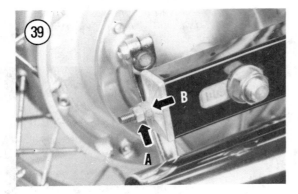

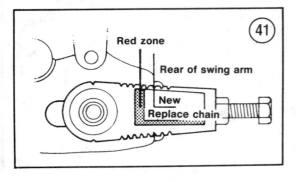

entire drive chain. If the drive chain cannot be adjusted within the limit of adjustment, the drive chain is excessively worn and stretched and should be replaced as described in Chapter Ten. Drive chain replacement numbers are listed in **Table 7**. Always replace both sprockets when replacing the drive chain; never install a new chain over worn sprockets.

WARNING
Excess free play can result in chain breakage which could cause frame damage and lead to a serious accident.

4. When the adjustment is correct, sight along the chain from the rear sprocket to see that it is correctly aligned as follows:

    a. It should leave the top of the rear sprocket in a straight line. If it is cocked to one side or the other, the rear wheel is incorrectly aligned and must be corrected.

    b. Turn the adjusters counter to one another until the chain and sprocket are correctly aligned.

    c. When the alignment is correct, readjust the free play as described in this chapter and tighten the adjuster locknuts securely.

    d. Tighten the axle nut to the torque specifications listed in **Table 4**.

5. After adjusting the drive chain, adjust the rear brake pedal free play as described under *Rear Brake Adjustment* in this chapter.

Drive Chain Cleaning, Inspection and Lubrication (Non O-ring Type)

At the interval listed in **Table 1**, remove, thoroughly clean and lubricate the drive chain.

1. Disconnect the master link (**Figure 43**) and remove the chain from the motorcycle.

2. Immerse the chain in a pan of cleaning solvent and allow it to soak for about a half hour. Move it around and flex it during this period so that dirt between the pins and rollers can work its way out.

3. Scrub the rollers and side plates with a stiff brush and rinse away loosened grit. Rinse it a couple of times to make sure all dirt and grit is washed out. Hang up the chain and allow it to thoroughly dry.

4. After cleaning the chain, examine it carefully for wear or damage. If any signs are visible, replace the chain.

5. Lay the chain alongside a ruler (**Figure 44**) and compress the links together. Then stretch them apart. If more than 0.6 mm (1/4 in.) of movement is possible, replace the chain; it is too worn to be used again.

> *CAUTION*
> *Always check both sprockets (**Figure 45**) every time the chain is removed. If any wear is visible on the teeth, replace the sprocket. Never install a new chain over worn sprockets or a worn chain over new sprockets.*

6. Check the inner faces of the inner plates (**Figure 46**). They should be lightly polished on both sides. If they show considerable wear on both sides, the sprockets are not aligned. Adjust alignment as described in Step 4 of *Drive Chain Adjustment* in this chapter.

> *WARNING*
> *Be careful when heating the grease in the next step. If the grease is heated excessively it may reach its flashpoint, resulting in a dangerous and difficult to extinguish fire. Never heat the grease with an open flame or on a hot plate. Heat it only by placing the grease pan in a larger pan containing about an inch of boiling water, and only after the water has been removed from the heat source.*

7. Lubricate the chain with a good grade of chain lubricant carefully following the manufacturer's instructions. As an alternative, lubricate by soaking in a pan of heated all-purpose grease such as Castrol Graphited Grease, Shell Retinax A or DC, Mobilgrease MP, or Marfax All-Purpose Grease. Heating permits the grease to penetrate the rollers and pins, but extreme care must be taken. After the chain has soaked in the grease for about a half hour, remove it from the pan and wipe off all the excess grease with a clean rag.

8. Reinstall the chain on the motorcycle. Use a new clip on the master link and install it so that the closed end of the clip faces the direction of the chain travel (**Figure 47**).

9. Adjust chain free play as described under *Drive Chain Adjustment* in this chapter.

Drive Chain Cleaning, Inspection and Lubrication (O-ring Type)

At the interval listed in **Table 1**, remove and thoroughly clean and lubricate the drive chain.

> *CAUTION*
> *The drive chain is equipped with O-rings. These rubber O-rings can easily be damaged. Do not use a steam cleaner, a high-pressure washer or any solvent that may damage the rubber O-rings.*

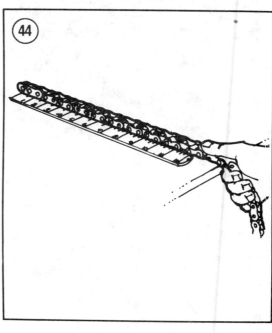

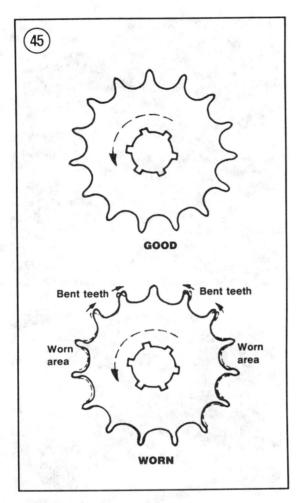

GOOD

Bent teeth   Bent teeth

Worn
area

Worn
area

WORN

3

1A. On all models equipped with a master link, disconnect the master link (**Figure 43**) and remove the chain from the motorcycle.

1B. On models without a master link, remove the drive chain as described under *Drive Chain Removal/Installation* in Chapter Ten.

2. Immerse the chain in a pan of diesel fuel, kerosene or non-flammable solvent and allow it to soak for about half an hour. Move it around and flex it during this period so that the dirt between the links, pins, rollers and O-rings may work its way out.

CAUTION
In the next step, do not use a wire brush or the O-rings will be damaged and the drive chain will have to be replaced.

3. Scrub the rollers and side plates with a medium soft brush and rinse away loosened dirt. Do not scrub hard as the O-rings may be damaged. Rinse it a couple of times to make sure all dirt and grit are washed out. Dry the chain with a shop cloth, then hang it up and allow the chain to thoroughly dry.

4. After cleaning the chain, examine it carefully for wear or damage. If any signs are visible, replace the chain.

NOTE
Always check both sprockets every time the chain is removed. If any wear is visible on the teeth, replace both sprockets. Never install a new chain over worn sprockets or a worn chain over new sprockets.

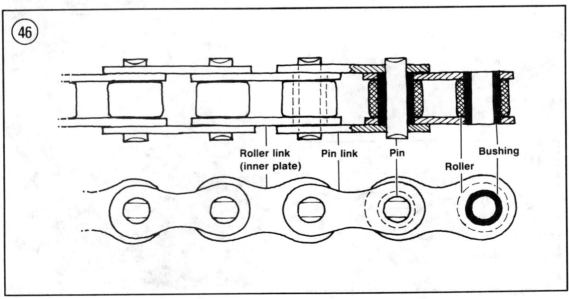

Roller link
(inner plate)   Pin link   Pin   Roller   Bushing

5. Lubricate the chain with SAE 80 or 90 weight gear oil or a good grade of chain lubricant (specifically formulated for O-ring chains), following the manufacturer's instructions.

6. Reinstall the chain on the motorcycle. Use a new clip on the master link and install it so that the closed end of the clip faces the direction of the chain travel (**Figure 47**).

7. Adjust chain free play as described under *Drive Chain Adjustment* in this chapter.

Drive Chain Slider
(Models So Equipped)

A plastic slider (**Figure 48**) is attached to the left-hand side of the swing arm directly below the upper run of the drive chain. If it is worn or damaged it must be replaced. The swing arm must be removed from the frame to replace the slider. Refer to *Swing Arm Removal/Installation* in Chapter Ten.

There is also a small metal oil guide plate directly below the lower run of the drive chain behind the drive sprocket. If damaged, remove the bolt (**Figure 49**) securing the plate and replace with a new one.

Front Fork Air Pressure Check
(Air Assist Forks)

Check the front fork air pressure when the forks are cold.

1. Place the bike on the center stand.

2. Remove the air valve cap (**Figure 50**).

3. Measure the air pressure with the air gauge furnished with the factory tool kit (or equivalent air gauge). The correct air pressure is 60-100 kPa (8-14 psi).

> *WARNING*
> *Never use any type of compressed gas as a lethal explosion may result. Never heat the fork assembly with a torch or place it near an open flame or extreme heat as this will also result in an explosion.*

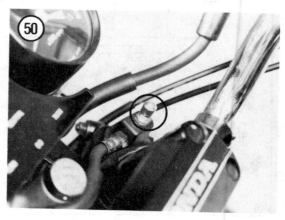

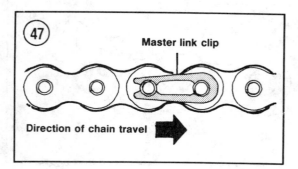

Master link clip

Direction of chain travel

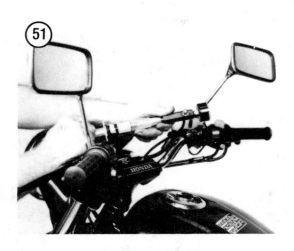

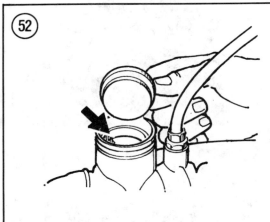

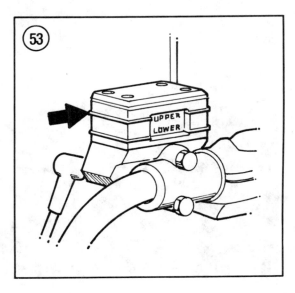

4. Adjust if necessary. Do not use compressed air; only use a small hand-operated air pump (**Figure 51**).

5. Remove the hand-held air pump and install the air valve cap.

Disc Brakes

The hydraulic brake fluid in the disc brake master cylinder should be checked at the interval listed in **Table 1**. The brake pads should also be checked for wear at the same time. Bleeding the system, servicing the brake system components and replacing the brake pads are covered in Chapter Eleven.

Disc Brake Fluid Level

The hydraulic brake fluid in the reservoir should be up to the upper line. Refer to the following figures:

   a. **Figure 52** for 1978 models.
   b. **Figure 53** for 1979-1980 models.
   c. **Figure 54** for 1981-on models.

If necessary, correct the level by adding fresh brake fluid.

1. Clean any dirt from the area around the cover before removing the cover.

> *WARNING*
> *Use brake fluid marked DOT 3 or DOT 4. Others may vaporize and cause brake failure. Do not intermix different brands or types of brake fluid as they may not be compatible. Do not intermix silicone based (DOT 5) brake fluid as it can cause brake component damage leading to brake system failure.*

> *CAUTION*
> *Be careful when adding brake fluid. Do not spill it on plastic, painted or plated surfaces as it will destroy the finish. Wash off the area immediately with soapy water and thoroughly rinse it off with clean water.*

2A. On CB400A and 1978 CB400T models, perform the following:
   a. Unscrew the cover.
   b. Fill the reservoir almost to the top lip and screw on the cover securely.
2B. On all other models, perform the following:
   a. Remove the screws securing the cover (**Figure 55**) and remove the cover, diaphragm plate (models so equipped) and diaphragm.
   b. Fill the reservoir almost to the top lip; insert the diaphragm plate (models so equipped), diaphragm and the cover loosely.

Disc Brake Lines

Check the brake line between the master cylinder and the brake caliper assembly. If there is any leakage, tighten the connections and bleed the brakes as described under *Bleeding the System* in Chapter Eleven. If tightening the connection does not stop the leak or if the brake line is obviously damaged, cracked or chafed, replace the brake line and bleed the system as described in Chapter Eleven.

Disc Brake Pad Wear

Inspect the brake pads for excessive or uneven wear or scoring of the disc. If the pads are worn to the wear groove, the pads must be replaced. If pad replacement is necessary, refer to Chapter Eleven.

> *CAUTION*
> *Always replace both pads in each caliper at the same time to maintain even pressure on the brake disc.*

Disc Brake Fluid Change

Every time the reservoir cap is removed, a small amount of dirt and moisture enters the brake fluid system. The same thing happens if a leak occurs or any part of the hydraulic brake system is loosened or disconnected. Dirt can clog the system and cause unnecessary wear. Water in the brake fluid vaporizes at high temperature, impairing the hydraulic action and reducing the brake's stopping ability.

To maintain peak braking efficiency, change the brake fluid at the interval listed in **Table 1**. To change brake fluid, follow the *Bleeding the System* procedure in Chapter Eleven. Continue adding new brake fluid to the master cylinder and bleed the

fluid out at the caliper until the brake fluid leaving the caliper is clean and free of contaminants.

> *WARNING*
> *Use brake fluid marked DOT 3 or DOT 4. Others may vaporize and cause brake failure. Do not intermix different brands or types of brake fluid as they may not be compatible. Do not intermix silicone based (DOT 5) brake fluid as it can cause brake component damage leading to brake system failure.*

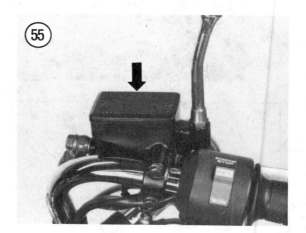

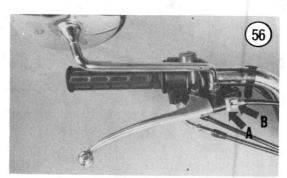

Front Drum Brake Adjustment

The front brake cable should be adjusted so that there is 3/4 to 1-1/4 in. (20-30mm) of brake lever movement required to actuate the brake, but it must not be so closely adjusted that the brake shoes contact the drum with the lever relaxed. The primary adjustment should be made with the control lever adjuster.

1. Loosen the locknut (A, **Figure 56**) and turn the adjusting barrel (B, **Figure 56**) in order to achieve the correct amount of free play. Tighten the locknut (A).

2. Because of normal brake wear, this adjustment will eventually be "used up." It is then necessary to loosen the locknut (A) and screw the adjusting barrel (B) all the way in toward the hand grip. Tighten the locknut (A).

3. At the brake plate on the wheel, loosen the locknut (C, **Figure 57**) and adjust the adjustment nut (D, **Figure 57**) until the brake lever can be used once again for fine adjustment. Be sure to tighten the locknut (C).

4. When the two arrows on the brake arm and brake plate align the brake shoes must be replaced. Refer to Chapter Eleven.

Rear Brake Height Adjustment

1. Place the motorcycle on the center stand.

2A. On Rebel 450 models, loosen the locknut and turn the adjustment bolt (**Figure 58**) until the brake pedal is at the desired height.

2B. On all models except Rebel 450, loosen the locknut (A, **Figure 59**) and turn the adjustment bolt (B, **Figure 59**) until the brake pedal is at the desired height.

3. Tighten the locknut and adjust switch as described under *Rear Brake Light Switch Adjustment* in Chapter Eight.

Rear Brake Free Play Adjustment

The rear brake pedal should be adjusted so that there is 20-30 mm (3/4-1 1/4 in.) of brake pedal movement required to actuate the brake, but it must not be so closely adjusted that the brake shoes contact the drum with the pedal relaxed.

1. Place the motorcycle on the center stand.

2. At the brake arm, turn the adjust nut (**Figure 60**) on the brake rod until the correct amount of free play can be achieved.

3. When the two arrows (**Figure 61**) on the brake arm and brake plate align, the brake shoes must be replaced. Refer to Chapter Eleven.

Clutch Adjustment

In order for the clutch to fully engage and disengage there must be 10-20 mm (3/8-3/4 in.) free play at the lever end (**Figure 62**).

1. On models so equipped, slide back the rubber boot covering the clutch adjuster and locknut (A, **Figure 63**).

2. Loosen the locknut (B, **Figure 63**) and turn the adjuster (C, **Figure 63**) in or out to obtain the correct amount of free play. Tighten the locknut (B).

> *CAUTION*
> *Do not screw the adjuster out so that there are more than 8 mm (0.3 in.) of threads exposed between it and the locknut.*

3. Start the engine, pull the clutch lever in and shift into first gear. If shifting is difficult, if bike creeps when stopped or if the clutch slips accelerating in high gear, the clutch will have to be adjusted at the clutch housing.

4. At the clutch lever, loosen the locknut (B, **Figure 63**) and screw the adjuster (C, **Figure 63**) in all the way toward the hand grip. Tighten the locknut (A).

5. At the clutch housing, loosen the locknut (A, **Figure 64**) and turn the adjuster (B, **Figure 64**) in or out to obtain the correct amount of free play and tighten the locknut (B).

6. If necessary, do some final adjusting at the clutch lever as described in Step 1.

7. Road test the bike to make sure the clutch fully disengages when the lever is pulled in; if it does not, the bike will creep in gear when stopped. Also, make sure the clutch fully engages; if it does not, it will slip, particularly when accelerating in high gear.

Throttle Operation/Adjustment

The throttle grip should have 2-6 mm (0.08-0.24 in.) rotational play (**Figure 65**). If adjustment is

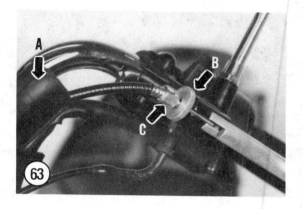

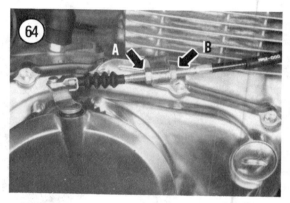

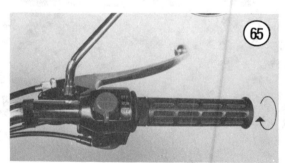

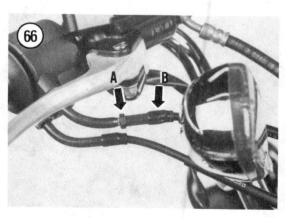

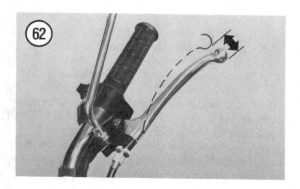

necessary, loosen the cable locknut (A, **Figure 66**) and turn the adjuster (B, **Figure 66**) in or out to achieve the proper play. Tighten the locknut (A).

Check the throttle cables from grip to carburetors. Make sure they are not kinked or chafed. Replace them if necessary.

Make sure that the throttle grip rotates smoothly from fully closed to fully open. Check at center, full left and full right position of the steering.

Air Filter Element Cleaning

The air filter element should be removed and cleaned (or replaced depending on model) at the interval indicated in **Table 1** and replaced whenever it is damaged or starts to deteriorate.

The air filter removes dust and abrasive particles before the air enters the carburetors and engine. Without the air filter, very fine particles could enter into the engine and cause rapid wear of the piston rings, cylinders and bearings. They also might clog small passages in the carburetors. Never run the bike without the element installed.

Proper air filter servicing can ensure long service from your engine.

Rebel 450

1. Place the bike on the centerstand.
2. Remove the Allen screws (**Figure 67**) securing the air filter case cover and remove the cover.
3. Remove the remaining Allen screw (**Figure 68**) securing the air filter case inner cover and remove the inner cover.
4. Remove the air filter element (**Figure 69**) from the air box.
5. Inspect the wire screen (**Figure 70**) for dirt and foreign matter. If dirty, remove the screen and thoroughly clean in solvent. Blow dry with compressed air and reinstall.

6. Wipe out the interior of the air box with a shop rag dampened in cleaning solvent. Remove any foreign matter that may have passed through a broken element.

7. Install a new air filter element into the air box. Make sure it seats correctly onto the air box.

8. Inspect the rubber seal around the perimeter of the air filter case inner cover for deterioration and damage; replace if necessary.

9. Install the air filter case inner cover and screws. Tighten the screws securely.

10. Install the air filter case cover and screws. Tighten the screws securely.

CB400T and CM400T

The air filter must be cleaned at the interval listed in **Table 1**.

1. Remove the seat.

2. Remove the screws (**Figure 71**) securing the air filter top cover and remove it.

3. Remove the air filter element (**Figure 72**) and the perforated grill (**Figure 73**).

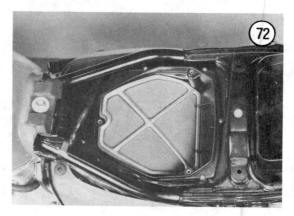

> *CAUTION*
> *Do not wring or twist the element as it will be torn or the individual foam cells will be damaged. Squeeze the element during the cleaning and oiling procedures.*

4. Clean the element gently in cleaning solvent until all dirt is removed. Squeeze out the solvent and dry thoroughly in a clean shop cloth until all solvent residue is removed. Let it dry for about one hour.

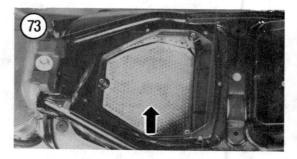

> *CAUTION*
> *Inspect the element; if it is torn or broken in any area it should be replaced. Do not run with a damaged element as it may allow dirt to enter the engine.*

5. Pour a small amount of SAE 80 or 90 gear oil or special foam air filter oil onto the element and work it into the porous foam material. Gently squeeze the element to remove the oil from the element leaving it slightly wet with the oil. Do not oversaturate the element as too much oil will restrict air flow. The element will be discolored by the oil and should have an even color indicating that the oil is distributed evenly. Let it dry for another hour before installation. If installed too soon, the chemical carrier in the special foam air filter oil will be drawn into the engine and may cause damage.

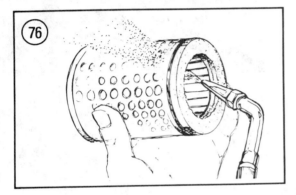

6. Wipe out the interior of the air box with a shop rag dampened in cleaning solvent. Remove any foreign matter that may have passed through a broken element.

7. Inspect the seal around the perimeter of the cover; replace if necessary.

8. Install the element by reversing these steps.

All other models

The filter element should be checked and blown clean with compressed air at the interval listed in **Table 1** or more frequently if used in dusty areas.

1. Remove the seat.

2. Remove the screws securing the air filter top cover (**Figure 74**) and remove it.

3. Lift up and remove the air filter element (**Figure 75**).

4. Tap the element to loosen the dust then blow it out with compressed air (**Figure 76**).

> *CAUTION*
> *Apply compressed air to the inside of the filter element only. Air pressure applied to the outside of the element will force dirt into the pores of the element material and destroy its filtering ability.*

5. Inspect the element; if it is torn or broken in any area, it should be replaced.

6. Wipe out the interior of the air box with a shop rag and cleaning solvent. Remove any foreign matter that may have passed through a broken filter element.

7. Install by reversing these removal steps.

Fuel Line Inspection

Inspect the fuel line (**Figure 77**) from the fuel tank to the carburetor. If it is cracked or starting to deteriorate it must be replaced. Make sure the small hose clamps are in place and holding securely.

> *WARNING*
> *A damaged or deteriorated fuel line presents a very dangerous fire hazard to both the rider and the bike if fuel should spill onto a hot engine or exhaust pipe.*

Fuel Strainer
(1982-on Models)

1. Turn the fuel shutoff valve to the OFF position.

2. Remove the fuel cup (**Figure 78**), O-ring seal and filter screen from the bottom of the fuel shutoff valve. Dispose of fuel remaining in the fuel cup properly.

3. Clean the filter screen with a medium soft toothbrush and blow out with compressed air. Replace the filter screen if it is broken in any area.

4. Wash the fuel cup in kerosene to remove any residue or foreign matter. Thoroughly dry with compressed air.

5. Align the index marks on the filter screen and the fuel shutoff valve body (**Figure 79**).

6. Install the O-ring seal and screw on the fuel cup.

7. Hand-tighten the fuel cup and then tighten to a final torque specification listed in **Table 4**. Do not overtighten the fuel cup as it may be damaged.

8. Turn the fuel shutoff valve to the ON position and check for leaks.

Wheel Bearings

The wheel bearings should be cleaned and repacked at the interval listed in **Table 1** or whenever there is a likelihood of water contamination. The correct service procedures are covered in Chapter Nine and Chapter Ten.

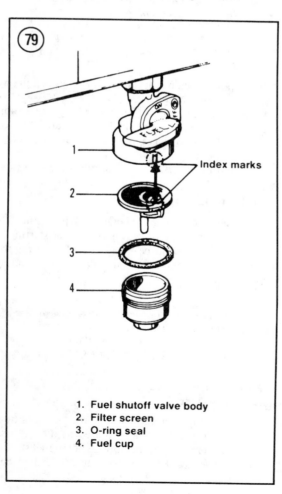

1. Fuel shutoff valve body
2. Filter screen
3. O-ring seal
4. Fuel cup

Index marks

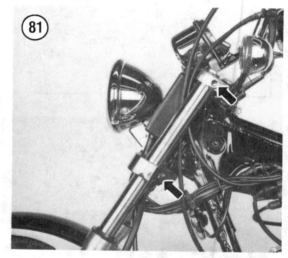

Front Suspension Inspection

The front suspension should be checked at the interval indicated in **Table 1**.

1. Visually inspect all components of the front suspension. If any signs of damage are apparent, the front suspension components must be repaired as described in Chapter Nine.

2. Check the tightness of the handlebar holder bolts (**Figure 80**) securing the handlebar.

3. Make sure the upper and lower fork bridge bolts (**Figure 81**) are tight.

4. On models so equipped, make sure the front axle nut (**Figure 82**) is tight and that the cotter pin is in place.

5. Make sure the front axle holder nuts (**Figure 83**) are tight and that the front axle (**Figure 84**) is tight.

> *WARNING*
> *If any of the previously mentioned bolts and nuts are loose, refer to Chapter Nine for correct procedures and torque specifications.*

Rear Suspension Check

1. Place wood block(s) under the frame to support the bike securely with the rear wheel off the ground.

2. Push hard on the rear wheel (sideways) to check for side play in the rear swing arm bearings.

3. Make sure the swing arm pivot bolt nut is tight (**Figure 85**).

4. Make sure the shock absorber upper and lower bolts are tight (**Figure 86**).

5. Make sure the rear axle nut (**Figure 87**) is tight and on models so equipped that the cotter pin is in place.

> *WARNING*
> *If any of the previously mentioned bolts and nuts are loose, refer to Chapter Ten for correct procedures and torque specifications.*

Nuts, Bolts and Other Fasteners

Constant vibration can loosen many of the fasteners on the bike. Check the tightness of all fasteners, especially those on:

a. Engine mounting hardware.
b. Engine crankcase covers.
c. Handlebar and front steering components.
d. Gearshift lever.
e. Kickstarter lever.
f. Brake pedal and lever.
g. Exhaust system.

Balancer Chain Adjustment
(1978 CM400T I, CM400T II, CM400A)

NOTE
*Adjust the balancer chain **only** if it becomes noisy.*

1. Place the bike on the center stand.
2. Drain the engine oil as described under *Changing Oil and Filter* in this chapter.
3. Remove the right-hand cover.
4. On manual transmission models, remove 2 bolts securing the clutch bracket (**Figure 88**); remove it and the cable from the clutch arm. Remove the tachometer drive cable if so equipped.
5. Remove the bolt and nut clamping the kickstarter arm (A, **Figure 89**) to the shaft and remove it. Remove the bolt securing the front right-hand footpeg and remove the footpeg assembly.

6. Remove the exhaust system as described under *Exhaust System Removal/Installation* in Chapter Seven.
7. On manual transmission models, remove bolts (**Figure 89**) securing the right-hand engine cover and remove the engine cover.
8. On automatic transmission models, remove the bolts (**Figure 90**) securing the outer side cover and remove. Remove the torque converter (**Figure 91**) by pulling it straight off the transmission input shaft. Remove the bearing(s). There are 2 caged bearings; during removal, one or more may stay on the shaft.

9. On automatic transmission models, remove the bolts (**Figure 92**) securing the inner side cover and remove the inner side cover.

NOTE
*Do not lose the oil check valve and spring (A, **Figure 92**).*

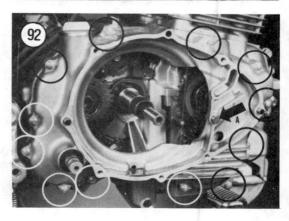

10. Loosen the 8 mm adjusting nut (A, **Figure 93**). The balancer chain will not automatically adjust to

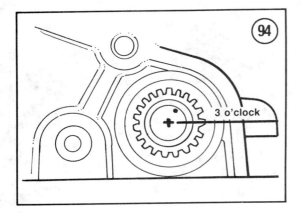

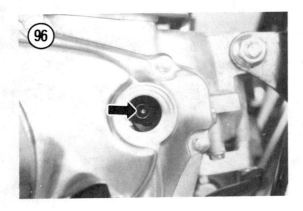

the correct tension. Tighten the nut to the torque specification listed in **Table 4**.

11. If after loosening the 8 mm nut, the adjuster plate bottoms out on the stud; it will have to be repositioned. Remove the 8 mm nut (A, **Figure 93**) and the 10 mm nut (B, **Figure 93**).

12. Remove the adjuster plate (C, **Figure 93**) and reposition it on the balancer shaft.

NOTE
When reinstalling the adjuster plate, center it within the threaded stud.

13. Torque the 8 mm and 10 mm nuts to the torque specification listed in **Table 4**.

CAUTION
The chain must be replaced if the punch mark on the end of the balancer shaft is below the 3 o'clock position (Figure 94). Refer to Crankcase Disassembly/Assembly in Chapter Four.

14. Install by reversing the removal steps.

15. Fill the crankcase with the recommended type and quantity of engine oil as described in this chapter.

Balance Chain Adjustment (All Other Models)

NOTE
Adjust the chain only if it becomes noisy.

1. Place the bike on the center stand.

2. Unscrew the inspection cap (**Figure 95**) from the right-hand engine cover.

3. Loosen the 8 mm adjusting nut (**Figure 96**). The balancer chain will now automatically adjust to the correct tension. Tighten the nut to the torque specification listed in **Table 4**.

4. If after loosening the 8 mm nut, the adjuster plate bottoms out on the stud, it will have to be repositioned. Perform Steps 1-15, *Balancer Chain Adjustment (1978 CM400T I, CM400T II, CM400A),* as described in this chapter.

Camshaft Chain Tensioner Adjustment (All Models Except Rebel 450)

NOTE
The Rebel 450 has an automatic cam chain tensioner assembly with no provisions for adjustment.

1. Place the bike on the center stand.

2. Start the engine, warm it up and allow it to idle.

NOTE
Figure 97 *is shown with the carburetor assembly removed for clarity.*

3. Loosen the camshaft chain tensioner locknut (**Figure 97**).

4. Let the engine remain at idle speed (1,200 ± 100 rpm); the chain tensioner will automatically locate itself to the right tension.

5. Tighten the locknut securely.

Sidestand Rubber

The rubber tip on the sidestand kicks the stand up if you should forget. If it wears down to the molded line (**Figure 98**) replace the rubber as it will no longer be effective.

TUNE-UP

A complete tune-up should be performed at the interval indicated in **Table 1** with normal riding. More frequent tune-ups may be required if the bike is ridden primarily in dusty areas.

The number of definitions of the term "tune-up" is probably equal to the number of people defining it. For the purposes of this book, a tune-up is general adjustment and maintenance to ensure peak engine performance.

Table 8 summarizes tune-up specifications.

The spark plug should be routinely replaced at every other tune-up or if the electrodes show signs of erosion. Have new parts on hand before you begin.

The air filter element should be cleaned or replaced before doing other tune-up procedures as described in this chapter.

Because different systems in an engine interact, the procedures should be done in the following order.

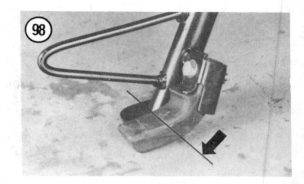

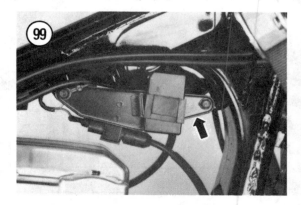

a. Clean or replace the air filter element.
b. Tighten the cylinder head bolts.
c. Adjust the valve clearances.
d. Check or replace the spark plug.
e. Check the ignition system.
f. Synchronize carburetors and set idle speed.

To perform a tune-up on your Honda, you will need the following tools and equipment:

a. 18 mm spark plug wrench.
b. Socket wrench and assorted sockets.
c. Spark plug wire feeler gauge and gapper tool.
d. Portable tachometer.

Cylinder Head Bolts

1. Place the bike on the center stand and remove the right- and left-hand side covers.
2. Remove the seat.
3. Remove the fuel tank as described in Chapter Seven.
4. On 1986-1987 models, remove screws securing the CDI unit/ignition coil bracket (**Figure 99**) and move the bracket assembly out of the way.
5. On California models so equipped, disconnect and remove the air injection control valve and hoses from the cam cover.
6. Disconnect the cam cover breather tube (**Figure 100**) from the cam cover.
7. Remove the bolts (**Figure 101**) on each side securing the cam cover. Rotate the cover forward and slide it off to one side.
8. Tighten the bolts in the sequence shown in **Figure 102**. Torque the bolts to the torque specification listed in **Table 4**.

> *NOTE*
> *On some models, the inner 4 bolts can be reached through holes (**Figure 103**) in the frame.*

The fuel tank and cam cover should be left off at this time for the following procedures.

Valve Clearance Adjustment

Valve clearance adjustment must be made with the engine cool, at room temperature (below 35° C/95° F). The correct valve clearance for all models is listed in **Table 8**. The exhaust valve is toward the front of the engine (near to the exhaust pipe) and the intake valves are located toward the rear of the engine (near to the carburetor intake port).

1. Remove the spark plugs from the cylinder head.
2A. On Rebel 450 models, perform the following:
   a. Remove the bolt and nut clamping the shift lever to the shaft and remove the shift lever (A, **Figure 104**).

b. Remove the bolt securing the front left-hand footpeg and remove the footpeg (B, **Figure 104**).

c. Remove the bolts securing the left-hand engine cover and remove the cover (C, **Figure 104**).

2B. On models other than Rebel 450, perform the following:

a. Remove the bolt and nut (A, **Figure 105**) clamping the shift lever to the shaft and remove the shift lever.

b. Remove the bolts (B, **Figure 105**) securing the left-hand engine cover and remove it.

3. Use the alternator rotor bolt and rotate the engine *counterclockwise* as viewed from the left-hand side of the bike. Rotate the engine until the engine timing "T" mark on the alternator flywheel aligns with the mark on the crankcase (**Figure 106**). One of the pistons must be at top dead center (TDC) on the compression stroke.

> *NOTE*
> *A cylinder on TDC will have all of its rocker arms loose, indicating that both intake valves and the exhaust valve are closed.*

4. With the engine timing mark on the "T," see if all 3 rocker arms for that cylinder are loose. If not, rotate the engine an additional 360° until all 3 rocker arms have free play.

5. Check the clearance on all 3 valves on that cylinder by inserting a flat feeler gauge between the adjusting screw and the valve stem. When the clearance is correct, there will be a slight drag on the feeler gauge when it is inserted and withdrawn.

6. To correct the valve clearance, loosen the locknut and turn the adjuster in or out so a slight resistance is felt on the feeler gauge. Hold the adjuster to prevent it from turning further and tighten the locknut securely (**Figure 107**). Recheck the clearance to make sure the adjuster did not slip when the locknut was tightened; readjust if necessary.

7. Rotate the engine 360° *counterclockwise* and make sure the "T" mark on the alternator flywheel aligns with the mark on the crankcase (**Figure 106**). Repeat Steps 7 and 8 for the other cylinder.

8. When all clearances have been checked and adjusted, install the left-hand engine cover, front footpeg, gearshift lever, spark plugs and the cam cover. Make sure that the cam cover gasket is aligned and in good condition. Reinstall the breather tube, fuel tank and the seat.

Compression Test

The results, when properly interpreted, can indicate general cylinder, piston ring, and valve condition.

1. Warm the engine to normal operating temperature. Ensure that the choke valve and throttle valve are completely open.
2. Remove the spark plugs.
3. Connect the compression tester to one cylinder following manufacturer's instructions.
4. Have an assistant crank the engine over until there is no further rise in pressure.
5. Remove the tester and record the reading.

6. Repeat Steps 3-5 for the other cylinder.

When interpreting the results, actual readings are not as important as the difference between the readings. Refer to **Table 8** for specified compression pressures for all models. A maximum difference of 400 kPa (56 psi) between the 2 cylinders is acceptable. Greater differences indicate worn or broken rings, leaky or sticky valves, blown head gasket or a combination of all.

If a low reading (10% or more) is obtained on one of the cylinders, it indicates valve or ring trouble. To determine which, pour about a teaspoon of engine oil through the spark plug hole onto the top of the piston. Turn the engine over once to clear some of the excess oil, then take another compression test and record the reading. If the compression returns to normal, the valves are good but the rings are defective on that cylinder. If compression does not increase, the valves require servicing. A valve could be hanging open, burned or a piece of carbon could be on a valve seat.

Spark Plug Selection

Spark plugs are available in various heat ranges, hotter or colder than the plugs originally installed at the factory.

Select a plug of the heat range designed for the loads and conditions under which the bike will be run. Use of incorrect heat ranges can cause a seized piston, scored cylinder wall or damaged piston crown.

> *NOTE*
> *For NGK and ND spark plugs, higher plug numbers designate colder plugs; lower plug numbers designate hotter plugs. For example, an NGK DPR9EA-9 plug is colder than a DPR7EA-9 plug.*

In general, use a hot plug for low speeds and low temperatures. Use a cold plug for high speeds, high engine loads and high temperatures. The plug should operate hot enough to burn off unwanted deposits, but not so hot that it is damaged or causes preignition. A spark plug of the correct heat range will show a light tan color on the portion of the insulator within the cylinder after the plug has been in service.

The reach (length) of a plug is also important. A longer than normal plug could interfere with the piston, causing permanent and severe damage; refer to **Figure 108**.

Refer to **Table 8** for Honda factory recommended spark plug heat ranges.

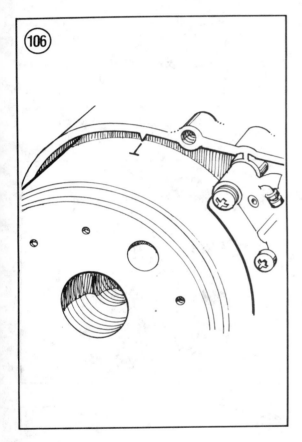

Spark Plug Removal/Cleaning

1. Grasp the spark plug lead as near the plug as possible and pull it off the plug (**Figure 109**). If it is stuck to the plug, twist it slightly to break it loose.
2. Use compressed air and blow away any dirt that has accumulated on the cylinder head around the spark plug.

> *CAUTION*
> *The dirt could fall into the cylinder when the plug is removed, causing serious engine damage.*

3. Remove the spark plug with a 18 mm spark plug wrench.

> *NOTE*
> *If the plug is difficult to remove, apply penetrating oil, like WD-40 or Liquid Wrench around the base of the plug and let it soak in about 10-20 minutes.*

4. Inspect the plug carefully. Look for a broken center porcelain, excessively eroded electrodes and excessive carbon or oil fouling. If present, replace the plug. If deposits are light, the plug may be cleaned in solvent with a wire brush or cleaned in a special spark plug sandblast cleaner. Regap the plug as explained in the following section.

Gapping and Installing the Plug

A spark plug should be carefully gapped to ensure a reliable, consistent spark. You must use a special spark plug gapping tool and a wire feeler gauge.

1. Remove the new spark plugs from the box. Do *not* screw on the small piece that may be loose in each box (**Figure 110**). If the small piece is installed, unscrew it as it is not to be used.
2. Insert a wire feeler gauge between the center and side electrode of the plug (**Figure 111**). The correct

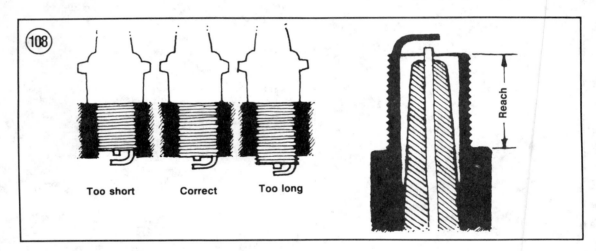

Too short   Correct   Too long

Reach

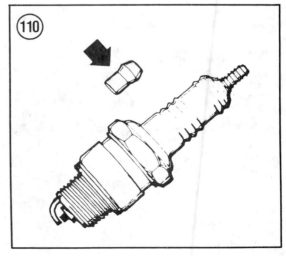

gap is listed in **Table 8**. If the gap is correct, you will feel a slight drag as you pull the wire through. If there is no drag, or the gauge won't pass through, bend the side electrode with a gapping tool (**Figure 112**) to set the proper gap.

3. Put a small drop of oil on the threads of the spark plug.

4. Screw the spark plug in by hand until it seats. Very little effort is required. If force is necessary, you have the plug cross-threaded; unscrew it and try again.

5. Use a spark plug wrench and tighten the plug an additional 1/4 to 1/2 turn after the gasket has made contact with the head. If you are installing an old, regapped plug and reusing the old gasket, only tighten an additional 1/4 turn.

CAUTION
Do not overtighten. This will only squash the gasket and destroy its sealing ability.

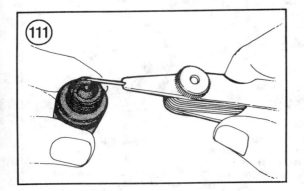

6. Install the spark plug leads; rotate them slightly in both directions and make sure they are on tight.

Reading Spark Plugs

Much information about engine and spark plug performance can be determined by careful examination of the spark plug. This information is only valid after performing the following steps.

1. Ride the bike a short distance at full throttle in any gear.

2. Turn the engine kill switch to the OFF position before closing the throttle and simultaneously shift to NEUTRAL; coast and brake to a stop.

3. Remove the spark plug and examine it. Compare it to **Figure 113**.

4. If the plugs are defective, replace them. If its condition indicates other engine problems, the engine cannot be properly tuned until repairs are made.

Capacitor Discharge Ignition (CDI)

All models are equipped with a capacitor discharge ignition (CDI). This system, unlike a battery or magneto ignition system, uses no breaker points or other moving parts.

Since there are no components to wear, adjusting the ignition timing is not necessary even after engine disassembly. The timing should not change for the life of the bike.

The only two items that could cause the timing to vary are the CDI unit and/or the alternator. Check the timing with the following procedure; if it is incorrect, check out both of these units as described in Chapter Eight.

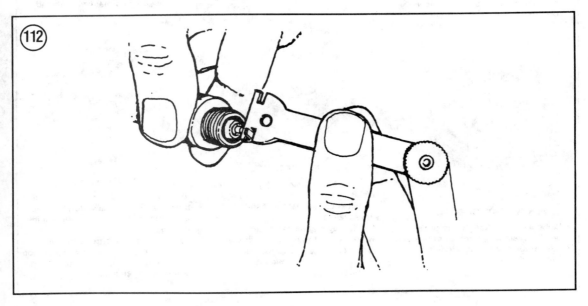

(113)   SPARK PLUG CONDITION

NORMAL

- Identified by light tan or gray deposits on the firing tip.
- Can be cleaned.

GAP BRIDGED

- Identified by deposit buildup closing gap between electrodes.
- Caused by oil or carbon fouling. If deposits are not excessive, the plug can be cleaned.

OIL FOULED

- Identified by wet black deposits on the insulator shell bore and electrodes.
- Caused by excessive oil entering combustion chamber due to worn rings and pistons, excessive clearance between valve guides and stems, or worn or loose bearings. Can be cleaned. If engine is not repaired, use a hotter plug.

CARBON FOULED

- Identified by black, dry fluffy carbon deposits on insulator tips, exposed shell surfaces and electrodes.
- Caused by too cold a plug, weak ignition, dirty air cleaner, too rich a fuel mixture, or excessive idling. Can be cleaned.

LEAD FOULED

- Identified by dark gray, black, yellow, or tan deposits or a fused glazed coating on the insulator tip.
- Caused by highly leaded gasoline. Can be cleaned.

WORN

- Identified by severely eroded or worn electrodes.
- Caused by normal wear. Should be replaced.

FUSED SPOT DEPOSIT

- Identified by melted or spotty deposits resembling bubbles or blisters.
- Caused by sudden acceleration. Can be cleaned.

OVERHEATING

- Identified by a white or light gray insulator with small black or gray brown spots and with bluish-burnt appearance of electrodes.
- Caused by engine overheating, wrong type of fuel, loose spark plugs, too hot a plug, or incorrect ignition timing. Replace the plug.

PREIGNITION

- Identified by melted electrodes and possibly blistered insulator. Metallic deposits on insulator indicate engine damage.
- Caused by wrong type of fuel, incorrect ignition timing or advance, too hot a plug, burned valves, or engine overheating. Replace the plug.

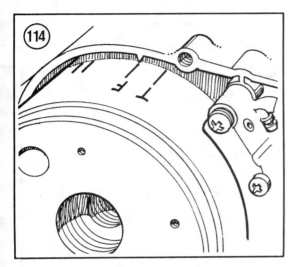

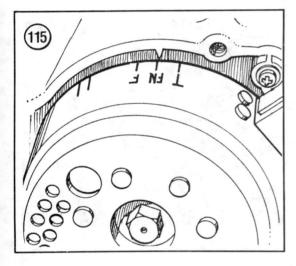

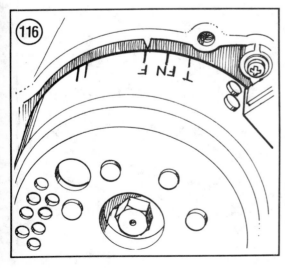

NOTE
Before starting on this procedure, check all electrical connections related to the ignition system. Make sure all connections are tight and free of corrosion and that all ground connections are tight.

1. Place the bike on the center stand or place wood blocks under the frame.

2A. On Rebel 450 models, perform the following:

   a. Remove the bolt and nut clamping the shift lever to the shaft and remove the shift lever (A, **Figure 104**).

   b. Remove the bolt securing the front left-hand footpeg and remove the footpeg (B, **Figure 104**).

   c. Remove the bolts securing the left-hand engine cover and remove the cover (C, **Figure 104**).

2B. On all other models, perform the following:

   a. Remove the bolt and nut (A, **Figure 105**) clamping the shift lever to the shaft and remove the shift lever.

   b. Remove the bolts (B, **Figure 105**) securing the left-hand engine cover and remove it.

3. Attach a timing light to either spark plug lead.

4. Place the bike on the center stand and start the engine. Let it warm up and idle at 1,200 ±100 rpm. Adjust if necessary as described under *Carburetor Idle Speed Adjustment* in this chapter.

5. Direct the timing light to the timing marks on the alternator flywheel and check the timing as follows:

   a. On *manual transmission* models the timing is correct if the "F" on the flywheel aligns with the mark on the crankcase (**Figure 114**).

   b. On *automatic transmission* models, with the transmission in NEUTRAL position, the timing is correct if the "FN" on the flywheel aligns with the pointer on the crankcase (**Figure 115**) and with the transmission in either gear, the timing is correct if the "F" aligns with the pointer on the crankcase (**Figure 116**).

6. Increase engine speed to between 4,500-5,350 rpm. The advance timing is correct, for both manual and automatic transmission models, if the mark on the crankcase aligns between the two lines on the flywheel (**Figure 117**).

Carburetor Synchronization

Before synchronizing the carburetors, the valve clearance must be properly adjusted.

This procedure requires a special tool to measure the manifold vacuum in both cylinders simultaneously.

1. Start the engine and let it warm up to operating temperature. Make sure the choke knob is all the way in and open.

2. Shut off the engine.

3. Remove the fuel tank. There should be enough fuel in the float bowls to run the bike for this procedure.

> *WARNING*
> *Do not rig up a temporary fuel supply as this presents a real fire danger. If you start to run out of fuel during the test, shut off the engine and momentarily install the fuel tank to refill the carburetor float bowls, then proceed with the test.*

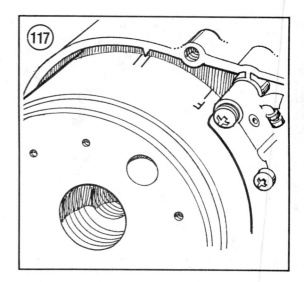

4A. On Rebel 450 models, disconnect the vacuum lines (**Figure 118**) from the cylinder head just above the rubber intake tubes. There is one for each cylinder.

4B. On all other models, remove the plugs (**Figure 119**) from the cylinder head just above the rubber intake tubes. There is one on each cylinder.

5. Connect the vacuum lines from the synchronizing tool, following the manufacturer's instructions.

6. Start the engine.

7. The carburetors are synchronized if both have the same gauge reading. If not, proceed as follows.

8. Set the engine idle speed to 1,200 ±100 rpm.

> *NOTE*
> *The figures shown in Step 9A and Step 9B are shown with the carburetor assembly removed for clarity. Do **not** remove the carburetor assembly for this procedure.*

9A. On Rebel 450 models, turn the adjusting screw (**Figure 120**) on the right-hand carburetor in either direction to achieve a balanced vacuum between the 2 carburetors.

9B. On all other models, loosen the locknut (A, **Figure 121**) and turn the adjusting screw (B, **Figure 121**). Turn the screw in either direction to achieve a balanced vacuum between the 2 carburetors.

> *NOTE*
> *The left-hand carburetor has no adjusting screw. Synchronize the right-hand carburetor to the left-hand carburetor.*

10. Adjust until the vacuum differential between the 2 carburetors is within 40 mm Hg (1.6 in. Hg).

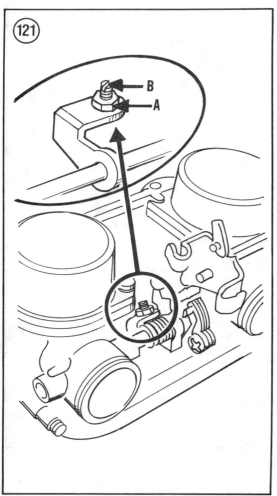

11. On all models except Rebel 450, tighten the locknut (A, **Figure 121**) securely.

12. Remove the vacuum lines.

13A. On Rebel 450 models, connect the vacuum lines (**Figure 118**) onto the cylinder head just above the rubber intake tubes. There is one for each cylinder.

13B. On all other models, install the 2 plugs (**Figure 119**) into the cylinder head just above the rubber intake tubes. There is one on each cylinder.

Carburetor Idle Adjustment

Before making this adjustment, the air filter must be clean, the carburetors must be synchronized as previously described and the engine must have adequate compression. See *Compression Test* in this chapter. Otherwise this procedure cannot be done properly.

1. Connect a portable tachometer to the engine following the manufacturer's instructions.

2. Start the engine and let it warm up to operating temperature. Make sure the choke knob is all the way in and open.

3. Rotate the black idle adjust screw (**Figure 122**), located between the 2 carburetors, to obtain the idle speed listed in **Table 8**.

4. Open and close the throttle a couple of times and make sure the idle speed does not change.

> *WARNING*
> *With the engine idling, move the handlebar from side to side. If idle speed increases during this movement, the throttle cable needs adjusting or may be incorrectly routed through the frame. Correct this problem immediately. Do not ride the vehicle in this unsafe condition.*

5. Turn the engine off and disconnect the portable tachometer.

Table 1 SCHEDULED MAINTENANCE

Every 300 miles (500 km) **or when dry**	• Lubricate and adjust the drive chain

Every 600 miles
(1,000 km)
	• Check tire inflation pressure
	• Check and adjust valve clearance
	• Adjust cam chain tensioner (models so equipped
	  with a cam chain adjuster)
	• Change engine oil
	• Check and adjust idle speed
	• Inspect brake system, examine drum brake shoes and
	  disc brake pads for wear
	• Check and adjust clutch lever free play
	• Check wheel spoke condition (models so equipped)
	• Inspect wheel rim condition (ComStar and ComCast)
	• Check wheel runout
	• Check wheel bearings for smooth operation
	• Lubricate all control cables
	• Check battery electrolyte level and condition
	• Lubricate side stand pivot point
	• Lubricate rear brake pedal and shift lever pivot
	• Inspect front suspension and steering for looseness

Every 4,000 miles
(6,400 km)
	• Check fuel shutoff valve and clean filter
	• Inspect crankcase ventilation hoses for cracks
	  or loose hose clamps—drain out all residue
	  (models so equipped)
	• Replace both spark plugs
	• Inspect brake fluid level
	• Clean and lubricate drive chain

Every 8,000 miles
(12,800 km)
	• Complete engine tune-up
	• Inspect fuel lines for chafed, cracked or
	  swollen ends
	• Inspect and adjust throttle operation
	• Inspect and adjust choke operation
	• Synchronize carburetors
	• Inspect secondary air supply hoses for cracks
	  or loose hose clamps (models so equipped)
	• Check engine mounting bolts and nuts for tightness
	• Inspect all suspension components for wear
	• Inspect drive chain slider for wear
	• Lubricate rear swing arm bushings or bearings

Every 12,000 miles **(19,200 km)**	• Replace air filter element * • Adjust engine balancer chain • Inspect evaporative emission hoses for cracks or loose hose clamps (models so equipped) • Change oil in front forks. • Change disc brake fluid • Repack wheel bearings with grease
* Replace sooner if ridden in dusty areas.	

Table 2 TIRE PRESSURES *

Model	Up to 206 lbs (90 kg)		Up to vehicle load limit	
	psi	kg/cm²	psi	kg/cm²
CB400T, CB400A				
Front	24	1.75	24	1.75
Rear	32	2.25	36	2.50
1979-1980 CM400T, 1979-1980 CM400A, CM400E				
Front	24	1.75	24	1.75
Rear	28	2.0	36	2.50
1981 CM400A				
Front	28	2.0	28	2.0
Rear	28	2.0	36	2.50
1981 CM400E				
Front	24	1.75	28	2.0
Rear	28	2.0	36	2.50
1981 CB400T, 1981 CM400C, CM400T				
Front	28	2.0	28	2.0
Rear	28	2.0	36	2.50
CM450A, CM450C, CM450T				
Front	28	2.0	28	2.0
Rear	28	2.0	36	2.50
CM450E				
Front	24	1.75	28	2.0
Rear	24	1.75	36	2.50
CB450SC				
Front	28	2.0	28	2.0
Rear	28	2.0	36	2.50
Rebel 450				
Front	28	2.0	28	2.0
Rear	28	2.0	28	2.0

* Tire inflation pressure for factory equipped tires. Aftermarket tire inflation pressure may vary according to the manufacturer's instructions.

Table 3 STATE OF CHARGE

Specific Gravity	State of Charge
1.110-1.130	Discharged
1.140-1.160	Almost discharged
1.170-1.190	One-quarter charged
1.200-1.220	One-half charged
1.230-1.250	Three-quarters charged
1.260-1.280	Fully charged

Table 4 MAINTENANCE AND TUNE-UP TORQUE SPECIFICATIONS

Item	N·m	ft.-lb.
Oil filter cover bolt	29-31	21-22
Oil drain bolt		
1978-1984	25-35	18-25
1985-on	32-38	23-27
Fork cap bolt	15-30	11-22
1982-1985 air-assist models		
and Rebel 450	15-30	11-22
1986 CM450SC	16-20	12-14
Fork bridge bolts		
Upper (1982-on)	9-13	7-9
Lower (1982-on)	18-25	13-18
Front fork interconnecting air hose (1982-on)		
Air connector-to-fork cap bolt	4-7	3-5
Air hose-to-fork cap bolt	4-7	3-5
Air hose-to-connector	15-20	11-14
Handlebar holder bolts	18-25	13-18
Rear axle nut		
Rebel 450	80-100	58-72
CB450SC	90-100	65-72
All other models	68-100	50-72
Fuel strainer cup	3-5	2-4
(models so equipped)		
Balancer chain		
8 mm adjust nut	20-24	15-18
Adjuster plate		
8 mm nut	20-24	15-18
10 mm nut	30-35	22-25
Cylinder head bolts	30-35	22-25

Table 5 ENGINE OIL CAPACITY

Engine size	Oil drain		Rebuild	
	U.S. qt.	Liter	U.S. qt.	Liter
Manual transmission	2.6	2.5	3.2	3.0
Automatic transmission	2.6	2.5	3.5	3.3

Table 6 FRONT FORK OIL CAPACITY *

Model	cc	fl. oz.
CB400T	175	5.9
CM400A, CM400C, CM400T, CB45OT	172	5.8
CM400E	135	4.6
CM450A, CM450C	105	6.9
CM450SC	185	2.3
Rebel 450	114	4.5

* Capacity for each fork leg.

Table 7 DRIVE CHAIN REPLACEMENT NUMBERS

Model	Number
CB400T, CB400A, CB450T, CM400E	DID 50DS-100L or RK 50KS-100L
CM400A, CM400C, CM400T	DID 50DS-102L or RK 50KS-102L
CM450A, CM450C, CM450E	DID 50DS-102L or RK 50KS-102L
CB450SC	DID 50H1-106LE or Takasago 520-106LE
Rebel 450	DID 525V or RK525 MO-21

3

Table 8 TUNE-UP SPECIFICATIONS

Valve clearance	
Intake	0.08-0.12 mm (0.003-0.005 in.)
Exhaust	0.12-0.16 mm (0.005-0.006 in.)
Compression pressure	
1979-1985	1,172-1,368 kPa (171-199 psi)
1986 CB450SC	1,000-1,400 kPa (145-205 psi)
Rebel 450	1,019-1,215 kPa (157-185 psi)
Spark plug type	
Standard heat range	
1978-1981	ND X24ES-U or NGK D8EA
1982	ND X24ESR-U or NGK DR8ES-L
1983-on	ND X24EPR-U9 NGK DPR8EA-9
Spark plug gap	
1978-1981	0.6-0.7 mm (0.024-0.028 in.)
1982-on	0.8-0.9 mm (0.032-0.036 in.)
Idle speed	
Manual transmission	1,200 ± 100 rpm
Automatic transmission	1,250 ± 100 rpm

CHAPTER FOUR

ENGINE

The engine is an air-cooled 4-stroke, 2-cylinder, single overhead camshaft design with three valves per cylinder. Three main bearings support the counterbalanced crankshaft that has two secondary chain driven vibration counter-balancers. The camshaft, driven by a Hy-Vo chain, operates the valves via rocker arms. A single rocker arm on each cylinder operates both intake valves; each valve has its own adjuster.

The oil pump supplies oil under pressure throughout the engine and is chain-driven by the crankshaft.

This chapter contains removal, inspection, service and reassembly procedures for the Honda Twin. Service procedures for the engine are virtually the same for both the manual and automatic transmission versions. Where differences occur they are identified.

From 1982-on, the engine displacement was increased from 395 cc (24.1 cu. in.) to 477 cc (27.3 cu. in.). The displacement increase is achieved through a larger bore with the stroke remaining the same as on the previous models.

Although the clutch and transmission are mounted within the engine, they are covered separately in Chapters Five and Six to simplify the presentation of this material.

Before beginning any engine work, re-read the service hints in Chapter One. You will do a better job with this information fresh in your mind.

Refer to **Table 1** and **Table 2** for engine specifications and to **Table 3** for torque specifications. **Tables 1-4** are located at the end of this chapter.

ENGINE PRINCIPLES

Figure 1 explains how the engine works. This will be helpful when troubleshooting or repairing your engine.

SERVICING ENGINE IN FRAME

Many components can be serviced while the engine is mounted in the frame (the bike's frame is a great holding fixture—especially when breaking loose stubborn bolts and nuts):

a. Cylinder head.
b. Camshaft and rocker arms.
c. Cylinder and pistons.
d. Oil pump and filter.
e. Gearshift mechanism.
f. Clutch or torque converter.
g. Carburetors.
h. Alternator and electrical systems.

4-STROKE PRINCIPLES

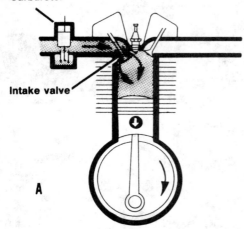

Carburetor

Intake valve

A

As the piston travels downward, the exhaust valve is closed and the intake valve opens, allowing the new air-fuel mixture from the carburetor to be drawn into the cylinder. When the piston reaches the bottom of its travel (BDC), the intake valve closes and remains closed for the next 1 1/2 revolutions of the crankshaft.

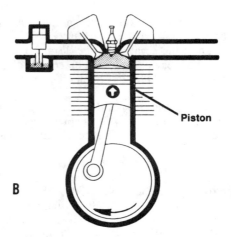

Piston

B

While the crankshaft continues to rotate, the piston moves upward, compressing the air-fuel mixture.

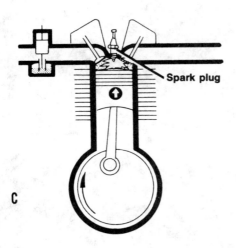

Spark plug

C

As the piston almost reaches the top of its travel, the spark plug fires, igniting the compressed air-fuel mixture. The piston continues to top dead center (TDC) and is pushed downward by the expanding gases.

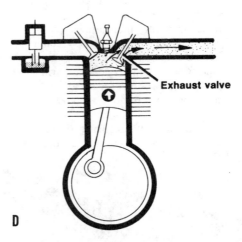

Exhaust valve

D

When the piston almost reaches BDC, the exhaust valve opens and remains open until the piston is near TDC. The upward travel of the piston forces the exhaust gases out of the cylinder. After the piston has reached TDC, the exhaust valve closes and the cycle starts all over again.

ENGINE

Removal/Installation
(Rebel 450)

1. Place wood blocks under the frame to support the bike securely.
2. Remove any accessories such as fairings and crash bars.
3. Disconnect the negative battery lead.
4. Drain the engine oil as described under *Changing Oil and Filter* in Chapter Three.
5. Remove the seat.
6. Remove the fuel tank as described under *Fuel Tank Removal/Installation* in Chapter Seven.
7. Disconnect the cam cover breather tube (**Figure 2**).
8. Disconnect the spark plug wires (**Figure 3**) and tie them up out of the way.
9. Remove the carburetors as described under *Carburetor Removal/Installation* in Chapter Seven.
10. Remove the exhaust system as described under *Exhaust System Removal/Installation* in Chapter Seven.
11. Remove the bolt and nut clamping the shift lever (A, **Figure 4**) to the shaft and remove the shift lever from the shaft.
12. Remove the Allen bolts securing the left-hand footpeg (B, **Figure 4**) and remove the left-hand footpeg and shift lever assembly.
13. Remove the bolt and nut clamping the brake pedal arm (A, **Figure 5**) to the shaft and remove the brake pedal arm from the shaft.
14. Remove the Allen bolts securing the right-hand footpeg (B, **Figure 5**). Remove the right-hand footpeg, brake pedal and arm assembly.
15. Remove the bolts securing the left-hand crankcase cover and remove the cover (C, **Figure 4**).
16. Remove the bolts securing the drive chain sprocket guide plate. Rotate the guide plate in

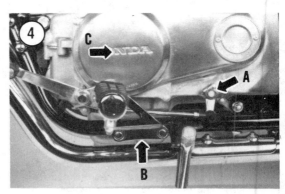

either direction, disengage it from the splines and remove the guide. Remove the sprocket and drive chain.

17. Disconnect the neutral/overdrive switch, pulse generator and alternator electrical connectors located under the seat.

18. Disconnect the starter electrical wire (**Figure 6**).

19. Loosen the clutch cable locknut (A, **Figure 7**) and adjuster (B, **Figure 7**), then disconnect the clutch cable from the clutch actuating arm.

20. If the engine is going to be totally disassembled, remove the following components as described in their respective chapters:

    a. Cylinder head and cylinder (this chapter).

    b. Pistons and rings (this chapter).

    c. Alternator (this chapter).

    d. Clutch (Chapter Five).

21. Take a final look all over engine to make sure everything has been disconnected.

> *NOTE*
> *Place wooden blocks under the crankcase to support engine after mounting bolts have been removed.*

22. Place a suitable size jack under the engine. Place a wood block between the engine and the jack to protect the crankcase. Apply just enough jack pressure to take the weight of the engine.

23. Remove the bolts and nuts securing the following engine mounting plates:

    a. Engine upper mounting plates (**Figure 8**).

    b. Engine front mounting plates (**Figure 9**).

    c. Engine rear upper mounting plates (A, **Figure 10**).

24. Remove the nuts and through-bolts from the front, upper rear and lower rear (B, **Figure 10**) portions of the engine. Remove the mounting plates also.

4

25. Apply additional jack pressure to raise the engine up slightly to clear the frame.

26. Remove the engine from the right-hand side frame and take to workbench for further disassembly.

27. Install by reversing the removal steps.

28. Tighten engine mounting bolts and nuts to specification in **Table 3**.

29. Fill the crankcase with the recommended type and quantity of engine oil. Refer to Chapter Three.

Removal/Installation
(All Models Except Rebel 450)

1. Place the bike on the center stand or place wood blocks under the engine to support the bike securely.

2. Remove the right- and left-hand side covers and accessories such as fairings and crash bars.

3. Disconnect the negative battery lead.

4. Drain the engine oil as described under *Changing Oil and Filter* in Chapter Three.

5. Remove the seat.

6. Remove the fuel tank as described under *Fuel Tank Removal/Installation* in Chapter Seven.

7. Disconnect the cam cover breather tube (**Figure 11**).

8. Disconnect the spark plug wires (**Figure 12**) and tie them up out of the way.

9. Disconnect the wire from the neutral safety switch (**Figure 13**).

10. Remove the bolts securing the rear upper engine mounting plates (**Figure 14**) and remove the mounting plates.

11. Remove the carburetors as described under *Carburetor Removal/Installation* in Chapter Seven.

12. Remove the bolt and nut clamping the shift lever (**Figure 15**) to the shaft and remove the shift lever.

13. Remove the exhaust system as described under *Exhaust System Removal/Installation* in Chapter Seven.

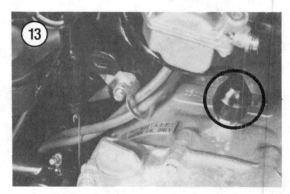

14. Remove the bolts (**Figure 16**) securing the left-hand crankcase cover and remove the cover.

15. Remove the bolts (**Figure 17**) securing the drive chain sprocket and remove the sprocket and drive chain.

16. Disconnect the electrical leads from the alternator to the electrical connector near the voltage regulator/rectifier.

17. On models equipped with an *automatic transmission,* perform the following:

    a. Remove the shield covering the oil pressure sending unit (**Figure 18**).

    b. Disconnect the electrical wire (A, **Figure 19**) from the sending unit.

18. On electric starter models, disconnect the starter electrical wire (B, **Figure 19**).

19. On models equipped with a *manual transmission,* disconnect the clutch cable from the clutch actuating arm.

20. On models so equipped, disconnect the tachometer drive cable from the left-hand crankcase cover.

21. If the engine is going to be totally disassembled, remove the following components as described in their respective chapters:

    a. Cylinder head and cylinder (this chapter).

    b. Pistons and rings (this chapter).

    c. Alternator (this chapter).

    d. On *manual transmission* models, remove the clutch (Chapter Five).

    e. On *automatic transmission* models, remove the torque converter and shift components (Chapter Six).

22. Take a final look all over engine to make sure everything has been disconnected.

23. Place a suitable size jack under the engine. Place a wood block between the engine and the jack to protect the crankcase. Apply just enough jack pressure to take the weight of the engine.

24. Remove the front bolts and nuts and the rear bolts and nuts securing the engine into the frame (**Figure 20**).

25. Lower the jack to allow the engine to slip out of the frame attachment points. Remove the engine from the frame and take to workbench for further disassembly.

26. Install by reversing the removal steps. The upper rear bolt has the electrical ground strap and bracket for the carburetor drain tubes attached to it (**Figure 21**).

27. Tighten engine mounting bolts and nuts to specification in **Table 3**.

28. Fill the crankcase with the recommended type and quantity of engine oil. Refer to Chapter Three.

CYLINDER HEAD, CAMSHAFT AND ROCKER ARM ASSEMBLIES (1978-1981)

The camshaft is driven by a Hy-Vo chain off of the timing sprocket on the camshaft.

The cylinder head, rocker arm assemblies and camshaft can be removed with the engine in the frame.

Cylinder Head, Camshaft and Rocker Arm Removal

CAUTION
To prevent any warpage and damage, remove the cylinder head only when the engine is at room temperature.

The cylinder head can be removed with the engine in the frame.

1. Place the bike on the center stand or place wood blocks under the engine.

2. Remove the seat and both side covers.

3. Disconnect the negative battery lead.

4. Remove the fuel tank as described under *Fuel Tank Removal/Installation* in Chapter Seven.

5. Remove the bolts (**Figure 14**) and nuts securing the rear upper engine mounting plates and remove the plates.

6. Remove the carburetors as described under *Carburetor Removal/Installation* in Chapter Seven.

7. Remove the exhaust system as described under *Exhaust System Removal/Installation* in Chapter Seven.

8. Remove the spark plug wires and spark plugs (**Figure 12**).

9. Disconnect the breather tube (**Figure 11**).

10. Remove the bolts (**Figure 22**) securing the cam cover and remove the cam cover and gasket.

11. Remove the bolts (**Figure 23**) securing the left-hand crankcase cover and remove the cover and gasket.

12. Use the alternator rotor bolt and rotate the engine until one of the cylinders is at top dead center on the compression stroke. This is to minimize the amount of cam pressure on the camshaft holders during the following steps.

NOTE
*In the following step, on some models, the inner 4 bolts can be reached through holes in the frame (**Figure 24**).*

13. Loosen all cylinder head bolts using the sequence shown in **Figure 25**. After loosening all 8 bolts, remove them.

14. Remove the rocker arm assemblies (**Figure 26**).

15. Remove the top bolt (**Figure 27**) securing the cam chain tensioner.

16. Remove the bolts securing the chain sprocket to the cam (**Figure 28**). Do not drop the bolts as they will fall into the crankcase. If this happens, the crankcase will have to be separated to retrieve the bolts.

17. Slide the chain and the sprocket to the left and off to the shoulder on the cam.

18. Pull the chain off the sprocket (**Figure 29**) and remove the sprocket.

19. Tie the chain up to the frame with a piece of wire (**Figure 30**).

NOTE
Do not drop the cam chain or it will drop into the crankcase.

20. Remove the cam from the cylinder head.

21. Loosen the head by tapping around the perimeter with a rubber or soft-faced mallet. If necessary, *gently* pry the cylinder head loose with a

broad-tipped screwdriver only in the ribbed areas of the fins as shown in **Figure 31** and **Figure 32**.

> *CAUTION*
> *Remember, the cooling fins are fragile and may be damaged if tapped or pried on too hard.*

> *CAUTION*
> *Do not pull both the cylinder head and the cylinder off as an assembly at this time. The upper end of the cam chain tensioner is secured between the cylinder and the cylinder head and the lower end is attached to the upper crankcase half.*

22. Remove the head by pulling straight up and off the cylinder.

23. Remove the front cam chain guide. Place a clean shop rag (**Figure 33**) into the cam chain slot in the cylinder to prevent the entry of foreign matter.

Cylinder Head Inspection

1. Remove all traces of gasket material from the head and the cylinder mating surface.

2. *Without* removing the valves, remove all carbon deposits from the combustion chambers with a wire brush. A blunt screwdriver or chisel may be used if care is taken not to damage the head or valves.

3. After all carbon is removed from combustion chambers and valve intake and exhaust ports, clean the entire head in solvent.

4. Clean away all carbon on the piston crowns. Do not remove carbon ridge at the top of the cylinder bore.

5. Check for cracks in the combustion chamber and exhaust ports. Cracked heads must be replaced.

6. Inspect the valves and valve guides as described under *Valves and Valve Components* in this chapter.

Rocker Mechanism
Disassembly/Inspection/Assembly

It is important that all parts be assembled in their original positions as shown in **Figure 34**.

Before disassembling, mark the parts with an "R" (right-hand cylinder) or "L" (left-hand cylinder).

Honda made a running change during the 1979 model year relating to the type of spring used on the rocker arm shafts. A coil type spring was used originally, but was changed to a wave type washer.

1. Push one of the rocker arm shafts out of the holder.

2. Remove the spring (or the wave washer) and the rocker arm.

3. Push the other rocker shaft out and remove the spring (or wave washer) and the rocker arm.

4. Clean all parts in solvent and dry thoroughly.

5. Inspect the rocker arm bore and bearing faces for signs of wear or scoring. Measure the inside diameter of the rocker arm bore (**Figure 35**) with a micrometer and check against measurements given in **Table 1**. Replace if worn to the service limit or greater.

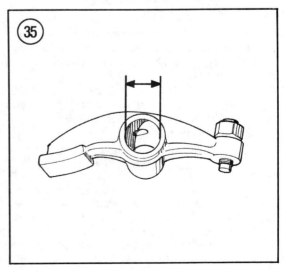

6. Inspect the rocker arm shafts for signs of wear or scoring. Measure the outside diameter of the rocker arm shaft (**Figure 36**) with a micrometer and check against measurements given in **Table 1**. Replace if worn to the service limit or less.

7. Inspect the rocker arm shaft bore in the rocker arm holder. Measure the inside diameter of the rocker arm shaft bore (**Figure 37**) with a micrometer and check against measurements given in **Table 1**. Replace if worn to the service limit or greater.

8. Check the springs (or wave washers) for distortion or breakage; replace as necessary.

9. Coat the rocker arm shafts, rocker arm bore and holder bore with fresh engine oil or assembly oil.

10. Slide the rocker shafts into the holder while assembling the rocker arms and springs (or wave washers) on the shaft.

Camshaft Inspection

1. Check the bearing journals for wear and scoring. Replace the camshaft if necessary.

2. Check cam lobes for wear. The lobes should not be scored and the edges should be square. Slight damage may be removed with a silicon carbide oilstone. Use No. 100-120 grit initially, then polish with a No. 280-320 grit.

3. Measure the height of each cam lobe with a micrometer as shown in **Figure 38** and check against the dimensions listed in **Table 1**. Replace the shaft if worn to the service limit dimension or less.

4. Check camshaft bearing bores in the cylinder head and the rocker shaft holder for wear or damage; replace as a set if necessary.

Cylinder Head, Camshaft and Rocker Arm Installation

1. Be sure that the location dowels are in position. The dowels with O-rings are at the rear (**Figure 39**).

2. Install a new head gasket and front cam chain guide (**Figure 40**).

3. Slide the cylinder head onto the cylinder.

4. Remove the bolt and nut clamping the shift lever (A, **Figure 41**) to the shaft and remove it.

5. If not already removed, remove the bolt (B, **Figure 41**) securing the footpeg and remove the footpeg.

6. If not already removed, remove the bolts securing the left-hand crankcase cover (**Figure 42**) and remove the cover and gasket.

7. Use the alternator rotor bolt and rotate the engine *counterclockwise* until the "T" timing mark on the alternator flywheel aligns with the pointer on the crankcase (**Figure 43**).

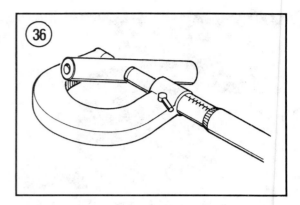

8. Coat the cam bearing surfaces with assembly oil and install cam with the notch straight up.

9. Position the cam sprocket with the timing marks toward the left-hand side.

10. Install the cam chain sprocket onto the cam, but not onto the cam shoulder.

11. Position the sprocket so the line is horizontal and install the cam chain onto it.

CAUTION
*The notch on the cam must point straight up (A, **Figure 44**) and the line on the cam chain sprocket must be horizontal (B, **Figure 44**). The "T" on the alternator flywheel must align with the pointer on the crankcase (**Figure 45**). Valve timing depends on the proper relationship of all of these parts. Very expensive damage could result from improper installation.*

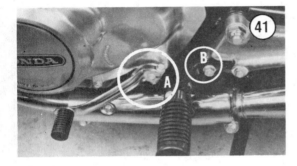

12. Slide the cam chain sprocket up onto the shoulder of the cam and install the bolts. Tighten the bolts to the torque specification listed in **Table 3**.

13. Make sure the locating dowels (**Figure 46**) are in position.

14. Install both rocker arm assemblies.

NOTE
*The inner 4 bolts have copper washers (A, **Figure 47**) and the outer 4 bolts hold the rocker arm retainer (B, **Figure 47**).*

15A. On 1980-1981 CB400T models, make sure the cylinder head bolts equipped with a rubber seal are installed as shown in A, **Figure 48**. Install the cylinder head bolts.

15B. On all other models, install the cylinder head bolts.

16. Tighten the bolts in the sequence shown in **Figure 48**. Tighten to the torque specification listed in **Table 3**.

17. Adjust cam chain tensioner as described under *Camshaft Chain Tensioner Adjustment* in this chapter.

18. Adjust the valves as described under *Valve Clearance Adjustment* in Chapter Three.

NOTE
Figure 49 *is shown with the rocker arm assembly removed for clarity.*

19. Fill the pockets in the head (**Figure 49**) with engine oil until the cam lobes are submerged in oil.

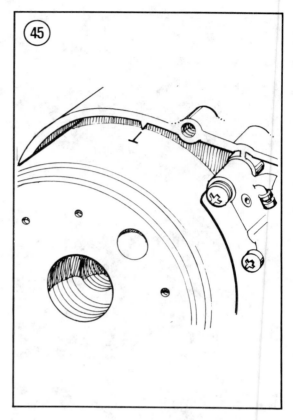

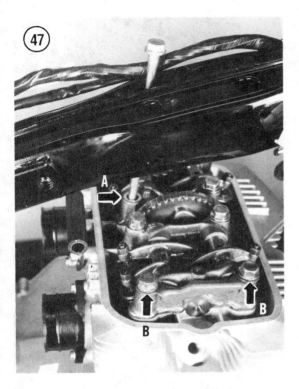

20. Make sure the cam cover gasket is in place and is in good condition; replace if necessary. Install the cam cover and bolts. Tighten the bolts securely.

21. Install the carburetors, spark plug, and exhaust system.

22. Install the upper engine mounting plates and bolts (**Figure 50**) and tighten to the torque specification listed in **Table 3**.

23. Install the fuel tank, seat, and side covers.

24. Start the engine and check for leaks.

CYLINDER HEAD, CAMSHAFT AND ROCKER ARM ASSEMBLIES (1982-ON)

The camshaft is driven by a Hy-Vo chain off of the timing sprocket on the camshaft.

The cylinder head, rocker arm assemblies and cam can be removed with the engine in the frame.

Cylinder Head, Camshaft and Rocker Arm Removal

CAUTION
To prevent any warpage and damage, remove the cylinder head only when the engine is at room temperature.

1. Place the bike on the center stand or place on wood blocks to support the bike securely.

2. Remove both side covers.

3. Disconnect the battery negative lead.

4. Remove the fuel tank as described under *Fuel Tank Removal/Installation* in Chapter Seven.

5A. On CB450SC models, perform the following.

   a. On California models, disconnect hoses from the air injection control valve.

   b. Remove the bolt securing the CDI unit bracket. Move the CDI unit out of the way.

   c. Disconnect the breather tube.

   d. Remove the bolts securing the reed valve housing and remove the housing from the cam cover.

   e. On California models, remove the bolts securing the charcoal canister and move the canister out of the way. Mark any hoses and their respective fitting if you unhook any hoses.

   f. Remove the spark plug wires and spark plugs.

   g. Remove the bolts and nuts (A, **Figure 51**) securing the rear upper engine mounting plates and remove the plates.

   h. Remove the bolts (B, **Figure 51**) securing the cam cover and remove the cam cover and gasket.

5B. On Rebel 450 models, perform the following:

   a. Remove the bolt securing the CDI unit bracket (**Figure 52**). Move the CDI unit out of the way.

   b. Disconnect the breather tube (**Figure 53**).

   c. Remove the spark plug wires and spark plugs (**Figure 54**).

   d. Remove the bolts (**Figure 55**) on each side securing the cam cover and remove the cam cover and gasket.

   e. Remove the bolts (**Figure 56**) and nuts securing the rear upper engine mounting plates and remove the plates.

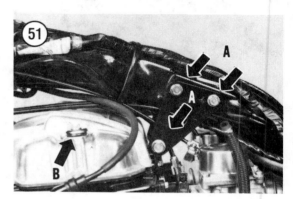

6. Remove the carburetors as described under *Carburetor Removal/Installation* in Chapter Seven.

7. Remove the exhaust system as described under *Exhaust System Removal/Installation* in Chapter Seven.

8. Remove the bolt and nut clamping the shift lever to the shaft and remove the shift lever.

9. Remove the bolt securing the footpeg and remove the footpeg.

10. Remove the bolts securing the left-hand crankcase cover and remove the cover and gasket.

11. Use the alternator rotor bolt and rotate the engine until one of the cylinders is at top dead center (TDC) on the compression stroke. This is to minimize the amount of cam pressure on the camshaft holders during the following steps. A

cylinder at TDC will have play in both of its rocker arms indicating that all 3 valves are completely closed.

12. On all models except Rebel 450, remove the cam chain tensioner bolt (**Figure 57**) and sealing washer.

13. Hold onto each oil pipe fitting with a wrench and remove each bolt (**Figure 58**) securing the rocker arm assembly oil pipe to each rocker arm assembly.

14. Remove the upper and lower bolts and sealing washers (one on each side of each oil pipe fitting) securing the external oil pipe to the cylinder head and to the crankcase. Remove the external oil pipe.

15. Remove the rocker arm assembly oil pipe from the rocker arm assemblies. Don't lose the O-ring seal in the front of the oil pipe receptacle.

4

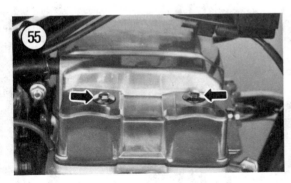

16. Loosen the cylinder head bolts following the sequence shown in **Figure 59**. On some models, the inner 4 bolts can be reached through the holes in the frame. After loosening all bolts, remove them.

17. Remove both rocker arm assemblies.

18. On Rebel 450 models, to allow maximum slack on the cam chain, the tension on the cam chain tensioner must be released. Perform the following:

   a. Cut a piece of wire approximately 2 mm (0.08 in.) in diameter and about 38 mm (1 1/2 in.) long. A straightened No. 2 paper clip will work.

   b. Pull the tip of the cam chain tensioner up with a pair of pliers until the hole in the tip is visible.

   c. Hold the tip up and insert the piece of cut wire into the hole in the tip (**Figure 60**).

   d. Bend the end of the wire over a little so it will not accidentally fall out during this procedure.

19. Remove the bolts (**Figure 61**) securing the cam chain sprocket to the cam. Do not drop the bolts as they will drop into the crankcase. If this happens, the crankcase must be separated to retrieve the bolts.

20. Slide the cam chain and sprocket to the left and off of the shoulder on the cam.

21. Pull the cam chain off of the sprocket and remove the sprocket.

NOTE
Do not drop the cam chain as it will drop into the crankcase.

22. Tie the cam chain up to the frame with a piece of wire.

23. Remove the cam from the cylinder head.

24. On Rebel 450 models, remove the bolts securing the cam chain tensioner to the cylinder head and remove the tensioner assembly.

CAUTION
Remember, the cooling fins are fragile and may be damaged if pried too hard.

25. Loosen the cylinder head by tapping around the perimeter with a plastic or soft-faced mallet. If

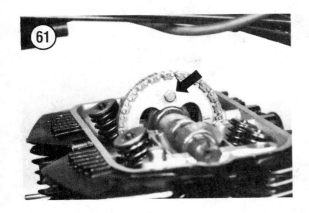

necessary, *gently* pry the head loose with a broad-tipped screwdriver only in the ribbed areas of the fins.

CAUTION
Do not pull both the cylinder head and cylinder off as an assembly. The upper end of the cam chain tensioner is secured between the cylinder and the cylinder head and the lower end is attached to the upper crankcase half.

26. Pull the cylinder head straight up and off of the cylinder.
27. Place a clean shop cloth into the cam chain slot in the cylinder to prevent the entry of foreign matter.

Cylinder Head Inspection

1. Remove all traces of gasket material from the cylinder head and the mating surface of the cylinder.
2. *Without removing the valves*, remove all carbon deposits from the combustion chambers with a wire brush. A blunt screwdriver or chisel may be used if care is taken not to damage the head, the valves or the spark plug hole threads.
3. After all carbon is removed from the combustion chambers and intake and exhaust ports, clean the entire head in solvent. Dry thoroughly with compressed air.
4. Clean away all carbon deposits on the piston crown. Do not remove the carbon ridge at the top of the cylinder bore.
5. Check for cracks in the combustion chamber and exhaust ports. A cracked head must be replaced.
6. Check the condition of the valves and valve guides as described under *Valves and Valve Components* in this chapter.

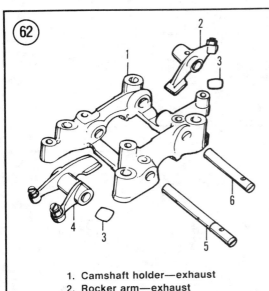

1. Camshaft holder—exhaust
2. Rocker arm—exhaust
3. Wave washer
4. Rocker arm—intake
5. Rocker arm shaft—intake
6. Rocker arm shaft—exhaust

Rocker Mechanism
Disassembly/Inspection/Assembly

It is important that all parts be assembled in their original positions as shown in **Figure 62**. Before disassembling, mark the parts with an "R" (right-hand cylinder) or "L" (left-hand cylinder).
1. Using a suitable size pin driver, drive out the rocker arm shaft stopper pins (**Figure 63**).

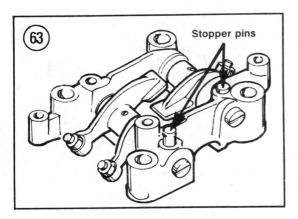

Stopper pins

2. Push one of the rocker arm shafts out of the holder.

3. Remove the wave washer and the rocker arm.

4. Push the other rocker shaft out and remove the wave washer and the rocker arm.

5. Clean all parts in solvent and thoroughly dry.

6. Inspect the rocker arm bore and bearing faces for signs of wear or scoring. Measure the inside diameter of the rocker arm bore (**Figure 64**) with a micrometer and check against measurements given in **Table 2**. Replace if worn to the service limit or greater.

7. Inspect the rocker arm shafts for signs of wear or scoring. Measure the outside diameter of the rocker arm shaft (**Figure 65**) with a micrometer and check against measurements given in **Table 2**. Replace if worn to the service limit or less.

8. Inspect the rocker arm shaft bore in the rocker arm holder. Measure the inside diameter of the rocker arm shaft bore (**Figure 66**) with a micrometer and check against measurements given in **Table 2**. Replace if worn to the service limit or greater.

9. Check the wave washers for distortion or breakage. Replace as necessary.

10. Coat the rocker arm shafts, rocker arm bore and holder bore with fresh engine oil or assembly oil.

11. Slide the rocker shafts into the holder while assembling the rocker arms and wave washers on the shaft.

> *NOTE*
> *Use a flat-bladed screwdriver to rotate the rocker arm shafts.*

12. Align the stopper pin holes in the rocker arm shafts with the holes in the rocker arm holder. Install the rocker arm shaft stopper pins (**Figure 63**). If they will not completely seat, tap them in with a plastic mallet until they are completely seated.

Camshaft Inspection

1. Check the bearing journals for wear and scoring. Replace the camshaft if necessary.

2. Check cam lobes for wear. The lobes should not be scored and the edges should be square. Slight damage may be removed with a silicon carbide oilstone. Use No. 100-120 grit initially, then polish with a No. 280-320 grit.

3. Measure the height of each cam lobe with a micrometer as shown in **Figure 67** and check against the dimensions listed in **Table 2**. Replace the shaft if worn to the service limit dimension or less.

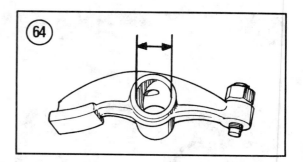

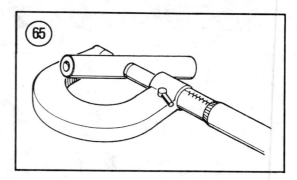

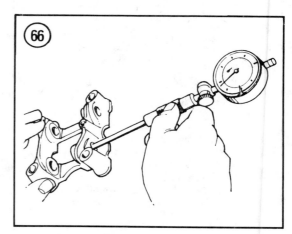

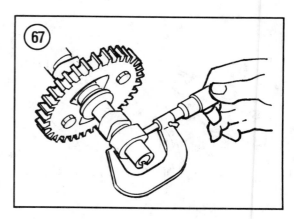

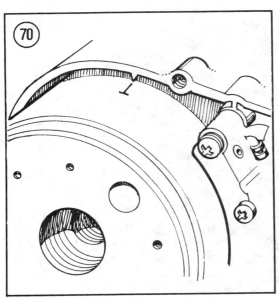

4. Check camshaft bearing bores in the cylinder head and the rocker shaft holder for wear or damage. Replace as a set if necessary.

Cylinder Head, Camshaft and Rocker Arm Installation

1. Be sure that the locating dowels are in position in the receptacles at the front of the cylinder (A, **Figure 68**).

2. Install a new head gasket (B, **Figure 68**).

3. Slide the cylinder head onto the cylinder.

4A. On Rebel 450 models, install the cam chain tensioner assembly into the cylinder head. Install the silver bolt at the top and the golden bolt at the bottom. Tighten both bolts securely.

4B. On all models except Rebel 450, loosen the cam chain tensioner locknut and pull the tensioner assembly (**Figure 69**) straight up as far as it will go. Tighten the locknut.

5. Using the alternator bolt, rotate the engine *counterclockwise* until the "T" on the alternator flywheel aligns with the pointer on the crankcase (**Figure 70**).

6. Coat the cam bearing surfaces with assembly oil and install the cam with the notch *straight up*.

7. Position the cam sprocket with the timing marks facing toward the left-hand side of the engine.

8. Install the cam chain sprocket onto the cam, but not onto the cam shoulder. Position the sprocket so the timing line is horizontal.

9. Install the cam chain onto the cam sprocket.

> *CAUTION*
> *The notch on the cam must point straight up and the timing line on the cam chain sprocket must be horizontal (**Figure 71**). The "T" on the alternator flywheel must align with the pointer on the crankcase (**Figure 70**). Valve timing depends on the proper relationship of all of these parts. Very expensive damage could result from improper installation.*

10. Slide the cam chain and sprocket up onto the shoulder of the cam and install the 2 bolts (**Figure 61**). Tighten the sprocket bolts to the torque specification listed in **Table 3**.

11. Make sure the locating dowels are in position in the rocker arm assemblies (**Figure 72**). Install both rocker arm assemblies.

> *NOTE*
> *The inner 4 bolts have copper washers and the outer 4 bolts hold the rocker arm shaft retainers (A, **Figure 73**). The front bolts are longer than the rear bolts.*

12. Install the cylinder head bolts. Make sure the 2 bolts with the rubber seal (just above the threads) are installed in the left-hand side inner holes (B, **Figure 73**).

13. Tighten the cylinder head bolts in the sequence shown in **Figure 74**. Tighten to the torque specification listed in **Table 3**.

14. On Rebel 450 models, perform the following:
   a. Straighten the end of the wire installed in the cam chain tensioner tip.
   b. Using a pair of pliers, pull up on the tip of the cam chain tensioner and remove the wire from the tensioner tip.

c. Make sure the tip slides down after the wire is removed. If necessary, *gently* tap on the tip with a plastic mallet. The tip must move down to apply the proper tension on the cam chain.

CAUTION
To avoid damage to the oil pipe assembly, hold onto the flat portion of the oil line fitting with a wrench when tightening the bolts.

15. Apply a light coat of grease to the O-ring seal to hold it in place during installation. Install the O-ring seal (**Figure 75**) into the front of the receptacle in the rocker arm assembly oil pipe and install the oil pipe. Install the oil pipe bolts (**Figure 76**). Hold each oil pipe fitting with a wrench (**Figure 58**) and tighten each bolt securely.

NOTE
Make sure the O-ring seal is still in place in the receptacle in the rocker arm assembly oil pipe.

16. Position the external oil pipe onto the engine. Install a washer on each side of the upper fitting on the oil pipe and install the bolt through the fitting, through the cylinder head wall and into the rocker arm assembly oil pipe (**Figure 77**). Tighten only finger-tight.

17. Install a washer on each side of the lower fitting of the oil pipe (**Figure 78**) and install the shorter bolt through the fitting and into the crankcase. Tighten only finger-tight.

CAUTION
To avoid damage to the oil pipe assembly, hold onto the flat portion of the oil line fitting with a wrench when tightening the bolts.

18. Hold each oil pipe fitting with a wrench and tighten the upper and lower bolts securely.

NOTE
The cam chain tensioner is automatic on Rebel 450 models and does not require any adjustment after installation.

19. On all models except Rebel 450, adjust the cam chain tensioner as described under *Camshaft Chain Tensioner Adjustment* in this chapter.

20. Adjust the valves as described under *Valve Clearance Adjustment* in Chapter Three.

21. Fill in the pockets in the head with engine oil until the cam lobes are submerged in oil.

22A. On CB450SC models, perform the following:
   a. Install the cam cover and gasket. Tighten the bolts securely.
   b. Install the upper engine mounting plates, bolts and nuts. Tighten the bolts and nuts to the torque specifications listed in **Table 3**.
   c. Install the spark plugs and wires.
   d. On California models, install the charcoal canister and reconnect any disconnected hoses. Make sure the hoses are attached to the correct fittings as marked during the removal step.
   e. Install the reed valve housing and tighten the bolts securely.
   f. Connect the breather tube.
   g. Install the CDI unit and bracket. Tighten the bolts securely.
   h. On California models, connect hoses onto the air injection control valve.

22B. On Rebel 450 models, perform the following:
   a. Install the rear upper engine mounting plates, bolts and nuts. Tighten the bolts and nuts to the torque specifications listed in **Table 3**.
   b. Install the cam cover and gasket. Tighten the bolts securely.
   c. install the spark plugs and wires.
   d. Connect the breather tube.
   e. Install the CDI unit and bracket. Tighten the bolts securely.

23. Install the carburetors and exhaust system.

24. Install the fuel tank, seat and side covers.

25. Start the engine and check for leaks.

VALVES AND VALVE COMPONENTS

A general practice among those who do their own service is to remove the cylinder head and take it to a machine shop or dealer for inspection and service. This is usually the best approach even for experienced mechanics.

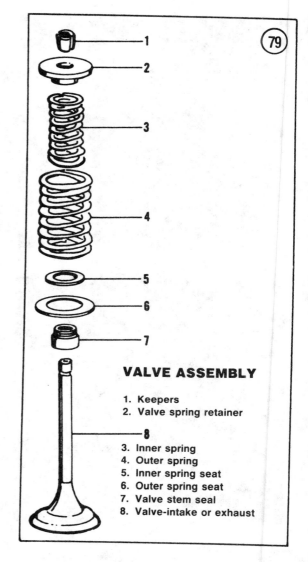

VALVE ASSEMBLY

1. Keepers
2. Valve spring retainer
3. Inner spring
4. Outer spring
5. Inner spring seat
6. Outer spring seat
7. Valve stem seal
8. Valve-intake or exhaust

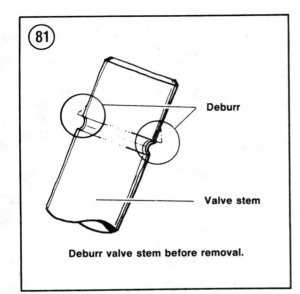

Deburr

Valve stem

Deburr valve stem before removal.

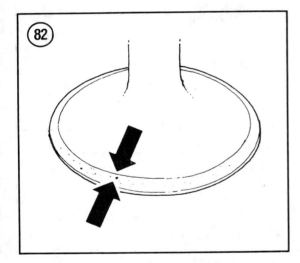

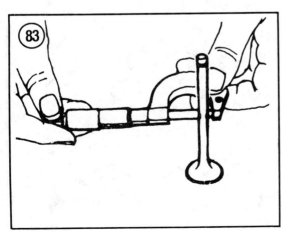

This procedure is included for those who choose to do their own valve service.

Due to the number of models and years covered in this book, the special Honda tools required for valve service are listed in **Table 4**.

Removal

Refer to **Figure 79** for this procedure.

1. Remove the cylinder head as described in this chapter.

> *CAUTION*
> *To avoid loss of spring tension, do not compress the springs any more than necessary to remove the keepers.*

2. Compress the valve springs with a valve compressor tool (**Figure 80**). Remove the valve keepers and release the compression. Remove the valve compressor tool.

3. Remove the valve spring retainer and valve springs.

> *NOTE*
> *The valve spring seat and valve stem seal will stay in the cylinder head.*

4. Remove the valve spring seat and the valve stem seal.

5. Before removing the valve, remove any burrs from the valve stem (**Figure 81**). Otherwise the valve guide will be damaged.

6. Mark all parts as they are disassembled so that they will be installed in their same locations.

Inspection

1. Clean valves with a wire brush and solvent.

2. Inspect the contact surface of each valve for burning or pitting (**Figure 82**). Unevenness of the contact surface is an indication that the valve is not serviceable. The valve contact surface *cannot* be ground as it has a special coating. If defective the valve(s) must be replaced.

3. Measure the valve stem for wear (**Figure 83**). Compare with specifications given in **Table 1** or **Table 2**.

4. Remove all carbon and varnish from the valve guide as described in this chapter.

5. Insert each valve in its guide. Hold the valve with the head just slightly off the valve seat and rock it sideways. If it rocks more than slightly, the guide is probably worn and should be replaced. As a final check, measure the valve guides.

6. Measure each valve spring free length with a vernier caliper (**Figure 84**). All should be within the length specified in **Table 1** or **Table 2** with no signs of bends or distortion. Replace defective springs in pairs (inner and outer).

7. Check the valve spring retainer and valve keepers. If they are in good condition they may be reused; replace as necessary.

8. Inspect the valve seats. If worn or burned, they must be reconditioned. This should be performed by a dealer or qualified machine shop.

Installation

1. Install the valve stem seal.

2. Coat the valve stems with molybdenum disulfide grease. To avoid damage to the valve stem seal, turn the valve slowly while inserting the valve into the cylinder head.

3. Install the valve spring seat.

> *NOTE*
> *Install the valve springs with their closer wound coils facing the cylinder head.*

4. Install the inner and outer springs.

5. Install the valve spring retainer.

> *CAUTION*
> *To avoid loss of spring tension, do not compress the springs any more than necessary to install the keepers.*

6. Compress the valve springs with a compressor tool (**Figure 80**) and install the valve keepers. Remove the compressor tool.

7. After all springs have been installed, gently tap the end of the valve stems with a soft aluminum or brass drift and hammer. This will ensure that the keepers are properly seated.

Valve Guide Inspection

1. Remove the valves as described in this chapter.

2. Ream out each valve guide prior to measuring the guide. Use a valve guide reamer for your specific model and year as listed in **Table 4** or equivalent.

> *CAUTION*
> ***Always** rotate the valve guide reamer **clockwise**. If the reamer is rotated counterclockwise, damage to a good valve guide will occur.*

3. Insert the valve guide reamer into the valve guide and rotate the reamer *clockwise* as shown in **Figure 85**. Continue to rotate the reamer and work it down through the entire length of the valve guide.

4. Rotate the reamer *clockwise* and remove all carbon buildup and varnish within the valve guide.

5. Rotate the reamer *clockwise* and withdraw the reamer from the valve guide. Remove the reamer.

6. Repeat Steps 3-5 for all other valve guides.

7. Thoroughly clean the cylinder head and valve guides with solvent and dry with compressed air.

8. Using a bore gauge, measure the inside diameter of each valve guide (**Figure 86**). Record the measurement for each valve guide.

9. Subtract the valve stem dimension from the valve guide dimension. This will give the

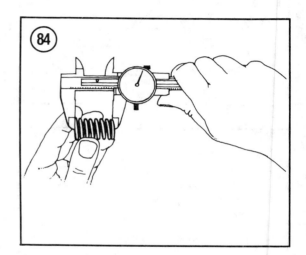

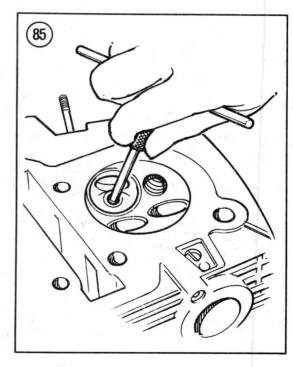

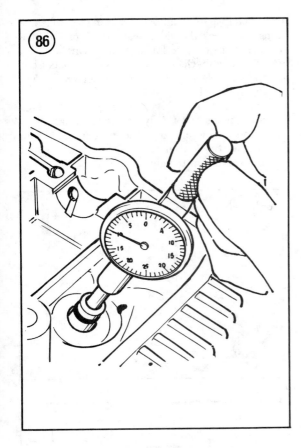

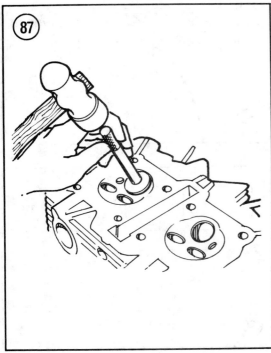

clearance. Compare to the dimension listed in **Table 1** or **Table 2**. If the valve stem-to-valve guide dimension exceeds the service limit, determine if a new guide with the standard dimension would bring the clearance within tolerance. If it will, replace the valve guides as described in this chapter.

10. If the valve stem-to-valve guide clearance exceeds the service limits with new guide, replace the valve also.

Valve Guide Replacement

When valve guides are worn so that there is excessive stem-to-guide clearance or valve tipping, the guides must be replaced. Replace both, even if only one is worn. This job should only be done by a dealer as special tools are required as well as considerable expertise. If the valve guides are replaced, also replace both valves as well.

The following procedure is provided if you choose to perform this task yourself.

CAUTION
*There **may** be a residual oil or solvent odor left in the oven after heating the cylinder head. If you use a household oven first check with the person who uses the oven for food preparation to avoid getting into trouble.*

1. The valve guides are installed with a slight interference fit. The cylinder head must be heated in an oven (or on a hot plate) to a temperature between 100-150° C (212-300° F). An easy way to check the proper temperature is to drop tiny drops of water on the cylinder head; if they sizzle and evaporate immediately, the temperature is correct.

CAUTION
Do not heat the cylinder head with a torch (propane or acetylene); never bring a flame into contact with the cylinder head or valve guide. The direct heat will destroy the case hardening of the valve guide and will likely cause warpage of the cylinder head.

2. Remove the cylinder head from the oven using kitchen pot holders, heavy gloves or heavy shop cloths—it is very *hot*.

3. Turn the cylinder head upside down on wood blocks. Make sure the cylinder is properly supported on the wood blocks.

4. From the combustion chamber side of the cylinder, drive out the old valve guide (**Figure 87**) with a hammer and valve guide remover for your specific model and year as listed in **Table 4** or equivalent. Remove the special tool.

5. While heating up the cylinder head, place the new valve guides in a freezer if possible. Chilling them will slightly reduce their overall diameter while the hot cylinder head is slightly larger due to heat expansion. This will make valve guide installation much easier.

6. Install a new O-ring seal onto the valve guide.

7. While the cylinder head is still hot, drive in the new valve guide into place in the cylinder head.

NOTE
The same Honda special tool is used for both removal and installation of the valve guide.

8. From the top side (valve side) of the cylinder, drive in the new valve guide with a hammer and valve guide remover for your specific model and year as listed in **Table 4** or equivalent. Drive the valve guide in until it completely seats in the cylinder head. Remove the special tool.

9. Ream the new valve guide as follows:

a. Ream out the new valve guide. Use a valve guide reamer for your specific model and year as listed in **Table 4** or equivalent.

CAUTION
Always rotate the valve guide reamer clockwise. If the reamer is rotated counterclockwise, damage to a good valve guide will result.

b. Apply cutting oil to both the new valve guide and the valve guide reamer.

c. Insert the valve guide reamer into the valve guide and rotate the reamer *clockwise* as shown in **Figure 85**. Continue to rotate the reamer and work it down through the entire length of the valve guide. Apply additional cutting oil during this procedure.

d. Rotate the reamer *clockwise* until the reamer has traveled all the way through the new valve guide.

e. Rotate the reamer *clockwise* and withdraw the reamer from the valve guide. Remove the reamer.

10. Repeat Step 9 for all other valve guides.

11. Thoroughly clean the cylinder head and valve guides with solvent to wash out all metal particles. Dry with compressed air.

12. Reface the valve seats as described in this chapter.

Valve Seat Inspection

1. Remove the valves as described in this chapter.

2. The most accurate method for checking the valve seal is to use Prussian blue or machinist's

dye, available from auto parts stores or machine shops. To check the valve seal with Prussian blue or machinist's dye, perform the following:

a. Thoroughly clean off all carbon deposits from the valve face with solvent or detergent, then dry thoroughly.

b. Spread a thin layer of Prussian blue or machinist's dye evenly on the valve face.

c. Moisten the end of a suction cup valve tool (**Figure 88**) and attach it to the valve. Insert the valve into the guide.

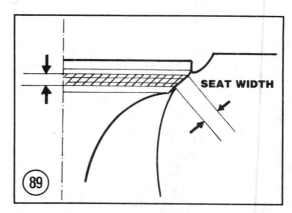

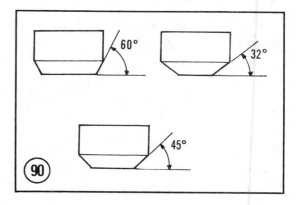

d. Using the suction cup tool, tap the valve up and down in the cylinder head. Do *not* rotate the valve or a false indication will result.

e. Remove the valve and examine the impression left by the Prussian blue or machinist's dye. If the impression left by the dye on the valve or in the cylinder head is not even and continuous and the valve seat width (**Figure 89**) is not within specified tolerance

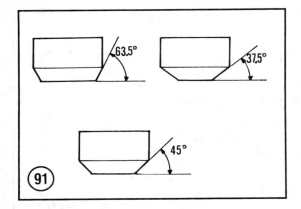

listed in **Table 1**, the cylinder head valve seat must be reconditioned.

3. Closely examine the valve seat in the cylinder head. It should be smooth and even with a polished seating surface.

4. If the valve seat is okay, install the valves as described in this chapter.

5. If the valve seat is not correct, recondition the valve seat as described in this chapter.

Valve Seat Reconditioning

Special valve cutter tools and considerable expertise are required to properly recondition the valve seats in the cylinder head. You can save considerable money by removing the cylinder head and taking just the cylinder head to a dealer or machine shop to have the valve seats ground.

The following procedure is provided if you choose to perform this task yourself.

Honda valve seat cutters and a grinder are available from a Honda dealer or from machine shop supply outlets. Follow the manufacturer's instruction in regard to operating the cutters and grinder. You will need the following 3 cutters:

a. Rebel 450: one 32°, one 45° and one 60° (**Figure 90**).

b. All models except Rebel 450: one 37.5°, one 45° and one 63.5° (**Figure 91**).

1. Use the 45 degree cutter and descale and clean the valve seat with one or two turns (**Figure 92**).

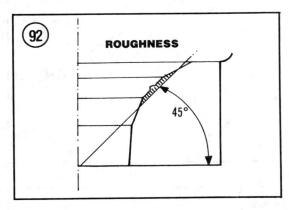

CAUTION
Measure the valve seat contact area in the cylinder head after each cut to make sure the contact area is correct and to prevent removing too much material. If too much material is removed, the cylinder head must be replaced.

2. Inspect the valve seat-to-valve face impression as follows:

a. Spread a thin layer of Prussian blue or machinist's dye evenly on the valve face.

b. Moisten the end of a suction cup valve tool (**Figure 88**) and attach it to the valve. Insert the valve into the guide.

c. Using the suction cup tool, tap the valve up and down in the cylinder head. Do *not* rotate the valve or a false indication will result.

d. Remove the valve and examine the impression left by the Prussian blue or machinist's dye.

e. Measure the valve seat width as shown in **Figure 93**. Refer to **Table 1** or **Table 2** for the seat. If the valve seat is burned or pitted, turn the 45 degree cutter an additional turn or two.

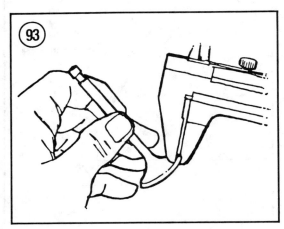

3A. On Rebel 450 models, perform the following:
  a. Use the 32 degree cutter and remove the top 1/4 of the existing valve seat material (**Figure 94**).
  b. Use the 60 degree cutter and remove the bottom 1/4 of the existing valve seat material (**Figure 95**).
  c. Install the 45 degree finish cutter and cut the valve seat to the proper width (**Figure 96**) listed in **Table 1** or **Table 2**. Make sure all pitting and irregularities are removed. Repeat Steps 2-5 if necessary.

3B. On all models except Rebel 450, perform the following:
  a. Use the 37.5 degree cutter and remove the top 1/4 of the existing valve seat material (**Figure 97**).
  b. Use the 63.6 degree cutter and remove the bottom 1/4 of the existing valve seat material (**Figure 98**).
  c. Install the 45 degree finish cutter and cut the valve seat to the proper width (**Figure 96**) listed in **Table 1** or **Table 2**. Make sure all pitting and irregularities are removed. Repeat Steps 2-5 if necessary.

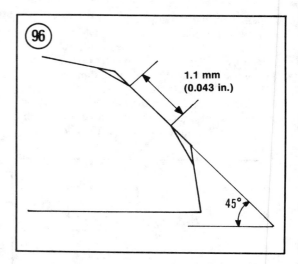

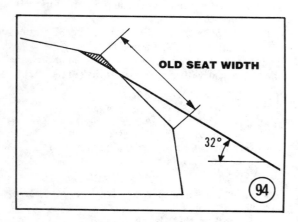

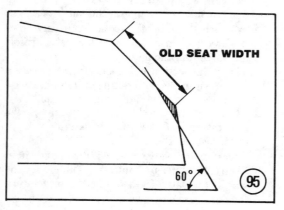

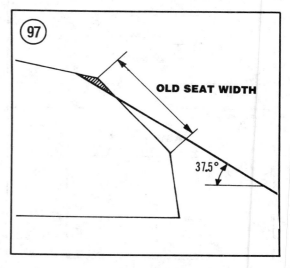

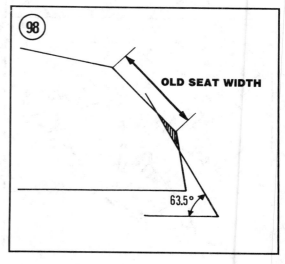

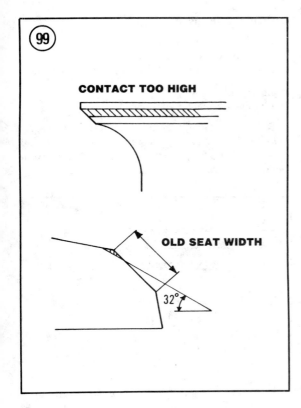

(99)

CONTACT TOO HIGH

OLD SEAT WIDTH

32°

4. Spread a thin layer of Prussian blue or machinist's dye evenly on the valve face.

5. Moisten the end of a suction cup valve tool (**Figure 88**) and attach it to the valve. Insert the valve into the guide.

6. Using the suction cup tool, tap the valve up and down in the cylinder head. Do *not* rotate the valve or a false indication will result.

7. Remove the valve and examine the impression left by the Prussian blue or machinist's dye.

8A. On Rebel 450 models, if the contact area is too *high* on the valve, the seat must be lowered.

    a. Use the 32 degree cutter and remove a portion of the top area of the valve seat material (**Figure 99**).

    b. If the contact area is too *low* on the valve, the seat must be lowered.

    c. Use the 60 degree cutter and remove a portion of the lower area of the valve seat material (**Figure 100**).

    d. Install the 45 degree finish cutter and cut the valve seat to the proper width (**Figure 96**) listed in **Table 1** or **Table 2**. Make sure all pitting and irregularities are removed.

8B. On all models except Rebel 450, if the contact area is too *high* on the valve, the seat must be lowered.

    a. Use the 37.5 degree cutter and remove a portion of the top area of the valve seat material (**Figure 101**).

    b. If the contact area is too *low* on the valve, the seat must be lowered.

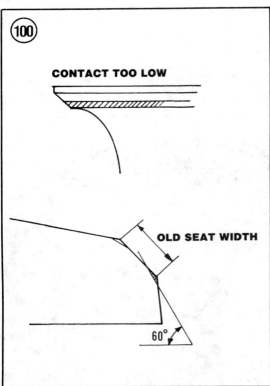

(100)

CONTACT TOO LOW

OLD SEAT WIDTH

60°

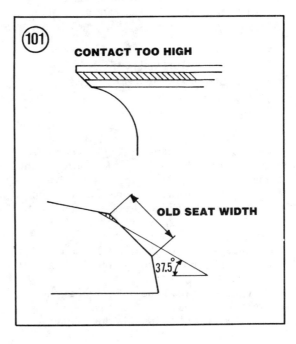

(101)

CONTACT TOO HIGH

OLD SEAT WIDTH

37.5°

c. Use the 63.5 degree cutter and remove a portion of the lower area of the valve seat material (**Figure 102**).

d. Install the 45 degree finish cutter and cut the valve seat to the proper width (**Figure 96**) listed in **Table 1** or **Table 2**. Make sure all pitting and irregularities are removed.

9. After cutting the seat, apply a small amount of lapping compound to the valve face.

10. Moisten the end of a suction cup valve tool (**Figure 88**) and attach it to the valve. Insert the valve into the guide.

CAUTION
Do not allow any lapping compound to enter the valve guide area as it will damage the valve guide.

11. Lap the valve *lightly*. Do *not* apply heavy pressure or the valve facing material will be removed.

12. Check that the finish has a smooth and velvety surface. The final seating will take place when the engine is first run.

13. Thoroughly clean the cylinder head and all valve components in solvent or detergent and hot water.

14. Install the valve assemblies and fill the ports with solvent to check for leaks. If any leaks are present, the valve seats must be inspected for foreign matter or burrs that may be preventing a proper seal.

15. If the cylinder head and valve components were cleaned in detergent and hot water, apply a light coat of engine oil to all bare metal surfaces that can rust.

CAMSHAFT CHAIN TENSIONER

Replacement
(Rebel 450)

1. Remove the rocker arm assemblies and camshaft. Perform Steps 1-23 of *Cylinder Head, Camshaft and Rocker Arm Removal* in this chapter.

2. Remove the bolts securing the cam chain tensioner to the cylinder head and remove the tensioner assembly.

3. Install the cam chain tensioner assembly into the cylinder head. Install the silver bolt at the top and the golden bolt at the bottom. Tighten both bolts securely.

4. Install the camshaft and rocker arm assemblies. Perform Steps 5-25 of *Cylinder Head, Camshaft and Rocker Arm Installation* in this chapter.

Tensioner Adjustment
(Rebel 450)

The cam chain tensioner is automatic on Rebel 450 models and does not require any adjustment.

Replacement
(All Models Except Rebel 450)

1. Remove the cylinder head as described under *Cylinder Head Removal* in this chapter.

2. Remove the spring pin clip and pin (**Figure 103**) securing the cam chain tensioner slipper to the

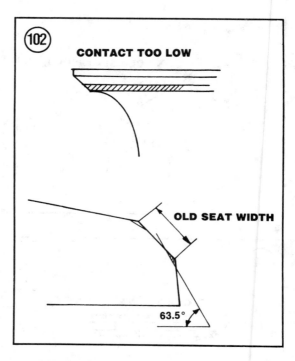

CONTACT TOO LOW

OLD SEAT WIDTH

63.5°

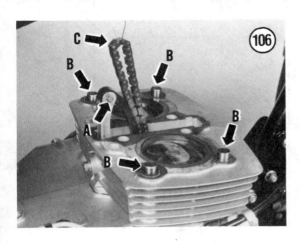

tensioner base. Remove the slipper from the tensioner base and the cylinder.

3. Remove the locknut, washer and O-ring securing the tensioner base to the cylinder and remove the tensioner base assembly.

4. Install the cam chain tensioner assembly into the cylinder. Install a new O-ring, the washer and locknut.

5. Pull the tensioner base all the way up until it stops, then tighten the locknut securely.

6. Install the tensioner slipper into the cylinder. Move the slipper back into position and install the pin and spring pin.

7. Install the cylinder head as described under *Cylinder Head Installation* in this chapter.

Tensioner Adjustment
(All Models Except Rebel 450)

1. Place the bike on the center stand.
2. Start engine; warm it up and allow it to idle.

NOTE
Figure 104 *is shown with the carburetor assembly removed for clarity.*

3. Loosen the camshaft chain tensioner locknut (**Figure 104**).
4. Let the engine remain at idle speed ($1,200 \pm 100$ rpm); the chain tensioner will automatically locate itself to the correct tension.
5. Tighten the locknut securely.

CYLINDER

This procedure is shown with both the 1978-1981 model engine and the 1982-on model engine. The procedures are the same on both models except where noted.

Removal

1. Remove the cylinder head as described under *Cylinder Head Removal* in this chapter.
2. Remove the head gasket and the front chain guide (A, **Figure 105**).
3. Remove the cam chain tensioner locknut, washer, and O-ring (B, **Figure 105**).
4. Remove the cam chain tensioner spring clip and pin (A, **Figure 106**).
5. Remove the 4 locating dowels (B, **Figure 106**).
6. Pull the cylinder straight up and off of the pistons.
7. Wire the cam chain up to the frame (C, **Figure 106**) to prevent if from falling into the crankcase.
8. Remove the 2 alignment dowels and the 2 oil control orifices from the top of the crankcase.

Inspection

The following procedure requires the use of highly specialized and expensive measuring instruments. If such equipment is not readily available, have the measurements performed by a dealer or qualified machine shop.

1. Soak with solvent any old cylinder head gasket material on the cylinder. Use a broad-tipped *dull* chisel and gently scrape off all gasket residue. Do not gouge the sealing surface as oil and air leaks will result.

2. Measure each cylinder bore with a cylinder gauge (**Figure 107**) or inside micrometer at the points shown in **Figure 108**. Measure in 2 axes—in line with the piston-pin and at 90° to the pin. If the taper or out-of-round is 0.05 mm (0.002 in.) or greater, the cylinders must be rebored to the next oversize and new pistons installed. Always rebore both cylinders even though only one may require it.

NOTE
New pistons should be obtained before the cylinders are rebored so that the pistons can be measured. Slight manufacturing tolerances must be taken into account to determine the actual size and working clearance.

3. Check the cylinder walls for scratches; if evident, the cylinder(s) should be rebored.

NOTE
*The maximum wear limit on the cylinders is listed in **Table 1** or **Table 2**. If either cylinder is worn to this limit, it must be replaced. Never rebore a cylinder if the finished rebore diameter will be this dimension or greater.*

NOTE
After having the cylinders rebored, wash it thoroughly in hot soapy water. This is the best way to clean the cylinders of all fine grit material left from the bore job. After washing the cylinders, run a clean white cloth through them; the cloth should show no traces of dirt or other debris. If the rag is dirty, the cylinders are not clean enough and must be rewashed. After the cylinders are thoroughly clean, dry and lubricate the cylinder walls with clean engine oil to protect the cylinder liners from rust.

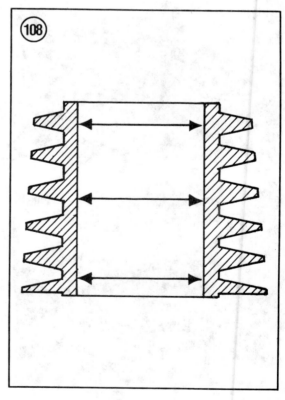

Installation

1. Check that the top surface of the crankcase and the bottom surface of the cylinder are clean before installation.

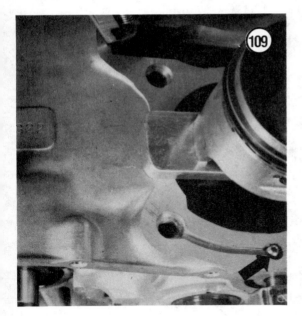

2. On 1978-1981 models, make sure that the oil control orifice (**Figure 109**), at each end of the crankcase, is clean. This is necessary to allow good oil flow.

3. Install a new cylinder base gasket (A, **Figure 110**) and the locating dowels (B, **Figure 110**).

4. Install a piston holding fixture under each piston (C, **Figure 110**).

NOTE
The fixtures may be purchased or may be homemade units of wood. See ***Figure 111*** *for dimensions.*

5. Make sure the end gaps of the piston rings are *not* lined up with each other—they must be staggered (**Figure 112**). Lightly oil the piston rings and cylinder bores with assembly oil or new engine oil.

6. Untie the cam chain wire and retie it to the top of the cylinder.

7. Carefully install the cylinder onto the pistons. Untie the wire and feed the cam chain and wire up through the opening in the cylinder and tie the wire to the bike's frame. Slide the cylinder down onto the pistons. Compress each piston ring with your fingers, as the cylinder starts to slide over the ring.

8. Slide the cylinder down until it bottoms on the piston holding fixtures (**Figure 113**).

9. Remove the piston holding fixtures and push the cylinder all the way down.

10. Install the cylinder head as described under *Cylinder Head Installation* in this chapter.

11. Install the cam chain tensioner as described under *Cam Chain Tensioner Replacement* in this chapter.

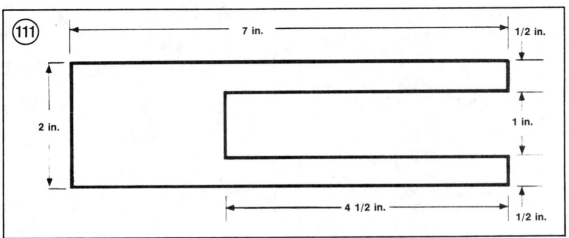

12. Install the cam chain front guide and a new head gasket.

13. Install the cylinder head as described under *Cylinder Head Installation* in this chapter.

PISTONS, PISTON PINS AND PISTON RINGS

The steel piston pins are a precision fit in the aluminum pistons. The piston pins are held in place by a clip at each end.

Piston Removal

1. Remove the cylinder head and cylinder as described in this chapter.

> *WARNING*
> *The edges of all piston rings are very sharp. Be careful when handling them to avoid cut fingers.*

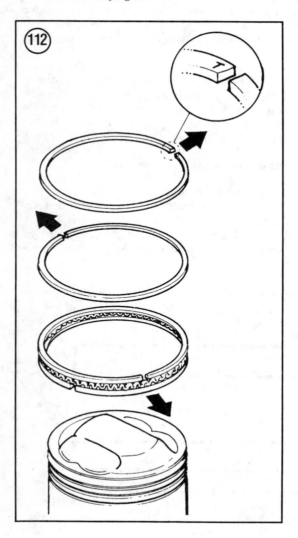

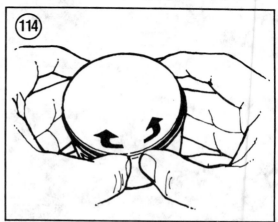

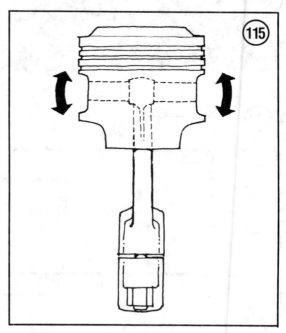

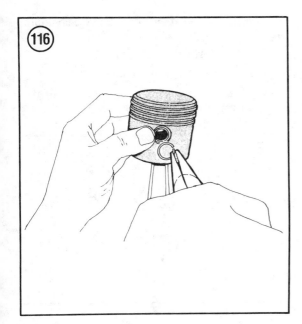

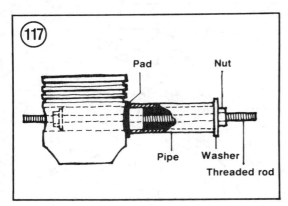

Pad   Nut

Pipe   Washer

Threaded rod

4

2. Remove the top ring with a ring expander tool or by spreading the ends with your thumbs just enough to slide the ring up over the piston (**Figure 114**). Repeat for the remaining rings.

3. Before removing the piston, hold the rod tightly and rock the piston as shown in **Figure 115**. Any rocking motion (do not confuse with the normal sliding motion) indicates wear on the piston pin, piston pin bore or connecting rod small-end bore (more likely a combination of these).

NOTE
Wrap a clean shop cloth under the piston so that the piston pin clip will not fall into the crankcase.

4. Lightly mark the top of the piston with an "L" (left-hand side) or "R" (right-hand side) so that they will be installed into the correct cylinder.

5. Remove the clip from each side of the piston pin bore (**Figure 116**) with a small screwdriver or scribe. Hold your thumb over one edge of the clip when removing it to prevent the clip from springing out.

6. Use a proper size wooden dowel or socket extension and push out the piston pin.

CAUTION
Be careful when removing the pin to avoid damaging the connecting rod. If it is necessary to gently tap the pin to remove it, be sure that the piston is properly supported so that lateral shock is not transmitted to the lower connecting rod bearing.

7. If the piston pin is difficult to remove, heat the piston and pin with a butane torch. The pin will probably push right out. Heat the piston to only about 140° F (60° C), i.e., until it is too warm to touch, but not excessively hot. If the pin is still difficult to push out, use a homemade tool as shown in **Figure 117**.

8. Lift the piston off the connecting rod.

9. If the piston is going to be left off for some time, place a piece of foam insulation tube over the end of the rod to protect it.

10. Repeat Steps 5-9 for the other piston.

Inspection

1. Carefully clean the carbon from the piston crown with a chemical remover or with a soft scraper (**Figure 118**). Do not remove or damage the carbon ridge around the circumference of the piston above the top ring. If the pistons, rings and cylinders are found to be dimensionally correct and can be reused, removal of the carbon ring from

the top of the piston or the carbon ridge from the top of the cylinder will promote excessive oil consumption in this cylinder.

CAUTION
Do not wire brush the piston skirts.

2. Examine each ring groove for burrs, dented edges and wide wear. Pay particular attention to the top compression ring groove as it usually wears more than the other grooves.
3. Make sure the oil holes in the piston pin area of the piston are clear.
4. If damage or wear indicates piston replacement, select a new piston as described under *Piston Clearance* in this chapter.
5. Oil the piston pin and install it in the connecting rod. Slowly rotate the piston pin and check for radial play (**Figure 119**). If any play exists, the piston pin should be replaced, providing the rod bore is in good condition.
6. Measure the inside diameter of the piston pin bore with a snap gauge and measure the outside diameter of the piston pin with a micrometer (**Figure 120**). Compare with dimensions given in **Table 1** or **Table 2**. Replace the piston and piston pin as a set if either or both are worn.
7. Check the piston skirt for galling and abrasion which may have been caused by piston seizure. If light galling is present, smooth the affected area with No. 400 emery paper and oil or a fine oilstone. However, if galling is severe or if the piston is deeply scored, replace it.

Piston Clearance

1. Make sure the pistons and cylinder walls are clean and dry.
2. Measure the inside diameter of the cylinder bore at a point 13 mm (1/2 in.) from the upper edge with a bore gauge (**Figure 121**).
3. Measure the outside diameter of each piston across the skirt (**Figure 122**) at right angles to the piston pin. Measure at a distance 10 mm (0.40 in.) up from the bottom of the piston skirt.
4. Piston clearance is the difference between the maximum piston diameter and the minimum cylinder diameter. Subtract the dimension of the piston from the cylinder dimension and compare to the dimension listed in **Table 1** or **Table 2**. If the clearance exceeds that specified, the cylinders should be rebored to the next oversize and a new pistons installed.
5. To establish a final overbore dimension with new pistons, add the piston skirt measurement to the specified clearance. This will determine the dimension for the cylinder overbore size.

Remember, do not exceed the cylinder maximum service limit inside diameter indicated in **Table 1** or **Table 2**.

Piston Installation

1. Apply molybdenum disulfide grease to the inside surface of the connecting rod.

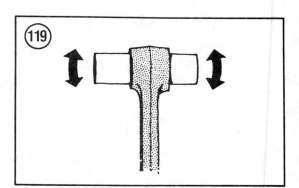

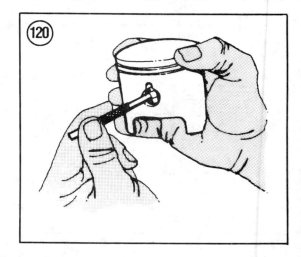

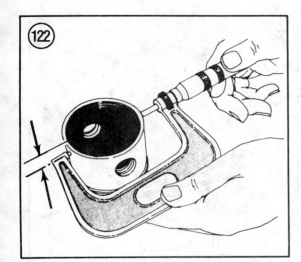

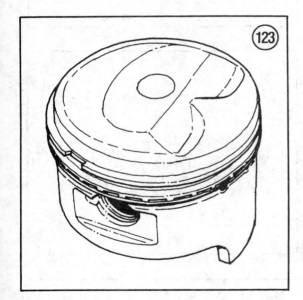

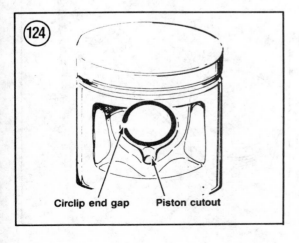

Circlip end gap   Piston cutout

2. Oil the piston pin with assembly oil or fresh engine oil and install it in the piston until its end extends slightly beyond the inside of the boss.

3. Place the piston over the connecting rod. If you are reusing the same pistons and connecting rods, match the pistons to the rod from which it came. The double intake valve relief on top of the piston (**Figure 123**) must be located at the rear toward the intake port or the rear of the engine.

4. Line up the piston pin with the hole in the connecting rod. Push the piston pin through the connecting rod and into the other side of the piston until it is even with the piston pin clip grooves.

CAUTION
If it is necessary to tap the piston pin into the connecting rod, do so gently with a block of wood or a soft-faced hammer. Make sure you support the piston to prevent the lateral shock from being transmitted to the connecting rod bearing.

NOTE
*In the next step, install the clips with the gap away from the cutout in the piston (**Figure 124**).*

5. Install new piston pin clips in both ends of the pin boss. Make sure they are seated in the grooves in the piston.

6. Check the installation by rocking the piston back and forth around the pin axis and from side to side along the axis. It should rotate freely back and forth but not from side to side.

7. Repeat Step 1-6 for the other piston.

8. Install the piston rings as described in this chapter.

9. Install the cylinder and cylinder head as described in this chapter.

Piston Ring Replacement

WARNING
The edges of all piston rings are very sharp. Be careful when handling them to avoid cut fingers.

NOTE
Install all rings with their markings facing up. The second ring has a keystone cross-section—the outer face is tapered.

1. Remove the top ring by spreading the ends with your thumbs just enough to slide the ring up over the piston (**Figure 114**). Repeat for the remaining rings.

2. Carefully remove all carbon buildup from the ring grooves with a broken piston ring (**Figure 125**). Inspect the grooves carefully for burrs, nicks or broken and cracked lands. Recondition or replace the piston if necessary.

3. Roll each ring around its piston groove as shown in **Figure 126** to check for binding. Minor binding may be cleaned up with a fine-cut file.

4. Measure the side clearance of each ring in its groove with a flat feeler gauge (**Figure 127**) and compare to dimensions given in **Table 1** or **Table 2**. If the clearance is greater than specified, the rings must be replaced. If the clearance is still excessive with the new rings, the piston must also be replaced.

5. Measure each ring for wear. Place each ring, one at a time, into the cylinder and push it in about 20 mm (3/4 in.) with the crown of the piston to ensure that the ring is square in the cylinder bore. Measure the gap with a flat feeler gauge (**Figure 128**) and compare to dimensions in **Table 1**. If the gap is greater than specified, the rings should be replaced. When installing new rings, measure their end gap in the same manner as for old ones. If the gap is less than specified, carefully file the ends (**Figure 129**) with a fine-cut file until the gap is correct.

NOTE
Install the compression rings with their markings facing up. The second ring has a keystone cross-section—the outer face is tapered.

6. Install the piston rings in the order shown in **Figure 130**.

7. Install the oil ring spacer first, then the side rails. Some new oil ring side rails do not have top and bottom designations. If reassembling used parts, install the side rails as they were removed.

8. Install the second compression ring, then the top by carefully spreading the ends of the ring with your thumbs and slipping the ring over the top of the piston. Remember that the marks on the piston rings are toward the top of the piston.

9. Make sure the rings are seated completely in their grooves all the way around the piston and that the ends are distributed around the piston as shown in **Figure 112**. The important thing is that the ring gaps are not aligned with each other when installed.

10. If new rings were installed, measure the side clearance of each ring in its groove with a flat feeler gauge (**Figure 127**) and compare to dimensions given in **Table 1**.

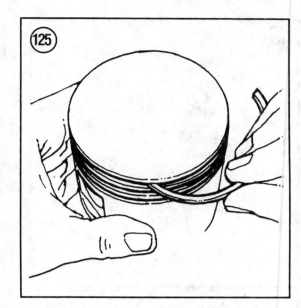

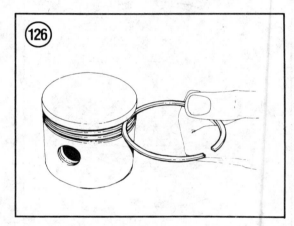

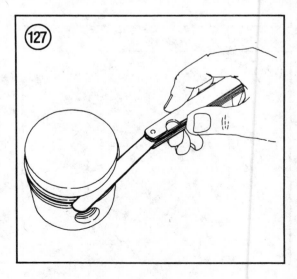

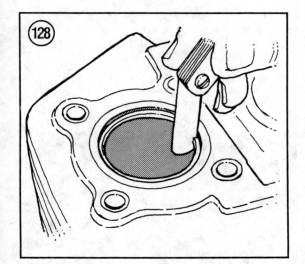

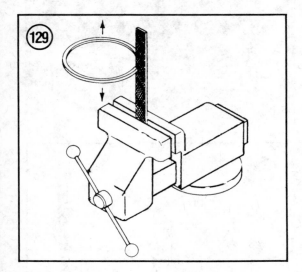

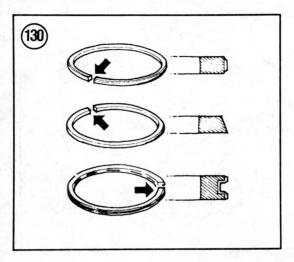

11. Follow the *Break-in Procedure* in this chapter if new pistons or new piston rings have been installed or the cylinders were rebored or honed.

ALTERNATOR

Rotor Removal/Installation (Rebel 450 Models)

Refer to **Figure 131** for this procedure.

1. Shift the transmission into gear.

2. Remove the bolt and nut clamping the shift lever (A, **Figure 132**) to the shaft and remove the shift lever from the shaft.

3. Remove the Allen bolts (B, **Figure 132**) securing the left-hand footpeg and remove the left-hand footpeg and shift lever assembly.

4. Remove the bolts securing the left-hand crankcase cover (C, **Figure 132**) and remove the cover.

5. Have an assistant apply the rear brake.

6. Loosen, then remove bolt and washer securing alternator rotor.

7. Screw a flywheel puller (Honda part No. 07933-3950000, or equivalent) in all the way until it stops.

8. Tap on the end of the puller with a hammer to break the rotor loose. If the rotor will not break loose, tap on the cross bar with a plastic mallet until the flywheel disengages.

9. Remove the rotor and puller.

> *CAUTION*
> *Do not try to remove the rotor without a puller; any attempt to do so will damage the crankshaft and/or rotor. Many aftermarket pullers are available from most motorcycle dealers or mail order houses. The cost of a puller is about $10 and it makes an excellent addition to any mechanic's tool box. If you can't borrow one, have a dealer remove the rotor for you.*

10. Don't lose the Woodruff key on the crankshaft.

> *NOTE*
> *The rotor is permanently magnetized and cannot be remagnetized. If it is dropped, the magnetism can be lost. There is no way to check it except by replacing it with a good one.*

11. Carefully inspect the inside of the rotor for small bolts, washers, or other metal "trash" that may have been picked up by the magnets. These small metal bits can cause severe damage to the stator assembly components.

12. Install by reversing these removal steps, noting the following.

13. Make sure the Woodruff key is in place in the slot in the crankshaft. Align the keyway in the rotor with the key when installing the rotor.

14. Be sure to install the washer before installing the rotor nut.

15. Apply blue Loctite (Lock N' Seal No. 242) to the threads on the crankshaft, then install the rotor bolt.

16. Tighten the rotor bolt to the torque specification listed in **Table 3**.

Stator/Pulse Generator Assembly Removal/Installation (Rebel 450)

Test procedures for the alternator rotor and stator assembly are covered in Chapter Eight.

Refer to **Figure 131** for this procedure.

1. Remove the alternator rotor as described in this chapter.

2. Remove the seat.

3. Disconnect the alternator electrical connectors (**Figure 133**) from the chassis wiring harness.

4. Carefully remove the electrical wire harness from the retaining clips on the frame.

5. Remove the bolts securing the stator and pulse generator assembly to the left-hand crankcase housing. Pull the grommet and electrical harness

out of the left-hand crankcase and remove the stator/pulse generator assembly.

> *NOTE*
> *The pulse generator and its wiring harness are separate from the stator assembly. If either one is faulty, either can be replaced separately.*

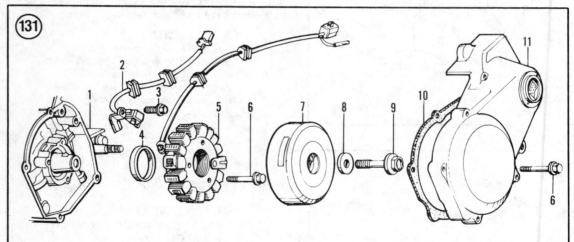

ALTERNATOR (REBEL 450)

1. Crankcase
2. Pulse generator/wiring harness
3. Bolt
4. Oil seal
5. Stator assembly
6. Bolt
7. Rotor
8. Washer
9. Bolt
10. Gasket
11. Crankcase cover

6. Inspect the stator assembly for loose screws, chafed or damaged wires or any visible damage. Replace the stator assembly if any item is damaged.

7. Install by reversing these removal steps, noting the following.

8. Apply a small amount of blue Loctite (Lock N' Seal No. 242) to the stator mounting bolts.

9. Install the bolts and tighten them securely.

10. Make sure the electrical connectors are tight.

Rotor Removal/Installation
(All Models Except Rebel 450)

Refer to **Figure 134** for this procedure.

1. Remove the bolt and nut clamping the shift lever (A, **Figure 135**) to the shaft and remove it. Remove bolt (B, **Figure 135**) securing the front footpeg and remove the footpeg.

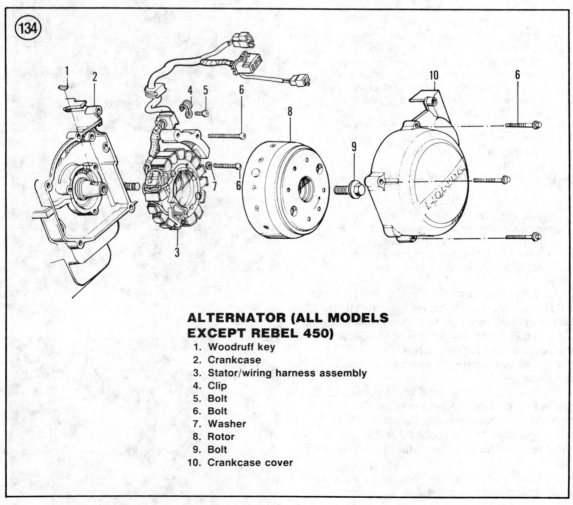

ALTERNATOR (ALL MODELS EXCEPT REBEL 450)

1. Woodruff key
2. Crankcase
3. Stator/wiring harness assembly
4. Clip
5. Bolt
6. Bolt
7. Washer
8. Rotor
9. Bolt
10. Crankcase cover

2. Remove the bolts (**Figure 136**) securing the left-hand crankcase cover and remove the cover.

3. Disconnect the 2 electrical connectors from the alternator to the voltage regulator/rectifier (**Figure 137**).

4. Loosen, then remove bolt securing alternator rotor with a socket and impact driver (**Figure 138**).

> *NOTE*
> *To prevent the flywheel from turning while removing the nut, secure it with a holding tool (**Figure 139**).*

5. Screw a flywheel puller (Honda part No. 07933-3950000, or equivalent) in all the way until it stops (**Figure 140**).

6. Tap on the end of the puller with a hammer to break the rotor loose. If the rotor will not break loose, tap on the cross bar with a plastic mallet until the flywheel disengages.

7. Remove the rotor and puller.

> *CAUTION*
> *Do not try to remove the rotor without a puller; any attempt to do so will damage the crankshaft and/or rotor. Many aftermarket pullers are available from most motorcycle dealers or mail order houses. The cost of a puller is about $10 and it makes an excellent addition to any mechanic's tool box. If you can't borrow one, have a dealer remove the rotor for you.*

8. Don't lose the Woodruff key on the crankshaft.

> *NOTE*
> *The rotor is permanently magnetized and cannot be remagnetized. If it is dropped, the magnetism can be lost. There is no way to check it except by replacing it with a known good one.*

9. Carefully inspect the inside of the rotor (**Figure 141**) for small bolts, washers or other metal "trash" that may have been picked up by the magnets. These small metal bits can cause severe damage to the stator assembly components.

10. Install by reversing these removal steps, noting the following.

11. Make sure the Woodruff key is in place in the slot in the crankshaft. Align the keyway in the rotor with the key when installing the rotor.

12. Apply blue Loctite (Lock N' Seal No. 2114) to the threads on the crankshaft, then install the rotor bolt.

13. Tighten the rotor bolt to the torque specification listed in **Table 3**.

Stator/Pulse Generator Assembly Removal/Installation
(All Models Except Rebel 450)

Test procedures for the alternator rotor and stator assembly are covered in Chapter Eight.

Refer to **Figure 134** for this procedure.

1. Remove the alternator rotor as described in this chapter.

2. Disconnect the alternator electrical connectors (**Figure 137**) from the chassis wiring harness.

3. Carefully remove the electrical wire harness from the retaining clips on the frame and on the crankcase.

4. Remove the screws and washers securing the stator and pulse generator assembly to the left-hand crankcase housing. Refer to **Figure 142** for manual transmission models or **Figure 143** for automatic transmission models. Pull the grommet and electrical harness out of the left-hand crankcase and remove the stator/pulse generator assembly.

NOTE
The pulse generator, stator assembly and their wiring harnesses are one complete assembly. If either one is faulty, both must be replaced as an assembly.

5. Inspect the stator assembly for loose screws, chafed or damaged wires or any visible damage. Replace the stator assembly if any item is damaged.

6. Install by reversing these removal steps, noting the following.

7. Apply a small amount of blue Loctite (Lock N' Seal No. 242) to the stator mounting screws.

8. Install the screws and tighten the screws securely.

9. Make sure the electrical connectors are tight.

OIL PUMP

The oil pump is located on the right-hand side of the engine forward of the clutch or torque converter assembly. The oil pump can be removed with the engine in the frame.

Refer to the following illustrations for this procedure:

   a. **Figure 144**: Rebel 450.
   b. **Figure 145**: CB400A.
   c. **Figure 146**: for all other models.

Removal/Installation
(Manual Transmission)

1. Drain the engine oil, as described under *Changing Oil and Filter* in Chapter Three.

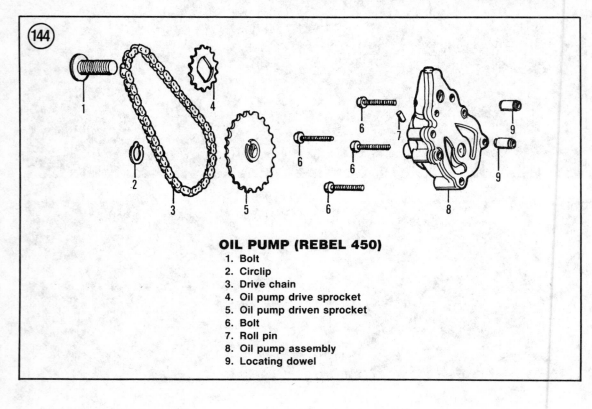

OIL PUMP (REBEL 450)
1. Bolt
2. Circlip
3. Drive chain
4. Oil pump drive sprocket
5. Oil pump driven sprocket
6. Bolt
7. Roll pin
8. Oil pump assembly
9. Locating dowel

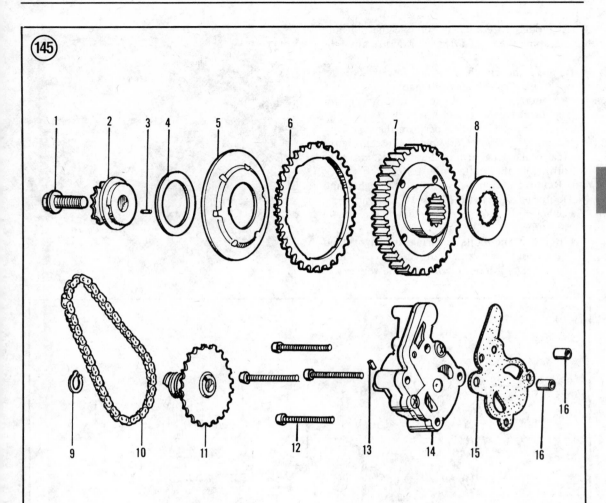

4

OIL PUMP (CB400A)
1. Bolt
2. Oil pump drive sprocket
3. Roll pin
4. Spring washer
5. Sub-gear plate
6. Primary drive sub-gear
7. Primary drive gear
8. Splined washer
9. Circlip
10. Drive chain
11. Oil pump driven sprocket
12. Bolt
13. Roll pin
14. Oil pump assembly
15. Gasket
16. Locating dowel

2. On models so equipped, remove the bolt and nut clamping the kickstarter lever and remove the lever.

3. Remove the clutch cable as described under *Clutch Cable Replacement* in Chapter Five.

4. On models so equipped, disconnect the tachometer drive cable.

5A. On Rebel 450 models, perform the following:

  a. Remove the bolt (A, **Figure 147**) securing the rear brake pedal arm to the shaft. Remove the arm from the shaft.

  b. Remove the bolts securing the right-hand footpeg assembly (B, **Figure 147**). Remove the right-hand footeg and rear brake pedal assembly.

  c. Remove the bolts securing the right-hand crankcase cover and remove the cover and gasket. Don't loose the locating dowels.

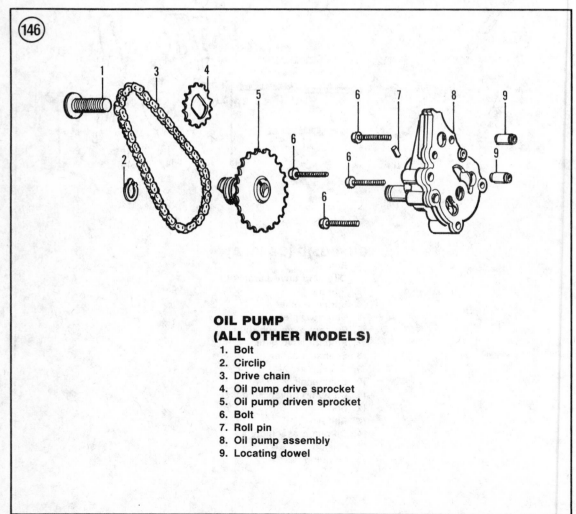

**OIL PUMP
(ALL OTHER MODELS)**
1. Bolt
2. Circlip
3. Drive chain
4. Oil pump drive sprocket
5. Oil pump driven sprocket
6. Bolt
7. Roll pin
8. Oil pump assembly
9. Locating dowel

5B. On models except Rebel 450, remove the bolts securing the right-hand crankcase cover and remove the cover and gasket. Don't lose the locating dowels.

6. Place a copper washer (or copper penny) between the clutch outer housing gear and the primary drive gear. This will prevent the primary drive gear from rotating while loosening the bolt securing the gear.

NOTE
The following steps are shown with the clutch removed for clarity. It is not necessary to remove the clutch for this procedure.

7. Loosen, then remove the bolt securing the primary drive gear (**Figure 148**) and oil pump drive sprocket to the crankshaft. Remove the copper washer (or copper penny).

8. Remove the oil pump drive sprocket and the chain (**Figure 149**).

9. Remove the circlip (**Figure 150**) securing the driven gear and tachometer drive gear (models so equipped) to the oil pump shaft.

10. Remove the oil pump driven sprocket (**Figure 151**).

11. Remove the screws (**Figure 152**) securing the oil pump to the crankshaft and remove the oil pump assembly.

12. Remove the old gasket (**Figure 153**) and discard the gasket.

13. Inspect the oil pump as described under *Oil Pump Disassembly/Inspection/Assembly (All Models)* in this chapter.

14. Install by reversing the removal steps, noting the following.

15. Install a new oil pump gasket.

16. Make sure the locating dowels are in place on the backside of the oil pump before installation.

17. Align the flats on the oil pump drive sprocket with the flats on the crankshaft and install the drive sprocket.

18. Align the groove in the backside of the oil pump driven sprocket with the oil pump shaft drive pin, then install the oil pump driven sprocket.

19. Tighten the primary drive gear bolt to the torque specification listed in **Table 3**.

20. Make sure the right-hand crankcase locating dowels are in place and install a new gasket. Tighten the crankcase cover bolts securely.

21. Fill the crankcase with the recommended type and quantity of engine oil. Refer to Chapter Three.

**Removal/Installation
(Automatic Transmission)**

1. Drain the engine oil, as described under *Changing Engine Oil and Filter* in Chapter Three.

2. Remove the torque converter as described under *Torque Converter Removal/Installation* in Chapter Six.

3. Remove the bolts securing the inner crankcase cover (A, **Figure 154**) and remove the cover and gasket. Don't lose the locating dowels.

> *NOTE*
> *Do not lose the oil check valve and spring (B, **Figure 154**).*

4. Temporarily reinstall the 2 needle bearings and the torque converter, onto the transmission shaft.

5. Place a copper washer (or copper penny) between the torque converter drive gear and the primary drive gear. This will prevent the primary drive gear from rotating while loosening the bolt securing the gear.

6. Loosen, then remove the bolt (**Figure 155**) securing the primary drive gear and oil pump drive sprocket to the crankshaft. Remove the copper washer (or copper penny).

7. Remove the torque converter and needle bearings.

8. Remove the oil pump drive sprocket and the chain (**Figure 156**).

9. Remove the circlip (**Figure 157**) securing the driven sprocket to the oil pump shaft.

10. Remove the oil pump driven sprocket.

11. Remove the screws securing the oil pump to the crankshaft and remove the oil pump assembly.

12. Remove the old gasket and discard the gasket.

13. Inspect the oil pump as described under *Oil Pump Disassembly/Inspection/Assembly (All Models)* in this chapter.

14. Install by reversing the removal steps, noting the following.

15. Install a new oil pump gasket.

16. Make sure the locating dowels are in place on the backside of the oil pump before installation.

17. Align the flats on the oil pump drive sprocket with the flats on the crankshaft and install the sprocket.

18. Align the groove in the backside of the oil pump driven sprocket with the oil pump shaft drive pin, then install the oil pump driven sprocket.

19. Tighten the primary drive gear bolt to the torque specification listed in **Table 3**.

20. Make sure the right-hand crankcase locating dowels are in place and install a new gasket. Tighten the inner crankcase cover bolts securely.

21. Fill the crankcase with the recommended type and quantity of engine oil. Refer to Chapter Three.

Disassembly/Inspection/Assembly

Replacement parts are *not* available for the oil pump. If any of the parts are faulty, the entire oil pump assembly must be replaced.

NOTE
Honda does not provide oil pump specifications for all models.

1. Remove the drive pin from the snap ring grove end of the shaft.

2. Remove the Phillips head screws (A, **Figure 158**) securing the pump cover to the body.

3. Remove the cover (B, **Figure 158**) and the thrust washer.

4. Remove the shaft and drive pin and the inner and outer rotors. Inspect both rotors for scratches and abrasions. Replace the oil pump assembly if evidence of this is found.

5. Inspect the oil pump body and cover for cracks.

6. Inspect the teeth on the drive and driven sprocket. Replace both sprockets if the teeth are damaged or any are missing on either sprocket.

7. Inspect the drive chain for wear or damage. Replace if necessary.

8. Clean all parts in solvent and dry thoroughly. Coat all parts with fresh engine oil before assembly.

9. Position the outer rotor with the punch mark facing out and install the outer rotor into the oil pump body.

10. Position the inner rotor with the drive pin grooves facing out and install the inner into the outer rotor and the oil pump body.

11. Using a flat feeler gauge measure the clearance between the outer rotor and the oil pump body (**Figure 159**). Compare to specifications listed in **Table 1** or **Table 2**. If the clearance is worn to the service limit dimension or greater, replace the oil pump assembly.

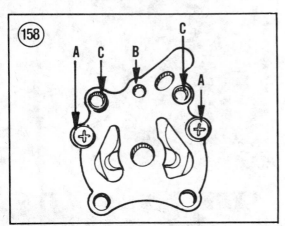

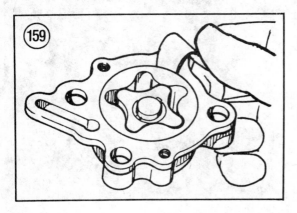

4

12. Using a flat feeler gauge measure the clearance between the inner rotor tip and the outer rotor (**Figure 160**). Compare to specifications listed in **Table 1** or **Table 2**. If the clearance is worn to the service limit dimension or greater, replace the oil pump assembly.

13. Place a straightedge across both rotors and the oil pump body. Insert a flat feeler gauge between the rotors and the body (**Figure 161**). Compare to specifications listed in **Table 1** or **Table 2**. If the clearance is worn to the service limit dimension or greater, replace the oil pump assembly.

14. Install the drive pin into the shaft.

15. Position the shaft with the snap ring groove end going in first and install the shaft into the inner rotor and oil pump body.

16. Align the drive pin with the grooves in the inner rotor. Push the shaft in until it bottoms out.

17. Install the thrust washer onto the shaft.

18. If removed, install the dowel pins (C, **Figure 158**).

19. Install the cover and Phillips head screw. Tighten the screw securely.

20. Install the other drive pin into the end of the shaft with the snap ring groove.

OIL COOLER
(1982-ON EXCEPT REBEL 450)

NOTE
The Rebel 450 is not equipped with an oil cooler.

Removal/Installation

1. Drain the engine oil as described under *Changing Engine Oil and Filter* in Chapter Three.

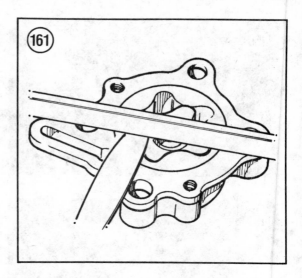

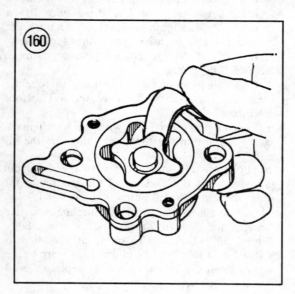

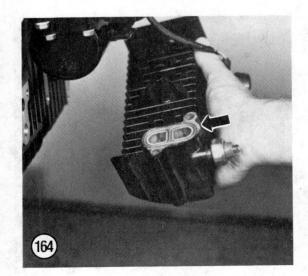

164

165

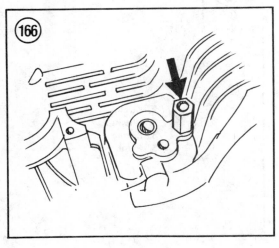

166

2. Remove the bolts (**Figure 162**) securing the shield covering the oil pressure switch and remove the shield.

3. Disconnect the electrical wire from the oil pressure switch (**Figure 163**).

4. Move the oil drain pan, used during engine oil draining, under the oil cooler as additional oil will drain out.

5. Remove the bolts securing the oil cooler to the crankcase and remove the oil cooler.

6. Don't lose the rubber seal (**Figure 164**) on the oil cooler.

7. Install by reversing these removal steps, noting the following.

8. Inspect the rubber seal for damage or deterioration (**Figure 164**); replace if necessary.

9. Clean the mating surfaces of both the oil cooler and the crankcase (**Figure 165**) where they join each other.

10. Tighten the mounting bolts securely.

11. Refill the engine with the recommended type and quantity of oil. Refer to Chapter Three.

OIL PRESSURE RELIEF VALVE

The oil pressure relief valve was relocated on the 1979 CB400T I, the CB400T II and the CB400A models during the mid-1979 model year. The relief valve was relocated to the base of the lower crankcase beginning with the following engine serial numbers:

    a. CB400T I: 2050501-on through end of 1979.

    b. CB400T II: 4067096-on through end of 1979.

    c. CB400A: 2057123-on through end of 1979.

On all other models, the oil pressure relief valve is located below the oil pump on the right-hand side of the crankcase.

Removal/Inspection/Installation

1A. On *manual transmission* models, to gain access to the relief valve, perform Steps 1-5 *Oil Pump Removal/Installation* in this chapter.

1B. On *automatic transmission* models, to gain access to the relief valve, perform Steps 1-4 *Oil Pump Removal/Installation* in this chapter.

1C. On CB400T I and CB400T II models from mid-1979 to the end of the 1979 model runs (see previously noted engine serial numbers) perform Steps 1-14, *Crankcase Disassembly* in this chapter.

2A. On CB400T I and CB400T II models from mid-1979 to the end of the 1979 model runs (see previously noted engine serial numbers), unscrew the pressure relief valve (**Figure 166**) from the crankcase.

NOTE
*Figure 167 is shown with the oil pump
gear and chain removed for clarity. It is
not necessary to remove either in order
to remove the relief valve.*

2B. On all other models, unscrew the pressure
relief valve (**Figure 167**) from the crankcase.

3. From the backside of the valve, push on the
plunger; it should move freely. It will take some
effort to push it though, as it would normally open
under 382-510 kPa (55-74 psi) of oil pressure.

4. If it will not move, remove the circlip, washer,
spring and plunger (**Figure 168**) from the body.

5. Wash all parts in solvent and dry with
compressed air. Make sure that the relief holes in
the body are clean.

6. If the spring is broken or the plunger or body
damaged, the entire assembly must be replaced as
replacement parts are not available.

7. Coat all parts with assembly oil and reassemble
all parts into the body. Make sure the circlip is
correctly seated in the body groove.

8. Install the pressure relief valve into the
crankcase and tighten securely.

CRANKCASE AND BALANCER SYSTEM

Service to the lower end requires that the
crankcase assembly be removed from the
motorcycle frame.

While the engine is still in the frame it is easier
to remove the cylinder head, cylinder, pistons,
electric starter, alternator and clutch or torque
converter assembly. In addition, the decrease of
engine weight makes it easier to remove the
crankcase from the frame.

This procedure is shown with an engine
equipped with a *manual transmission*; the
procedure is the same for both the manual and
automatic transmissions.

The balancer system for 1978-1981 is shown in
Figure 169 or **Figure 170** for 1982-on models.

Disassembly

1. Remove the engine as described under *Engine
Removal/Installation* in this chapter. Perform the
steps for total disassembly described in the engine
removal procedure.

2. Place the engine on a workbench upside down
on a couple of 2×4 in. wood blocks. This is to
protect the protruding connecting rod ends.

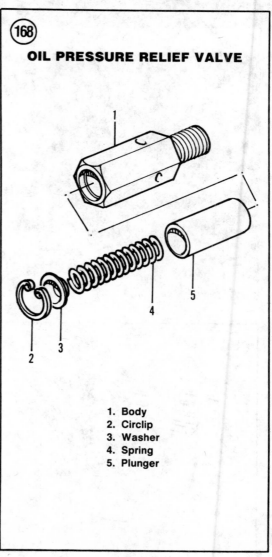

OIL PRESSURE RELIEF VALVE

1. Body
2. Circlip
3. Washer
4. Spring
5. Plunger

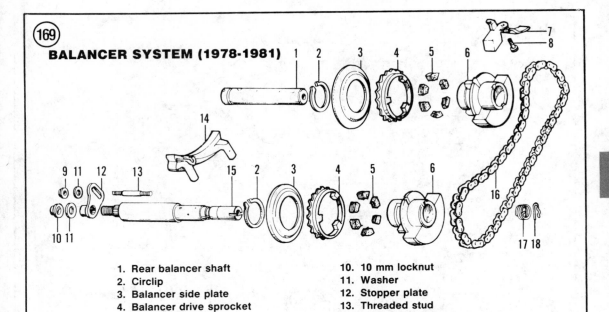

④

⑯⑨ **BALANCER SYSTEM (1978-1981)**

4

1. Rear balancer shaft
2. Circlip
3. Balancer side plate
4. Balancer drive sprocket
5. Rubber dampers
6. Balancer weight
7. Drive chain guard plate
8. Screw
9. 8 mm locknut

10. 10 mm locknut
11. Washer
12. Stopper plate
13. Threaded stud
14. Drive chain slipper
15. Front balancer shaft
16. Drive chain
17. Balancer shaft return spring
18. Lock pin

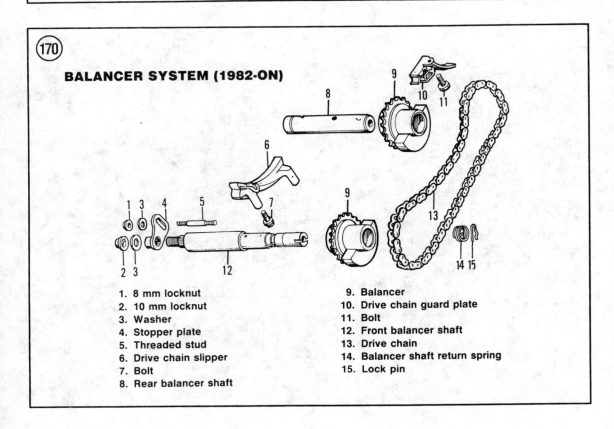

⑰⓪ **BALANCER SYSTEM (1982-ON)**

1. 8 mm locknut
2. 10 mm locknut
3. Washer
4. Stopper plate
5. Threaded stud
6. Drive chain slipper
7. Bolt
8. Rear balancer shaft

9. Balancer
10. Drive chain guard plate
11. Bolt
12. Front balancer shaft
13. Drive chain
14. Balancer shaft return spring
15. Lock pin

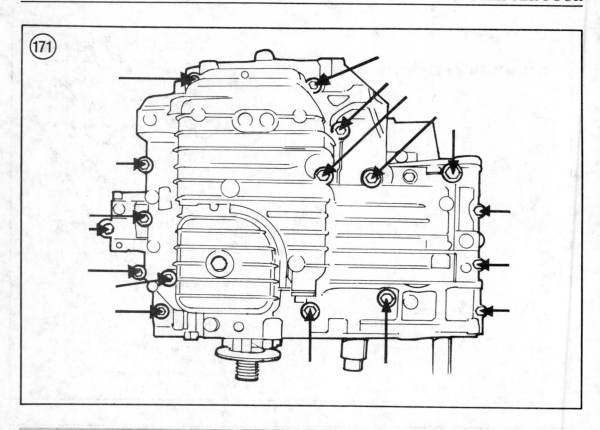

3. Remove the bolts securing the crankcase halves together (**Figure 171**). Tap the lower crankcase with a plastic mallet and separate the halves.

CAUTION
*If it is necessary to pry the halves apart, do it very **carefully** so that you do not mar the gasket surfaces. If you do, the cases will leak and must be replaced.*

NOTE
The "L" and "R" marks should relate to the right- and left-hand side of the engine as it sits in the bike frame—not as it sits on your bench upside down.

4. Remove the nuts (**Figure 172**) on the connecting rod caps and remove the connecting rods. Mark them "L" (left-hand side) and "R" (right-hand side) so that they will be installed in the same cylinder.
5. Remove the balancer chain tensioner adjustment nut (**Figure 173**). It is not necessary to remove the arm.
6. Remove the bolts (**Figure 174**) securing the oil strainer and remove the oil strainer assembly.
7. Using the torque pattern shown in **Figure 175**, loosen, then remove the bolts securing the main bearing cap assembly.

8. Pull out the rear balancer shaft (**Figure 176**) and remove the rear balancer.

9. Remove the bolt (A, **Figure 177**) securing the balancer chain slipper (B, **Figure 177**) and remove the slipper assembly.

10. Remove the rear counterbalancer (**Figure 178**).

11. Remove the balancer chain guard plate.

12A. On electric starter models, lift out the crankshaft, oil seal and the cam chain (**Figure 179**).

12B. On kickstarter only models, lift out the crankshaft, oil seal and the cam chain (**Figure 180**).

13. On 1979-1981 models, remove the cam chain tensioner slipper (**Figure 181**). On 1982 and later models, the slipper is removed during cylinder removal.

14. Remove the spring clip and spring (**Figure 182**), then pull out the shaft securing the front balancer. Remove the front balancer and the chain.

NOTE
Remember that the left-hand side refers to the engine as it sits in the bike's frame—not as it sits on your workbench.

15. Remove the main bearing inserts from the upper crankcase (**Figure 183**) and from the main

bearing cap assembly (**Figure 184**). Mark the backside of the inserts with a "1" (left-hand cylinder) and "2" (right-hand cylinder) and "U" (upper) or "L" (lower).

16. Remove the crankshaft and connecting rods as described under *Crankshaft and Connecting Rods Removal/Installation* in this chapter.

17. To remove the transmission assemblies, refer to *Manual Transmission Removal* in Chapter Five or *Automatic Transmission Removal* in Chapter Six.

4

Inspection

1. Thoroughly clean the inside and outside of both crankcase halves with cleaning solvent. Dry with compressed air. Make sure there is no solvent residue left in the cases as it will contaminate the new engine oil.

2. Carefully inspect the cases for cracks and fractures, especially in the lower areas; they are vulnerable to rock damage. Also check the areas around the stiffening ribs, around bearing bosses and threaded holes. If damage is found, have it repaired by a shop specializing in the repair of precision aluminum castings or replace the crankcase halves as a set.

Assembly

NOTE
If reusing the old bearings, make sure that they are installed in the same location as noted in Step 15, of Removal.

1. Install the main bearing inserts into the upper crankcase (**Figure 183**) and into the main bearing cap assembly (**Figure 184**).
2. Install the transmission assemblies; refer to *Manual Transmission Installation* in Chapter Five or *Automatic Transmission Installation* in Chapter Six.
3. Install the crankshaft and connecting rods as described under *Crankshaft and Connecting Rods Removal/Installation* in this chapter.
4. Install the front balancer shaft and front balancer with the chain side on the right-hand side.

NOTE
Balancer shaft punch mark position indications—i.e., 10 o'clock and 6 o'clock, are to be read with the upper crankcase positioned upside down as shown in Figure 185.

5. Rotate the balancer shaft until the punch mark, on the end of the shaft, is at the 10 o'clock position. Install the spring and spring clip (**Figure 182**).
6. Turn the balancer shaft *clockwise* about 250° or until the punch mark is at the 6 o'clock position. Center the adjuster plate within the threaded stud, then install the adjuster plate and the 10 mm self-locking nut (A, **Figure 185**).
7. Again, center the adjuster plate within the threaded stud and install the 8 mm self-locking adjustment nut (B, **Figure 185**). Tighten the adjustment nut finger-tight at this time.
8. Do *not* allow the adjuster plate to move, then tighten the 10 mm nut (A) to the torque specification listed in **Table 3**.
9. Loosen the 8 mm nut (B), rotate the adjuster plate completely clockwise *and tighten the 8 mm nut to the torque specification listed in* **Table 3**.
10. On 1979-1981 models, install the cam chain tensioner slipper (**Figure 181**). On 1982 and later models, the slipper is installed during cylinder installation.

NOTE
Before installation, coat all bearing surfaces with assembly oil and install the oil seal onto the crankshaft.

11A. On electric starter models, perform the following:
  a. Install the overrunning clutch and starter gear onto crankshaft before installation. installation.
  b. Install the cam chain onto the crankshaft and install this assembly into the crankcase (**Figure 179**).
11B. On kickstarter only models, install the cam chain onto the crankshaft and install this assembly into the crankcase (**Figure 180**).
12. Install the balancer chain guard plate.

CAUTION
The front counterbalance mark **TC** *must be horizontal and align with the web on the crankcase (**Figure 186**). The rear counterbalance mark* **TH** *must be horizontal and align with the ledge of the main bearing cap assembly (**Figure 187**) when it is installed. This alignment is necessary for proper engine operation.*

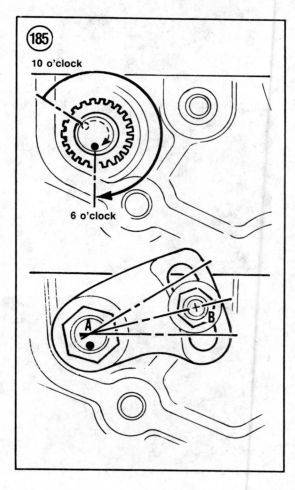

13. Rotate the crankshaft to top dead center (TDC) and install the rear counterbalancer and chain (**Figure 178**).

14. Install the balancer chain over the balancer chain slipper, and install the slipper (B, **Figure 177**) into the main bearing cap assembly.

15. Install the shaft (**Figure 176**) into the rear balancer which is already installed in the main bearing cap assembly.

16. Make sure all alignment dowels and bearing inserts are in place in the main bearing cap assembly (**Figure 184**).

17. Install the main bearing cap assembly onto the upper crankcase half.

CAUTION
*Make sure the alignment of both the front and rear counter balancers are still correct. See **Figure 186** and **Figure 187**. If not, adjust the counterbalancers on the chain until they are correct. This alignment is necessary for proper engine operation.*

18. Using the torque pattern shown in **Figure 175** tighten the 6 mm and 8 mm bolts to the torque specification listed in **Table 3**.

19. Install the oil strainer as follows:

a. Install the oil strainer (A, **Figure 188**).

b. Rotate the slot on the balancer shaft to vertical (**Figure 189**) in order to install the attachment bolt.

c. Install the bolt (B, **Figure 188**) and tighten to the torque specification listed in **Table 3**.

20. Loosen the 8 mm adjustment nut (**Figure 190**). The balancer chain will now automatically adjust to the correct tension. Tighten the nut to the torque specification listed in **Table 3**.

21. If removed, install the oil filter seal ring (**Figure 191**).

22. Install the locating dowels (**Figure 192**) into the lower crankcase.

23. Make sure case half sealing surfaces are perfectly clean and dry.

NOTE
Use Three Bond, Gasgacinch Gasket Sealer or equivalent. When selecting an equivalent, avoid thick and hard setting materials.

24. Apply a light coat of gasket sealer, or equivalent, to the sealing surfaces of both halves. Cover only flat surfaces, not curved bearing surfaces. Make the coating as thin as possible or the case can shift and hammer out bearings. Join both halves and tap them together lightly with a plastic mallet—do not use a metal hammer as it will damage the case.

NOTE
Refer to Figure 193 for correct crankcase bolt length placement.

25. Install the crankcase bolts and tighten in a crisscross pattern. Tighten to the torque specification listed in **Table 3**.

26. Install the engine as described under *Engine Removal/Installation* in this chapter.

27. Fill the crankcase with the recommended type and quantity of engine oil. Refer to Chapter Three.

CRANKSHAFT AND CONNECTING RODS

Crankshaft Removal/Installation

1. Split the crankcase and remove the crankshaft as described under *Crankcase Disassembly* in this chapter.

2. On electric starter models, remove the starter gear and clutch as described under *Starter Gear and Clutch Removal/Installation* in this chapter.

3. On electric starter models, install the starter gear and clutch as described under *Starter Gear and Clutch Removal/Installation* in this chapter.

4. Install the crankshaft and assemble the crankcase as described under *Crankcase Assembly* in this chapter.

Crankshaft Inspection

1. Clean crankshaft thoroughly with solvent. Clean oil holes with rifle cleaning brushes; dry thoroughly with compressed air. Lightly oil all journal surfaces immediately to prevent rust.

2. Carefully inspect each main bearing journal (A, **Figure 194**) and connecting rod bearing journal (B, **Figure 194**) for scratches, ridges, scoring, nicks, etc. Very small nicks and scratches may be removed with crocus cloth. More serious damage must be removed by grinding, a job for a machine shop.

3. Inspect the cam chain and balancer chain sprocket teeth (C, **Figure 194**). If damaged, the crankshaft must be replaced.

4. If the surface finish on all journals is satisfactory, take the crankshaft to your dealer or local machine shop. They can check out-of-roundness, taper and wear on the journals. They can also check crankshaft alignment and inspect for cracks. Check against measurements given in **Table 1** or **Table 2**.

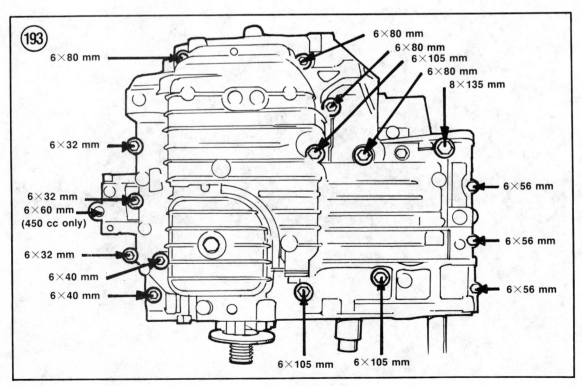

Main Bearing and Journal Inspection

1. Check each main bearing insert for evidence of wear, abrasion and scoring. If the bearings are good, they may be reused. If any insert is questionable, replace the entire set.
2. Install the bearing inserts in upper case half and main bearing cap assembly (**Figure 195**).
3. Set the crankshaft in place.
4. Place a piece of Plastigage over each main bearing journal parallel to the crankshaft. Do not place the Plastigage material over an oil hole in the crankshaft.

CAUTION
Do not rotate the crankshaft while the Plastigage is in place.

5. Install the main bearing cap assembly and tighten the bolts using the torque pattern shown in **Figure 196**. Tighten to the torque specification listed in **Table 3**.
6. Remove the bolts and the main bearing cap assembly.
7. Measure the width of the flattened Plastigage according to manufacturer's instructions. Measure at both ends of the Plastigage strip (**Figure 197**). A difference of 0.001 in. or more indicates a tapered journal. Confirm with a micrometer. Bearing clearance for new bearings is listed in **Table 1** or **Table 2**.
8. Remove the Plastigage strips from the main bearing journals.

Connecting Rod Inspection

1. Check each connecting rod for obvious damage such as cracks and burns.
2. Check the piston pin bushing for wear or scoring.
3. Take the connecting rods to a machine shop and check the alignment for twisting and bending.
4. Examine the bearing inserts for wear, scoring, or burning. They are reusable if in good condition. Make a note of the bearing size (if any) stamped on the back of the insert if the bearing is to be discarded; a previous owner may have used undersized bearings.
5. Check bearing clearance and connecting rod side play as described under *Connecting Rod Bearing and Crankpin Inspection*.

Connecting Rod Bearing and Crankpin Disassembly

1. Remove the crankshaft and connecting rods assembly as described under *Crankshaft and*

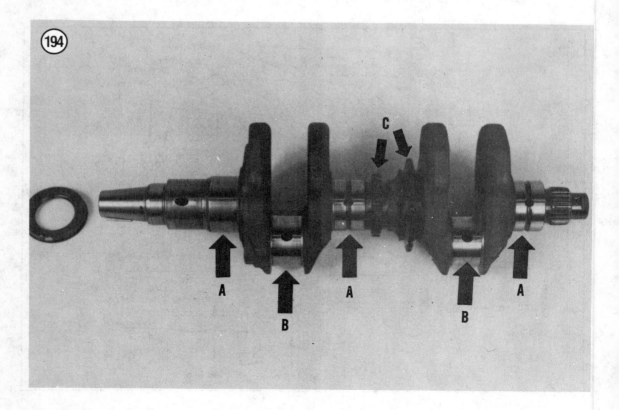

Connecting Rod Removal/Installation in this chapter.

> *NOTE*
> *Before disassembling, mark the rods and end caps. Number them with a "1" (left-hand cylinder) or "2" (right-hand cylinder). The left-hand side refers to the engine sitting in the bike's frame—not as it sits on your workbench.*

2. If not already removed, remove the nuts securing the connecting rod end caps and remove the end caps. Remove both connecting rods from the crankshaft.

3. If the bearing inserts are going to be removed for cleaning, perform the following;

    a. Remove the connecting rod bearing inserts from each connecting rod.

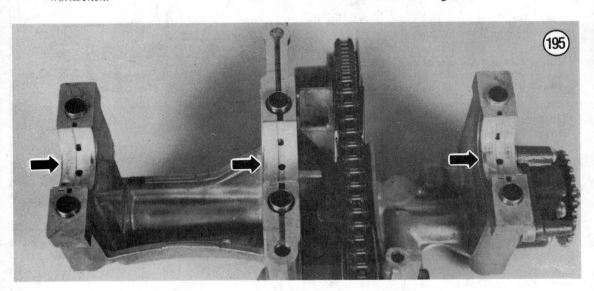

b. Mark the backside of the inserts with a "1"
(left-hand cylinder) and "2" (right-hand
cylinder) and "U" (upper) or "L" (lower).

CAUTION
*If the old bearings are reused, be sure
that they are installed in their exact
original locations.*

4. If removed, reinstall the bearing inserts into the
connecting rods and end caps.
5. Wipe bearing inserts and crankpins clean.
Check again that the inserts and crankpins are in
good condition.
6. Place a piece of Plastigage on one crankpin
parallel to the crankshaft. Do not place the
Plastigage material over an oil hole in the
crankshaft.

CAUTION
*Do not rotate crankshaft while
Plastigage is in place.*

7. Install one of the connecting rods and its cap.
Tighten the cap nuts to the torque specification
listed in **Table 3**.
8. Remove the nuts securing the connecting rod
end cap and remove the end cap. Remove the
connecting rod from the crankshaft.
9. Measure width of flattened Plastigage according
to the manufacturer's instructions. Measure at
both ends of the strip. A difference of 0.025 mm
(0.001 in.) or more indicates a tapered crankpin.
Bearing clearance for a new bearing are listed in
Table 1 or **Table 2**.
10. Repeat Steps 6-9 for the other connecting rod.
11. Remove the Plastigage strips from the
connecting rod bearing journals.
12. Measure the inside diameter of the small ends
of the connecting rods with an inside dial gauge as
shown in **Figure 198**. If worn to the service limit
dimension listed in **Table 1** or **Table 2** or greater,
replace the connecting rod.
13. Lubricate bearings, crankpins and rod caps.
14. Install the connecting rods and end caps onto
the step crankshaft. Refer to marks made in Step 1
and Step 2 for correct connecting rod-to-rod cap-to-
cylinder location. Tighten the nuts to the torque
specification listed in **Table 3**.
15. Rotate the crankshaft to be sure bearings are
not too tight.
16. Insert a feeler gauge between connecting rods.
Side clearance should be as listed in **Table 1** or
Table 2. Replace any rod with excessive side
clearance.

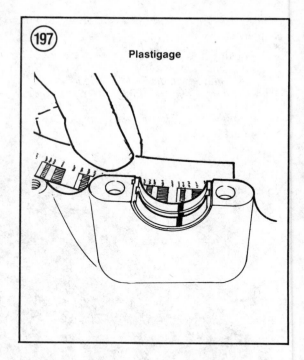

(197) Plastigage

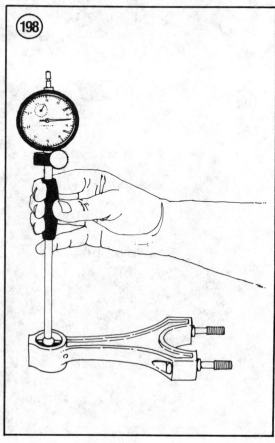

(198)

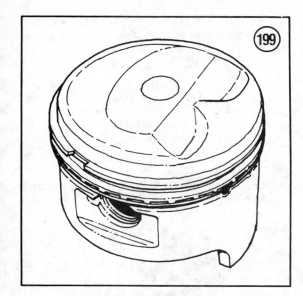

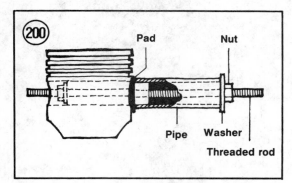

Pad   Nut

Pipe   Washer

Threaded rod

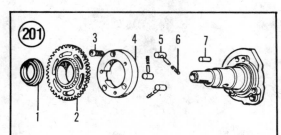

ELECTRIC STARTER GEARS

1. Oil seal
2. Starter drive gear
3. Torx bolt
4. Starter clutch
5. Roller
6. Spring
7. Dowel pin

17. Remove the nuts securing the connecting rod end caps and remove the end caps. Remove the connecting rods from the crankshaft.

Connecting Rod Bearing and Crankpin Assembly

1. Coat the connecting rod bushings, piston pins and piston holes with assembly lubricant.

2. The connecting rods must be installed onto the crankshaft with the oil hole and/or the bearing code number facing toward the *rear* of the engine. Keep this relationship in mind when installing the piston onto the connecting rod in the next step.

3. Place the piston over the connecting rod as follows:

   a. If you are reusing the same pistons and connecting rods, match the pistons to the rod from which it came. Refer to marks made during disassembly.

   b. The double intake valve relief on top of the piston (**Figure 199**) and the oil hole and/or bearing code number must be positioned to the *rear* of the engine.

4. Install the piston pin as follows:

   a. Insert the piston pin and tap it with a plastic mallet until it starts into the connecting rod bushing.

   b. If it does not slide in easily, heat the piston until it is too warm to touch, but not excessively hot (140° F or 60° C).

   c. Continue to drive the piston in while holding the piston so that the rod does not have to take any shock. Otherwise, it may be bent.

   d. Drive the pin in until it is centered in the rod. If the pin is still difficult to install, use the homemade tool (**Figure 200**), but eliminate the piece of pipe.

5. Install the rings as described under *Piston Ring Replacement* in this chapter.

6. Insert the bearing inserts into each connecting rod and the bearing cap. Make sure the insert locating tangs are locked into place.

CAUTION
If the old bearings are reused, be sure they are installed in their exact original locations as noted during disassembly.

ELECTRIC STARTER GEARS

Refer to **Figure 201** for this procedure.

Drive Gear and Clutch Removal/Inspection/Installation

1. Remove the crankshaft as described under *Crankshaft Removal/Installation* in this chapter.

2. Remove the crankshaft oil seal.

3. Remove the starter drive gear (**Figure 202**).

4. Remove the Torx bolts (**Figure 203**) securing the starter clutch to the crankshaft. Use an impact driver and special Torx driver bit for a 6 mm bolt.

5. Inspect the gear for chipped or missing teeth. Look for uneven or excessive wear on the gear faces; replace if necessary.

6. Check the rollers in the starter clutch for uneven or excessive wear; replace as a set if any are bad.

7. Install by reversing the removal steps.

8. Tighten the Torx bolts to the torque specification listed in **Table 3**.

Idle Gear
Removal/Inspection/Installation

1. Remove the lower crankcase as described under *Crankcase Removal/Installation* in this chapter.

2. Remove the bolt (**Figure 204**) securing the shaft.

3. Pull out the shaft and remove the idle gear.

4. Inspect the gear for chipped or missing teeth.

5. Measure the inner diameter of the idle gear and the outer diameter of the shaft with vernier caliper or micrometer. Replace if the difference between the two parts is 0.10 mm (0.004 in.) or greater.

KICKSTARTER
(MANUAL TRANSMISSION)

Not all models with a manual transmission are equipped with a kickstarter.

Refer to **Figure 205** for this procedure.

Removal/Disassembly

1. Place the bike on the center stand or place wood blocks under the engine to support the bike securely.

2. Drain the engine oil as described under *Changing Oil and Filter* in Chapter Three.

3. Remove the right-hand side cover.

4. Remove the bolts (**Figure 206**) securing the clutch bracket. Remove the bracket, then remove the cable from the clutch arm.

5. On models so equipped, disconnect the tachometer drive cable.

6. Remove the bolt and nut clamping the kickstarter lever (**Figure 207**) to the shaft and remove the lever.

7. Remove the exhaust system as described under *Exhaust System Removal/Installation* in Chapter Seven.

8. Remove the bolts securing the right-hand engine cover and remove the cover and gasket. Don't lose the locating dowels.

> *NOTE*
> *Steps 9 and 10 are shown with the clutch and shifting mechanism removed for clarity. It is not necessary to remove either assembly for this procedure.*

9. Remove the spring collar and the kickstarter return spring (**Figure 208**).

10. Remove the thrust washer, rachet spring and kickstarter rachet (**Figure 209**) from the kickstarter spindle.

11. In order to remove the kickstarter gear and kickstarter spindle, it is necessary to remove the engine and split the crankcase halves. Refer to *Crankcase Disassembly* in this chapter.

12. Remove the E-clip and washer (A, **Figure 210**).

13. Withdraw the kickstarter spindle (B, **Figure 210**) and remove the starter pinion.

Assembly/Installation

1. Install by reversing the removal steps.

2. Apply assembly oil to all sliding surfaces of all parts.

3. Hook the end of the return spring onto the web on the crankcase (**Figure 211**).

4. Fill the crankcase with the recommended type and quantity of motor oil. Refer to Chapter Three.

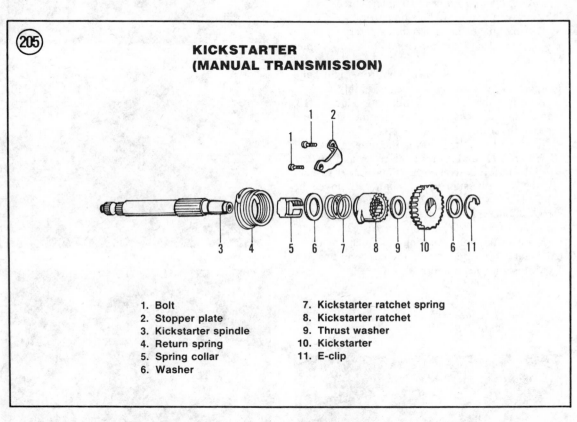

(205)

KICKSTARTER
(MANUAL TRANSMISSION)

1. Bolt
2. Stopper plate
3. Kickstarter spindle
4. Return spring
5. Spring collar
6. Washer
7. Kickstarter ratchet spring
8. Kickstarter ratchet
9. Thrust washer
10. Kickstarter
11. E-clip

(206)

(207)

KICKSTARTER
(AUTOMATIC TRANSMISSION)

Refer to **Figure 212** for this procedure.

Removal

1. Place the bike on the center stand or place wood blocks under the engine to support the bike securely.

2. Drain the engine oil as described under *Changing Oil and Filter* in Chapter Three.

3. Remove the right-hand side cover.

4. Remove the exhaust system as described under *Exhaust System Removal/Installation* in Chapter Seven.

5. Remove the bolt securing the front right-hand footpeg and remove the footpeg assembly.

6. Remove the bolt and nut (A, **Figure 213**) clamping the kickstarter arm to the shaft and remove the arm.

7. Remove the bolts securing the outer side cover (B, **Figure 213**) and remove the cover and gasket.

8. Pull the torque converter (**Figure 214**) straight off the transmission input shaft. Remove the needle bearing. There are 2 needle bearings. During removal, one or more may stay on the shaft or may come off with the torque converter.

9. Remove the bolts securing the inner side cover (A, **Figure 215**) and remove the cover and gasket. Don't lose the locating dowels.

NOTE
*Don't lose the oil check valve and spring (B, **Figure 215**).*

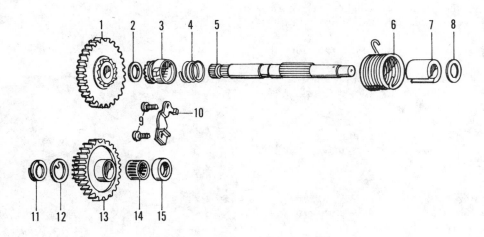

**KICKSTARTER
(AUTOMATIC TRANSMISSION)**

1. Kickstarter gear
2. Washer
3. Kickstarter ratchet
4. Kickstarter ratchet spring
5. Kickstarter spindle
6. Return spring
7. Collar
8. Thrust washer

9. Bolt
10. Stopper plate
11. Spiral spring retainer
12. Splined thrust washer
13. Kickstarter idle gear
14. Needle bearing
15. Collar

10. Remove the kickstarter gear (**Figure 216**) and washer (A, **Figure 217**).

11. Remove the spiral spring retainer and thrust washer (B, **Figure 217**) securing the kickstarter idle gear.

12. Remove the kickstarter idle gear (**Figure 218**) and bearing (**Figure 219**).

13. Remove the shift plate and washer (**Figure 220**).

14. Remove the bolt and nut (**Figure 221**) securing the shift lever to the shaft and remove the shift lever.

15. Push down on the shift arm and from the left-hand side push the shift lever shaft toward the right. Remove the shift lever shaft (**Figure 222**).

16. Remove the kickstarter idle gear bushing (A, **Figure 223**).

17. Remove the bolts securing the holding bar (B, **Figure 223**) and remove the holding bar.

18. Withdraw the kickstarter spindle assembly (**Figure 224**).

> *NOTE*
> *Be sure to remove the thrust washer from the inner surface of the crankcase (**Figure 225**).*

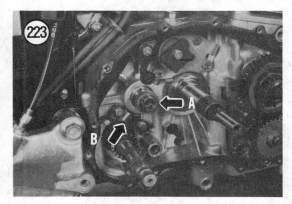

19. In order to remove the starter gear, it is necessary to remove the engine and split the crankcase halves. Refer to *Crankcase Disassembly* in this chapter.

20. Remove the bolt (**Figure 226**) securing the spindle. Slide the spindle out and remove the starter gear.

21. From the inner surface of the inner side cover, remove the circlip (**Figure 227**) securing the kickstarter clutch disc and spring.

22. Remove the clutch disc (**Figure 228**) and spring (**Figure 229**).

Inspection

1. Check the operation of the kickstarter rachet to the starter gear. Look for uneven wear.

2. Slide the kickstarter gear on the kickstarter spindle and check for ease of movement.

3. Check for uneven wear on the sliding surfaces.

4. Check for broken or missing teeth on the starter gear and kickstarter idle gear; replace any parts as necessary.

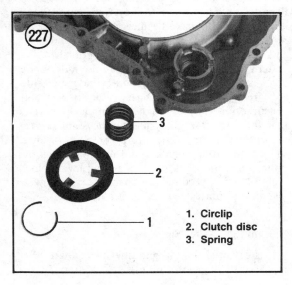

1. Circlip
2. Clutch disc
3. Spring

Installation

1. Install by reversing the removal steps.
2. Apply assembly oil to all sliding surfaces of all parts.
3. Install the steel thrust washer (**Figure 225**) with the machined side toward the spring, away from the crankcase face. Apply some grease to the back side of the washer to hold it in place.
4. Hook the spring end onto the web on the crankcase, and wind the spring up a little. Install the holding plate (**Figure 230**) and bolts, then tighten the bolts securely. Be sure that the cam on the kickstarter ratchet is under the holding plate.
5. Install the torque converter as described under *Torque Converter Installation* in Chapter Six.

BREAK-IN

Following cylinder servicing (boring, honing, new rings, etc.) and major lower end work, the engine should be broken in just as though it were new. The performance and service life of the engine depend greatly on a careful and sensible break-in.

For the first 800 km (500 miles), no more than one-third throttle should be used and speed should be varied as much as possible within the one-third throttle limit. Prolonged, steady running at one speed, no matter how moderate, is to be avoided, as is hard acceleration.

Following the 800 km (500-mile) service, increasingly more throttle can be used but full throttle should not be used until the motorcycle has covered at least 1,600 km (1,000 miles) and then it should be limited to short bursts until 2,410 km (1,500 miles) have been logged.

The mono-grade oils recommended for break-in and normal use provide a more superior bedding pattern for rings and cylinders than do multi-grade oils. As a result, piston ring and cylinder bore life are greatly increased. During this period, oil consumption may be higher than normal. It is therefore important to frequently check and correct the oil level. At no time, during break-in or later, should the oil level be allowed to drop below the bottom line on the dipstick; if the oil level is low, the oil will become overheated resulting in insufficient lubrication and increased wear.

800 km (500 Mile) Service

It is essential that oil and filter be changed after the first 800 km (500 miles). In addition, it is a good idea to change the oil and filter at the completion of break-in (about 2.410 km/1,500 miles) to ensure that all of the particles produced during break-in are removed from the lubrication system. The small added expense may be considered a smart investment that will pay off in increased engine life.

Table 1 ENGINE SPECIFICATIONS (400 CC MODELS)

	Specification	Wear limit
General		
Type and number of cylinders	Vertical parallel twin	
Bore × stroke	70.7×50.6 mm (2.776×1.992 in.)	
Displacement	395.0 cc (24.1 cu. in.)	
Compression ratio	9.3:1	
Compression pressure	1,172-1,368 kPa (171-199 psi)	
Cylinders		
Bore	70.50-70.51 mm (2.775-2.776 in.)	70.60 mm (2.78 in.)
Cylinder/piston clearance	—	0.10 mm (0.004 in.)
Out-of-round	—	0.10 mm (0.004 in.)
Pistons		
Outer diameter	70.74-70.49 mm (2.774-2.775 in.)	70.40 mm (2.772 in.)
Clearance in bore	—	0.10 mm (0.004 in.)
Piston pin bore	17.002-17.008 mm (0.6694-0.6696 in.)	17.04 mm (0.671 in.)
Piston pin outer diameter	16.994-17.000 mm (0.6690-0.6693 in.)	16.98 mm (0.669 mm)
Piston to piston pin clearance	—	0.04 mm (0.0016 in.)
Piston rings		
Number per piston		
Compression	2	—
Oil control	1	—
Ring end gap		
Top and second	0.2-0.4 mm (0.008-0.016 in.)	0.60 mm (0.024 in.)
Oil control (side rail)	0.2-0.9 mm (0.008-0.035 in.)	1.10 mm (0.043 in.)
Ring side clearance		
Top	0.03-0.06 mm (0.001-0.002 in.)	0.10 mm (0.004 in.)
Second	0.025-0.055 mm (0.01-0.002 in.)	0.10 mm (0.004 in.)
Crankshaft		
Main bearing journal oil clearance	0.020-0.044 mm (0.0008-0.0017 in.)	0.08 mm (0.003 in.)
Crankpin oil clearance	0.020-0.044 mm (0.0008-0.0017 in.)	0.08 mm (0.003 in.)
Runout	—	0.05 mm (0.002 in.)
Connecting rods		
Big end side clearance	0.05-0.25 mm (0.002-0.010 in.)	0.35 mm (0.014 in.)
Piston pin hole inner diameter	17.016-17.034 mm (0.6699-0.6706 in.)	17.06 mm (0.672 in.)

(continued)

Table 1 ENGINE SPECIFICATIONS (400 CC MODELS) (continued)

	Specification	Wear limit
Counterbalance		
Balancer inner diameter	18.010-18.028 mm (0.7090-0.7098 in.)	18.04 mm (0.710 in.)
Shaft outer diameter	17.966-17.984 mm (0.7073-0.7080 in.)	17.95 mm (0.707 in.)
Balancer-to-shaft clearance	—	0.08 mm (0.003 in.)
Camshaft		
Cam lobe height		
Intake	37.008-37.208 mm (1.457-1.465 in.)	36.9 mm (1.45 in.)
Exhaust	37.040-37.240 mm (1.458-1.466 in.)	36.9 mm (1.45 in.)
Oil clearance		
Ends	0.040-0.144 mm (0.0016-0.0056 in.)	0.20 mm (0.0079 in.)
Center	0.090-0.191 mm (0.0035-0.0075 in.)	0.23 mm (0.0091 in.)
Runout	—	0.10 mm (0.004 in.)
Valves		
Valve stem-to-guide clearance		
Intake and exhaust	—	0.10 mm (0.004 in.)
Valve guide inner diameter		
Intake	5.500-5.510 mm (0.2165-0.2169 in.)	5.60 mm (0.220 in.)
Exhaust	6.600-6.610 mm (0.2589-0.2604 in.)	6.70 mm (0.264 in.)
Valve stem outer diameter		
Intake	5.455-5.470 mm (0.2148-0.2154 in.)	5.44 mm (0.214 in.)
Exhaust	6.555-6.570 mm (0.2580-0.2587 in.)	6.54 mm (0.257 in.)
Valve seat width	1.1-1.3 mm (0.04-0.05 in.)	2.0 mm (0.08 in.)
Valve springs		
Free length (inner)		
Intake	36.6 mm (1.44 in.)	35.5 mm (1.40 in.)
Exhaust	40.8 mm (1.61 in.)	39.5 mm (1.56 in.)
Free length (outer)		
Intake	50.6 mm (1.99 in.)	49.0 mm (1.93 in.)
Exhaust	51.1 mm (2.01 in.)	49.5 mm (1.95 in.)
Rocker assembly		
Rocker arm bore inner diameter	12.000-12.018 mm (0.4724-0.4731 in.)	12.03 mm (0.474 in.)
Rocker shaft outer diameter	11.966-11.984 mm (0.4711-0.4718 in.)	11.95 mm (0.470 in.)
Camshaft holder inner diameter	12.000-12.027 mm (0.4724-0.4735 in.)	12.05 mm (0.474 in.)
Oil pump		
Inner to outer rotor tip clearance	—	0.10 mm (0.004 in.)
Outer rotor to body clearance	—	0.35 mm (0.014 in.)
Rotor to body clearance	—	0.10 mm (0.004 in.)

Table 2 ENGINE SPECIFICATIONS (450 CC MODELS)

	Specification	Wear limit
General		
Type and number of cylinders	Vertical parallel twin	
Bore×stroke	75.0×50.6 mm (2.95×1.99 in.)	
Displacement	477.0 cc (27.3 cu. in.)	
Compression ratio	9.3:1	
Compression pressure		
1986 CB450SC	1,000-1,400 kPa (145-205 psi)	
Rebel 450	1,019-1,215 kPa (157-185 psi)	
Cylinders		
Bore	75.00-75.01 mm (2.9538-2.9531 in.)	75.10 mm (2.957 in.)
Cylinder/piston clearance	—	0.10 mm (0.004 in.)
Out-of-round and taper	—	0.10 mm (0.004 in.)
Pistons		
Outer diameter	74.96-74.99 mm (2.9512-2.9524 in.)	74.90 mm (2.949 in.)
Clearance in bore	—	0.10 mm (0.004 in.)
Piston pin bore	18.002-18.008 mm (0.7087-0.7090 in.)	18.04 mm (0.710 in.)
Piston pin outer diameter	17.994-18.000 mm (0.7084-0.7087 in.)	17.98 mm (0.708 mm)
Piston to piston pin clearance	—	0.04 mm (0.0016 in.)
Piston rings		
Number per piston		
Compression	2	—
Oil control	1	—
Ring end gap		
Top and second	0.1-0.3 mm (0.004-0.012 in.)	0.50 mm (0.020 in.)
Oil control (side rail)	0.2-0.9 mm (0.008-0.035 in.)	1.10 mm (0.043 in.)
Ring side clearance		
Top	0.03-0.06 mm (0.001-0.002 in.)	0.10 mm (0.004 in.)
Second	0.025-0.055 mm (0.01-0.002 in.)	0.10 mm (0.004 in.)
Crankshaft		
Main bearing journal oil clearance	0.020-0.045 mm (0.0008-0.0018 in.)	0.08 mm (0.003 in.)
Crankpin oil clearance	0.020-0.044 mm (0.0008-0.0017 in.)	0.08 mm (0.003 in.)
Runout	—	0.05 mm (0.002 in.)
Connecting rods		
Big end side clearance	0.05-0.25 mm (0.002-0.010 in.)	0.35 mm (0.014 in.)
Piston pin hole inner diameter	18.016-18.034 mm (0.7093-0.7100 in.)	18.06 mm (0.711 in.)

4

(continued)

Table 2 ENGINE SPECIFICATIONS (450 CC MODELS) (continued)

	Specification	Wear limit
Counterbalance		
Balancer inner diameter	18.010-18.028 mm (0.7090-0.7098 in.)	18.04 mm (0.710 in.)
Shaft outer diameter	17.966-17.984 mm (0.7073-0.7080 in.)	17.95 mm (0.707 in.)
Balancer-to-shaft clearance	—	0.08 mm (0.003 in.)
Camshaft		
Cam lobe height		
Intake	36.220-36.420 mm (1.4260-1.4339 in.)	36.10 mm (1.421 in.)
Exhaust	35.851-36.051 mm (1.4115-1.4193 in.)	35.75 mm (1.407 in.)
Oil clearance		
Ends	0.040-0.144 mm (0.0016-0.0056 in.)	0.20 mm (0.0079 in.)
Center	0.090-0.191 mm (0.0035-0.0075 in.)	0.23 mm (0.0091 in.)
Runout	—	0.10 mm (0.004 in.)
Valves		
Valve stem-to-guide clearance		
Intake and exhaust	—	0.10 mm (0.004 in.)
Valve guide inner diameter		
Intake	5.500-5.510 mm (0.2165-0.2169 in.)	5.60 mm (0.220 in.)
Exhaust	6.600-6.610 mm (0.2589-0.2604 in.)	6.70 mm (0.264 in.)
Valve stem outer diameter		
Intake	5.455-5.470 mm (0.2148-0.2154 in.)	5.44 mm (0.214 in.)
Exhaust	6.555-6.570 mm (0.2580-0.2587 in.)	6.54 mm (0.257 in.)
Valve seat width	1.1-1.3 mm (0.04-0.05 in.)	2.0 mm (0.08 in.)
Valve springs		
Free length (inner)		
Intake	36.6 mm (1.44 in.)	35.5 mm (1.40 in.)
Exhaust	40.8 mm (1.61 in.)	39.5 mm (1.56 in.)
Free length (outer)		
Intake	50.6 mm (1.99 in.)	49.0 mm (1.93 in.)
Exhaust	51.1 mm (2.01 in.)	49.5 mm (1.95 in.)
Rocker assembly		
Rocker arm bore inner diameter	12.000-12.018 mm (0.4724-0.4731 in.)	12.03 mm (0.474 in.)
Rocker shaft outer diameter	11.966-11.984 mm (0.4711-0.4718 in.)	11.95 mm (0.470 in.)
Oil pump (all models except Rebel 450)		
Inner to outer rotor tip clearance	0.02-0.07 mm (0.001-0.003 in.)	0.10 mm (0.004 in.)
Outer rotor to body clearance	0.15-0.22 mm (0.006-0.009 in.)	0.35 mm (0.014 in.)
Rotor to body clearance	0.02-0.07 mm (0.001-0.003 in.)	0.10 mm (0.004 in.)

(continued)

Table 2 ENGINE SPECIFICATIONS (450 CC MODELS) (continued)

	Specification	Wear limit
Oil pump (all models except Rebel 450)		
Inner to outer	0.157 mm	0.20 mm (0.008 in.)
rotor tip clearance	(0.001-0.003 in.)	
Outer rotor to	0.15-0.21 mm	0.35 mm (0.014 in.)
body clearance	(0.006-0.008 in.)	
Rotor to body clearance	0.04-0.09 mm	0.12 mm (0.005 in.)
	(0.002-0.004 in.)	

Table 3 ENGINE TORQUE SPECIFICATIONS

Item	N·m	ft.-lb.
Engine mounting bolts and nuts		
Except Rebel 450		
8 mm bolt and nut	18-24	13-18
8 mm flange bolt and nut	15-22	20-30
10 mm flange bolt and nut	45-58	33-43
Engine mounting bolts and nuts		
Rebel 450		
Mounting bracket-to-frame bolts	24-30	17-22
Lower through-bolts and nuts	60-70	43-51
Upper through-bolts and nuts	35-45	25-33
Cam sprocket bolts		
1978-1981	18-22	13-16
1982-on	30-33	22-24
Cylinder head bolts		
1978-1981	30-33	22-24
1982-on	30-36	22-26
Alternator rotor bolt		
Rebel 450, CB450SC	110-130	80-94
All other models	100-120	72-87
Primary drive gear bolt	46-50	33-36
Balancer adjuster plate		
8 mm nut	20-25	14-18
10 mm nut	30-35	22-25
Main bearing cap assembly bolts		
8 mm bolts	10-14	7-10
10 mm bolts	33-37	24-27
Oil strainer bolt	10-14	7-10
Crankcase bolts		
6 mm bolts	10-14	7-10
8 mm bolts	22-28	16-20
Connecting rod end cap nuts	25-29	18-12
Starter clutch Torx bolts	33-37	24-27

4

Table 4 VALVE GUIDE SERVICE SPECIAL TOOLS

Model	Honda Part No.
Valve guide reamer	
400 cc models	
Intake (5.5 mm)	07984-2000000
Exhaust (6.6 mm)	07984-6110000
1982-1985 450 cc models	
Except Rebel 450 and CB450SC	
Intake (5.5 mm)	07984-3290100
Exhaust (6.6 mm)	07984-6570100
Rebel 450, CB450SC	
Intake	07984-2000000
Exhaust	07984-5510000
Valve guide remover (all models)	
Intake (5.5 mm)	07742-0010100 or 07942-3291000
Exhaust (6.6 mm)	07742-6570100 or 07942-6570100

CHAPTER FIVE

CLUTCH AND MANUAL TRANSMISSION

CLUTCH

The clutch on these models is a wet multi-plate type which operates immersed in the engine oil. All clutch parts can be removed with the engine in the frame.

The clutch outer housing on 1982-on models is equipped with damping springs instead of the previously used rubber dampers. When the rubber dampers age or deteriorate they compress and cause the clutch to rattle.

This procedure is typical for all models and is shown with different models and years. Where differences occur, they are identified.

Removal/Disassembly

Refer to **Figure 1** for this procedure.

1. Place the bike on the center stand or place wood blocks under the engine to support the bike securely.
2. Drain the engine oil as described under *Changing Oil and Filter* in Chapter Three.
3. On all models except Rebel 450, remove the right-hand cover.
4. Slacken the clutch cable at the hand lever on the handlebar as follows:

    a. On models so equipped, slide back the rubber boot covering the clutch adjuster and locknut (A, **Figure 2**).

    b. Loosen the locknut (B, **Figure 2**) and turn the adjuster (C, **Figure 2**) in to allow maximum slack in the clutch cable.

5. On models so equipped, remove the screw and withdraw the tachometer cable (**Figure 3**) from the right-hand crankcase cover. Reinstall the screw to avoid misplacing it.
6. On models so equipped, remove the bolt and nut (A, **Figure 4**) clamping the kickstarter arm to the shaft and remove the arm.

7A. On Rebel 450 models, perform the following:

    a. Loosen the clutch cable locknut (A, **Figure 5**) and screw in the adjuster (B, **Figure 5**) to allow slack in the clutch cable.

    b. Remove the bolts securing the clutch cable bracket.

    c. Disconnect the cable from the clutch arm.

    d. Remove the clamping bolt securing the brake rod to the brake shaft (A, **Figure 6**). Remove the brake rod from the shaft.

    e. Remove the Allen bolts (B, **Figure 6**) securing the right-hand footpeg assembly.

    f. Remove the brake pedal and right-hand footpeg assembly.

7B. On all models except Rebel 450, perform the following:

    a. Remove the bolts (A, **Figure 7**) securing the clutch cable bracket.

b. Disconnect the cable from the clutch arm (B, **Figure 7**) and remove the clutch cable and bracket.

c. Remove the bolt (B, **Figure 4**) securing the front right-hand footpeg assembly and remove the assembly.

d. Remove the nuts securing the right-hand exhaust pipe to the cylinder head. Loosen the clamping bolt securing the right-hand exhaust pipe to the collector and remove the right-hand exhaust pipe from the engine.

8. Remove the bolts securing the right-hand crankcase cover (**Figure 8**) and remove the cover and gasket. Don't lose the locating dowels.

9. On models so equipped, pull back on the rubber boot and remove the electrical wire from the oil pressure sending switch (**Figure 9**).

10. Remove the clutch bolts (**Figure 10**) in a crisscross pattern.

11. Remove the lifter plate, release bearing and the clutch springs.

12. Shift the transmission into gear and have a helper apply the rear brake.

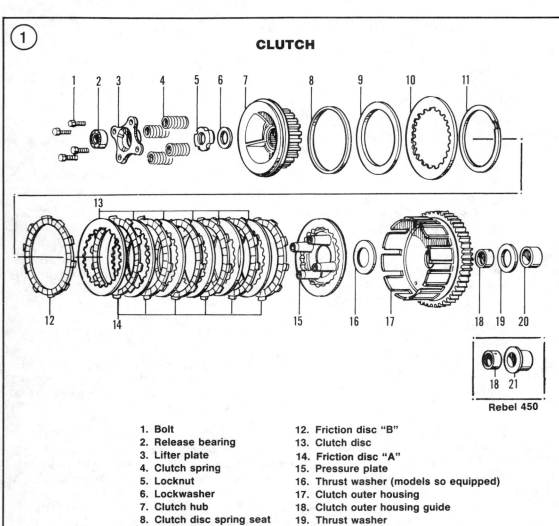

CLUTCH

Rebel 450

1. Bolt	12. Friction disc "B"
2. Release bearing	13. Clutch disc
3. Lifter plate	14. Friction disc "A"
4. Clutch spring	15. Pressure plate
5. Locknut	16. Thrust washer (models so equipped)
6. Lockwasher	17. Clutch outer housing
7. Clutch hub	18. Clutch outer housing guide
8. Clutch disc spring seat	19. Thrust washer
9. Clutch disc spring	20. Inner collar
10. Clutch plate "B"	21. Inner bushing (Rebel 450)
11. Set spring	

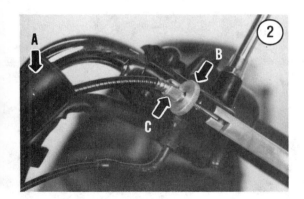

13. Loosen the clutch nut with a drift and hammer (**Figure 11**). Remove the clutch nut and lockwasher.

> *NOTE*
> *The clutch nut can also be loosened with the use of a special Honda tool (Locknut Wrench, part No. 07716-0020203).*

14. Remove the clutch hub (**Figure 12**).
15. Remove the clutch plates and friction discs (**Figure 13**).

> *NOTE*
> *The outermost friction disc "B" (**Figure 1**) is thicker than the other friction discs. Remember this when installing the friction discs.*

16. Remove the pressure plate (**Figure 14**).
17. On models so equipped, remove the thrust washer.

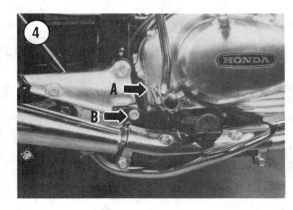

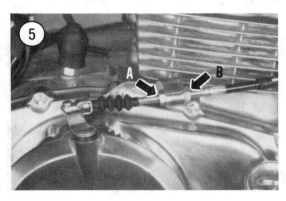

18. Remove the clutch outer housing (**Figure 15**).

19A. On Rebel 450 models, remove the clutch outer housing guide and inner collar from the transmission shaft.

19B. On all models except Rebel 450, perform the following:

a. Remove the clutch outer housing guide (**Figure 16**) and thrust washer (**Figure 17**).

b. If the crankcase is going to be disassembled, remove the inner collar on the transmission shaft.

20. Inspect all components as described in this chapter.

Inspection

1. Clean all parts in a petroleum-based solvent such as kerosene and dry thoroughly with compressed air.

2. Measure the free length of each clutch spring with a vernier caliper as shown in **Figure 18**. Replace all springs if any have sagged to the service limit dimension listed in **Table 1** or less.

3. Measure the thickness of each friction disc at several places around the disc as shown in **Figure 19**. Replace if worn to the service limit dimension listed in **Table 1** or less. Friction disc "B" is the outermost friction disc; it is located against the clutch hubs and has wide tabs.

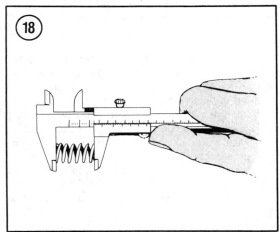

4. Check the clutch plates for warpage on a surface plate such as a piece of plate glass (**Figure 20**). Replace any plates that are warped to the service limit listed in **Table 1** or greater.

NOTE
If any of the friction discs, clutch plates or clutch springs require replacement, you should consider replacing all of them as a set to retain maximum clutch performance.

5. Inspect the teeth of the clutch outer housing for damage. Remove any small nicks on the gear teeth with an oilstone. If damage is severe, the housing must be replaced.

6. Inspect the slots in the clutch outer housing for cracks, nicks or galling where they come in contact with the friction disc tabs. If any severe damage is evident, the housing must be replaced.

7. Inspect the outer grooves in the clutch center; replace the clutch center if damage is apparent.

8. Measure the clearance between the clutch center and the clutch plate "B" (**Figure 21**) with a flat feeler gauge. The standard dimension is listed in **Table 1**. If the dimension is greater the clutch disc spring must be replaced. To replace the clutch disc spring:

    a. Remove the set spring from the clutch center and remove the clutch plate "B", the clutch disc spring and the clutch disc spring seat.

    b. Reinstall the clutch disc spring seat, clutch disc spring, clutch plate "B" and the set spring. Make sure to install the disc spring as shown in **Figure 22**.

    c. Make sure that the set ring is correctly seated in the groove in the clutch center.

9. Measure the inside diameter of the clutch outer housing where the outer guide rides. If worn to the

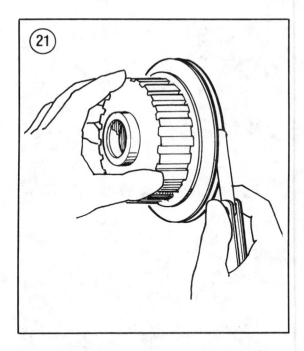

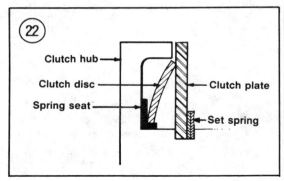

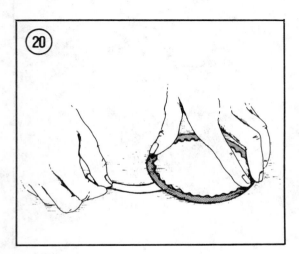

service limit dimension listed in **Table 1** or greater the clutch outer housing must be replaced.

10. Measure the outside diameter of the clutch outer guide. If worn to the service limit dimension listed in **Table 1** or less the clutch outer guide must be replaced.

Assembly/Installation

Refer to **Figure 1** for this procedure.

NOTE
If either or both friction discs and clutch plates have been replaced with new ones, apply new engine oil to all surfaces to avoid having the clutch lock up when used for the first time.

1A. On Rebel 450 models, install the inner collar and clutch outer housing guide onto the transmission shaft.

1B. On all models except Rebel 450, perform the following:

 a. If the crankcase was disassembled, install the inner collar onto the transmission shaft.

 b. Install the thrust washer (**Figure 17**) and the clutch outer housing guide (**Figure 16**).

2. Install the clutch outer housing (A, **Figure 23**).

3. On models so equipped, install the thrust washer (B, **Figure 23**).

4. Install the friction disc "B" onto the clutch center. This is the only friction disc with wide tabs.

5. Install a clutch plate and a friction disc. Continue to install a clutch plate, then a friction disc and alternate them until all are installed. Install the clutch pressure plate. Align all of the friction disc tabs.

6. Install all components assembled in Step 5 into the clutch outer housing (**Figure 24**).

7. Install the lockwasher (**Figure 25**). The word OUTSIDE must face toward the outside.

8. Temporarily install 2 clutch springs, 2 flat washers and 2 clutch bolts. Tighten the bolts completely; this will lock the clutch and prevent it from turning within itself. Shift the transmission into gear and have an assistant apply the rear brake.

9. Install the clutch nut (**Figure 26**) and tighten to the torque specification listed in **Table 2**. Use the same tool used for removal.

10. Remove the 2 clutch bolts and 2 washers and install the other clutch springs.

11. Install the lifter plate and the clutch bolts (**Figure 27**). Tighten the clutch bolts in a crisscross pattern in 2-3 stages.

12. On models so equipped, connect the electrical wire onto the oil pressure sending switch (**Figure 28**). Install the rubber boot over the sending switch.

13. Install a new gasket and locating dowels (**Figure 29**) and install the right-hand. crankcase cover.

14A. On Rebel 450 models, perform the following:
   a. Install the brake pedal and right-hand footpeg assembly.
   b. Install the Allen bolts securing the right-hand footpeg assembly and tighten securely.
   c. Install the brake rod onto the brake shaft and install the clamping bolt. Tighten the bolt securely.
   d. Install the clutch cable bracket and bolts. Tighten the bolts securely.
   e. Connect the cable onto the clutch arm.

14B. On all models except Rebel 450, perform the following:
   a. Install the clutch cable bracket and bolts. Tighten the bolts securely.
   b. Connect the cable onto the clutch arm.
   c. **Install the right-hand footpeg assembly and bolt. Tighten the bolt securely.**
   d. Install the right-hand exhaust pipe into the collector and into the cylinder head. First tighten the nuts securing the right-hand exhaust pipe to the cylinder head. Then tighten the clamping bolt securing the right-hand exhaust pipe to the collector. Tighten the nuts and bolts in this order to minimize exhaust leakage.

15. On models so equipped, install the kickstarter arm, bolt and nut. Tighten the bolt securely.

16. On models so equipped, install the tachometer cable into the right-hand crankcase cover and secure it with the screw.

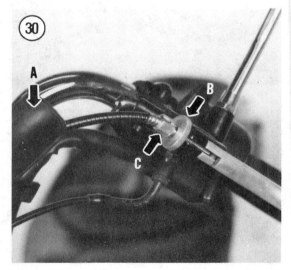

17. On all models except Rebel 450, install the right-hand cover.

18. Fill the crankcase with the recommended type and quantity of engine oil. Refer to Chapter Three.

19. Adjust the clutch cable as described under *Clutch Cable Adjustment* in Chapter Three.

CLUTCH CABLE

Removal/Installation

In time, the cable will stretch to the point where it is no longer useful and will have to be replaced.

> *NOTE*
> *Before removing the cable, make a drawing of the cable routing through the frame. It is easy to forget how it was, once it has been removed. Replace it exactly as it was, avoiding any sharp turns.*

1. Slacken the clutch cable at the hand lever on the handlebar as follows:
   a. On models so equipped, slide back the rubber boot covering the clutch adjuster and locknut (A, **Figure 30**).
   b. Loosen the locknut (B, **Figure 30**) and turn the adjuster (C, **Figure 30**) in to allow maximum slack in the clutch cable.

2A. On Rebel 450 models, perform the following:
   a. Completely unscrew the locknut (A, **Figure 31**) at the cable bracket.
   b. Disconnect the lower end of the cable from the clutch actuating operating lever.
   c. Slide the cable out from the cable bracket.

2B. On all models except Rebel 450, perform the following:
   a. Completely unscrew the locknut (A, **Figure 32**) at the cable bracket.
   b. Disconnect the lower end of the cable from the clutch actuating operating lever (B, **Figure 32**).

3. Remove the cable from the frame and replace with a new one.

4. Adjust the cable free play as described under *Clutch Cable Adjustment* in Chapter Three.

EXTERNAL GEARSHIFT MECHANISM

Refer to the following drawings for this procedure:
   a. **Figure 33**: CB400T I, CB400T II, CB400T, CM400T, CM400C, CM400E.
   b. **Figure 34**: CB450T, CB450SC, CM450E, CM450C.
   c. **Figure 35**: Rebel 450.

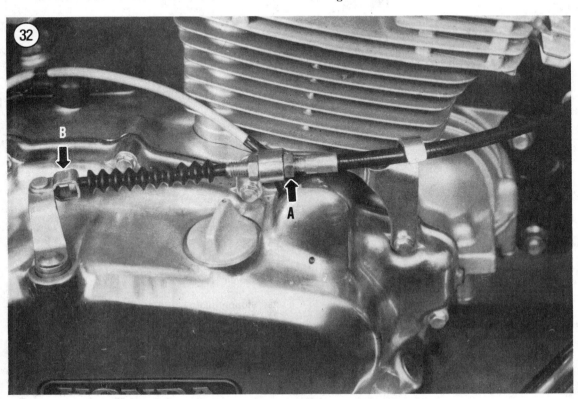

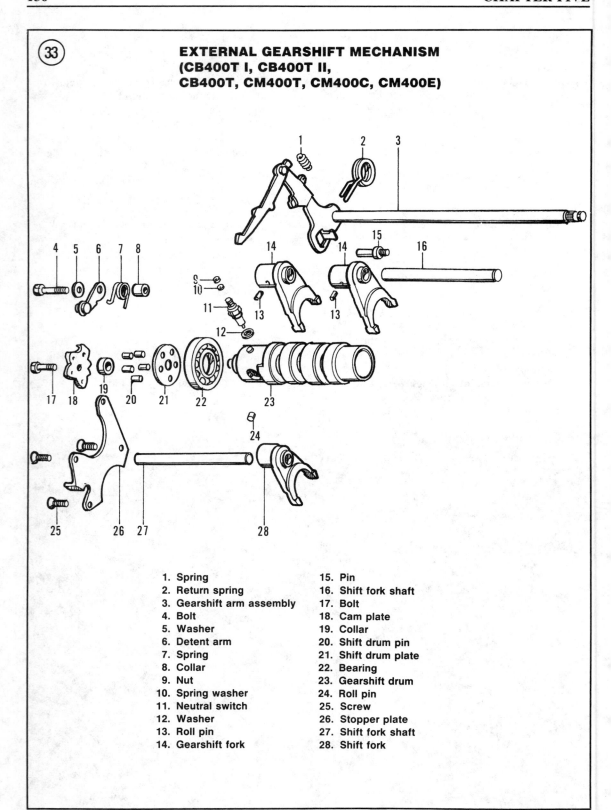

③③ EXTERNAL GEARSHIFT MECHANISM
(CB400T I, CB400T II,
CB400T, CM400T, CM400C, CM400E)

1. Spring	15. Pin
2. Return spring	16. Shift fork shaft
3. Gearshift arm assembly	17. Bolt
4. Bolt	18. Cam plate
5. Washer	19. Collar
6. Detent arm	20. Shift drum pin
7. Spring	21. Shift drum plate
8. Collar	22. Bearing
9. Nut	23. Gearshift drum
10. Spring washer	24. Roll pin
11. Neutral switch	25. Screw
12. Washer	26. Stopper plate
13. Roll pin	27. Shift fork shaft
14. Gearshift fork	28. Shift fork

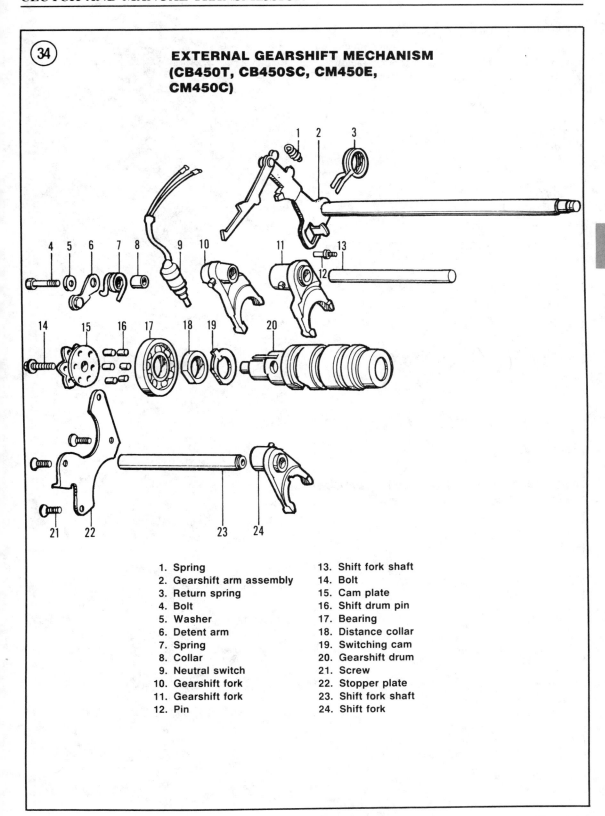

EXTERNAL GEARSHIFT MECHANISM (CB450T, CB450SC, CM450E, CM450C)

1. Spring
2. Gearshift arm assembly
3. Return spring
4. Bolt
5. Washer
6. Detent arm
7. Spring
8. Collar
9. Neutral switch
10. Gearshift fork
11. Gearshift fork
12. Pin
13. Shift fork shaft
14. Bolt
15. Cam plate
16. Shift drum pin
17. Bearing
18. Distance collar
19. Switching cam
20. Gearshift drum
21. Screw
22. Stopper plate
23. Shift fork shaft
24. Shift fork

Removal/Installation

1. Remove the clutch assembly as described under *Clutch Removal/Disassembly* in this chapter.

2. Loosen the bolt securing the detent arm about 3-4 turns (**Figure 36**).

3. Flip the detent arm out and off of the cam plate (**Figure 37**).

4. Disengage the spring from under the detent arm (**Figure 38**).

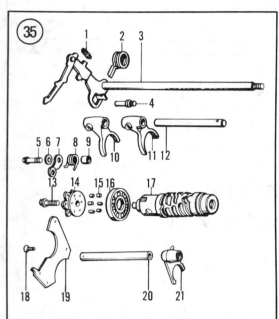

EXTERNAL GEARSHIFT MECHANISM (REBEL 450)

1. Spring
2. Return spring
3. Gearshift arm assembly
4. Pin
5. Bolt
6. Washer
7. Detent arm
8. Spring
9. Collar
10. Gearshift fork
11. Gearshift fork
12. Shift fork shaft
13. Bolt
14. Cam plate
15. Shift drum pin
16. Bearing
17. Gearshift drum
18. Screw
19. Stopper plate
20. Shift fork shaft
21. Shift fork

5A. On Rebel 450 models, perform the following:
 a. Remove the clamping bolt securing the gearshift pedal arm to the shift shaft (A, **Figure 39**). Remove the gearshift pedal arm from the shaft.
 b. Remove the Allen bolts (B, **Figure 39**) securing the left-hand footpeg assembly.
 c. Remove the gearshift pedal arm and the left-hand footpeg assembly.

5B. On all models except Rebel 450, loosen the bolt and nut (**Figure 40**) clamping the shift lever to the shaft and remove the shift lever.

6. Push down on the shift arm (**Figure 41**), then from the left-hand side, push the gearshift arm assembly toward the right-hand side.

7. Withdraw the gearshift arm assembly from the crankcase (**Figure 42**).

8A. On CB400T I, CB400T II, CB400T, CM400T, CM400C, CM400E models, perform the following:
 a. Remove the bolt securing the cam plate.
 b. Remove the cam plate and pins.
 c. Remove the collar, the shift drum pins and the shift drum plate. Don't lose the pin on the backside of the shift drum plate.

8B. On all other models, remove the bolt securing the cam plate and remove the cam plate and dowel pin (A, **Figure 43**).

9. Remove the bolt and washer (B, **Figure 43**) securing the detent arm and remove the detent arm, spring and collar.

10. If necessary, remove the screws securing the shift drum bearing retainer (C, **Figure 43**) and remove the retainer.

11. Install by reversing these removal steps, noting the following.

12. Apply a small amount of Loctite Lock N' Seal on the cam plate mounting bolt and tighten to the torque specification listed in **Table 2**.

13. Fill the crankcase with the recommended type and quantity of engine oil. Refer to Chapter Three.

14. Adjust the clutch cable as described under *Clutch Cable Adjustment* in Chapter Three.

5

MANUAL TRANSMISSION AND INTERNAL SHIFT MECHANISM

To gain access to the transmission and internal shift mechanism it is necessary to remove the engine from the frame and split the crankcase.

MANUAL TRANSMISSION

Removal (All Models)

1. Remove the engine as described under *Engine Removal/Installation* in Chapter Four. Perform the engine disassembly steps described in the engine removal procedure (remove cylinder head, cylinder, pistons, alternator, clutch).
2. Place the engine on the workbench upside down on a couple of 2×4 wood blocks. This is to protect the protruding connecting rods.

3. Remove the bolts securing the crankcase halves together (**Figure 44**). All of the bolts are in the lower crankcase half—none are in the top half. Tap around the perimeter of the lower crankcase half with a plastic mallet and separate the two halves.
4. Remove the bolts (**Figure 45**) securing the oil pickup and strainer assembly and remove the assembly. Don't lose the O-ring seal on the portion that goes into the main bearing cap assembly.
5. Remove the bolts (**Figure 46**) securing the main bearing cap assembly.
6. Lift up the main bearing cap assembly and pivot it away from the transmission components and the crankshaft assembly.
7. Remove the bolt (**Figure 47**) securing the rear chain guide and remove the guide.
8. Lift out the mainshaft assembly (A, **Figure 48**) and the countershaft assembly (B, **Figure 48**).

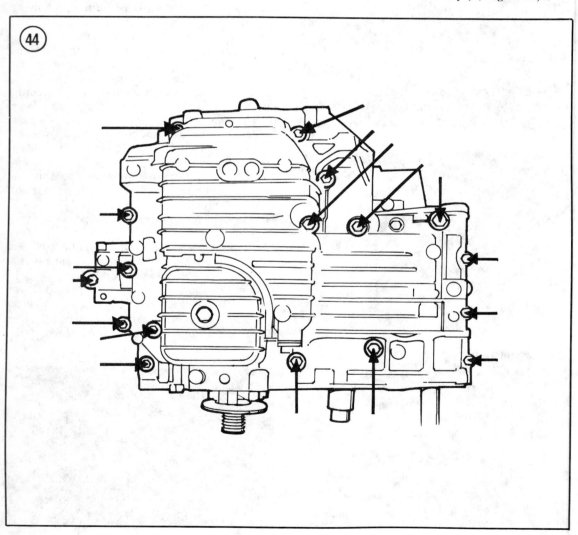

Installation (All Models)

1. Apply assembly oil to all bearing surfaces of the crankshaft and crankcase.

2. Make sure the locating pin (A, **Figure 49**) and the oil control orifice (B, **Figure 49**) are in place in the upper crankcase half. Position the shift forks as shown in **Figure 50**.

3. Install the mainshaft assembly (A, **Figure 48**). Make sure that the hole in the needle bearing race is facing down and aligns with the oil control orifice in the crankcase. Check that the alignment marks are flush with the crankcase surface.

4. Install the countershaft assembly (B, **Figure 48**). Make sure that the hole in the needle bearing race is facing down and aligns with the locating pin in

the crankcase. Check that the alignment marks are flush with the crankcase surface (**Figure 51**).
5. Install the rear chain guide and tighten the bolt securely (**Figure 47**).

> *CAUTION*
> *Alignment of the crankshaft to the balancers is very critical. The following steps must be performed correctly.*

6. Rotate the crankshaft until it is at TDC. When it is at TDC the alignment mark on one of the crankshaft counterbalancers will align with the crankcase surface as shown in **Figure 52** and **Figure 53**.
7. Lift the main bearing cap assembly temporarily into position.

> *CAUTION*
> *Alignment of the crankshaft to the balancers is very critical. All alignment marks must be aligned exactly or severe engine vibration will occur.*

8. With the crankshaft at top dead center, the following alignment marks must be correctly aligned.
   a. The front counter balance mark "TC" must be horizontal and align with the web on the crankcase. Refer to **Figure 54** and **Figure 55**.
   b. The rear counterbalance mark "TH" must be horizontal and align with the ledge of the main bearing cap assembly. Refer to **Figure 56** and **Figure 57**.

> *CAUTION*
> *Make sure the alignment of both the front and rear counter balancers are correct. If not, adjust the counterbalancers on the chain until they are. This alignment is necessary for proper engine operation and to avoid severe engine vibration.*

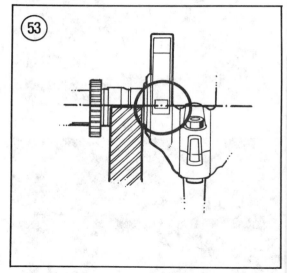

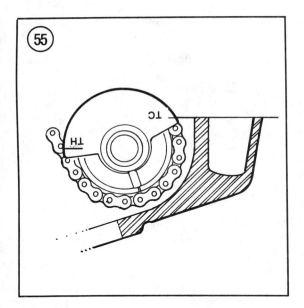

9. If the counterbalance marks are not correct, perform the following:

    a. Lift the main bearing cap assembly up and change the counterbalance weight's location on the chain.

    b. Reinstall the main bearing cap assembly.

    c. Recheck the marks as described in Step 8 and if necessary reposition the counterbalancers on the chain until *both alignment marks* are correct with the crankshaft at TDC.

10. Install the main bearing cap bolts and tighten in 2-3 stages in the sequence shown in **Figure 58** to the torque specifications listed in **Table 2**.

11. Install the oil pickup as follows:

    a. Make sure the O-ring is in place and install the oil pickup and strainer assembly.

    b. Install the front bolt.

    c. Rotate the rear balancer shaft (**Figure 59**) to vertical in order to install the rear bolt. Tighten both bolts securely.

5

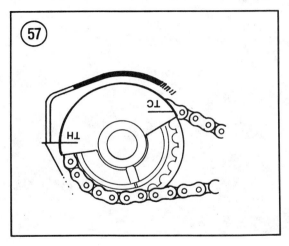

12. Install the oil filter seal ring (**Figure 60**) if it was removed.

13. Install the crankcase locating dowels (**Figure 61**).

14. Make sure both crankcase sealing surfaces are completely clean and free of old gasket sealing material.

15. Apply a light coat of gasket sealer to the sealing surface of the lower case half. Cover only flat surfaces, not curved bearing surfaces. Make the coating as thin as possible or the case can shift and hammer out the bearings.

> *NOTE*
> *Use Three Bond, Gasgacinch Sealer or equivalent. When selecting an equivalent, avoid thick or hard setting materials.*

16. Install all of the crankcase bolts and tighten in a crisscross pattern in 2-3 stages to the torque specification listed in **Table 2**.

17. Install the engine as described in Chapter Four.

Transmission Shaft Assembly
Preliminary Inspection (All Models)

Before disassembling the transmission shaft assemblies they should be cleaned and inspected. Place the assembled shaft into a large can or plastic bucket and thoroughly clean with solvent and a stiff brush. Dry with compressed air or let it sit on rags to drip dry. Repeat for the other shaft assembly.

1. After they have been cleaned, visually inspect the components of the assemblies for excessive wear. Any burrs, pitting or roughness on the teeth of a gear will cause wear on the mating gear. Minor roughness can be cleaned up with an oilstone but there's little point in wasting time attempting to remove deep scars.

> *NOTE*
> *Defective gears should be replaced. It's a good idea to replace the mating gear on the other shaft even though it may not show as much wear or damage.*

2. Carefully check the engagement dogs. If any are chipped, worn, rounded or missing, the affected gear must be replaced.

3. If possible, check the runout of each transmission shaft. Mount the shaft being checked in a lathe, on V-blocks or on some other suitable centering device. Place a dial indicator so that its plunger contacts a constant surface near the center of the shaft. Rotate the shaft and record the

extremes of the dial readings. The shaft should be replaced if the runout exceeds 0.04 mm (0.0016 in.).

4. Rotate the transmission bearings by hand. Check for roughness, noise and radial play. Any bearing that is suspect should be replaced.

5. If the transmission shafts are satisfactory and are not going to be disassembled, apply engine oil to all components and reinstall them in the crankcase as described in this supplement.

5-SPEED MANUAL TRANSMISSION (CB400T I, CB400T II, CM400T, CM400C, CM400E)

Mainshaft
Disassembly/Assembly

Refer to **Figure 62** for this procedure.

1. Remove the needle bearing assembly.

2. Slide off the washer and the 2nd gear.

3. Slide off the splined washer, the 5th gear and another splined washer.

4. Remove the circlip and the 3rd gear.

5. Remove the circlip.

6. Slide off the thrust washer and the 4th gear.

7. If necessary, remove the ball bearing from the shaft.

8. Check each gear for excessive wear and for chipped or missing teeth. Make sure the lugs on ends of gears are in good condition.

9. Make sure that all gears slide smoothly on the mainshaft splines.

10. Check the bearings. Make sure that they rotate smoothly with no signs of wear or damage.

11. Position the 4th gear with the flush side going on first and slide on the 4th gear and splined washer.

12. Install the circlip and slide on the 3rd gear.

13. Install the circlip and slide on the splined washer.

14. Position the 5th gear with the engagement lug receptacles side going on first and slide on the 5th gear.

15. Slide on the splined washer and the 2nd gear.

16. Slide on the washer and the needle bearing assembly.

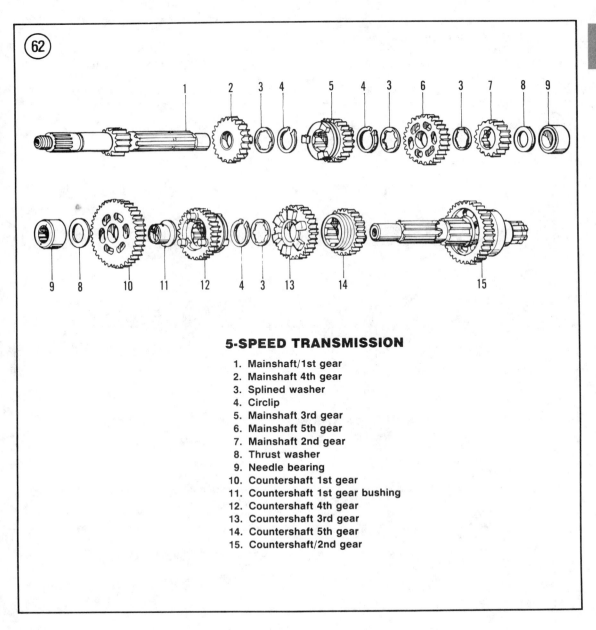

5-SPEED TRANSMISSION

1. Mainshaft/1st gear
2. Mainshaft 4th gear
3. Splined washer
4. Circlip
5. Mainshaft 3rd gear
6. Mainshaft 5th gear
7. Mainshaft 2nd gear
8. Thrust washer
9. Needle bearing
10. Countershaft 1st gear
11. Countershaft 1st gear bushing
12. Countershaft 4th gear
13. Countershaft 3rd gear
14. Countershaft 5th gear
15. Countershaft/2nd gear

Countershaft
Disassembly/Assembly

Refer to **Figure 62** for this procedure.
1. Remove the needle bearing assembly.
2. Slide off the washer, the 1st gear and the 1st gear bushing.
3. Slide off the 4th gear.
4. Remove the circlip and slide off the splined washer.
5. Slide off the 3rd gear and the 5th gear.
6. Remove the 2 oil seals from the sprocket end of shaft.

NOTE
The second gear is pressed onto the shaft. If removal is necessary, take the countershaft to a Honda dealer or machine shop. Have them remove the gear and install a new gear.

7. Clean all of the parts in solvent and dry thoroughly.
8. Check each gear for excessive wear and for chipped or missing teeth. Make sure the lugs on the ends of gears are in good condition.
9. Make sure that all gears slide smoothly on the countershaft splines.
10. Install the outer oil seal with the flush side out, toward the sprocket.
11. Position the 5th gear with the engagement lug side going on first and slide on the 5th gear.
12. Position the 3rd gear with the engagement lug side going on last and slide on the 3rd gear.
13. Slide on the splined washer and install the circlip.
14. Position the 4th gear with the *round* engagement lug side going on last and slide on the 4th gear.

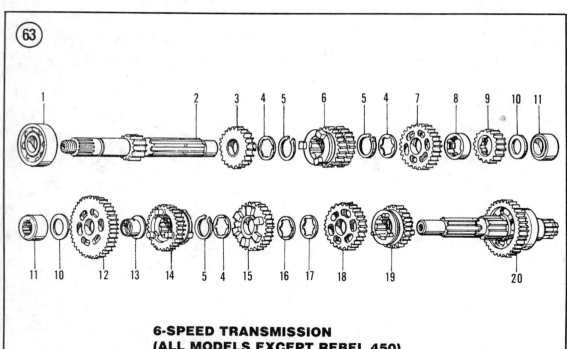

63

6-SPEED TRANSMISSION
(ALL MODELS EXCEPT REBEL 450)

1. Bearing
2. Mainshaft/1st gear
3. Mainshaft 5th gear
4. Splined washer
5. Circlip
6. Mainshaft 3rd/4th combination gear
7. Mainshaft 6th gear
8. Mainshaft 6th gear bushing
9. Mainshaft 2nd gear
10. Thrust washer
11. Needle bearing
12. Countershaft 1st gear
13. Countershaft 1st gear bushing
14. Countershaft 5th gear
15. Countershaft 4th gear
16. Splined collar
17. Lockwasher
18. Countershaft 3rd gear
19. Countershaft 6th gear
20. Countershaft/2nd gear

15. Slide on the 1st gear bushing.

16. Position the 1st gear with the flush side going on last and slide on the 1st gear.

17. Slide on the washer and the needle bearing assembly.

6-SPEED MANUAL TRANSMISSION

Refer to the following illustrations for this procedure:

a. **Figure 63**: CB400T, CB450T, CM450SC, CM450E and CM450C.

b. **Figure 64**: Rebel 450.

NOTE
The 6-speed transmission used among the various models is basically the same. On Rebel 450 models, there are some additional components (e.g. lockwashers). Where differences occur they are identified.

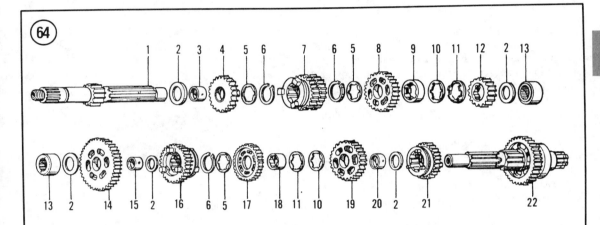

6-SPEED TRANSMISSION (REBEL 450)

1. Mainshaft/1st gear
2. Thrust washer
3. Mainshaft 5th gear bushing
4. Mainshaft 5th gear
5. Splined washer
6. Circlip
7. Mainshaft 3rd/4th combination gear
8. Mainshaft 6th gear
9. Mainshaft 6th gear bushing
10. Splined collar
11. Lockwasher
12. Mainshaft 2nd gear
13. Needle bearing
14. Countershaft 1st gear
15. Countershaft 1st gear bushing
16. Countershaft 5th gear
17. Countershaft 4th gear
18. Countershaft 4th gear bushing
19. Countershaft 3rd gear
20. Countershaft 3rd gear bushing
21. Countershaft 6th gear
22. Countershaft/2nd gear

5

Mainshaft
Disassembly/Inspection/Assembly

NOTE
*A helpful "tool" that should be used for transmission disassembly is a large egg flat (the type that restaurants get their eggs in). As you remove a part from the shaft set it in one of the depressions in the same position from which it was removed (**Figure 65**). This is an easy way to remember the correct relationship of all parts.*

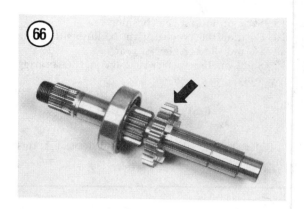

1. If not cleaned in the *Preliminary Inspection* sequence, place the assembled shaft into a large can or plastic bucket and thoroughly clean with solvent and a stiff brush. Dry with compressed air or let it sit on rags to drip dry.
2. Remove the needle bearing assembly and the thrust washer.
3. Slide off the 2nd gear.
4. On Rebel 450 models, perform the following:
   a. Slide off the lockwasher.
   b. Rotate the splined collar in either direction to clear the transmission spline grooves, then slide the splined collar off.
5. Slide off the 6th gear and the 6th gear bushing.
6. Slide off the splined washer and remove the circlip.
7. Slide off the 3rd/4th combination gear.
8. Remove the circlip and splined washer.
9A. On Rebel 450 models, slide off the 5th gear, the 5th gear bushing and the thrust washer.
9B. On all models except Rebel 450, slide off the 5th gear.

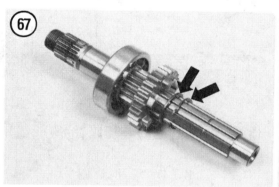

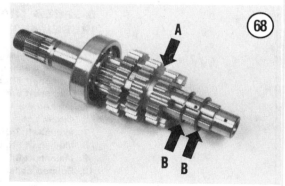

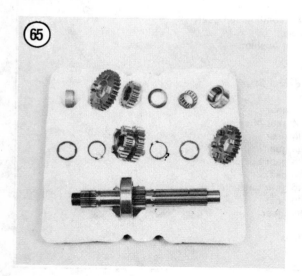

10. Check each gear for excessive wear, burrs, pitting or chipped or missing teeth. Make sure the lugs on the gears are in good condition.

NOTE
Defective gears should be replaced. It is a good idea to replace the mating gear on the countershaft even though it may not show as much wear or damage.

NOTE
The 1st gear is part of the shaft; therefore, if the gear is defective the shaft must be replaced.

11. Make sure that all gears slide smoothly on the mainshaft splines.

NOTE
It is a good idea to replace all circlips every other time the transmission is disassembled to ensure proper gear alignment.

12. Slide on the 5th gear (**Figure 66**) and install the splined washer and circlip (**Figure 67**).
13. Position the 3rd/4th combination gear with the larger 4th gear going on first. Slide on the 3rd/4th combination gear (A, **Figure 68**) and install the circlip and the splined washer (B, **Figure 68**).
14. Slide on the 6th gear bushing (**Figure 69**).
15. Slide on the 6th gear (**Figure 70**).
16. On Rebel 450 models, perform the following:
   a. Slide on the splined collar and rotate it in either direction so its tangs are engaged in the groove in the transmission shaft.
   b. Slide on the lockwasher so its tangs go into the open areas of the splined collar and lock the collar in place.
17. Slide on the 2nd gear and the thrust washer (**Figure 71**).
18. Install the needle bearing (**Figure 72**) and the needle bearing outer race (**Figure 73**).

**Countershaft
Disassembly/Inspection/Assembly**

Refer to **Figure 63** and **Figure 64** for this procedure.

NOTE
Use the same large egg flat (used on the mainshaft disassembly) during countershaft disassembly (Figure 74). This is an easy way to remember the correct relationship of all parts.

1. If not cleaned in the *Preliminary Inspection* sequence, place the assembled shaft into a large can or plastic bucket and thoroughly clean with solvent and a stiff brush. Dry with compressed air or let it sit on rags to drip dry.

2. Remove the needle bearing assembly.

3. Slide off the thrust washer, 1st gear and the 1st bushing.

4. On Rebel 450 models, slide off the thrust washer.

5. Slide off the 5th gear and remove the circlip and thrust washer.

6A. On Rebel 450 models, slide off the 4th gear and the 4th gear bushing.

6B. On all models except Rebel 450, slide off the 4th gear.

7. Slide off the splined collar, then rotate the splined washer in either direction so its tangs will clear the transmission spline grooves and slide the splined washer off of the shaft.

8A. On Rebel 450 models, slide off the 3rd gear, the 3rd gear bushing and the thrust washer.

8B. On all models except Rebel 450, slide off the 3rd gear.

9. Slide off the 6th gear.

10. Check each gear for excessive wear, burrs, pitting or chipped or missing teeth. Make sure the lugs on the gears are in good condition.

NOTE
Defective gears should be replaced. It is a good idea to replace the mating gear on the mainshaft even though it may not show as much wear or damage.

11. Make sure that all gears slide smoothly on the countershaft splines.

NOTE
It is a good idea to replace the circlip every other time the transmission is disassembled to ensure proper gear alignment.

12. Position the 6th gear with the shift fork groove side going on last and slide on the 6th gear (**Figure 75**).

13A. On Rebel 450 models, slide on the thrust washer, the 3rd gear bushing and the 3rd gear.

13B. On all models except Rebel 450, slide on the 3rd gear (**Figure 76**).

14. Slide on the splined collar (**Figure 77**). Rotate the splined collar in either direction so its tangs are engaged into the groove in the raised splines of the transmission shaft (A, **Figure 78**).

15. Slide on the splined lockwasher (B, **Figure 78**) so that the tangs go into the open areas of the splined collar and lock the collar in place (**Figure 79**).

16A. On Rebel 450 models, slide on the 4th gear bushing and 4th gear.

16B. On all models except Rebel 450, slide on the 4th gear (A, **Figure 80**).

17. Slide on the splined washer and install the circlip (B, **Figure 80**).

18. Slide on the 5th gear (A, **Figure 81**).

19. On Rebel 450 models, slide on the thrust washer.

20. Slide on the 1st gear bushing (B, **Figure 81**).

21. Position the 1st gear with the flush side going on last and slide on the 1st gear (**Figure 82**).

22. Slide on the thrust washer (**Figure 83**).

23. Install the needle bearing (**Figure 84**) and the needle bearing outer race (**Figure 85**).

24. After assembly is complete make sure the circlip is seated correctly in the countershaft groove.

> *NOTE*
> *After both transmission shafts have been assembled, mesh the two assemblies together in the correct position (**Figure 86**). Check that all gears meet correctly. This is your last check before installing the assemblies into the crankcase; make sure they are correctly assembled.*

INTERNAL SHIFT MECHANISM

The gearshift drum and forks are basically the same for both the 5-speed and 6-speed transmission. The only difference being the shift fork finger width specification and the shape of the shift forks.

Refer to the following illustrations for this procedure:

a. **Figure 87**: CB400T I, CB400T II, CB400T, CM400T, CM400C, CM400E.

b. **Figure 88**: CB450T, CB450SC, CM450E, CM450C.

c. **Figure 89**: Rebel 450.

Disassembly

1. Remove the transmission assemblies as described under *Transmission Removal/ Installation* in this chapter.

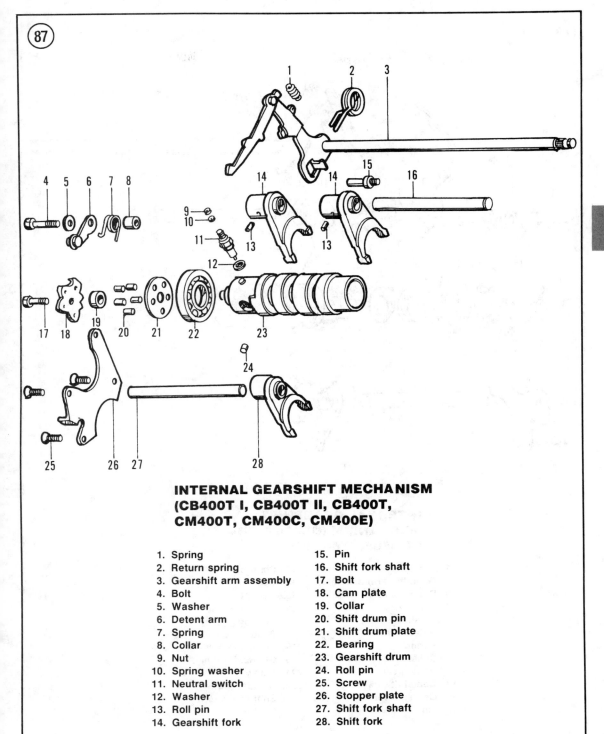

INTERNAL GEARSHIFT MECHANISM (CB400T I, CB400T II, CB400T, CM400T, CM400C, CM400E)

1. Spring
2. Return spring
3. Gearshift arm assembly
4. Bolt
5. Washer
6. Detent arm
7. Spring
8. Collar
9. Nut
10. Spring washer
11. Neutral switch
12. Washer
13. Roll pin
14. Gearshift fork
15. Pin
16. Shift fork shaft
17. Bolt
18. Cam plate
19. Collar
20. Shift drum pin
21. Shift drum plate
22. Bearing
23. Gearshift drum
24. Roll pin
25. Screw
26. Stopper plate
27. Shift fork shaft
28. Shift fork

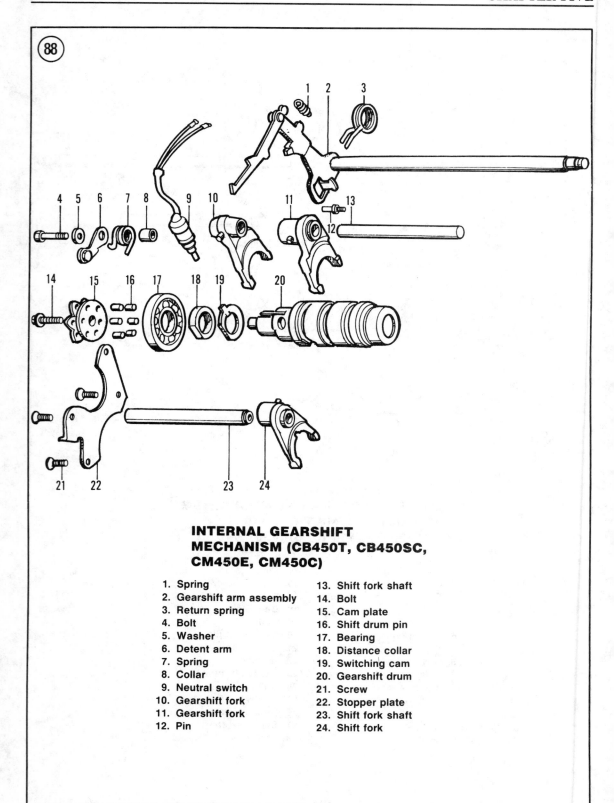

INTERNAL GEARSHIFT MECHANISM (CB450T, CB450SC, CM450E, CM450C)

1. Spring
2. Gearshift arm assembly
3. Return spring
4. Bolt
5. Washer
6. Detent arm
7. Spring
8. Collar
9. Neutral switch
10. Gearshift fork
11. Gearshift fork
12. Pin
13. Shift fork shaft
14. Bolt
15. Cam plate
16. Shift drum pin
17. Bearing
18. Distance collar
19. Switching cam
20. Gearshift drum
21. Screw
22. Stopper plate
23. Shift fork shaft
24. Shift fork

2. Remove the bolt and washer (A, **Figure 90**) securing the shift detent arm. Remove the shift detent arm, spring and collar.

3. Remove the screws (B, **Figure 90**) securing the shift drum bearing retainer (C, **Figure 90**) and remove the retainer.

4. Slide out the shift fork shaft and remove the center shift fork (**Figure 91**).

5. Slide out the rear shift fork shaft (A, **Figure 92**) and remove both the right and left shift forks (B, **Figure 92**).

6. Slide out the shift drum (A, **Figure 93**) and the bearing (B, **Figure 93**).

7. Wash all parts in solvent and dry thoroughly.

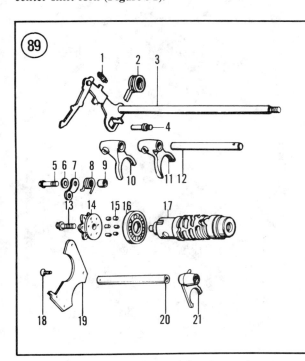

INTERNAL GEARSHIFT MECHANISM (REBEL 450)

1. Spring
2. Return spring
3. Gearshift arm assembly
4. Pin
5. Bolt
6. Washer
7. Detent arm
8. Spring
9. Collar
10. Gearshift fork
11. Gearshift fork
12. Shift fork shaft
13. Bolt
14. Cam plate
15. Shift drum pin
16. Bearing
17. Gearshift drum
18. Screw
19. Stopper plate
20. Shift fork shaft
21. Shift fork

Inspection

1. Measure the inside diameter of the shift forks with an inside micrometer (**Figure 94**). Replace the ones that are worn to the service limit listed in **Table 3** or greater.

2. Measure the width of the gearshift fingers with a micrometer (**Figure 95**). Replace the ones that are worn to the service limit listed in **Table 3** or less.

3. Measure the outside diameter of the shift fork shafts with a micrometer. Replace the ones that are worn to the service limit listed in **Table 3** or less.

4. Check the shift drum bearing. Make sure it rotates smoothly with no signs of wear or damage.

5. Make sure all shift forks slide easily on the shift fork shafts. If there is any binding, either the shift fork(s) or shaft must be replaced.

6. Check the grooves in the shift drum for wear or roughness. If any of the groove profiles have excessive wear or damage, replace the shift drum.

7. Inspect the bearing surface in the crankcase where the shift fork shafts and the shift drum ride. Check for scoring or scratches. If severely damaged, the crankcase must be replaced.

Assembly

1. Coat the bearing surface with assembly oil and insert the shift drum and bearing into the crankcase.

> *NOTE*
> *Make sure all guide pins are installed in the shift forks before installation.*

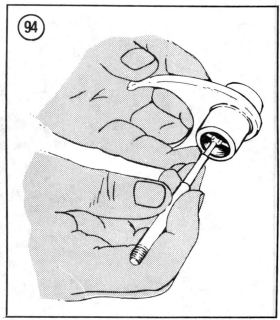

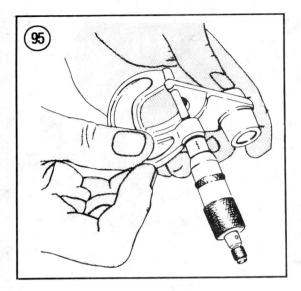

2. Insert the rear shift fork shaft and install the right and left shift forks with the shoulders facing away from the centerline of the crankcase (**Figure 92**).

3. Insert the front shift fork shaft and install the center shift fork with the shoulder facing away from the centerline of the crankcase (**Figure 91**).

NOTE
Apply Locite Lock N' Seal to the three screws before installation and stake them afterwards.

4. Install the shift drum bearing retainer and screws.

5. Install the collar, spring and the shift detent arm. Install the bolt and washer and tighten the bolt securely.

6. Install the transmission assemblies as described in this chapter.

Tables are on the following pages.

Table 1 CLUTCH SPECIFICATIONS

Item	New	Wear limit
Disc thickness		
A disc	2.7 mm (0.106 in.)	2.3 mm (0.090 in.)
B disc	3.0 mm (0.118 in.)	2.6 mm (0.102 in.)
Plate warpage	—	0.20 mm (0.008 in.)
Spring free length		
400 models	42.75 mm (1.68 in.)	41.25 mm (1.62 in.)
Rebel 450	46.6 mm (1.83 in.)	45.2 mm (1.79 in.)
All 450 cc models		
except Rebel 450	42.5 mm (1.67 in.)	41.0 mm (1.61 in.)
Clutch outer housing I.D.		
400 cc	33.000-33.025 mm (1.299-1.300 in.)	33.07 mm (1.302 in.)
450 cc	32.000-32.025 mm (1.2598-1.2608 in.)	32.07 mm (1.263 in.)
Clutch outer housing guide O.D.		
400 cc	32.950-32.975 mm (1.297-1.298 in.)	32.90 mm (1.295 in.)
450 cc	31.959-31.975 mm (1.2582-1.2589 in.)	31.90 mm (1.256 in.)
Clutch center-to-clutch		
plate "B" clearance	—	0.1-0.5 mm (0.004-0.020 in.)

Table 2 CLUTCH AND GEARSHIFT LINKAGE TORQUE SPECIFICATIONS

Item	N•m	ft.-lb.
Clutch nut		
Rebel 450	55-60	40-43
CB450SC	46-60	33-43
All other models	46-50	33-36
Camplate bolt	8-12	6-9
Main bearing cap assembly bolts		
8 mm bolts	10-14	7-10
10 mm bolts	33-37	24-27
Crankcase bolts		
6 mm bolts	10-14	7-10
8 mm bolts	22-28	16-20

Table 3 INTERNAL SHIFT MECHANISM SPECIFICATIONS

Item	Standard	Wear limit
400 cc		
Shift drum outer diameter	34.950-34.975 mm (1.3760-1.3770 in.)	34.90 mm (1.374 in.)
Case inner diameter	35.00-35.025 mm (1.3780-1.3789 in.)	35.05 mm (1.380 in.)
Shift fork		
Finger width	5.93-6.00 mm (0.233-0.236 in.)	5.50 mm (0.217 in.)
Inner diameter	13.000-13.018 mm (0.5118-0.5125 in.)	13.05 mm (0.514 in.)
Shift fork shaft outer diameter	12.966-12.984 mm (0.5104-0.5112 in.)	12.95 mm (0.509 in.)
450 cc		
Shift drum outer diameter	34.950-34.975 mm (1.3760-1.3770 in.)	34.90 mm (1.374 in.)
Case inner diameter	35.00-35.025 mm (1.3780-1.3789 in.)	35.05 mm (1.380 in.)
Shift fork		
Finger width Mainshaft 3rd gear	5.93-6.00 mm (0.233-0.236 in.)	5.50 mm (0.217 in.)
Countershaft 5th and 6th gear	4.93-5.00 mm (0.194-0.197 in.)	4.85 mm (0.191 in.)
Inner diameter	13.000-13.018 mm (0.5118-0.5125 in.)	13.05 mm (0.514 in.)
Shift fork shaft outer diameter	12.966-12.984 mm (0.5104-0.5112 in.)	12.95 mm (0.509 in.)

5

CHAPTER SIX

TORQUE CONVERTER AND

AUTOMATIC TRANSMISSION

The automatic transmission uses a torque converter, instead of a clutch to transmit engine power to the transmission gears. The converter uses the same oil that lubricates the engine.

The two-speed system is shifted mechanically with a foot operated lever on the left-hand side.

The automatic transmission is used on the following models:

a. 1978 CB400A.
b. 1979-1981 CM400A.
c. 1982-1983 CM450A.

Table 1 and **Table 2** are located at the end of the chapter.

TORQUE CONVERTER

Removal

Refer to **Figure 1** for this procedure.

> *NOTE*
> *The torque converter can be removed with the engine in the frame.*

1. Place the bike on the center stand.
2. Drain the engine oil as described under *Changing Oil and Filter* in Chapter Three.
3. Remove the right-hand side cover.

4. Remove the bolt (**Figure 2**) securing the front right-hand footpeg and remove the footpeg assembly.
5. Remove the exhaust system as described under *Exhaust System Removal/Installation* in Chapter Seven.
6. Remove the bolt and nut (**Figure 3**) clamping the kickstarter arm and remove the arm.
7. Remove the bolts securing the outer side cover (**Figure 4**) and remove the cover and gasket. Don't lose the locating dowels.
8. Withdraw the torque converter (**Figure 5**) from the transmission shaft.
9. Withdraw the needle bearings. There are 2 needle bearings; during removal, one or both bearings may stay on the shaft.
10. Remove the oil check valve and spring (**Figure 6**) from the crankcase cover.

Inspection

1. Clean all of the parts in solvent and dry thoroughly.
2. Inspect the kickstarter driven gear (A, **Figure 7**) and the primary driven gear (B, **Figure 7**) for excessive wear and for chipped or missing teeth; replace as necessary.

3. Check the bearings (C, **Figure 7**). Make sure that they operate smoothly and with no signs of wear.

NOTE
The torque converter housing assembly is a sealed unit and cannot be serviced. If damaged, it must be replaced as a unit.

4. Measure the inside diameter of the kickstarter driven gear with an inside micrometer; replace if worn to the wear limit listed in **Table 1**.

5. Measure the check valve spring length in the relaxed position. Use a vernier caliper as shown in **Figure 8**. Replace the spring if it has sagged to the service limit listed in **Table 1**.

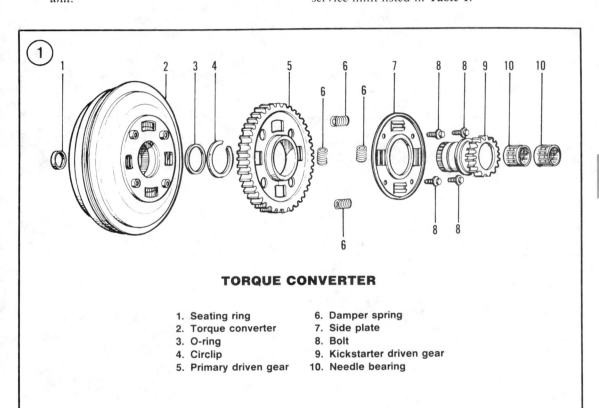

TORQUE CONVERTER

1. Seating ring
2. Torque converter
3. O-ring
4. Circlip
5. Primary driven gear
6. Damper spring
7. Side plate
8. Bolt
9. Kickstarter driven gear
10. Needle bearing

Driven and Kickstarter Gears
Removal/Inspection/Installation

1. Remove any needle bearings that may still be inside the kickstarter gear on the backside of the torque converter.

2. Remove the bolts (**Figure 9**) securing the side plate and the gears to the torque converter housing. Remove the side plate, damper springs and the gear assembly.

3. Remove the circlip securing the kickstarter driven gear to the primary driven gear and separate the gears.

4. Remove the damper springs.

5. Measure the damper springs' length in the relaxed position. Use a vernier caliper as shown in **Figure 8**. Replace the spring if it has sagged to the service limit listed in **Table 1**. For maximum performance, replace all 4 springs as a set even though only one requires replacement.

6. Install the kickstarter driven gear into the primary driven gear.

7. Install the circlip securing the kickstarter driven gear to the primary driven gear.

8. Install a new O-ring onto the kickstarter driven gear.

9. Install the gear assembly into the torque converter housing.

10. Install the damper springs and the side plate.

11. Apply Loctite Lock N' Seal to the bolt threads before installation. Install the bolts and tighten securely.

Torque Converter
Installation

1. Coat the inside of the kickstarter gear and the bearings with assembly oil. Install the bearings onto the transmission shaft.

2. Place the transmission into either gear. Align the teeth of the split drive gear (**Figure 10**) where

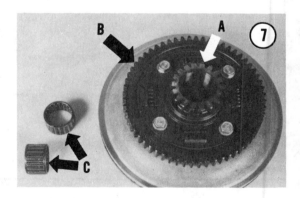

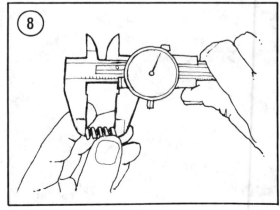

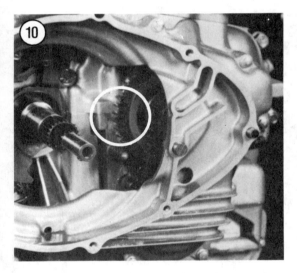

they mesh with the driven gear on the torque converter.

> *NOTE*
> *The drive gear is split; the outer thin gear is spring loaded and has one more tooth than the main gear. This helps to reduce noise and backlash.*

3. Install the torque converter onto the transmission shaft; it will go on only so far and then stop.

> *CAUTION*
> *Do not force it on any further.*

4. Have an assistant turn the rear wheel slowly, thus turning the transmission mainshaft. This enables the splines of the transmission shafts and those within the torque converter housing to align. When they are aligned, slide the torque converter housing on the remaining distance. It is also necessary to align the split drive gear on the crankshaft to the converter at the same time.

5. Make sure the converter is all the way on and check alignment with crankshaft gear.

6. Install the oil check valve and spring (**Figure 6**) into the receptacle in the crankcase cover.

7. Make sure the locating dowels are in place and install a new side cover gasket.

8. Install the outer side cover and bolts. Tighten the bolts securely.

9. Install the kickstarter arm, exhaust system, footpeg and side cover.

10. Fill the crankcase with the recommended type and quantity of engine oil. Refer to Chapter Three.

AUTOMATIC TRANSMISSION

The crankcase must be split to gain access to the transmission components.

Removal

1. Remove the engine as described under *Engine Removal/Installation* in Chapter Four.

> *NOTE*
> *Removal of the cylinder head and cylinder is not necessary.*

2. Remove the bolts securing the oil cooler and remove the oil cooler (**Figure 11**).

3. Place the engine upside down on the workbench. If the cylinder head, cylinder, and pistons were removed, place the engine on a couple of 2×4 wood blocks to protect the protruding connecting rods.

4. Remove the bolts (**Figure 12**) securing the crankcase halves together. Tap the lower crankcase with a plastic mallet and separate the two halves. If the case halves will not separate, take the crankcase assembly to a dealer and have it separated. Do not risk expensive crankcase damage with improper tools or techniques.

CAUTION
Never pry the case halves apart. Doing so may result in oil leaks, requiring replacement of the halves.

5. Remove the countershaft assembly (**Figure 13**).
6. Lift out the mainshaft/statorshaft assembly (**Figure 14**).
7. Remove the neutral safety switch, located on top of the upper crankcase.

Installation

Before installation, coat all bearings and bearing surfaces with assembly oil.
1. Install the mainshaft/statorshaft assembly. Make sure the holes in the bearing races (**Figure 15**) are facing down and that they align with the oil control orifice (A, **Figure 16**) and the locating pin (B, **Figure 16**) in the crankcase.
2. Install the countershaft assembly. Make sure that the locating hole in the bearing race is facing down and aligns with the locating pin (A, **Figure 17**) in the crankcase. Also the metal ring in the oil seal (A, **Figure 18**) must seat correctly in the crankcase groove (B, **Figure 17**).
3. Make sure the oil filter ring seal (A, **Figure 19**) is in place.

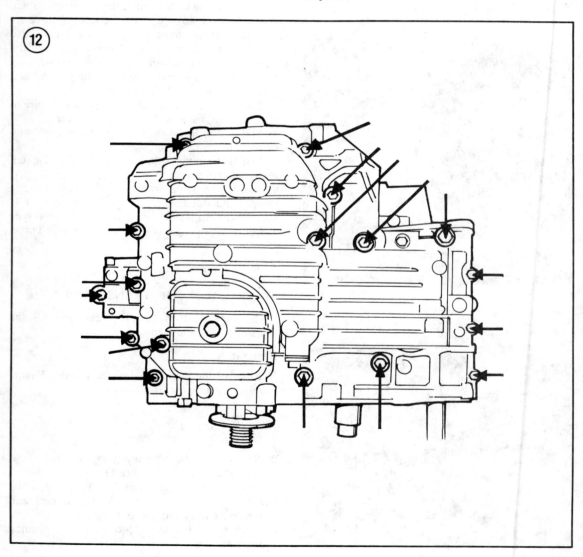

4. Install the 2 locating dowels (B, **Figure 19**) into the lower crankcase.

5. Make sure both crankcase sealing surfaces are perfectly clean and dry.

6. Apply a light coat of gasket sealer to the sealing surfaces of both halves. Cover only flat surfaces, not curved bearing surfaces. Make the coating as thin as possible or the case can shift and hammer out the bearings. Join halves and tap lightly with a plastic mallet—do not use a metal hammer as it will damage the case.

NOTE
Use Three Bond gasket sealer or equivalent. When selecting an equivalent, avoid thick and hard setting materials.

7. Install and tighten the bolts to the torque specification listed in **Table 2**.

8. Install the engine as described under *Engine Removal/Installation* in Chapter Four.

9. Fill the crankcase with the recommended type and quantity of engine oil. Refer to Chapter Three.

6

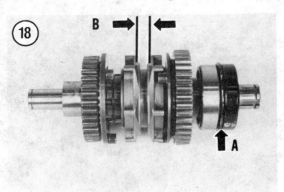

Mainshaft and Statorshaft
Disassembly/Assembly

Refer to **Figure 20** for this procedure.
1. Slide the statorshaft off the mainshaft.
2. Remove the outer race, needle bearing, and washer.
3. Remove the snap ring (**Figure 21**) securing the bearing and slide off the bearing.
4. Assemble by reversing the disassembly steps. Make sure that the snap ring is correctly seated in the mainshaft groove.

Mainshaft and Statorshaft
Inspection

1. Clean all parts in solvent and dry thoroughly. Use compressed air for the bearings, do not let them spin while drying.
2. Check the gears for excessive wear and for chipped or missing teeth.
3. Make sure the splines are in good condition.
4. Check the bearing. Make sure that it operates smoothly with no signs of wear or damage; replace if necessary.
5. Clean out the oil holes on both shafts (**Figure 22**).

6. Measure the outside diameter of the mainshaft where the statorshaft rides. Refer to **Table 1**. If the shaft is worn to the service limit or less, replace the shaft.
7. Measure the inside diameter of the statorshaft bushing where it rides on the mainshaft. Refer to **Table 1**. If the bushing is worn to the service limit or greater, replace the statorshaft bushing.

Countershaft
Disassembly/Assembly

Refer to **Figure 20** for this procedure.
1. Remove the outer race (**Figure 23**) and the outer needle bearing (**Figure 24**).
2. Slide off the high gear assembly (**Figure 25**).
3. Remove the inner needle bearing (**Figure 26**).
4. Remove the snap ring (**Figure 27**) retaining the engaging dog. Keep the shaft upright after removing the snap ring.
5. Place the shaft over a receptacle, like a metal pie tin, then slowly slide the engaging dog off of the shaft (**Figure 28**). There are 45 loose balls inside; don't lose any.
6. Turn shaft over and remove both oil seals.

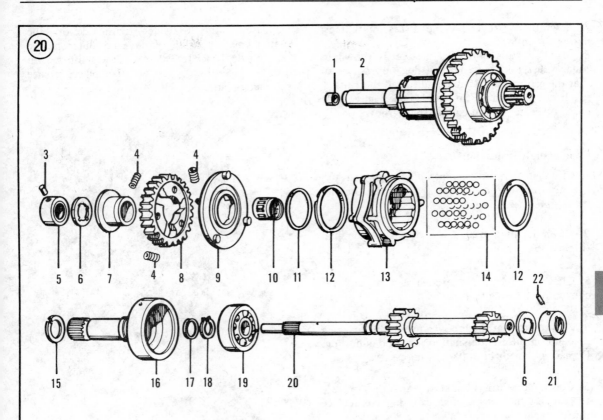

AUTOMATIC TRANSMISSION
1. Collar
2. Countershaft
3. Pin
4. Spring
5. Outer needle bearing
6. Splined washer
7. High gear center
8. High gear
9. High gear shifter plate
10. Inner needle bearing
11. Circlip
12. Internal double coil ring
13. Gear shifter
14. Steel balls
15. Oil seal
16. Stator shaft
17. Oil seal
18. Circlip
19. Bearing
20. Mainshaft
21. Needle bearing
22. Pin

6

7. Assemble by reversing the disassembly steps, noting the following.

8. Install 5 balls into each groove as shown in **Figure 29**. Hold the engaging dog up enough so that the grooves are visible and install the balls.

9. Install the snap ring and make sure it is correctly seated in the countershaft groove.

Countershaft Inspection

1. Clean all parts in solvent and dry thoroughly. Use compressed air for the bearings. Do not let them spin while drying.

2. Clean out all oil passageways in the countershaft (**Figure 30**).

3. Check the gears for excessive wear and for chipped or missing teeth.

4. Make sure that the grooves inside the engaging dog and on the countershaft are in good condition. Replace either or both parts if necessary.

5. Check the bearings. Make sure that they operate smoothly with no signs of wear or damage; replace if necessary.

6. Check the loose balls for wear or damage; replace all if any are bad.

7. Measure the outside diameter of the countershaft where the inner and outer needle bearing ride. Refer to **Table 1**. If the shaft is worn to the service limit or less at either place, replace the countershaft.

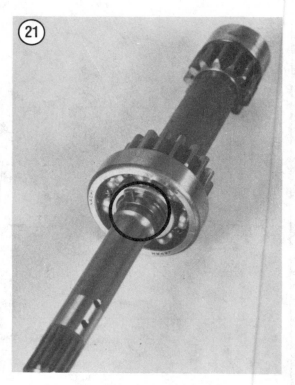

8. Disassemble the high gear assembly.

9. Measure the inside diameter of the high gear center. Refer to **Table 1**. If the high gear center is worn to the service limit or greater, replace the high gear center.

10. Measure the high gear damper springs' length in the relaxed position. Use a vernier caliper as shown in **Figure 31**. Replace the spring if it has sagged to the service limit listed in **Table 1**. For maximum performance, replace all 4 springs as a set even though only one requires replacement.

11. Reassemble the high gear assembly.

12. Measure the gear shifter groove width (B, **Figure 18**). Refer to **Table 1**. If the groove is worn

to the service limit or greater, replace the gear shifter.

INTERNAL SHIFT MECHANISM

Refer to **Figure 32** for this procedure.

Removal/Installation

1. Remove the torque converter as described under *Torque Converter Removal/Installation* in this chapter.

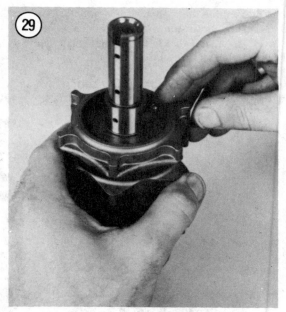

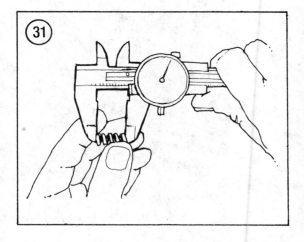

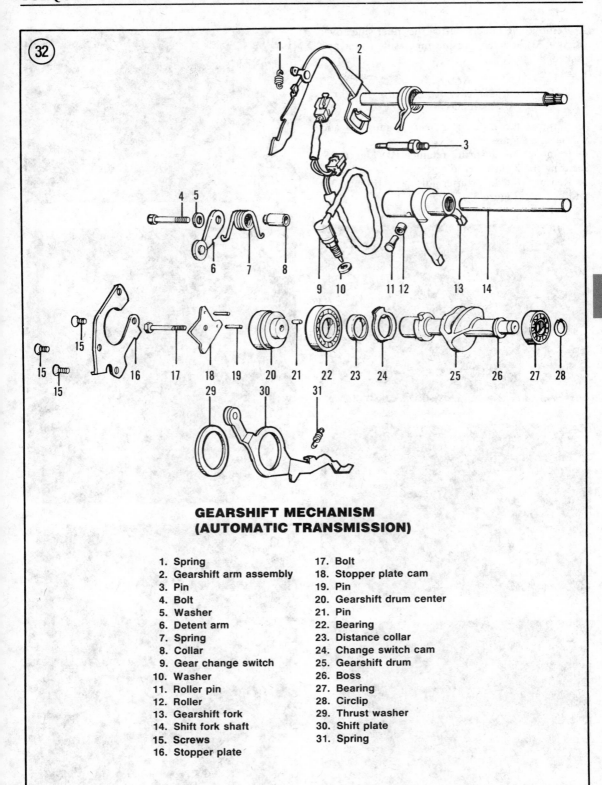

**GEARSHIFT MECHANISM
(AUTOMATIC TRANSMISSION)**

1. Spring
2. Gearshift arm assembly
3. Pin
4. Bolt
5. Washer
6. Detent arm
7. Spring
8. Collar
9. Gear change switch
10. Washer
11. Roller pin
12. Roller
13. Gearshift fork
14. Shift fork shaft
15. Screws
16. Stopper plate
17. Bolt
18. Stopper plate cam
19. Pin
20. Gearshift drum center
21. Pin
22. Bearing
23. Distance collar
24. Change switch cam
25. Gearshift drum
26. Boss
27. Bearing
28. Circlip
29. Thrust washer
30. Shift plate
31. Spring

2. Remove the bolts securing the inner side cover
(**Figure 33**) and remove the inner side cover and
gasket.

NOTE
Do not lose the oil check valve and
*spring (A, **Figure 33**).*

3. Remove the kickstarter gear (**Figure 34**) and
washer (A, **Figure 35**).
4. Remove spiral spring retainer (B, **Figure 35**)
securing the kickstarter idle gear.
5. Remove the kickstarter idle gear (**Figure 36**)
and bearing (**Figure 37**).

6. Remove the shift plate and washer (**Figure 38**).

7. Remove the bolt and nut (**Figure 39**) securing the shift lever to the shaft and remove the shift lever.

8. Push down on the shift arm and, from the left-hand side, push the shift lever shaft (**Figure 40**) toward the right and remove the shaft assembly.

9. Loosen the bolt (**Figure 41**) securing the detent arm.

10. Flip the pawl out and off of the cam plate (**Figure 42**) and disengage the spring from under the pawl (**Figure 43**). Remove the bolt and remove the pawl.

11. Install by reversing the removal steps.

GEARSHIFT DRUM AND FORK

Refer to **Figure 32** for this procedure.

Disassembly

1. Perform Steps 1-7 of *Transmission Disassembly* in this chapter.

2. Remove the bolts securing the shift detent arm and remove the shift dent arm.

3. Remove the screws (**Figure 44**) securing the bearing plate and let the bearing plate move down (**Figure 45**) sufficiently to allow access to the shift fork shaft.

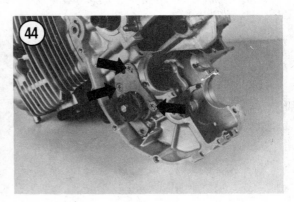

4. Slide out the shift fork shaft and remove the shift fork (A, **Figure 46**) and the shaft (B, **Figure 46**).

5. Slide out the shift drum and bearing plate (**Figure 47**).

6. Wash all of the parts with solvent and dry thoroughly.

Inspection

1. Measure the inside diameter of the shift fork with an inside micrometer (**Figure 48**). Refer to **Table 1**. If the shift fork is worn to the service limit or greater, replace the shift fork.

2. Measure the width of the gearshift finger with a micrometer (**Figure 49**). Refer to **Table 1**. If the shift fork finger is worn to the service limit or less, replace the shift fork.

3. Measure the outside diameter of the shift fork shaft with a micrometer. Refer to **Table 1**. If the shift fork shaft is worn to the service limit or less, replace the shift fork shaft.

4. Check the shift drum bearings. Make sure they operate smoothly with no signs of wear or damage.

5. Remove the roller pin and the roller from the shift fork.

6. Measure the outside diameter of the roller pin with a micrometer. Refer to **Table 1**. If the roller pin is worn to the service limit or less, replace the shift fork roller pin.

7. Measure the outside diameter of the roller with a micrometer. Refer to **Table 1**. If the roller OD is worn to the service limit or less, replace the shift fork roller.

8. Measure the inside diameter of the roller with a micrometer. Refer to **Table 1**. If the roller ID is worn to the service limit or greater, replace the shift fork roller.

Assembly

> *NOTE*
> *Make sure that the guide pin and roller are in place on the shift fork before the installation.*

1. Coat the bearing surfaces with assembly oil, slip the bearing plate onto the shift drum and insert shift drum into the crankcase (**Figure 47**). Do not install the 3 screws at this time.

2. Insert the shift fork shaft and install the shift fork (**Figure 45**).

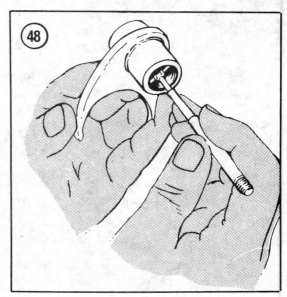

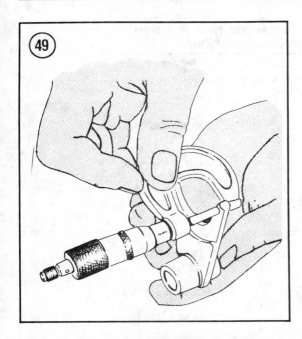

NOTE
Apply Loctite Lock N' Seal to the screw threads before installation.

3. Install the screws securing the bearing plate. Tighten the screws securely and stake them afterwards.
4. Install the bolt and shift detent arm.
5. Perform Steps 1-9 of *Transmission Assembly* in this chapter.

OIL COOLER

This procedure is shown with the exhaust system removed for clarity. It is not necessary to remove it.

Removal/Installation

1. Remove bolts (**Figure 50**) securing the cover plate and remove the cover plate.
2. Remove the electrical wire from the oil pressure sending unit (**Figure 51**).
3. Place a drip pan under the cooler as some oil will drain out when the cooler is removed.
4. Remove the bolts securing the oil cooler to the crankcase and remove the oil cooler.
5. Install by reversing the removal steps. Make sure that the sealing surface of the crankcase is clean.
6. Start engine and check for leaks. Turn engine off and check for correct oil level; add oil if necessary.

Inspection

Make sure that the inlet and outlet holes in the crankcase and cooler (A, **Figure 52**) are clean and unobstructed.

If the oil has been contaminated, wash out the interior with solvent and thoroughly dry with compressed air.

Check the sealing gasket (B, **Figure 52**). Replace if broken or deteriorated.

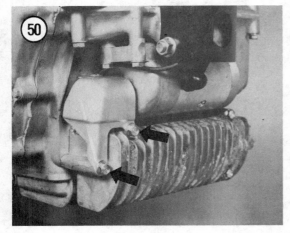

6

Table 1 TORQUE CONVERTER, AUTOMATIC TRANSMISSION AND SHIFT MECHANISM SPECIFICATIONS

Item	Specification	Wear limit
Torque Converter		
Kickstarter driven gear inner diameter	30.000-30.021 mm (1.181-1.182 in.)	30.03 mm (1.182 in.)
Check valve spring free length	18.5 mm (0.73 in.)	16.7 mm (0.66 in.)
Damper spring free length	18.0 mm (0.71 in.)	16.0 mm (0.63 in.)
Automatic Transmission		
Mainshaft outer diameter (at end)	15.966-15.984 mm (0.6286-0.6293 in.	15.95 mm (0.628 in.)
Stator shaft outer diameter At the inner roller bearing location	24.974-24.993 mm (0.9832-0.9840 in.	25.97 mm (0.983 in.)
At the outer roller bearing location	19.980-19.993 mm (0.7866-0.7871 in.)	19.95 mm (0.785 in.)
Stator shaft bushing inner diameter	16.000-16.018 mm (0.6299-0.6306 in.)	16.05 mm (0.632 in.)
Gear center inner diameter	30.014-30.027 mm (1.1817-1.822 in.)	30.04 mm (1.183 in.)
Gear backlash	0.045-0.140 mm (0.0018-0.0055 in.)	0.2 mm (0.008 in.)
Minimum clearance end of dog	—	0.3 mm (0.012 in.)
Gear shifter groove width	6.10-6.18 mm (0.240-0.243 in.)	6.4 mm (0.25 in.)
Shift Mechanism		
Shift fork roller pin outer diameter	5.950-6.00 mm (0.234-0.236 in.)	5.93 mm (0.233 in.)
Shift fork roller Inner diameter	6.05-6.10 mm (0.2380-0.240 in.)	6.15 mm (0.242 in.)
Outer diameter	9.9-10.0 mm (0.390-0.394 in.)	9.8 mm (0.386 in.)
Shift fork finger width	5.9-6.0 mm (0.232-0.236 in.)	5.8 mm (0.228 in.)
Shift fork shaft outer diameter	12.973-12.984 mm (0.5107-0.5112 in.)	12.97 mm (0.510 in.)
Shift drum groove width	10.05-10.15 mm (0.396-0.400 in.)	10.4 mm (0.41 in.)

Table 2 AUTOMATIC TRANSMISSION TORQUE SPECIFICATIONS

Item	N·m	ft.-lb.
Crankcase bolts		
6 mm bolts	10-14	7-10
8 mm bolts	22-28	16-20

6

CHAPTER SEVEN

FUEL EXHAUST SYSTEMS

The fuel system consists of the fuel tank, shutoff valve, fuel filter, two Keihin constant velocity carburetors and an air filter.

The exhaust system consists of two exhaust pipes and two mufflers.

This chapter includes service procedures for all parts of the fuel and exhaust systems. Carburetor specifications are listed in **Table 1**.

Air filter service is described in Chapter Three.

CARBURETORS

In order to meet emission control regulations (U.S. only) the carburetors on 1980 and later models, are jetted for a "lean burn" operating condition and are thus equipped with an accelerator pump circuit to aid performance when accelerating. The accelerator pump assembly is part of the left-hand carburetor and the fuel is delivered to the right-hand carburetor via the accelerator pump joint pipe. After the accelerator pump assembly has been removed, disassembly is identical to a carburetor without an accelerator pump circuit.

CARBURETOR OPERATION

An understanding of the function of each of the carburetor components and their relationship to one another is a valuable aid for pinpointing a source of carburetor trouble.

The carburetor's purpose is to supply atomized fuel mixed in correct proportions with air that is drawn in through the air intake. At the primary throttle opening—at idle—a small amount of fuel is siphoned through the pilot jet by the incoming air. As the throttle is opened further, the air stream begins to siphon fuel through the main jet and needle jet. The tapered needle increases the effective flow capacity of the needle jet, as it is lifted with the air slide, in that it occupies progressively less of the area of the jet. In addition, the amount of cutaway in the leading edge of the throttle slide aids in controlling the fuel/air mixture during partial throttle openings.

At full throttle, the carburetor venturi is fully open and the needle is lifted far enough to permit the main jet to flow at full capacity.

CARBURETOR SERVICE

Carburetor service (removal and cleaning) should be performed when poor engine performance or hesitation is observed. If after servicing the carburetors and making the proper adjustments described in this chapter and Chapter

Three, the motorcycle does not perform correctly (and assuming that other factors affecting performance are correct, such as ignition timing and condition, valve adjustment, etc.), the motorcycle should be checked by a dealer or qualified performance specialist.

Alterations in jet size, throttle slide cutaway, changes in needle position, etc., should be attempted only if you're experienced in this type of "tuning" work; a bad guess could result in costly engine damage or, at the very least, poor performance.

Removal/Installation
(All Models Except Rebel 450)

1. Remove the seat and both side covers.
2. Remove the fuel tank as described in this chapter.
3. Disconnect the breather tube from the cam cover (**Figure 1**).
4. Remove the bolts (**Figure 2**) securing the rear upper engine mounting plates and remove the plates.
5. On CB450SC California models, remove the charcoal canister from the right-hand side of the carburetor assembly as described under *Charcoal Canister Removal/Installation* in this chapter.
6. Loosen the clamping screws on the rear rubber boots (A, **Figure 3**) and slide the clamps away from the carburetors.
7. Remove the bolts (B, **Figure 3**) securing the front rubber boots to the cylinder heads.
8. On CB450SC California models, disconnect the vent tube going to the purge control valve.
9. Pull the loose ends of the drain tubes free from the clamp on the right-hand crankcase cover (**Figure 4**).
10. Pull the carburetor assembly to the rear and push the front down as shown in **Figure 5**.

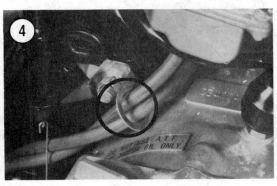

11. Pull the carburetor assembly to the left and disconnect the throttle cables (**Figure 6**) and the choke cable (**Figure 7**).

12. Install by reversing the removal steps, noting the following.

13. Attach the throttle PULL cable to the rear portion of the throttle cable mounting bracket on the carburetor assembly and the PUSH cable to the front portion.

14. Adjust the throttle as described under *Throttle Operation/Adjustment* in Chapter Three.

Removal/Installation (Rebel 450)

1. Remove the seat.

2. Remove the fuel tank as described in this chapter.

3. Disconnect the breather tube (**Figure 8**) from the cam cover.

4. Loosen the clamping screws on the front and rear rubber boots (A, **Figure 9**) and slide the clamps away from the carburetors.

5. Remove the bolts securing the air filter air box (B, **Figure 9**) and move the air box toward the rear.

6. On California models, disconnect the vent tube (C, **Figure 9**) going to the purge control valve.

7. Pull the loose ends of the vent tubes (D, **Figure 9**) free from the clamp on the side of the engine.

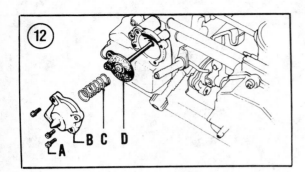

8. Pull the carburetor assembly to the rear and push the front down.

9. Pull the carburetor assembly to the left and disconnect the throttle cables (**Figure 6**) and the choke cable (**Figure 7**).

10. Install by reversing the removal steps, noting the following.

11. Attach the throttle PULL cable (A, **Figure 10**) to the rear portion of the throttle cable mounting bracket on the carburetor assembly and the PUSH cable (B, **Figure 10**) to the front portion.

12. Adjust the throttle as described under *Throttle Operation/Adjustment* in Chapter Three.

Disassembly/Assembly
(All Models Except Rebel 450)

Refer to **Figure 11** for this procedure.

1. On models equipped with an accelerator pump, perform the following:
   a. Remove the screws (A, **Figure 12**) securing the accelerator pump cover (B, **Figure 12**).
   b. Remove the cover and the spring (C, **Figure 12**).
   c. Carefully pull the accelerator pump rod assembly out (D, **Figure 12**). Don't lose the rubber boot that covers the rod while the rod is installed in the carburetor.

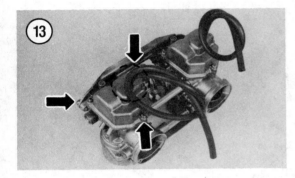

NOTE
The following figures are shown on a carburetor without the accelerator pump circuit.

2. Remove the screws (**Figure 13**) securing the float bowl and remove the float bowl.

3. Remove the O-ring seal (A, **Figure 14**) and the overflow line (B, **Figure 14**) from the float bowl.

4. Carefully push out the float pin (**Figure 15**).

5. Lift the float bowl assembly and the float valve needle out of the carburetor body (**Figure 16**).

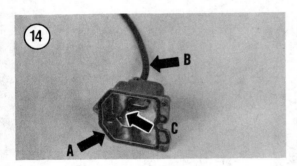

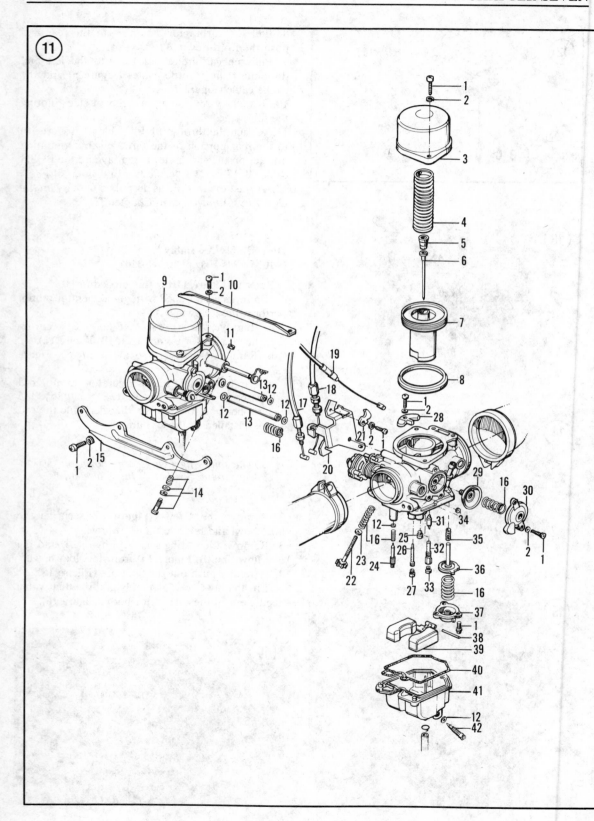

CARBURETOR
(ALL MODELS
EXCEPT REBEL 450)

1. Screw
2. Washer
3. Top cover
4. Spring
5. Jet needle holder
6. Jet needle
7. Vacuum piston
8. Seal ring
9. Complete carburetor assembly
10. Rear bracket
11. Nut
12. O-ring seal
13. Fuel line joint
14. Synchronizing screw
15. Front bracket
16. Spring
17. Throttle cable (push)
18. Throttle cable (pull)
19. Choke cable
20. Throttle and choke cable
    mounting bracket
21. Cable clamp
22. Throttle adjust screw
23. Washer
24. Spring
25. Plug
26. Needle jet holder
27. Primary main jet
28. Air jet cover
29. Air cutoff valve diaphragm
30. Cover
31. Float valve needle
32. Slow jet
33. Secondary main jet
34. Plug
35. Rubber boot
36. Accelerator pump rod assembly
37. Cover
38. Pivot pin
39. Float
40. O-ring gasket
41. Float bowl
42. Drain screw

6. Unscrew the primary main jet (A, **Figure 17**), the needle jet holder and the secondary main jet (B, **Figure 17**).

> *NOTE*
> *Before removing the pilot screw, record the number of turns necessary until the screw **lightly** seats. The pilot screw must be reinstalled to the exact same setting.*

7. Remove the pilot screw (C, **Figure 17**), the spring, the plain washer and the O-ring.
8. Remove the slow air jet rubber plug (D, **Figure 17**) and the slow air jet.
9. Remove the throttle adjust screw, washer and the spring (E, **Figure 17**).
10. Remove the screws (**Figure 18**) securing the top cover and remove the top cover.
11. Carefully pull out the spring (**Figure 19**) and the vacuum piston (**Figure 20**).

> *CAUTION*
> *Do not bend the needle on the piston.*

12. On the left-hand carburetor, remove the screws securing the air cutoff valve cover. Remove the cover, the spring and the diaphragm.
13. To disassemble the vacuum piston, perform the following:
   a. On models so equipped, remove the needle stopper.
   b. Unscrew the needle set screw.
   c. Withdraw the jet needle from the vacuum piston.

> *NOTE*
> *Further disassembly is neither necessary nor recommended. If throttle or choke shafts or butterflies are damaged, take the carburetor body to a Honda dealer for replacement.*

14. Repeat Steps 1-13 for the other carburetor. Do not intermix the parts—keep them separate so they will be reinstalled in the correct carburetor body.
15. Clean all parts, except rubber or plastic parts, in a good grade of carburetor cleaner. This solution is available at most automotive or motorcycle supply stores in a small, resealable tank with a dip basket for just a few dollars. If it is tightly sealed when not in use, the solution will last for several cleanings. Follow the manufacturer's instructions for correct soak time (usually about 1/2 hour).
16. Remove the parts from the cleaner and blow dry with compressed air. Blow out the jets with

compressed air. Do *not* use a piece of wire to clean them as minor gouges in the jet can alter flow rate and upset the fuel/air mixture.
17. Be sure to clean out the float bowl overflow tube (C, **Figure 14**) from both ends.
18. O-ring seals tend to become hardened after prolonged use and heat and therefore lose their ability to seal properly. Inspect the O-ring seal on the float bowl and all other locations; replace if necessary.
19. Inspect the accelerator pump diaphragm for cracks and for brittleness; replace if necessary. Make sure the rod is not bent and that it moves freely in its receptacle in the carburetor body.
20. Inspect the air cutoff valve diaphragm for cracks and for brittleness; replace if necessary.
21. Assemble all parts by reversing these disassembly steps, noting the following.
22. Check the float height as described under *Float Level Check* in this chapter.
23. Make sure the tabs on the accelerator pump diaphragm (D, **Figure 12**) are positioned correctly in the recesses in the float bowl.

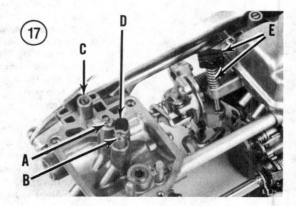

24. Adjust the pilot screw as described under *Pilot Screw Adjustment* in this chapter before installing the float bowl. If new pilot screws are installed, do not install the caps until pilot screw adjustment has been performed.

25. Synchronize and adjust the idle speed as described under *Tune-Up* in Chapter Three.

Disassembly/Inspection/Assembly (Rebel 450)

Refer to **Figure 21** for this procedure.

1. To disassemble the accelerator pump, perform the following:
   a. Remove the screws (A, **Figure 22**) securing the accelerator pump cover (B, **Figure 22**).
   b. Remove the cover and the spring (A, **Figure 23**).
   c. Carefully pull the accelerator pump rod assembly out (B, **Figure 23**). Don't lose the

rubber boot (**Figure 24**) that covers the rod while the rod is installed in the carburetor.

2. Remove the screws (**Figure 25**) securing the float bowl to the main body.

3. Remove the O-ring seal (**Figure 26**) and the accelerator pump rubber boot (**Figure 27**) from the float bowl.

4. Unscrew the drain screw assembly (**Figure 28**) from the float bowl.

5. Carefully push out the float pin (**Figure 29**).

6. Lift the float bowl assembly and the float valve needle out of the carburetor body (**Figure 30**).

7. Unscrew the slow jet (**Figure 31**).

8. Unscrew the main jet (**Figure 32**) and the needle jet holder (**Figure 33**).

NOTE
*Before removing the pilot screw, record the number of turns necessary until the screw **lightly** seats. The pilot screw must be reinstalled to the exact same setting.*

9. Remove the pilot screw (A, **Figure 34**), the spring, the plain washer and the O-ring.

10. Remove the throttle adjust screw, washer and the spring (B, **Figure 34**).

11. Remove the screws securing the top cover (A, **Figure 35**) and remove the top cover.

12. Carefully pull out the spring (**Figure 36**) and the vacuum piston (**Figure 37**).

CAUTION
Do not bend the jet needle on the piston.

13. On the left-hand carburetor, remove the screws (A, **Figure 38**) securing the air cutoff valve cover (B, **Figure 38**). Remove the cover, the spring (**Figure 39**) and the diaphragm (**Figure 40**).

14. To disassemble the vacuum piston, perform the following:
   a. Place an 8 mm socket down into the vacuum cylinder cavity. Place the socket on the needle holder and turn the holder 60° in either direction to unlock it from the tangs within the vacuum cylinder.
   b. Remove the needle holder and spring.
   c. Withdraw the jet needle from the vacuum piston (**Figure 41**).

NOTE
Further disassembly is neither necessary nor recommended. If throttle or choke shafts or butterflies are damaged, take the carburetor body to a Honda dealer for replacement.

7

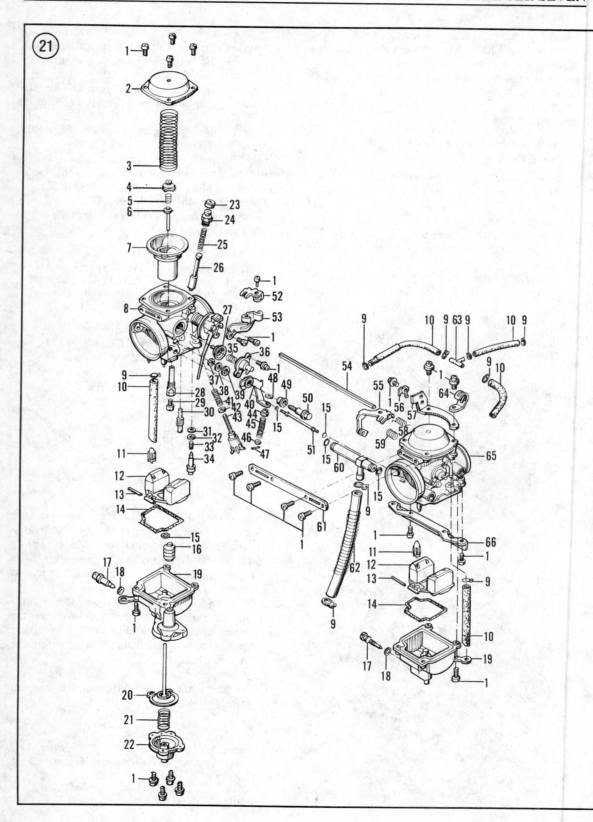

CARBURETOR (REBEL 450)

1. Screw
2. Top cover
3. Spring
4. Jet needle holder
5. Spring
6. Jet needle
7. Vacuum piston
8. Carburetor body
9. Hose clamp
10. Hose
11. Float valve needle
12. Float
13. Pivot pin
14. Gasket
15. O-ring seal
16. Rubber boot
17. Drain screw
18. Washer
19. Float bowl
20. Accelerator pump rod assembly
21. Spring
22. Cover
23. Cap
24. Choke nut
25. Spring
26. Choke valve
27. Air cut-off valve diaphragm
28. Needle jet holder
29. Main jet
30. Slow jet
31. O-ring
32. Washer
33. Spring

34. Pilot screw
35. Spring
36. Air cut-off valve cover
37. Lockwasher
38. Washer
39. Collar
40. Accelerator pump adjust arm
41. Spring
42. Washer
43. Throttle adjust screw
44. Collar
45. Spring
46. Washer
47. Cotter pin
48. Washer
49. Collar
50. Special screw
51. Fuel joint
52. Cable clamp
53. Throttle cable mounting bracket
54. Choke rod
55. Choke lever
56. Clip
57. Bracket
58. Spring
59. Spring
60. Fuel joint
61. Front bracket
62. Spring
63. "T" fitting
64. Hose clamp
65. Carburetor body
66. Rear bracket

7

15. Repeat Steps 1-14 for the other carburetor. Do not intermix the parts—keep them separate so they will be reinstalled in the correct carburetor body.

16. Clean all parts, except rubber or plastic parts, in a good grade of carburetor cleaner. This solution is available at most automotive or motorcycle supply stores in a small, resealable tank with a dip

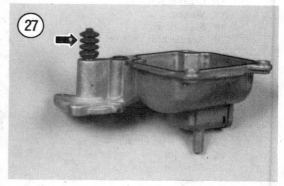

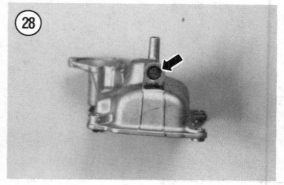

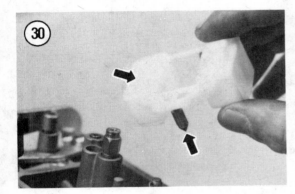

basket for just a few dollars. If it is tightly sealed when not in use, the solution will last for several cleanings. Follow the manufacturer's instructions for correct soak time (usually about 1/2 hour).

17. Remove the parts from the cleaner and blow dry with compressed air. Blow out the jets with compressed air.

7

Do *not* use a piece of wire to clean them as minor gouges in the jet can alter flow rate and upset the fuel/air mixture.

18. Be sure to clean out the float bowl overflow tube from both ends.

19. O-ring seals tend to become hardened after prolonged use and heat and therefore lose their ability to seal properly. Inspect the O-ring seal on the float bowl and all other locations; replace if necessary.

20. Inspect the accelerator pump diaphragm (A, **Figure 42**) for cracks and for brittleness; replace if necessary. Make sure the rod (B, **Figure 42**) is not bent and that it moves freely in its receptacle in the carburetor body.

21. Inspect the air cutoff valve diaphragm for cracks and for brittleness; replace if necessary.

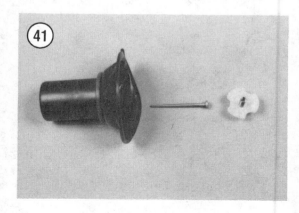

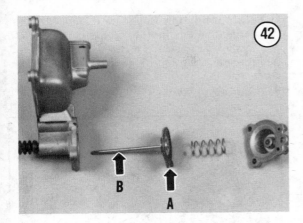

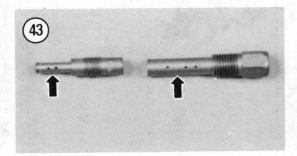

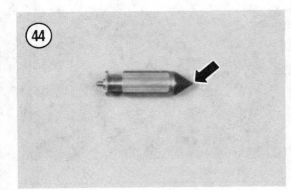

22. Make sure the small holes (**Figure 43**) in the needle jet holder and slow jet are clear. Blow out with compressed air if necessary.

23. Inspect the rubber tip (**Figure 44**) on the end of the float valve needle. Replace it if it has become hardened or starting to deteriorate.

24. Make sure the slow air jets (**Figure 45**) in the air horn are clear. Blow out with compressed air if necessary.

25. Assemble all parts by reversing these disassembly steps, noting the following.

26. Be sure to correctly align the small rubber seals (**Figure 46**) on the accelerator pump diaphragm with the holes in the float bowl housing.

27. Be sure to correctly align the small rubber seal (**Figure 47**) on the vacuum diaphragm with the hole in the float bowl housing.

7

28. In order to keep from distorting the rubber diaphragm portion of the vacuum piston, install the vacuum piston as follows:

    a. Insert the vacuum piston and spring into the carburetor body.

    b. Insert your finger into the carburetor bore and hold the vacuum piston up in the full throttle position.

    c. Turn the rubber diaphragm down and fit its sealing lips into the groove in the carburetor body.

    d. Hold the vacuum piston in this position until sub-step "e" is completed.

    e. Position the top cover so the raised cavity (B, **Figure 35**) aligns with the small hole (**Figure 47**), then install the top cover and at least 2 screws.

    f. Remove your finger and release the vacuum piston. Install the other screws. Tighten all screws securely.

29. Check and adjust, if necessary, the float height as described under *Float Level Check* in this chapter.

30. Adjust the pilot screw as described under *Pilot Screw Adjustment* in this chapter before installing the float bowl. If new pilot screws are installed, do not install the caps until pilot screw adjustment has been performed.

31. Synchronize and adjust the idle speed as described under *Tune-Up* in Chapter Three.

CARBURETOR ADJUSTMENTS

Float Level Check

1. Remove the carburetor assembly as described in this chapter.

2. Remove the screws (**Figure 25**) securing the float bowl and remove it.

3. Measure the height of the float above the carburetor body. Use a float gauge (**Figure 48**) and hold the carburetor inclined to approximately 15-45° from vertical. The correct height is listed in **Table 1**.

4. If the level is incorrect, replace the float. The float is a one piece molded plastic part and cannot be adjusted.

5. If the float level is set too high, the result will be a rich mixture. If it is set too low, the mixture will be too lean.

6. Reassemble and install the carburetor assembly.

Accelerator Pump Adjustment
(Models So Equipped)

1. Remove the carburetor assembly as described in this chapter.

2. Loosen the throttle stop screw (**Figure 49**). This will ensure that the throttle valve is closed.

3. Measure the distance between the accelerator pump rod and the adjusting arm (**Figure 50**). The correct clearance is listed in **Table 1**.

4. Adjust by carefully bending the adjusting arm.

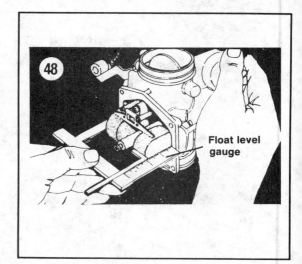

Float level gauge

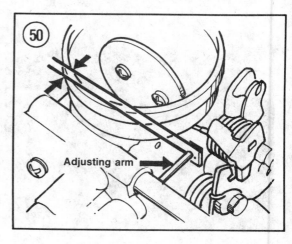

Adjusting arm

5. Measure the distance between the adjusting arm and the stopper (**Figure 51**) on the carburetor body. The correct clearance is listed in **Table 1**.

6. If necessary, adjust by bending the adjusting arm.

7. Install the carburetor assembly.

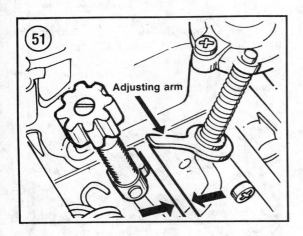

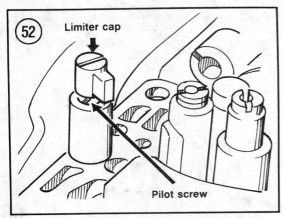

Pilot Screw Adjustment and New Limiter Cap Installation (1980-on U.S. Only)

NOTE
This procedure is to be performed only when a new pilot screw is installed. The pilot screw cannot be turned the required amount for this procedure with an old limiter cap already installed, since the limiter cap will bottom out on the stop on the float bowl chamber.

CAUTION
Do not try to remove the limiter cap from an oil pilot screw. The cap is bonded in place and if removal is attempted, the pilot screw will break.

To comply with emission control standards on 1980-on bikes sold in the U.S., a limiter cap is installed on each pilot screw to prevent the owner from readjusting the factory setting. It will allow a maximum of 7/8 of a turn of the screw to a *leaner mixture only*. The pilot screw is preset at the factory and should not be reset unless the carburetor has been overhauled.

1. For the preliminary adjustment, carefully turn the pilot screw on each carburetor (**Figure 52**) in until it seats lightly and then back it out the number of times listed in **Table 1**.

CAUTION
The pilot screw seat will be damaged if the screw is tightened against the seat. Also, do not try to remove an old limiter cap as the screw will be damaged and must be replaced.

2. Start the engine and let it reach normal operating temperature. Stop-and-go riding for approximately 10 minutes is sufficient.

3. Turn the engine off and connect a portable tachometer following the manufacturer's instructions. The bike's tachometer is not accurate enough at low rpm.

4. Start the engine and check the idle speed. If adjustment is necessary, use the throttle adjust screw (**Figure 53**) and adjust to the speed listed in **Table 1**.

5. Turn each pilot screw in or out to achieve the highest engine rpm.

6. Readjust the idle speed.

7. Turn the pilot screw on *either* carburetor in gradually until engine rpm is decreased by 100 rpm. Turn *this* pilot screw *out* an additional 3/8 turn and adjust idle speed.

8. Repeat Step 7 for the other carburetor.

9. Disconnect the portable tachometer.

10. To install new limiter caps, perform the following:

    a. Apply Loctite No. 601 (or equivalent) to the limiter cap.

    b. Position the limiter cap against the stop on the float bowl (**Figure 54**) or the mounting bracket (**Figure 55**) so that the pilot screw can only turn *clockwise*, not counterclockwise.

    c. Install the limiter cap on the pilot screw.

    d. Repeat sub-steps "a"-"c" for the other carburetor.

> *NOTE*
> *This prevents any adjustment that would enrich the mixture. With the limiter caps installed the pilot screw can be turned about 7/8 of a turn, toward a leaner mixture only.*

THROTTLE CABLE REPLACEMENT

Removal

1. Remove the carburetor assembly to a point where the throttle cables are accessible. Refer to *Carburetor Removal/Installation* in this chapter.

2. Loosen the nuts securing the throttle cables to the throttle cable mounting bracket.

3. Remove the throttle cables from the throttle cable mounting bracket and throttle wheel.

4. Remove the screws securing the upper and lower right-hand switch/throttle grip housing together (A, **Figure 56**).

5. Remove the throttle grip housing assembly from the handlebar and disengage the throttle cables from the throttle grip.

> *NOTE*
> *The piece of string attached in the next step will be used to pull the new throttle cable back through the frame so it will be routed in the exact same position as before.*

6. Tie a piece of heavy string or cord approximately 2-3 m (6-8 ft.) long to the carburetor end of the throttle cables. Wrap this end with masking or duct tape as it will be pulled through the frame loop during removal. Tie the other end of the string to the frame.

7. At the throttle lever end of the cables, pull the cables, and attached string, out through any frame loops or tabs and on some models, from behind the headlight housing. Make sure the attached string

follows the same path of the old cables through the frame and behind the headlight.

8. Remove the tape and untie the string from the old cables.

9. Lubricate the new cable as described under *Control Cable Lubrication* in Chapter Three.

10. Tie the string to the new throttle cables and wrap it with tape.

11. Carefully pull the string back through the frame routing the new cables through the same path as the old cables.

12. Remove the tape and untie the string from the cables and the frame.

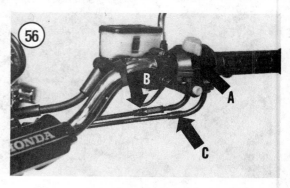

Installation

1. Apply grease to the sliding surface of the throttle grip and install it onto the handlebar. Align the punch mark on the handlebar with the slit in the throttle cover and tighten the forward screw first.

> *CAUTION*
> *The throttle cables are the push/pull type and must be installed as described in Step 2 and Step 3. Do **not** interchange the 2 cables.*

2. Attach the throttle "pull" cable to the *rear* portion of the throttle cable mounting bracket and

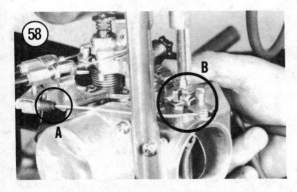

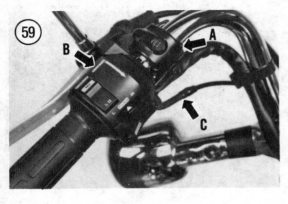

wheel (A, **Figure 57**). The other end of the cable is attached to the *front* receptacle (B, **Figure 56**) of the throttle/switch housing.

3. Attach the "push" cable to the *front* portion of the throttle cable mounting bracket and wheel (B, **Figure 57**). Attach the other end of the cable to the *rear* receptacle (C, **Figure 56**) of the throttle/switch housing.

4. Install the throttle/switch housing onto the handlebar and tighten the screws securely.

5. Operate the throttle grip and make sure the carburetor throttle linkage is operating correctly and with no binding. If operation is incorrect or there is binding, carefully check that the cable is attached correctly and there are no tight bends in the cables.

6. Install the carburetor assembly as described in this chapter.

7. Adjust the throttle cables as described under *Throttle Operation/Adjustment* in Chapter Three.

8. Test ride the bike slowly at first and make sure the throttle is operating correctly.

CHOKE CABLE REPLACEMENT

1. Remove the carburetor assembly to a point where the choke is accessible. Refer to *Carburetor Removal/Installation* in this chapter.

2. Loosen the screw clamping the choke cable to the carburetor assembly (A, **Figure 58**) and remove the choke cable from the choke arm (B, **Figure 58**).

> *NOTE*
> *The piece of string attached in the next step will be used to pull the new choke cable back through the frame so it will be routed in the same position as the old cable.*

3. Tie a piece of heavy string or cord approximately 3-4 m (6-8 ft.) long to the carburetor end of the choke cable. Wrap this end with masking or duct tape. Do not use an excessive amount of tape as it will be pulled through the frame loop during removal. Tie the other end of the string to the frame or air box.

4A. On Rebel 450 models, perform the following:
   a. Disconnect the electrical wires from the clutch switch.
   b. Remove the bolts securing the clutch lever bracket (A, **Figure 59**) and remove the bracket.
   c. Remove the screws securing the left-hand switch assembly (B, **Figure 59**) together and separate the switch assembly.
   d. Disconnect the choke cable (C, **Figure 59**) from the choke lever on the handlebar.

4B. On all models except Rebel 450, completely unscrew the locknut (**Figure 60**) securing the choke knob assembly to the handlebar base bracket.

5. At the choke lever or knob end of the cable, carefully pull the cable and attached string out through the electrical wire harness clips and through the fork area. Make sure the attached string follows the same path that the cable does through the frame and behind the fork area.

6. Remove the tape and untie the string from the old cable.

7. Lubricate the new cable as described under *Control Cable Lubrication* in Chapter Three.

> *NOTE*
> *Make sure the locknut is positioned on the string so it will be located below the mounting bracket when the cable is installed.*

8. Tie the string to the new choke cable and wrap it with tape.

9. Carefully pull the string back through the frame routing the new cable through the same path as the old cable.

10. Remove the tape and untie the string from the cable and the frame.

11A. On Rebel 450 models, perform the following:
   a. Connect the choke cable onto the choke lever on the handlebar.
   b. Assemble the left-hand switch assembly together and install the screws. Tighten the screws securely.
   c. Install the clutch lever bracket. Position the clamp with the UP mark facing up and install the bolts. Align the split in the bracket with the punch mark on the handlebar. Tighten the upper bolt first and then the lower bolt. Tighten the bolts securely.
   d. Connect the electrical wires onto the clutch switch.

11B. On all models except Rebel 450, screw the locknut onto the choke cable knob assembly and tighten securely.

12. Attach the choke cable to the carburetor choke lever.

13. Operate the choke lever or knob and make sure the carburetor choke linkage is operating correctly and with no binding. If operation is incorrect or there is binding, carefully check that the cable is attached correctly and there are no tight bends in the cable.

14. Install the carburetor assembly as described in this chapter.

FUEL SHUTOFF VALVE

Removal/Installation
(1978-1983)

> *WARNING*
> *Do not smoke or allow anyone to smoke in the immediate area while working on the fuel system. Be sure to work in a well-ventilated area and have a fire extinguisher, rated for gasoline fires, handy.*

1. Disconnect the battery negative lead.

2. Turn the shutoff valve to the OFF position (**Figure 61**).

3. Disconnect the flexible fuel line (A, **Figure 62**) from the carburetor.

4. Place the loose end in a clean, sealable metal container. This fuel can be reused if it is kept clean.

5. Open the valve to the RESERVE position (B, **Figure 62**).

6. Remove the fuel fill cap. This will allow air to enter the tank and speed up the flow of fuel. Drain the tank completely.

7. Remove the fuel shutoff valve by unscrewing the locknut (C, **Figure 62**) from the tank.

8. Stuff a clean lint-free cloth into the opening in the fuel tank to prevent any remaining fuel from draining out onto the engine or frame.

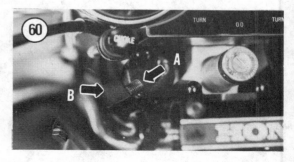

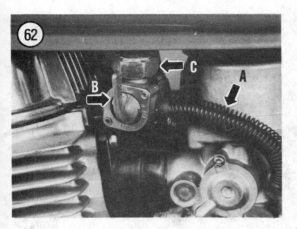

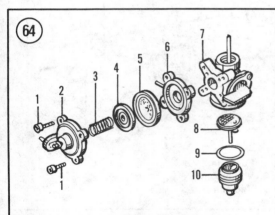

FUEL SHUTOFF VALVE
(1985-1986 CM450SC,
REBEL 450)

1. Screw
2. Cover
3. Spring
4. Backing plate
5. Diaphragm
6. Base
7. Valve body
8. Filter screen
9. O-ring seal
10. Cup

9. Remove the fuel filter from the shutoff valve. Clean with a medium soft toothbrush and blow dry with compressed air. Replace the filter if it is defective.

10. Install by reversing these removal steps, noting the following.

11. Install a new gasket between the shutoff valve and the fuel tank. Tighten the locknut securely.

12. Check for fuel leakage after installation is complete.

Removal/Installation
(Vacuum Operated Type,
1985-on)

The fuel shutoff valve on these models is controlled by engine vacuum. Fuel will *not* flow from the fuel shutoff valve without the engine running to create engine vacuum. If fuel does flow with the engine shut off, the valve or fuel valve diaphragm is faulty. Inspect the shutoff valve as described in this chapter. The fuel tank must be removed for shutoff valve removal, since there is no way to drain fuel from the tank before removing the shutoff valve.

> *WARNING*
> *Do not smoke or allow anyone to smoke in the immediate area while working on the fuel system. Be sure to work in a well-ventilated area and have a fire extinguisher, rated for gasoline fires, handy.*

1. Disconnect the battery negative lead.

2. Remove the fuel tank as described under *Fuel Tank Removal/Installation* in this chapter.

3. Remove the fuel shutoff valve by unscrewing the locknut (**Figure 63**) from the tank.

4. Stuff a clean lint-free cloth into the opening in the fuel tank to prevent the entry of foreign matter.

5. Remove the fuel filter from the shutoff valve. Clean with a medium soft toothbrush and blow dry with compressed air. Replace the filter if it is defective.

6. Install by reversing these removal steps, noting the following.

7. Install a new gasket between the shutoff valve and the fuel tank. Tighten the locknut securely.

8. Check for fuel leakage after installation is complete.

Vacuum Operation Inspection
(1985-on)

Refer to **Figure 64** for this procedure.

1. Disconnect the fuel line (**Figure 65**) going to the carburetor. Place a shop cloth over the loose end of the fuel line and drain any fuel remaining in the fuel line. The fuel line must be empty or you will get a false test reading.

2. Place the loose end of the fuel hose in a container.

3. Turn the fuel shutoff valve to the OFF position.

4. Turn the fuel shutoff valve to the ON position. Fuel should *not* flow from the end of the fuel line.

5. If fuel does flow out, disconnect the vacuum line (**Figure 66**) from the carburetor to the cylinder head. Clean out the vacuum line—it must not be blocked. Reconnect the vacuum line.

6. Repeat Step 4.

7. Disconnect the vacuum line from the cylinder head.

8. Attach a hand-operated vacuum pump to the loose end of the vacuum line (**Figure 67**).

9. Make sure the shutoff valve is still in the ON position.

10. Apply vacuum with the vacuum pump. Fuel should flow out with vacuum applied.

11. Disconnect the vacuum pump—fuel flow should stop flowing.

12. If the fuel shutoff valve does not operate properly, refer to **Figure 64** and disassemble the vacuum diaphragm as follows:

   a. Remove the screws securing the cover (**Figure 68**).

   b. Remove the cover, spring, backup plate and diaphragm.

   c. Clean all parts with a medium soft toothbrush and blow dry with compressed air. Make sure all air passages are free.

   d. Check the diaphragm for cracks or deterioration. If damaged, replace the shutoff valve assembly. Replacement parts are not available.

   e. Reassemble the vacuum diaphragm and tighten the cover screws securely.

13. Retest the shutoff valve. If it still does not operate correctly, replace the fuel shutoff valve.

FUEL TANK

Removal/Installation
(CB450SC)

1. Remove the seat and side covers.

2. Disconnect the battery negative lead.

3. Turn the fuel shutoff valve to the OFF position and remove the fuel line to the carburetors (A, **Figure 69**).

4. Disconnect the fuel shutoff valve's vacuum line from the cylinder head.

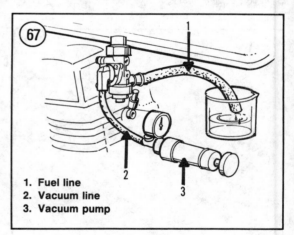

1. Fuel line
2. Vacuum line
3. Vacuum pump

5. Remove the rear mounting bolt, washer and collar (B, **Figure 69**) and move the rubber mounting pad out of the way.

6. Remove the front mounting bolt, collar and rubber cushion (C, **Figure 69**) on each side.

7A. On California models, partially pull the fuel tank up and disconnect the evaporative emission vacuum hose from the fuel tank. Remove the fuel tank from the frame.

7B. On all other models, pull the fuel tank up and remove it from the frame.

8. Install by reversing these removal steps, noting the following.

9. Be sure to reconnect the shutoff valve's vacuum line to the cylinder head. If the line is not connected, the valve will *not* operate at all.

Removal/Installation
(Rebel 450)

1. Remove both seats.

2. Disconnect the battery negative lead.

3. Turn the fuel shutoff valve to the OFF position (A, **Figure 70**) and remove the fuel line to the carburetors (B, **Figure 70**).

4. Disconnect the fuel shutoff valve's vacuum line (C, **Figure 70**) from the cylinder head.

5. Remove the rear mounting bolt, washer and collar (A, **Figure 71**).

6. Remove the front mounting bolt, collar and rubber cushion (B, **Figure 71**) on each side.

7A. On California models, partially pull the fuel tank up and disconnect the evaporative emission vacuum hose from the fuel tank. Remove the fuel tank from the frame.

7B. On all other models, pull the fuel tank up and remove it from the frame.

8. Install by reversing these removal steps, noting the following.

9. Be sure to reconnect the shutoff valve's vacuum line to the cylinder head. If the line is not connected, the fuel shutoff valve will *not* operate.

Removal/Installation
(All Other Models)

1. Remove the seat and both side covers.

2. Disconnect the battery negative lead.

3. Turn the fuel shutoff valve to the OFF position (**Figure 61**) and remove the fuel line to the carburetors.

4. Remove rear bolt and rubber pad (**Figure 72**) securing the fuel tank.

5. Pull the fuel tank up and remove it from the frame.

6. Install by reversing these removal steps.

FUEL FILTER

The bike is equipped with a small fuel filter screen in the fuel shutoff valve. Considering the dirt and residue that is often found in today's gasoline, it's a good idea to install an inline fuel filter to help keep the carburetor clean. A good quality inline fuel filter (A.C. part No. GF453 or equivalent) is available at most auto and motorcycle supply stores. Just cut the fuel line from the fuel tank to the carburetor and install the filter. Cut out a section of the fuel line the length of the filter so the fuel line does not kink and restrict fuel flow. Insert the fuel filter and make sure the fuel line is secured to the filter at each end.

GASOLINE/ALCOHOL BLEND TEST

Gasoline blended with alcohol is available in many areas. Most states and most fuel suppliers require labeling of gasoline pumps that dispense gasoline containing a certain percentage of alcohol (methyl or wood). If in doubt, ask the service station operator if their fuel contains any alcohol. A gasoline/alcohol blend, even if it contains co-solvents and corrosion inhibitors for methanol, may be damaging to the fuel system. It may also cause poor performance, hot engine restart or hot-engine running problems.

If you are not sure if the fuel you purchased contains alcohol, run this simple and effective test. A blended fuel doesn't look any different from straight gasoline so it must be tested.

WARNING
Gasoline is very volatile and presents an extreme fire hazard. Be sure to work in a well-ventilated area away from any open flames (including pilot lights on household appliances). Do not allow anyone to smoke in the area and have a fire extinguisher rated for gasoline fires handy.

During this test keep the following facts in mind:
  a. Alcohol and gasoline mix together.
  b. Alcohol mixes *easier* with water.
  c. Gasoline and water do *not* mix.

NOTE
If cosolvents have been used in the gasoline, this test may not work with water. Repeat this test using automotive antifreeze instead of water.

Use an 8 oz. transparent baby bottle with a sealable cap.

1. Set the baby bottle on a level surface and add water up to the 1.5 oz mark. Mark this line on the bottle with a fine-line permanent marking pen. This will be the reference line used later in this test.
2. Add the suspect fuel into the baby bottle up to the 8 oz. mark.
3. Install the sealable cap and shake the bottle vigorously for about 10 seconds.
4. Set the baby bottle upright on the level surface used in Step 1 and wait for a few minutes for the mixture to settle down.
5. If there is *no* alcohol in the fuel the gasoline/water separation line will be exactly on the 1.5 oz reference line made in Step 1.
6. If there *is* alcohol in the fuel the gasoline/water separation line will be *above* the 1.5 oz. reference line made in Step 1. The alcohol has separated from the gasoline and mixed in with the water (remember it is easier for the alcohol to mix with water than gasoline).
7. Discard the gasoline/water after the test.

WARNING
*After the test, discard the baby bottle or place it out of reach of small children. There will always be a gasoline and alcohol residue and it should **not** be used to drink out of.*

CRANKCASE BREATHER SYSTEM (1986-ON U.S. ONLY)

To comply with air pollution standards, the 1986-on models are equipped with a closed crankcase breather system. The system has a breather separator unit and the blowby gases from crankcase are recirculated into the fuel/air mixture and thus into the engine to be burned.

Refer to **Figure 73** for CB450SC models or **Figure 74** for Rebel 450 models.

Inspection/Cleaning

Make sure all hose clamps are tight. Check all hoses for deterioration and replace as necessary.

Remove the plug (**Figure 75**) from the drain hose and drain out all residue. This cleaning procedure should be done more frequently if a considerable amount of riding is done at full throttle or in the rain.

NOTE
Be sure to install the drain plug and clamp.

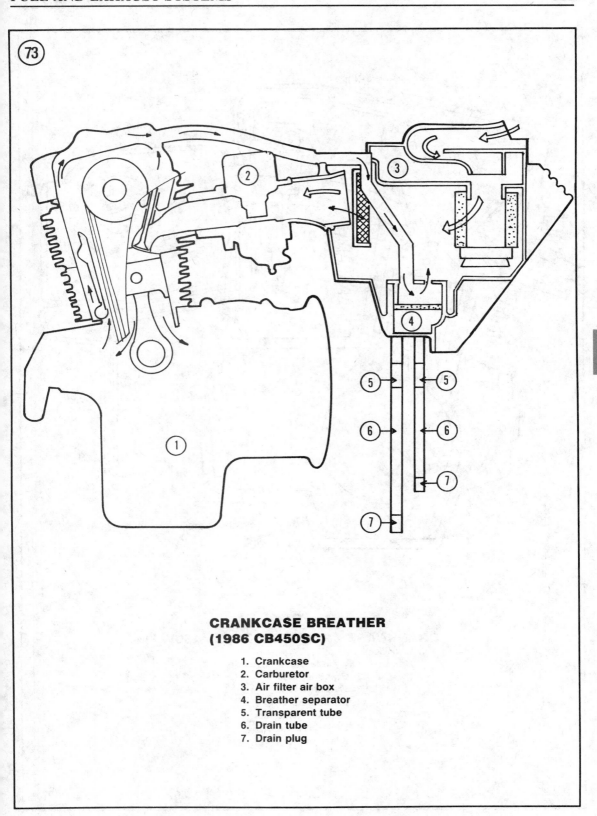

**CRANKCASE BREATHER
(1986 CB450SC)**

1. Crankcase
2. Carburetor
3. Air filter air box
4. Breather separator
5. Transparent tube
6. Drain tube
7. Drain plug

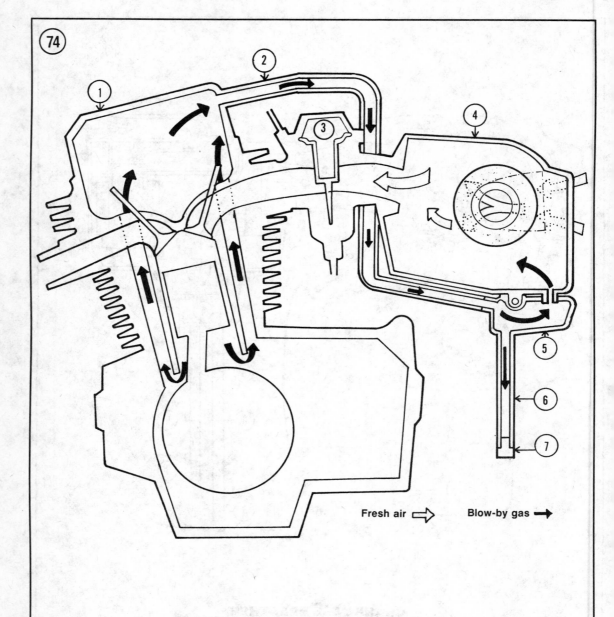

CRANKCASE BREATHER (REBEL 450)

1. Cylinder head cover
2. Breather hose
3. Carburetors
4. Air filter air box
5. Breather separator
6. Drain tube
7. Drain plug

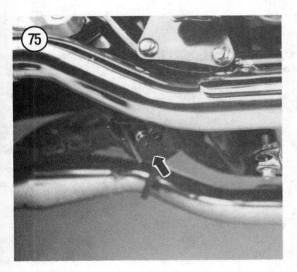

EVAPORATIVE EMISSION CONTROL SYSTEM (1985-ON CALIFORNIA MODELS ONLY)

Fuel vapor from the fuel tank is routed into a charcoal canister. This vapor is stored when the engine is not running. When the engine is running these vapors are drawn through a purge control (PC) valve and into the carburetors.

Make sure all hose clamps are tight. Check all hoses for deterioration and replace as necessary. Refer to **Figure 76** and **Figure 77**.

When removing the hoses from the PC valve, or any other related component, mark the hose and the fitting with a piece of masking tape and identify where the hose goes. There are many vacuum hoses on these models and reconnection can be confusing.

Refer to **Figure 78** for CB450SC models or **Figure 79** for Rebel 450 models.

Charcoal Canister Removal/Installation (CB450SC)

1. Remove both side covers and the seat.
2. Remove the fuel tank as described in this chapter.

NOTE
Before removing the hoses from the charcoal canister and PC valve, mark the hose and the fitting with a piece of masking tape and identify where the hose goes.

3. Remove the bolt securing the charcoal canister assembly to the frame.
4. Move the charcoal canister away from the carburetor assembly.
5. Disconnect the hose connecting the charcoal canister to the PC valve.
6. Note the routing of the vent hoses that are attached to the charcoal canister. Remove the charcoal canister from the frame.
7. Carefully remove the end cap from the canister case. Withdraw the canister from the canister case.
8. Install a new canister into the canister case and reinstall the cover.
9. Install by reversing these removal steps, noting the following.
10. Be sure to install the hose to the correct fitting on the PC valve.
11. Make sure the hoses are not kinked, twisted or in contact with any sharp surfaces.

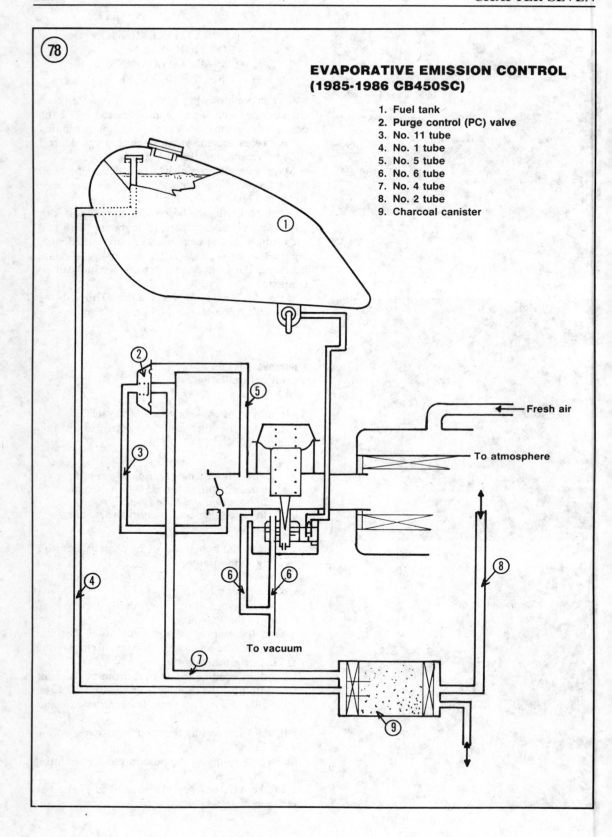

**EVAPORATIVE EMISSION CONTROL
(1985-1986 CB450SC)**

1. Fuel tank
2. Purge control (PC) valve
3. No. 11 tube
4. No. 1 tube
5. No. 5 tube
6. No. 6 tube
7. No. 4 tube
8. No. 2 tube
9. Charcoal canister

Fresh air

To atmosphere

To vacuum

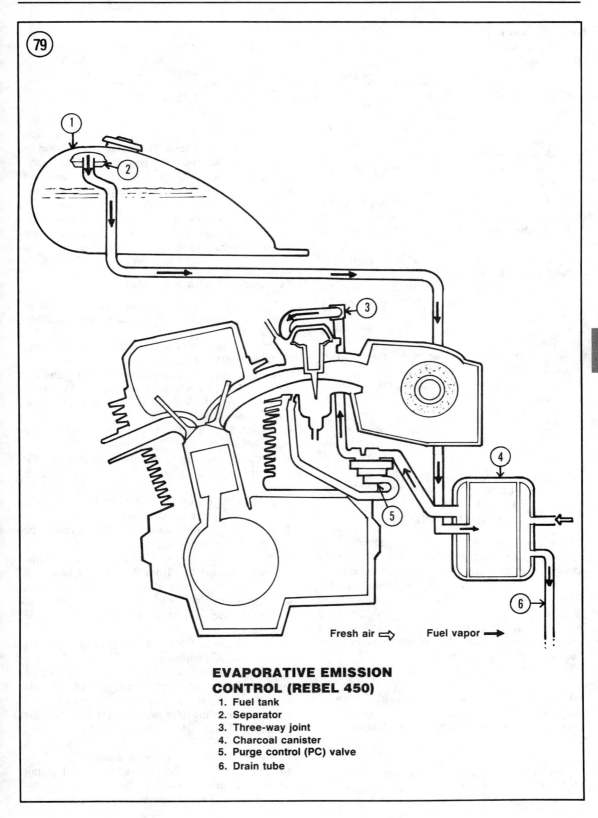

EVAPORATIVE EMISSION CONTROL (REBEL 450)
1. Fuel tank
2. Separator
3. Three-way joint
4. Charcoal canister
5. Purge control (PC) valve
6. Drain tube

Fresh air ⇨   Fuel vapor ➡

Charcoal Canister
Removal/Installation
(Rebel 450)

The charcoal canister is attached to the frame, just forward of the rear wheel.

NOTE
Before removing the hoses from the charcoal canister and PC valve, mark the hose and the fitting with a piece of masking tape and identify where the hose goes.

1. Remove the bolts and collars securing the charcoal canister assembly to the frame.
2. Move the charcoal canister down and away from the frame.
3. Disconnect the hose connecting the charcoal canister to the PC valve.
4. Note the routing of the vent hoses that are attached to the charcoal canister. Remove the charcoal canister from the frame.
5. Install by reversing these removal steps, noting the following.
6. Be sure to install the hose to the correct fitting on the PC valve.
7. Make sure the hoses are not kinked, twisted or in contact with any sharp surfaces.

EXHAUST EMISSION CONTROL SYSTEM (1986 CB450SC CALIFORNIA MODELS ONLY)

This model is equipped with a secondary air injection system that introduces fresh air from the air filter, through a reed valve and into the exhaust system (**Figure 80**). Fresh air is drawn into the exhaust port whenever there is a negative pressure pulse in the exhaust system. This fresh air helps promote the burning of unburned exhaust gases—thus reducing the hydrocarbons and carbon dioxide emissions into the air.

The reed valve assembly is located on top of the cam cover.

Make sure all hose clamps are tight. Check all hoses for deterioration and replace as necessary. There are no routine inspections or adjustment for this system.

NOTE
Neither the Rebel 450 nor the 1985 CB450SC California models are equipped with this system.

NOTE
Before removing the hoses from the system, mark the hose and the fitting with a piece of masking tape and identify where the hose goes.

EXHAUST SYSTEM

The exhaust system is a vital performance component and frequently, because of its design, it is a vulnerable piece of equipment. Check the exhaust system for deep dents and fractures and repair or replace them immediately. Check the muffler frame mounting flanges for fractures and loose bolts. Check the cylinder head mounting flanges for tightness. A loose exhaust pipe connection can rob the engine of power.

Removal/Installation
(All Models Except Rebel 450)

The exhaust system consists of two exhaust pipes, a common collector and two mufflers (**Figure 81**).
1. Loosen the clamping bolt securing the mufflers (A, **Figure 82**) to the collector.
2. Remove bolts securing the rear footpeg and the muffler (B, **Figure 82**). Remove the rear footpeg.
3. Slide the muffler out of the collector and remove the muffler.
4. Repeat Steps 1-3 for the other side and remove that muffler.
5. Remove the nuts and washers (**Figure 83**) securing the exhaust pipe flanges to the cylinder head.
6. Loosen the clamp bolt (**Figure 84**) securing the exhaust pipe to the collector inlet.
7. Remove the bolt on each side securing the collector to the crankcase.
8. Pull the collector down and forward until the exhaust pipes are free from the cylinder head and remove both exhaust pipes and the common collector assembly.
9. Inspect the gaskets at all joints; replace as necessary.
10. Be sure to install a new gasket in each exhaust port in the cylinder head.
11. Install the common collector and exhaust pipe assembly into position. Install the bolt on each side securing the common collector to the frame.
12. Install one cylinder head nut (at each exhaust port) only finger-tight until the muffler bolts and washers are installed.
13. Install the muffler onto the frame.
14. Install the rear footpeg assembly and install the bolts securing the rear footpeg and the muffler (B, **Figure 82**). Do not tighten the bolts at this time.

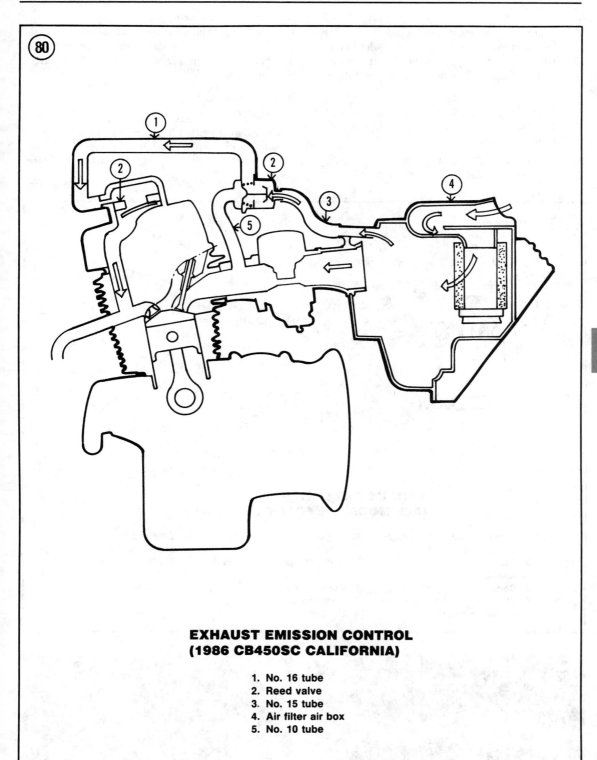

**EXHAUST EMISSION CONTROL
(1986 CB450SC CALIFORNIA)**

1. No. 16 tube
2. Reed valve
3. No. 15 tube
4. Air filter air box
5. No. 10 tube

Make sure each exhaust pipe inlet is correctly seated in each exhaust port in the cylinder head.

15. Install the other cylinder head nut on each exhaust pipe flange. Tighten both nuts securely.

NOTE
Tightening the cylinder head nuts first will minimize exhaust leaks at the cylinder head.

16. Tighten the muffler and rear footpeg assembly mounting bolts securely.

17. Tighten all clamping bolts securely.

18. After installation is complete, start the engine and make sure there are no exhaust leaks. Tighten all bolts and nuts securely.

Removal/Installation
(Rebel 450)

The exhaust system consists of two exhaust pipe and muffler assemblies. These 2 assemblies are joined together below the engine crankcase (**Figure 85**).

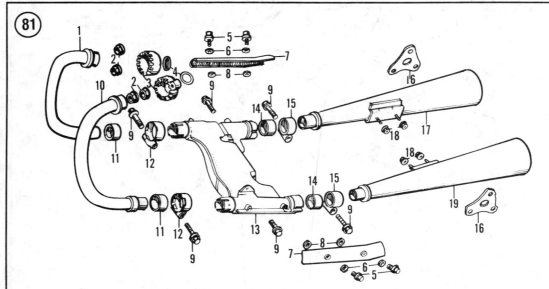

EXHAUST SYSTEM
(ALL MODELS EXCEPT REBEL 450)

1. Exhaust pipe—right-hand	8. Gasket	15. Clamp band
2. Flange nut	9. Bolt	16. Mounting bracket
3. Joint	10. Exhaust pipe—left-hand	17. Muffler—right-hand
4. Gasket	11. Gasket	18. Nut
5. Bolt	12. Clamp band	19. Muffler—left-hand
6. Washer	13. Common collector	
7. Protector plate	14. Gasket	

1. Remove the nuts (**Figure 86**) securing the exhaust pipe flanges to the cylinder head.

2. Loosen the clamp bolt (**Figure 87**) securing the exhaust crossover pipes together below the engine crankcase.

3. Remove the bolt (**Figure 88**) securing the exhaust pipe and muffler assembly to one side of the engine and frame.

4. Remove the exhaust pipe and muffler assembly from the frame and remove the assembly.

7

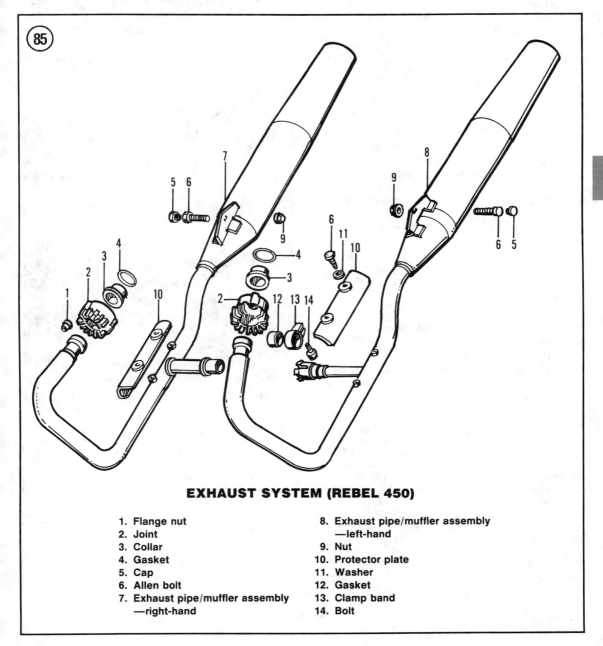

EXHAUST SYSTEM (REBEL 450)

1. Flange nut
2. Joint
3. Collar
4. Gasket
5. Cap
6. Allen bolt
7. Exhaust pipe/muffler assembly
   —right-hand
8. Exhaust pipe/muffler assembly
   —left-hand
9. Nut
10. Protector plate
11. Washer
12. Gasket
13. Clamp band
14. Bolt

5. Remove the bolt securing the other exhaust pipe and muffler assembly to the other side of the engine and frame.

6. Remove the exhaust pipe and muffler assembly from the frame and remove the assembly.

7. Inspect the gaskets at all joints; replace as necessary.

8. Be sure to install a new gasket in each exhaust port in the cylinder head.

9. Install the collar and new gasket into the cylinder head.

10. Install one of the exhaust pipe and muffler assemblies onto the engine and frame.

11. Install one cylinder head nut at the exhaust port. Tighten the nut only finger-tight until the muffler bolts are installed.

12. Install the bolt (**Figure 88**) securing the exhaust pipe and muffler assembly to one side of the engine and frame. Do not tighten the bolts at this time.

13. Install the other exhaust pipe and muffler assembly onto the engine and frame. Insert the crossover pipe into the crossover pipe on the other side. Tighten the clamping bolt securely.

14. Make sure each exhaust pipe inlet is correctly seated in each exhaust port in the cylinder head.

15. Install the other cylinder head nut on each exhaust pipe flange. Tighten both nuts securely.

NOTE
Tightening the cylinder head nuts first will minimize exhaust leaks at the cylinder head.

16. Tighten the muffler and rear footpeg assembly mounting bolts securely.

17. Tighten all clamping bolts securely.

18. After installation is complete, start the engine and make sure there are no exhaust leaks. Tighten all bolts and nuts securely.

Table 1 CARBURETOR SPECIFICATIONS

	1978 CB400A	1978-1979 CB400T
Model No.	VB24A	VB21A
Main jet No.		
Primary	72	75
Secondary	105	110
Initial pilot screw opening	1 3/4 turns out	1 1/2 turns out
Needle jet clip position from top	fixed	fixed
Float level	15.5 mm (0.61 in.)	14.5 mm (0.49 in.)
Idle speed	1,250 ±100 rpm	1,200 ±100 rpm

(continued)

Table 1 CARBURETOR SPECIFICATIONS (continued)

	1980-1981 CM400T	1982-1983 CM450A
Model No.	VB22A	VB24E
Main jet No.		
Primary	72	75
Secondary	118	108
Initial pilot screw opening	2 turns out	2 3/4 turns out
Needle jet clip position from top	fixed	fixed
Float level	15.5 mm (0.61 in.)	15.5 mm (0.61 in.)
Idle speed	1,200 ±100 rpm	1,250 ±100 rpm
Accelerator pump arm clearance		8.9 mm (3/8 in.)

	1980-1981 CB400T	1979 CM400A
Model No.	VB22B	VB24B
Main jet No.		
Primary	70	65
Secondary	110	110
Initial pilot screw opening	2 turns out	2 turns out
Needle jet clip position from top	fixed	fixed
Float level	15.5 mm (0.61 in.)	15.5 mm (0.61 in.)
Idle speed	1,200 ±100 rpm	1,250 ±100 rpm

	1980-1981 CM400A	1981 CM400C
Model No.	VB24C	VB22C
Main jet No.		
Primary	68	72
Secondary	112	118
Initial pilot screw opening	2 1/4 turns out	2 turns out
Needle jet clip position from top	fixed	fixed
Float level	15.5 mm (0.61 in.)	15.5 mm (0.61 in.)
Idle speed	1,250 ±100 rpm	1,200 ±100 rpm

	1980-1981 CM400E	1979 CM400T
Model No.	VB22E	VB21C
Main jet No.		
Primary	72	70
Secondary	118	112
Initial pilot screw opening	2 turns out	2 turns out
Needle jet clip position from top	fixed	fixed
Float level	15.5 mm (0.61 in.)	15.5 mm (0.61 in.)
Idle speed	1,200 ±100 rpm	1,200 ±100 rpm

7

(continued)

Table 1 CARBURETOR SPECIFICATIONS (continued)

	1982 CM450C	1982-1983 CM450E 1982-1983 CB450SC
Model No.	VB22G	VB22J
Main jet No.		
Primary	72	72
Secondary	115	115
Initial pilot screw opening	2 1/4 turns out	2 1/4 turns out
Needle jet clip position from top	fixed	fixed
Float level	15.5 mm (0.61 in.)	15.5 mm (0.61 in.)
Idle speed	1,200 ±100 rpm	1,200 ±100 rpm
Accelerator pump arm clearance	7.0 mm (1/4 in.)	7.0 mm (1/4 in.)

	1982 CM450SC	1983 CM450SC
Model No.	VB22G	VB22JN
Main jet No.	120	
Primary	72	—
Secondary	115	—
Slow jet	—	38
Initial pilot screw opening	2 1/2 turns out	2 1/2 turns out
Needle jet clip position from top	fixed	fixed
Float level	15.5 mm (0.61 in.)	15.5 mm (0.61 in.)
Idle speed	1,200 ±100 rpm	1,200 ±100 rpm
Accelerator pump arm clearance	7.0 mm (1/4 in.)	7.0 mm (1/4 in.)

	1985-1986 CM450SC 1985-1986 CB450SC	1986-1987 Rebel 450
Model No.		
49-state	VB2EA	VE24A
Calif.	VB2FA	VE28A
Main jet No.	125	120
Slow jet		1986—No. 35, 1987—No. 38
49-state	38	
Calif.	40	
Initial pilot screw opening	2 1/4 turns out	1986—2 1/4 turns out 1987—2 turns out
Needle jet clip position from top	fixed	fixed
Float level	15.5 mm (0.61 in.)	18.5 mm (0.73 in.)
Idle speed	1,200 ±100 rpm	1,200 ±100 rpm
Acclerator pump arm clearance	7.0 mm (1/4 in.)	2.5 mm(0.10 in.)

CHAPTER EIGHT

ELECTRICAL SYSTEM

The electrical system includes the following systems:

a. Charging system.
b. Ignition system.
c. Lighting system.
d. Turn signals.
e. Horn.

Tables 1-4 are located at the end of this chapter. Wiring diagrams are located at the end of this book.

CHARGING SYSTEM

The charging system consists of the battery, alternator and voltage regulator/rectifier. Refer to **Figure 1** for Rebel 450 models or **Figure 2** for all models except Rebel 450.

The alternator generates an alternating current (AC) which the rectifier converts to direct current (DC). The regulator maintains the voltage to the battery and load (lights, ignition, etc.) at a constant voltage regardless of variations in engine speed and load.

Leak Test

1. Turn the ignition switch to the OFF position.
2. Disconnect the battery negative lead (**Figure 3**).
3. Connect a voltmeter between the battery negative terminal and the negative cable.
4. The voltmeter should read 0 volts.
5. If there is a voltage reading, this indicates a voltage drain in the system that will drain the battery. Test all charging systems as described in this chapter.
6. Disconnect the voltmeter and reconnect the battery negative lead.

Charging System Test
(All 400 cc Models)

Whenever charging system trouble is suspected, make sure the battery is good before going any further. Clean and test the battery as described under *Battery Testing* in Chapter Three. Make sure all electrical connectors are tight and free of corrosion.

1. Disconnect the voltage regulator/rectifier black electrical wire, connect a 0-15 DC voltmeter and a 0-10 DC ammeter as shown in **Figure 4**.
2. Remove the right-hand side cover.
3. Connect the ammeter in series to the positive battery terminal. Connect the positive voltmeter terminal to the positive battery terminal and negative voltmeter terminal to ground.

CAUTION
Since the ammeter is connected between the positive battery terminal and the starter cable, the ammeter will burn out if the electric starter is used. Use the kickstarter only.

4. Start the engine with the kickstarter and run at 5,000 rpm. Minimum charging current should be 5 amperes. The voltmeter should read 14.5 volts.

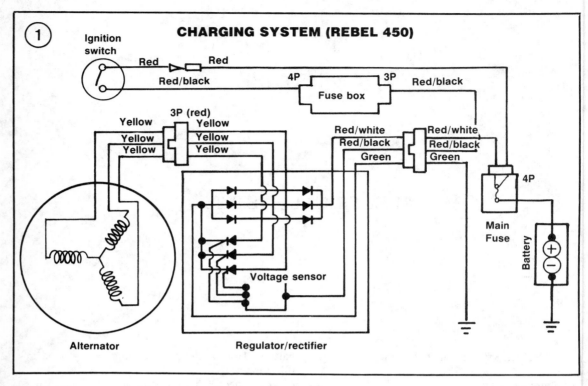

① **CHARGING SYSTEM (REBEL 450)**

Alternator

Regulator/rectifier

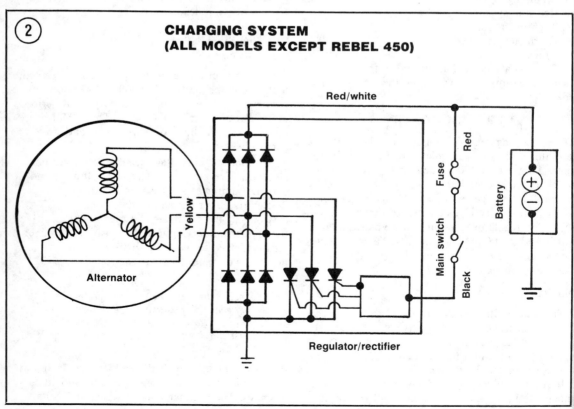

② **CHARGING SYSTEM (ALL MODELS EXCEPT REBEL 450)**

Alternator

Regulator/rectifier

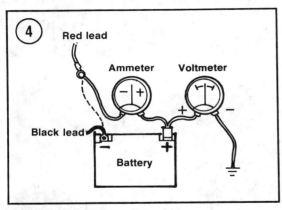

Red lead

Ammeter   Voltmeter

Black lead

Battery

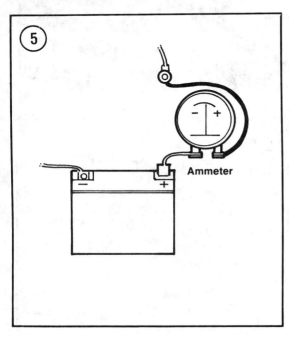

Ammeter

5. All of the measurements are made with lights on HIGH. If charging current is considerably lower than specified, check the alternator and voltage regulator/rectifier. It is less likely that the charging current is too high; in that case, the regulator is probably at fault.

6. Test the separate charging system components as described under appropriate heading in the following sections.

Charging System Test
(All 450 cc Models
Except Rebel 450)

Whenever a charging system trouble is suspected, make sure the battery is good before going any further. Clean and test the battery as described under *Battery Testing* in Chapter Three. Make sure all electrical connectors are tight and free of corrosion.

1. Remove the right-hand side cover.
2. Disconnect the battery positive (+) lead.
3. Connect the ammeter between the positive (+) terminal and the positive battery lead as shown in **Figure 5**.
4. Start the engine with the kickstarter.

CAUTION
Do not use the electric starter. The current surge may burn out the ammeter.

5. Turn the headlight to the HIGH beam position.
6. Increase engine speed to 2,000 rpm or higher several times.
7. Let the engine idle, then slowly increase engine speed.
8. Charging amperage should begin at 2,000 rpm and should be at a minimum of 5 amps at 5,000 rpms.
9. If the amperage is not within specifications, check the alternator and voltage regulator/rectifier as described in this chapter.
10. Shut the engine off and disconnect the ammeter from the battery.
11. Reconnect the battery positive (+) lead.
12. Install the right-hand side cover.

Charging System Test
(Rebel 450)

Whenever charging system trouble is suspected, make sure the battery is good before going any further. Clean and test the battery as described under *Battery Testing* in Chapter Three. Make sure all electrical connectors are tight and free of corrosion.

8

1. Start the engine and let it reach normal operating temperature; shut off the engine.

2. Connect a 0-15 DC voltmeter between the battery terminals. Do *not* disconnect the battery leads from the battery. With the engine off, there should be 12.4 volts present.

3. Start the engine and let it idle. Turn the headlight ON.

4. Gradually increase engine speed and check voltage output at various engine speeds.

5. The voltage should not exceed 14.0-15.0 volts at 5,000 rpm.

6. Shut the engine off.

7. If charging voltage is considerably lower than specified, check the alternator and voltage regulator/rectifier. It is less likely that the charging current is too high; in that case, the regulator is probably at fault. Test the separate charging system components as described under appropriate heading in the following sections.

8. Shut the engine off.

9. Disconnect the voltmeter from the battery terminals.

ALTERNATOR

An alternator is a form of electrical generator in which a magnetized field called a rotor revolves within a set of stationary coils called a stator. As the rotor revolves, alternating current is induced in the stator. The current is then rectified and used to operate the electrical accessories on the motorcycle and for charging the battery. The rotor is permanently magnetized.

Alternator rotor and stator assemblies removal and installation procedures are covered in Chapter Four.

Alternator Rotor Testing

The rotor is permanently magnetized and cannot be tested except by replacement with a rotor known to be good. A rotor can lose magnetism from old age or a sharp blow. If defective, the rotor must be replaced; it cannot be remagnetized.

Alternator Stator Testing
(1978-1981 CB400A, CB400T I, CB400T II, CB400T, CM400C and 1979 CM400T)

Disconnect the stator electrical leads at the voltage regulator/rectifier (**Figure 6**). Do not remove the stator assembly from the engine as it must be grounded to the engine for this test. Use an ohmmeter and measure the resistance between the terminals indicated in **Table 1**. Replace the stator if it does not meet the specifications listed in **Table 1**.

Alternator Stator and Ignition Pulser Testing (1980-1981 CM400T, CM400A, 1982-on CB450T, CB450SC, CM450C, CM450E, CM450A)

1. Disconnect the stator electrical connectors at the voltage regulator/rectifier (**Figure 7**). Do not

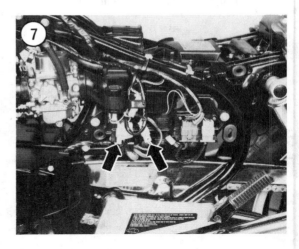

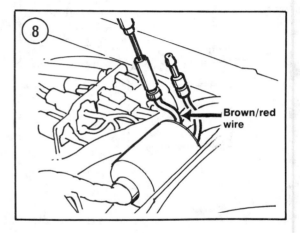

Brown/red wire

remove the stator assembly from the engine as it must be grounded to the engine for this test.

2. Use an ohmmeter set to R×10 and measure the resistance between the terminals indicated in **Table 1**.

3. Replace the stator if it does not meet the specifications listed in **Table 1**.

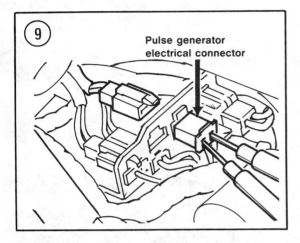

Pulse generator electrical connector

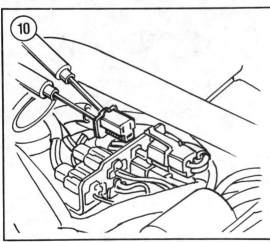

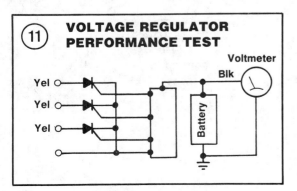

VOLTAGE REGULATOR PERFORMANCE TEST

Voltmeter
Blk

Yel
Yel
Yel
Battery

Alternator Exciter Coil Testing (Rebel 450)

1. Remove the seats.
2. Disconnect the brown/red wire going to the alternator stator.
3. Use an ohmmeter and measure the resistance between the brown/red wire and ground (**Figure 8**).
4. The specified resistance is 50-250 ohms.
5. Replace the stator assembly if it does not meet these specifications.
6. Reconnect the electrical wire connection and install the seats.

Alternator Pulse Generator Testing (Rebel 450)

1. Remove the seats.
2. Disconnect the 2-pin red electrical connector going to the alternator stator.
3. Use an ohmmeter and measure the resistance between the blue/yellow and the green wires (**Figure 9**) on the alternator stator side of the connector.
4. The specified resistance is 50-170 ohms.
5. Replace the stator assembly if it does not meet these specifications.
6. Reconnect the electrical connector and install the seats.

Alternator Charging Coil Testing (Rebel 450)

1. Remove the seats.
2. Disconnect the 3-pin red electrical connector going to the alternator stator.
3. Use an ohmmeter and measure the resistance between each yellow wire (**Figure 10**) on the alternator stator side of the connector.
4. The specified resistance is 0.6-1.1 ohms.
5. Replace the stator assembly if it does not meet these specifications.
6. Reconnect the electrical connector and install the seats.

VOLTAGE REGULATOR/RECTIFIER

Voltage Regulator Performance Test (All Models)

1. Connect a voltmeter across the battery (**Figure 11**).
2. Start the engine and let it idle.
3. Increase engine speed until the voltage going to the battery reaches 14.0-15.0 volts. At this point, the voltage regulator must divert the current to

ground. If this does not happen, the voltage regulator/rectifier must be replaced as described in this chapter.

Rectifier Testing
(All Models Except Rebel 450)

To test the rectifier portion of the voltage regulator/rectifier, disconnect the electrical connectors from the voltage regulator/rectifier. Refer to the following figures:

    a. A, **Figure 12**; 1978 CB400T, 1978 CB400A and 1982 CB450T.

    b. **Figure 13**: All other models except Rebel 450.

Refer to **Figure 14** and make the following measurements, using an ohmmeter set to R×10.

> *CAUTION*
> *Tests may be performed on the rectifier portion of the voltage regulator/rectifier unit but a good one may be damaged by someone unfamiliar with the test equipment. If you feel unqualified to perform the test, have the test made by a Honda dealer or substitute a known good unit for a suspected one.*

1. Connect either ohmmeter lead to the green rectifier lead. Connect the other ohmmeter lead to each of the yellow leads. These three measurements must be the same, either all very high resistance (2,000 ohm minimum) or very low resistance (5-40 ohms). If one or more differ, the voltage regulator/rectifier is faulty and the voltage regulator/rectifier assembly must be replaced.

2. Reverse the ohmmeter leads and repeat Step 1. This time, the readings must also be the same, but just the opposite from the measurements in Step 1. For example, if all readings in Step 1 were low, all readings in this step must be high and vice versa. If one or more differ, the voltage regulator/rectifier is faulty and the voltage regulator/rectifier assembly must be replaced.

3. Connect either ohmmeter lead to the red/white voltage regulator/rectifier lead. Connect the other ohmmeter lead to each of the yellow leads. These 3 measurements must be the same, either all very high or all very low. If one or more differ, the voltage regulator/rectifier is faulty and the voltage regulator/rectifier assembly must be replaced.

Voltage Regulator/Rectifier
Testing (Rebel 450)

1. Remove the seats.

2. Disconnect the electrical connector going to the voltage regulator (**Figure 15**).

> *CAUTION*
> *Tests may be performed on the voltage regulator/rectifier unit, but a good one may be damaged by someone unfamiliar with the test equipment. If you feel unqualified to perform the test, have the test made by a Honda dealer or substitute a known good unit for a suspected one.*

3. Use an ohmmeter and measure the resistance between each yellow wire on the alternator stator side of the connector. The specified resistance is 0.6-1.1 ohms.

4. Use a 12-V voltmeter and measure the voltage between the red/white and green wires. There should be battery voltage (12 volts).

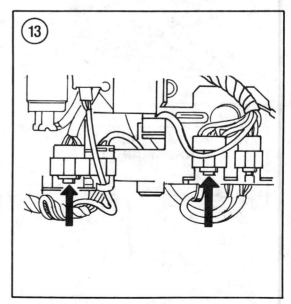

5. Turn the ignition switch to the ON position. Use a 12-V voltmeter and measure the voltage between the red/black and green wires. There should be battery voltage (12 volts).

6. If the voltage regulator fails any of these tests the unit is faulty and must be replaced as described in this chapter.

Voltage Regulator/Rectifier
Removal/Installation

1978 CB400T, 1978 CB400A, 1982 CB450T

1. Remove the right-hand side cover.
2. Disconnect the battery negative lead.
3. Remove the bolts (B, **Figure 12**) securing the voltage regulator/rectifier to the panel.

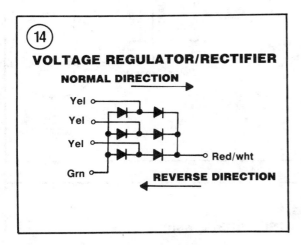

④

VOLTAGE REGULATOR/RECTIFIER

NORMAL DIRECTION →

Yel o

Yel o

Yel o

o Red/wht

Grn o

REVERSE DIRECTION ←

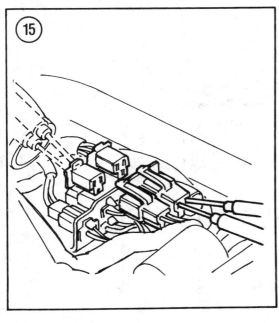

⑮

4. Disconnect the electrical connectors going to the voltage regulator/rectifier and remove the voltage regulator/rectifier.

5. Install a new voltage regulator/rectifier and reconnect the electrical connectors.

All other models except Rebel 450

1. Remove the right-hand side cover.
2. Disconnect the battery negative lead.
3. Remove the bolts securing the electrical panel to the frame.
4. Partially pull the electrical panel away from the frame.
5. Remove the bolts securing the voltage regulator/rectifier to the panel.
6. Disconnect the electrical wires going to the voltage regulator/rectifier and remove the voltage regulator/rectifier.
7. Install a new voltage regulator/rectifier and reconnect the electrical connectors. Reinstall the electrical panel and tighten the bolts securely.

Rebel 450

1. Remove the seats.
2. Remove the battery as described under *Battery* in Chapter Three.
3. Remove the bolts securing the battery tray.
4. Carefully pull the battery tray partially out from the frame.
5. Remove the bolts securing the voltage regulator/rectifier to the backside of the battery tray.
6. Disconnect the electrical wires going to the voltage regulator/rectifier and remove the voltage regulator/rectifier.
7. Install a new voltage regulator/rectifier and reconnect the electrical connectors. Reinstall the battery tray and battery.

IGNITION SYSTEM

All models are equipped with a capacitor discharge ignition (CDI) system, a solid-state system that uses no breaker points.

Alternating current from the alternator is rectified to direct current and is used to charge the capacitor. As the piston approaches the firing position, a pulse from the exciter coil is used to trigger the silicon controlled rectifier. The rectifier in turn allows the capacitor to discharge quickly into the primary circuit of the ignition coil, where the voltage is stepped up in the secondary circuit to a value sufficient to fire the spark plug.

8

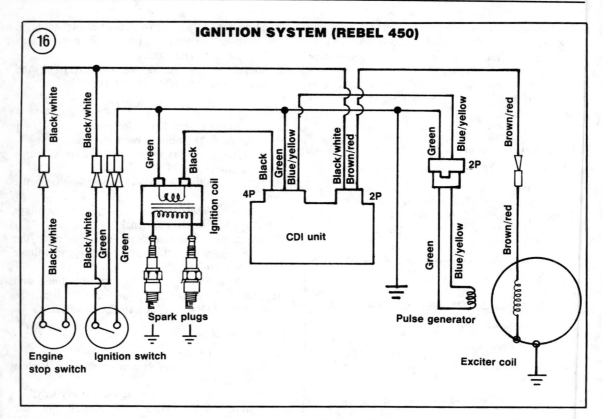

IGNITION SYSTEM (REBEL 450)

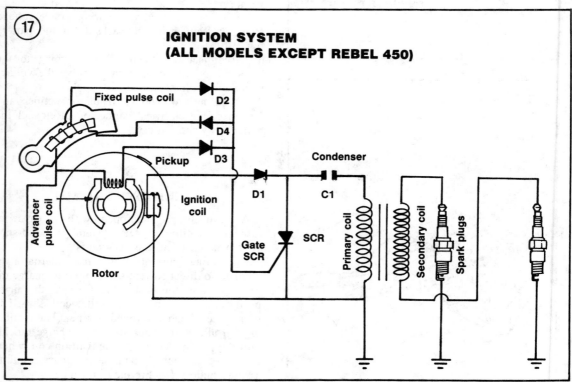

**IGNITION SYSTEM
(ALL MODELS EXCEPT REBEL 450)**

The ignition systems used among the different models are shown in the following illustrations:
a. **Figure 16**: Rebel 450.
b. **Figure 17**: All models except Rebel 450.

CDI Precautions

Certain measures must be taken to protect the capacitor discharge system. Instantaneous damage to the semiconductors in the system will occur if the following precautions are not observed.
1. Never disconnect any of the electrical connections while the engine is running.
2. Keep all connections between the various units clean and tight. Be sure that the wiring connectors are pushed together firmly to help keep out moisture.
3. Do not substitute another type of ignition coil.
4. The CDI unit is mounted within a rubber vibration isolator. Always be sure that the isolator is in place when installing the unit.

CDI Troubleshooting

Problems with the capacitor discharge system fall into one of the following categories. See **Table 2**.
a. Weak spark.
b. No spark.

CDI Testing (Rebel 450)

This test does not actually test the CDI unit, but tests all support components of the ignition circuit—switches, alternator exciter coil and pulse generator and the primary side of the ignition coil. If all of these support components check out okay, then the CDI unit is faulty and must be replaced.

This procedure covers only Rebel 450 models. Honda does not provide information on the new test procedures for the various other models covered in this book. If you suspect a faulty CDI unit, take your bike to a dealer and have them test it. Chances are they will perform a "remove and replace" test to see if the CDI unit is faulty. This type of test is expensive if performed by yourself. Remember if you purchase a new CDI unit and it does *not* solve your particular ignition system problem, you cannot return the CDI unit for a refund. Most motorcycle dealers will *not* accept returns on any electrical component since the component could be damaged internally even though it looks okay externally.

Honda does not recommend the CDI test procedures previously used by the factory. The previous test procedure was to measure the resistance values between the various connector pins on the CDI unit. This inspection method has been determined to be unreliable because of the following:
a. The wrong type of multimeter was used and would give incorrect resistance value readings.
b. The multimeter's battery voltage was low and would result in an incorrect resistance value reading.
c. Human error in performing the test and/or misreading the specifications in the resistance value reading table.
d. Varying manufacturing tolerances among the different CDI units of the same type for the same model.

1. Test the CDI's unit ability to produce a spark. Perform the following:
a. Disconnect the high voltage lead (**Figure 18**) from the spark plug. Remove the spark plug from the cylinder head.
b. Connect a new or known good spark plug to the high voltage lead. Place the spark plug base on a good ground like the engine cylinder head (**Figure 19**). Position the spark plug so you can see the electrodes.

> *WARNING*
> *If it is necessary to hold the high voltage lead, do so with an insulated pair of pliers. The high voltage generated by the CDI could produce serious or fatal shocks.*

> *NOTE*
> *The engine must be turned over **rapidly** since the ignition system does not produce a spark at a low rpm.*

8

c. Turn the engine over rapidly with the kickstarter or starter and check for a spark. If there is a fat blue spark, the CDI is okay.

d. If a weak spark or no spark is produced, continue with this procedure.

e. Reinstall the spark plug and connect the high voltage lead onto the spark plug.

2. Remove the seats.

3. Remove the fuel tank as described under *Fuel Tank Removal/Installation* in Chapter Seven.

4. Carefully pull the CDI unit and its rubber isolator (**Figure 20**) from the mounting tab on the mounting bracket.

5. Disconnect the electrical connectors from the backside of the CDI unit.

NOTE
For best results, in the following step, use a quality digital multimeter (Honda part No. KS-AHM-32-003) or equivalent. Install a fresh battery in the multimeter before performing these tests.

NOTE
*Make the resistance check between the electrical connector terminals on the **wire harness side** of the electrical connectors (**Figure 21**). Do **not** perform these tests on the terminals of the CDI unit.*

6. Use an ohmmeter and check for continuity between the black/white and green wires. Turn the ignition switch to the ON position and engine kill switch to the OFF position. There should be continuity (low resistance).

7. If either of the continuity checks failed in Step 6, then check the following:

a. Check for an open or short in the wire harness between each component.

b. Make sure all connections between the various components are clean and tight. Be sure that the electrical connectors are pushed together firmly to help keep out moisture.

8. If the wiring harness checks out okay, then test and inspect the following ignition system components as described in this chapter.

a. Ignition switch.

b. Engine stop switch.

9. Use an ohmmeter and check the resistance value between the black and the green wire terminals. The specified resistance is 0.1-0.3 ohms. If the resistance value is not within these specifications, inspect the ignition coil as described in this chapter.

10. Use an ohmmeter and check the resistance value between the blue/yellow and green wire terminals. The specified resistance is 50-170 ohms. If the resistance value is not within these specifications, inspect the pulse generator as described in this chapter.

11. Use an ohmmeter and check the resistance value between the black/red and green wire terminals. The specified resistance is 50-250 ohms. If the resistance value is not within these specifications, inspect the alternator exciter coil as described in this chapter.

12. If Steps 1-11 meet all specifications, then the CDI unit is faulty and must be replaced as described in this chapter.

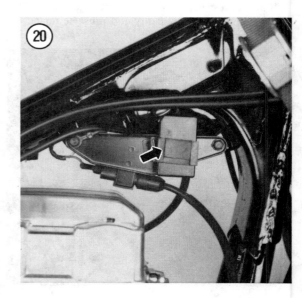

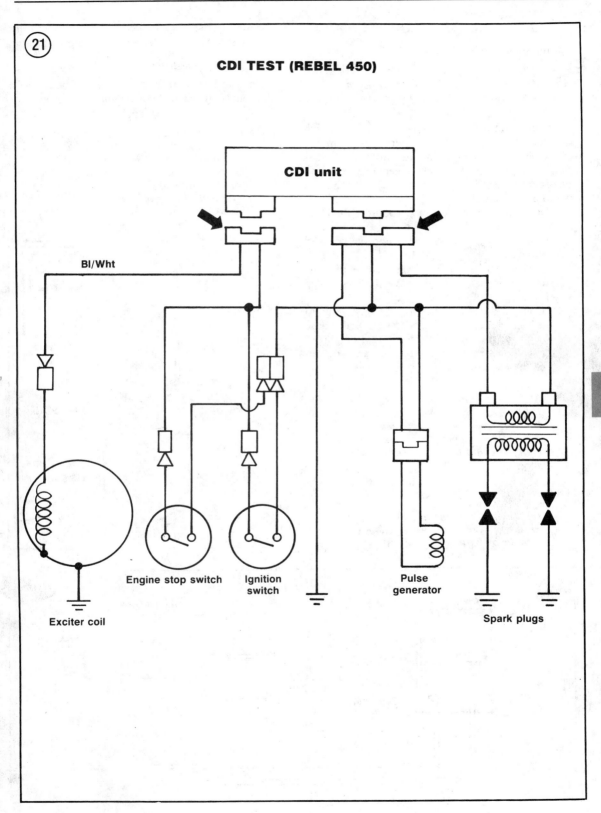

CDI TEST (REBEL 450)

CDI unit

Bl/Wht

Exciter coil

Engine stop switch

Ignition switch

Pulse generator

Spark plugs

8

IGNITION COIL

Testing (450 cc Models)

NOTE
Honda does not provide resistance specifications for the 400 cc models.

The ignition coil is a form of transformer which develops the high voltage required to jump the spark plug gap. The only maintenance required is that of keeping the electrical connections clean and tight and occasionally checking to see that the coil is mounted securely.

If the condition of the coil is doubtful, there are several checks which may be made.

First as a quick check of coil condition, perform the following:

a. Disconnect the high voltage lead (**Figure 18**) from the spark plug. Remove the spark plug from the cylinder head.

b. Connect a new or known good spark plug to the high voltage lead. Place the spark plug base on a good ground like the engine cylinder head (**Figure 19**). Position the spark plug so you can see the electrodes.

WARNING
If it is necessary to hold the high voltage lead, do so with an insulated pair of pliers. The high voltage generated by the CDI could produce serious or fatal shocks.

NOTE
*The engine must be turned over **rapidly** since the ignition system does not produce a spark at a low rpm.*

c. Turn the engine over rapidly with the kickstarter or starter and check for a spark. If there is a fat blue spark, the ignition coil is okay.

Refer to **Figure 22** for Rebel 450 or **Figure 23** for all models other than Rebel 450 for this procedure.

NOTE
In order to get accurate resistance measurements the coil must be have a minimum temperature of 20° C (68° F). If necessary, start the engine and let it warm up to normal operating temperature. If the engine won't start, warm the ignition coil with a hair drier.

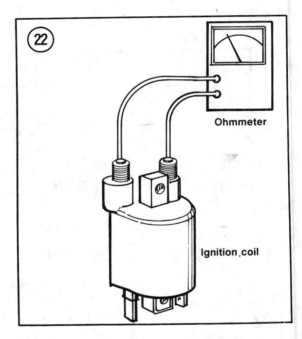

Ohmmeter

Ignition coil

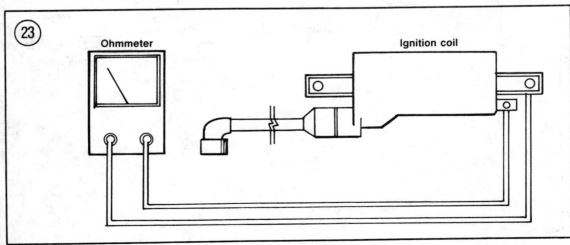

Ohmmeter

Ignition coil

1. Measure the coil primary resistance using an ohmmeter set at R×1. Measure the resistance between the 2 primary terminals. The value should be as follows:

 a. Rebel 450: 0.10-0.30 ohms.
 b. All models except Rebel 450: 0.55-0.65 ohms.

2. Disconnect with the high voltage leads (spark plug leads) from the spark plugs.

3. With the spark plug cap still installed to the high voltage lead (spark plug lead), measure the secondary resistance using an ohmmeter set at R×1,000. Measure the resistance between the two spark plug leads. The value should be as follows:

 a. Rebel 450: 7.4-11.1 k (7,400-11,100) ohms.
 b. All models except Rebel 450: 7.2-8.8 k (7,200-8,800) ohms.

4. On Rebel 450 models, if the resistance values in Step 3 are not correct, perform this test:
 a. Disconnect the high voltage leads (spark plug leads) from the ignition coil.
 b. Measure the secondary resistance using an ohmmeter set at R×K. Measure the resistance between the secondary terminals on the ignition coil. The value should be 3.7-4.5 k (3,700-4,500) ohms for.
 c. If the coil checks out okay with this test, inspect the spark plug leads for an open circuit, replace as necessary.
 d. Replace the coil or reinstall the high voltage leads onto the coil.

5. If the coil resistance does not meet either of these specifications, the coil must be replaced. If the coil exhibits visible damage, it should be replaced.

6. Reconnect all ignition coil wires to the ignition coil.

**Removal/Installation
(All Models Except Rebel 450)**

1. Remove the seat.
2. Remove the fuel tank as described under *Fuel Tank Removal/Installation* in Chapter Seven.
3. Disconnect the high voltage leads (A, **Figure 24**) from the spark plugs.
4. Remove the mounting bolts (B, **Figure 24**) and disconnect the electrical wires from the ignition coil.
5. Remove the ignition coil.
6. Install by reversing the removal steps. Make sure to route the spark plug wires to the correct cylinder: the right-hand ignition coil terminal to the right-hand spark plug and the left-hand ignition coil terminal to the left-hand spark plug.

**Removal/Installation
(Rebel 450)**

1. Remove the seats.
2. Remove the fuel tank as described under *Fuel Tank Removal/Installation* in Chapter Seven.
3. Disconnect the high voltage lead from the spark plugs (**Figure 25**).
4. Disconnect the electrical wires (A, **Figure 26**) from the ignition coil.
5. Carefully pull the ignition coil and the rubber isolator from the mounting tab on the frame (B, **Figure 26**).
6. Install by reversing these removal steps, noting the following.
7. Make sure all electrical connections are tight and free of corrosion.

8

STARTING SYSTEM

The starting system consists of the starter motor, starter gears, solenoid and the starter button.

When the starter button is pressed, it engages the starter solenoid switch that completes the circuit allowing electricity to flow from the battery to the starter motor.

Refer to the following illustrations for this procedure:

a. **Figure 27**: Rebel 450.

b. **Figure 28**: All models except Rebel 450 (manual transmission).

c. **Figure 29**: All models except Rebel 450 (automatic transmission).

CAUTION
Do not operate the starter for more than 5 seconds at a time. Let it rest approximately 10 seconds, then use it again.

The starter gears are covered in Chapter Four. **Table 3**, at the end of the chapter, lists possible starter problems, probable causes and most common remedies.

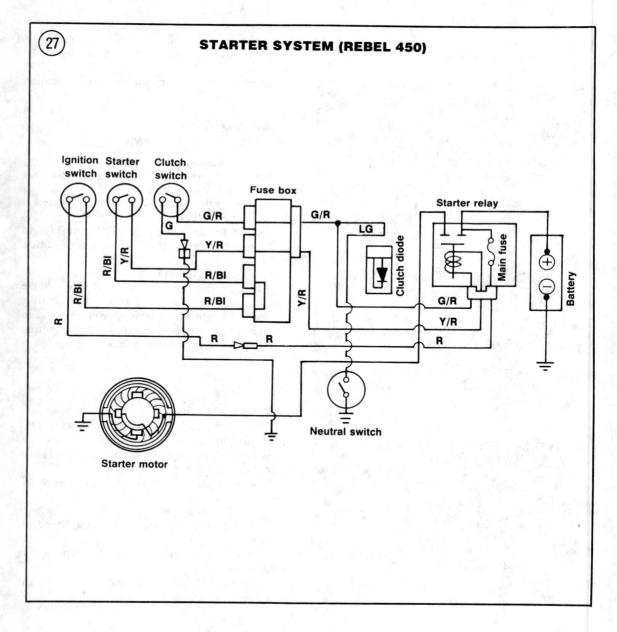

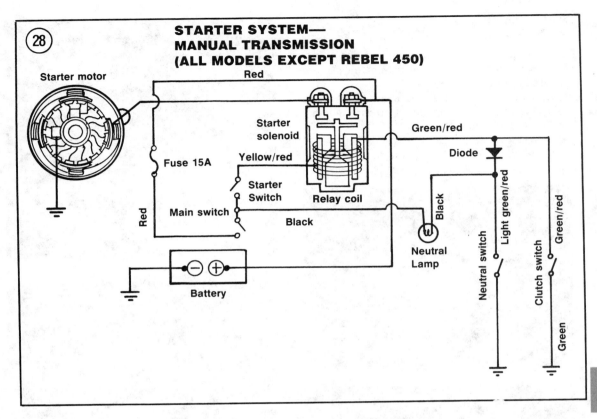

**(28) STARTER SYSTEM—
MANUAL TRANSMISSION
(ALL MODELS EXCEPT REBEL 450)**

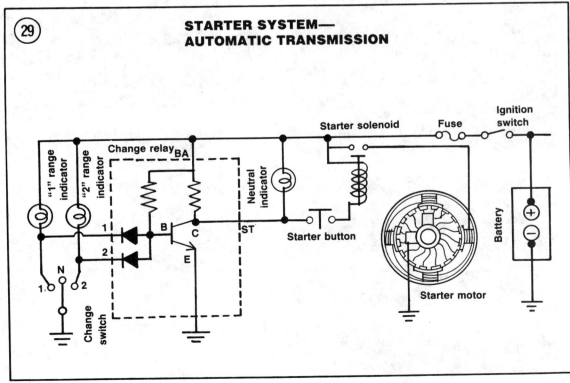

**(29) STARTER SYSTEM—
AUTOMATIC TRANSMISSION**

8

Starter Removal/Installation
(All Models Except Rebel 450)

1. Turn the ignition switch to the OFF position.
2. Disconnect the negative lead from the battery (**Figure 30**).
3. On automatic transmission models, remove the bolts (**Figure 31**) securing the oil pressure sending unit cover and remove the cover.
4. Disconnect the electrical cable (A, **Figure 32**) from the oil pressure sending unit.

5. Disconnect the starter electrical cable (B, **Figure 32**) from the starter.

6. Remove the bolts (C, **Figure 32**) securing the starter to the crankcase. Pull it to the right, carefully disengaging the gears and remove the starter.

7. Install by reversing the removal steps, noting the following.

8. Take care when installing the motor into the crankcase. Make sure that the gears mesh properly.

Starter Removal/Installation
(Rebel 450)

1. Turn the ignition switch to the OFF position.

2. Disconnect the negative lead from the battery **(Figure 33)**.

3. Disconnect the starter electrical cable **(Figure 34)** from the starter.

4. Remove the bolts securing the starter to the crankcase. Pull it to the right, carefully disengaging the gears, and remove the starter.

5. Install by reversing the removal steps, noting the following.

6. Take care when installing the motor into the crankcase. Make sure that the gears mesh properly.

Preliminary Inspection

The overhaul of a starter motor is best left to an expert. This procedure shows how to detect a defective starter.

Inspect the O-ring seal (A, **Figure 35**). O-ring seals tend to harden after prolonged use and heat and therefore lose their ability to seal properly; replace as necessary.

Inspect the gear (B, **Figure 35**) for chipped or missing teeth. If damaged, the starter assembly must be replaced.

Disassembly

Refer to **Figure 36** for this procedure.

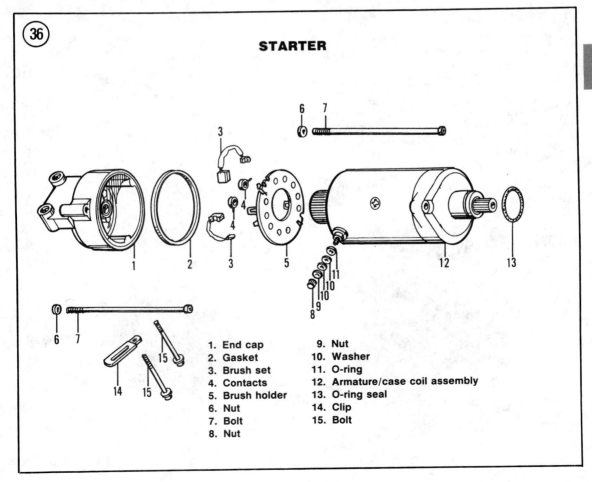

36 **STARTER**

1. End cap
2. Gasket
3. Brush set
4. Contacts
5. Brush holder
6. Nut
7. Bolt
8. Nut
9. Nut
10. Washer
11. O-ring
12. Armature/case coil assembly
13. O-ring seal
14. Clip
15. Bolt

8

1. Remove the case screws and washers (**Figure 37**), then separate the front and rear covers from the case.

> *NOTE*
> *Write down the number of shims used on the shaft next to the commutator and next to the rear cover. Be sure to install the same number when reassembling the starter.*

2. Remove the special washer and shims (**Figure 38**) from the front cover end of the shaft.

3. Remove the washers (**Figure 39**) from the armature end of the shaft.

4. Withdraw the armature coil assembly (**Figure 40**) from the front end of the case.

5. Remove the brush holder assembly (**Figure 41**) from the end of the case.

> *NOTE*
> *Before removing the nuts and washers, write down their description and order. They must be reinstalled in the same order to insulate this set of brushes from the case.*

6. Remove the nuts, washers and O-ring (A, **Figure 42**) securing the brush terminal set. Remove the brush terminal set (B, **Figure 42**).

> *CAUTION*
> *Do not immerse the wire windings in the case or the armature coil in solvent as the insulation may be damaged. Wipe the windings with a cloth lightly moistened with solvent and dry thoroughly.*

7. Clean all grease, dirt and carbon from all components.

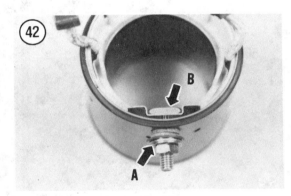

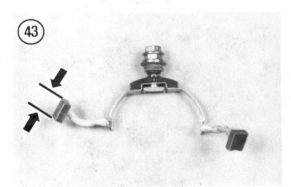

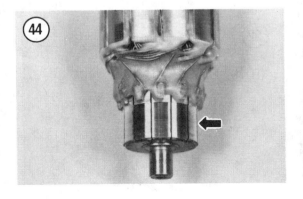

Inspection

1. Measure the length of each brush (**Figure 43**) with a vernier caliper. If the length is 6.5 mm (0.26 in.) or less for any one of the brushes, the brush holder assembly and brush terminal set must be replaced. The brushes cannot be replaced individually.

2. Inspect the commutator (**Figure 44**). The mica in a good commutator is below the surface of the copper bars. On a worn commutator the mica and copper bars may be worn to the same level (**Figure 45**). If necessary, have the commutator serviced by a dealer or electrical repair shop.

3. Inspect the commutator copper bars for discoloration. If a pair of bars are discolored, grounded armature coils are indicated.

4. Use an ohmmeter and perform the following:
   a. Check for continuity between the commutator bars (**Figure 46**); there should be continuity (indicated resistance) between pairs of bars.

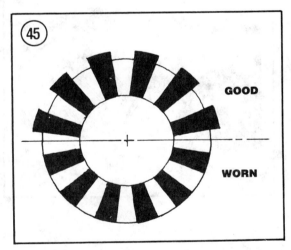

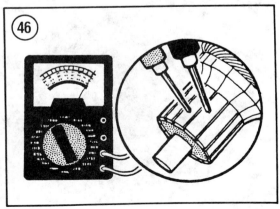

8

b. Check for continuity between the commutator bars and the shaft (**Figure 47**); there should be *no* continuity (infinite resistance).

c. If the unit fails either of these tests, the starter assembly must be replaced. The armature cannot be replaced individually.

5. Use an ohmmeter and perform the following:

a. Check for continuity between the starter cable terminal and the starter case; there should be continuity (indicated resistance).

b. Check for continuity between the starter cable terminal and the brush wire terminal; there should be *no* continuity (infinite resistance).

c. If the unit fails either of these tests, the starter assembly must be replaced. The case/field coil assembly cannot be replaced individually.

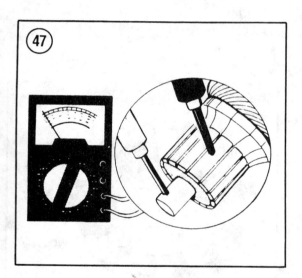

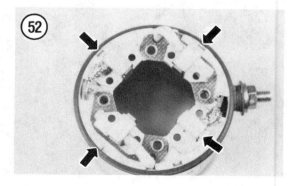

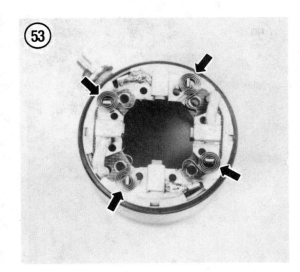

6. Inspect the oil seal and bushing (**Figure 48**) in the front cover for wear or damage. If either is damaged, replace the starter assembly as these parts are not available separately.

7. Inspect the bushing (**Figure 49**) in the rear cover for wear or damage. If it is damaged, replace the starter assembly as this part is not available separately.

Assembly

1. Install the brush holder assembly (**Figure 50**).

NOTE
In the next step, reinstall all parts in the same order as noted during removal. This is essential in order to insulate this set of brushes from the case.

2. Install the O-ring, washers and nuts (A, **Figure 42**) securing the brush terminal set to the case.

3. Install the brush holder assembly (**Figure 41**) onto the end of the case. Align the holder locating tab with the case notch (**Figure 51**).

4. Install the brushes into their receptacles (**Figure 52**).

5. Install the brush springs (**Figure 53**), but do not place them against the brushes at this time.

6. Insert the armature coil assembly (**Figure 40**) into the front end of the case. Do not damage the brushes during this step.

7. Bring the end of the spring up and onto the backside of the brush. Refer to **Figure 54** and **Figure 55** for correct spring-to-brush installation. Repeat for all remaining brushes.

8. Install the washers (**Figure 56**) onto the armature end of the shaft.

8

9. Align the raised tab on the brush holder with the locating notch (**Figure 57**) in the rear cover and install the rear cover.

10. Align the raised marks (**Figure 58**) on the rear cover with the case.

11. Install the shims and special washer (**Figure 59**) onto the front cover end of the shaft.

12. Install the front cover (A, **Figure 60**), then the case screws and washers (B, **Figure 60**). Tighten the screws securely (**Figure 61**).

STARTER SOLENOID

Testing (Rebel 450)

1. Remove the bolt securing the battery outer cover (**Figure 62**) and pivot the cover down.

2. Pivot the battery inner cover (**Figure 63**) down and out of the way.

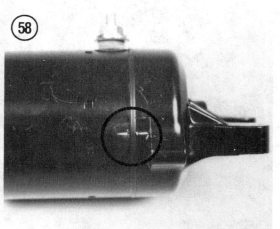

3. Remove the bolt securing the starter solenoid cover (**Figure 64**). Carefully disengage the locking tabs on the cover and remove the cover.

4. Pull the plastic cover (**Figure 65**) away from the electrical connector and the starter solenoid.

5. Shift the transmission into NEUTRAL.

6. Turn the ignition switch ON and pull the clutch lever in.

7. Press the START button. The solenoid should click. If it does not click the solenoid may be faulty and should be checked further.

8. Disconnect the electrical connector (**Figure 66**) from the top of the main fuse.

9. Remove the nuts and washers, then disconnect the electrical connectors from the starter solenoid.

8

10. Connect a 12-volt battery to the electrical connectors as follows (**Figure 67**):
  a. Yellow/red wire to the positive (+) battery terminal.
  b. Green/red wire to the negative (-) battery terminal.
11. With the 12-volt battery connected, connect an ohmmeter between the positive and negative terminals on top of the solenoid and check for continuity:
  a. If there is continuity (low resistance) the solenoid is okay.
  b. If there is no continuity (infinite resistance), the solenoid is faulty and must be replaced.
12. Turn the ignition switch OFF.
13. Disconnect the 12-volt battery from the electrical connectors.
14. Install both electrical wires to the solenoid and tighten the nuts securely. Make sure the electrical connectors are on tight and that the plastic boot is properly installed to keep out moisture.
15. Install the starter solenoid cover (**Figure 64**). Carefully engage the locking tabs on the cover and install the bolt. Tighten the bolt securely.
16. Pivot the battery inner cover up.
17. Pivot the battery outer cover up and install the bolt. Tighten the bolt securely.

Testing (All Models Except Rebel 450)

1. Remove the right-hand side cover.
2A. On 1986 CB450SC models, pull the plastic cover away from the top of the electrical connector and the starter solenoid.
2B. On all other models, pull the rubber cover (**Figure 68**) away from the top of the starter solenoid.
3. Shift the transmission into NEUTRAL.
4. Turn the ignition switch ON and pull the clutch lever in.
5. Press the START button. The solenoid should click. If it does not click the solenoid may be faulty and should be checked further.
6A. On 1986 CB450SC models, perform the following:
  a. Disconnect the electrical connector from the top of the main fuse.
  b. Remove the nuts and washers, then disconnect the electrical wires from the terminals on top of the solenoid.
6B. On all other models, remove the nuts and washers, then disconnect the electrical wires from the terminals on top of the solenoid.

7A. On 1986 CD450SC models, connect a 12-volt battery to the electrical connectors as follows: (**Figure 67**):
  a. Yellow/red wire to the positive (+) battery terminal.
  b. Green/red wire to the negative (-) battery terminal.
7B. On all other models, connect a 12-volt battery to the electrical connectors as follows: (**Figure 69**):
  a. Yellow/red wire to the positive (+) battery terminal.
  b. Green/red wire to the negative (-) battery terminal.
8. With the 12-volt battery connected, connect an ohmmeter between the positive and negative terminals on top of the solenoid and check for continuity:
  a. If there is continuity (low resistance) the solenoid is okay.
  b. If there is no continuity (infinite resistance), the solenoid is faulty and must be replaced.
9. Turn the ignition switch OFF.
10. Disconnect the 12-volt battery from the electrical connectors.
11. Install both electrical wires to the solenoid and tighten the nuts securely. Make sure the electrical connectors are on tight and that the rubber boot is properly installed to keep out moisture.

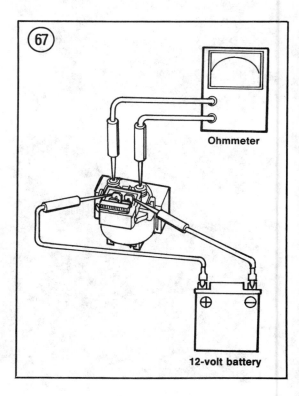

(67)

Ohmmeter

12-volt battery

Removal/Installation
(Rebel 450)

1. Remove the bolt securing the battery outer cover (**Figure 62**) and pivot the cover down.
2. Pivot the battery inner cover (**Figure 63**) down and out of the way.
3. Remove the bolt securing the starter solenoid cover (**Figure 64**). Carefully disengage the locking tabs on the cover and remove the cover.

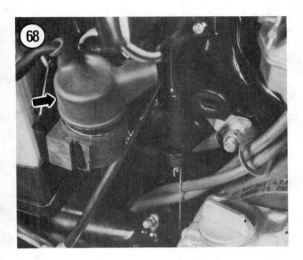

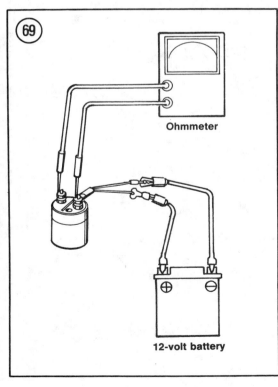

Ohmmeter

12-volt battery

4. Pull the plastic cover (**Figure 65**) away from the electrical connector and the starter solenoid.
5. Disconnect the electrical connector (**Figure 66**) from the top of the main fuse.
6. Remove the nuts and washers, then disconnect the electrical connectors from the starter solenoid.
7. Remove the solenoid from the rubber mount on the frame.
8. Replace by reversing these removal steps, noting the following.
9. Install both electrical wires to the solenoid and tighten the nuts securely. Make sure the electrical connectors are on tight and that the rubber boot is properly installed to keep out moisture.

Removal/Installation
(All Models Except Rebel 450)

1. Remove the right-hand side cover.
2A. On 1986 CB450SC models, pull the plastic cover away from the top of the electrical connector and the starter solenoid.
2B. On all other models, pull the rubber cover (**Figure 68**) away from the top of the starter solenoid.
3. On 1986 CB450SC models, disconnect the electrical connector from the top of the main fuse.
4. Remove the nuts and washers, then disconnect the electrical wires from the terminals on top of the solenoid.
5. Remove the solenoid from the rubber mount on the frame.
6. Replace by reversing these removal steps, noting the following.
7. Install both electrical wires to the solenoid and tighten the nuts securely. Make sure the electrical connectors are on tight and that the rubber boot is properly installed to keep out moisture.

LIGHTING SYSTEM

The lighting system consists of the headlight, taillight/brakelight combination, directional signals, warning lights, and speedometer and tachometer illumination lights. **Table 4** lists replacement bulbs for these components.

Always use the correct wattage bulb as indicated in this section. The use of a larger wattage bulb will give a dim light and a smaller wattage bulb will burn out prematurely.

Headlight Replacement
(Rebel 450)

Refer to **Figure 70** for this procedure.
1. Remove the screw (**Figure 71**) on each side securing the headlight lens assembly to the case.

8

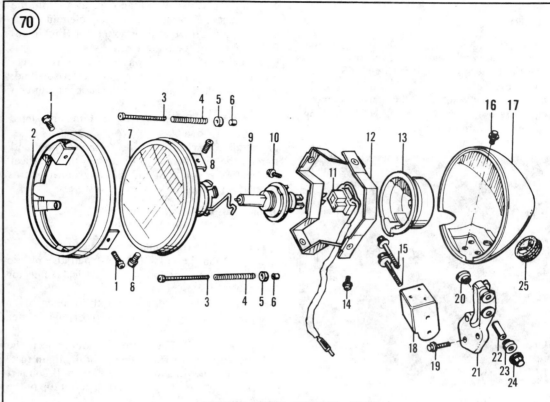

HEADLIGHT (REBEL 450)
1. Screw
2. Trim bezel
3. Adjust screw
4. Spring
5. Nut
6. Cover
7. Headlight lens
8. Screw
9. Bulb
10. Screw
11. Socket/wire harness assembly
12. Mounting bracket
13. Rubber dust cover
14. Screw
15. Bolt
16. Bolt
17. Case
18. Mounting bracket
19. Bolt
20. Rubber bushing
21. Case mounting bracket
22. Collar
23. Rubber bushing
24. Nut
25. Rubber grommet

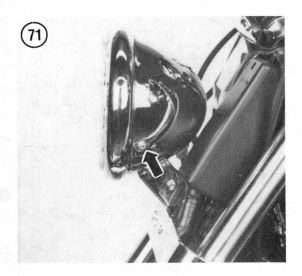

2. Pull the headlight lens assembly out and up at the bottom and unhook the assembly from the case.

3. Remove the headlight lens assembly.

4. Disconnect the electrical connector (**Figure 72**) from the backside of the headlight bulb.

5. Remove the rubber dust cover.

> *CAUTION*
> *Carefully read all instructions shipped with the replacement quartz bulb. Do not touch the bulb glass with your fingers because any traces of skin oil on the quartz halogen bulb will drastically reduce bulb life. Clean any traces of oil from the bulb with a cloth moistened in alcohol or lacquer thinner.*

6. Unhook the clip (A, **Figure 73**) and remove the light bulb (B, **Figure 73**). Replace with a new bulb.

7. To remove the trim bezel from headlight lens assembly, perform the following:

    a. Remove the adjusting screws (A, **Figure 74**) and the headlight mounting nuts (B, **Figure 74**).

    b. Remove the trim bezel from the headlight lens and mounting bracket assembly.

8. Install by reversing these removal steps, noting the following.

9. Don't forget the spring on each adjusting screw.

10. Adjust the headlight as described under *Headlight Adjustment* in this chapter.

**Headlight Replacement
(All Models Except Rebel 450)**

Refer to **Figure 75** for this procedure.

1. Remove the mounting screws on each side of the headlight housing.

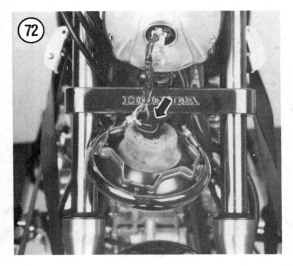

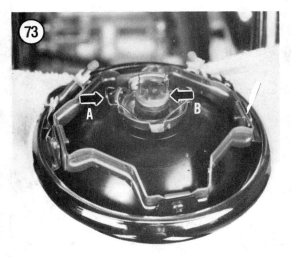

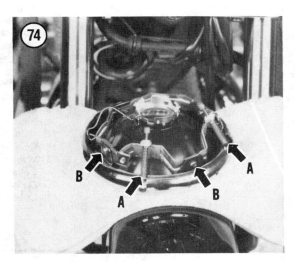

2. Pull the headlight assembly out and up at the bottom and unhook the unit from the case.

3. Remove the headlight assembly.

4. Disconnect the electrical connector from the backside of the headlight sealed beam unit.

5. Remove the 2 retaining screws (A, **Figure 76**) and the adjusting bolt, nut and spring (B, **Figure 76**).

6. Remove the trim bezel and the sealed beam.

7. Install by reversing these removal steps, noting the following.

8. Don't forget the spring on the adjusting bolt.

9. Adjust the headlight as described under *Headlight Adjustment* in this chapter.

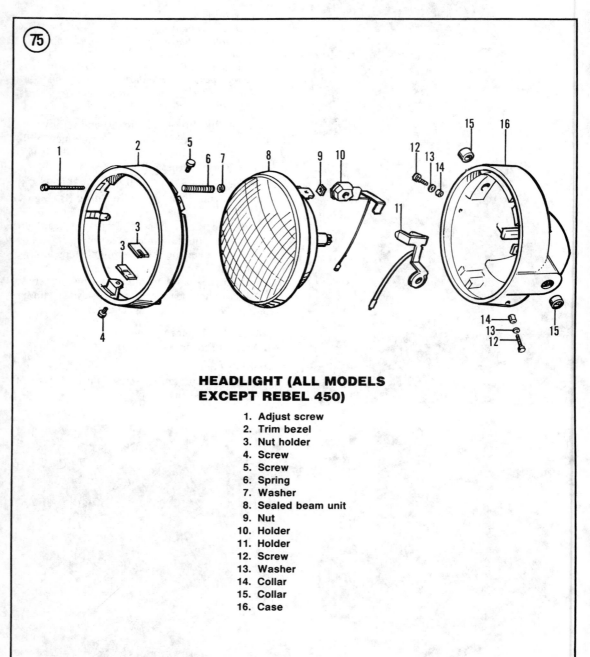

HEADLIGHT (ALL MODELS EXCEPT REBEL 450)

1. Adjust screw
2. Trim bezel
3. Nut holder
4. Screw
5. Screw
6. Spring
7. Washer
8. Sealed beam unit
9. Nut
10. Holder
11. Holder
12. Screw
13. Washer
14. Collar
15. Collar
16. Case

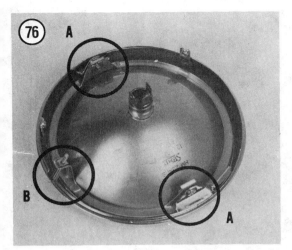

Headlight Adjustment
(All Models Except Rebel 450)

Adjust the headlight horizontally and vertically according to Department of Motor Vehicle regulations in your area.

To adjust the headlight horizontally, turn the screw (A, **Figure 77**). To adjust the headlight vertically, loosen the turn signal arms (B, **Figure 77**). Move headlight to desired position, then tighten screw and arms.

Headlight Adjustment
(Rebel 450)

Adjust the headlight horizontally and vertically according to Department of Motor Vehicle regulations in your area.

To adjust the headlight horizontally, turn the adjust screw (A, **Figure 78**). Turning the screw clockwise, move the light beam to the right of the rider.

To adjust the headlight vertically, turn the adjust screw (B, **Figure 78**). Turning the screw clockwise, move the light beam up.

Taillight Replacement
(All Models Except Rebel 450)

1. Remove the screws (**Figure 79**) securing the lens and remove the lens.
2. Wash out the inside and outside of the lens with a mild detergent and wipe dry.
3. Wipe off the reflective base surrounding the bulb with a soft cloth.
4. Replace the bulb and install the lens; do not overtighten screws or the lens may crack.

Taillight Replacement
(Rebel 450)

1. Remove the screws securing the lens (**Figure 80**) and remove the lens.

8

2. Wash out the inside and outside of the lens with a mild detergent and wipe dry.
3. Wipe off the reflective base surrounding the bulbs with a soft cloth.
4. Replace the bulbs (**Figure 81**) and install the lens; do not overtighten screws or the lens may crack.

License Plate Light Replacement (Rebel 450)

1. Remove the nuts on the backside of the case/lens assembly (**Figure 82**).
2. Remove the case/lens assembly.
3. Wash out the inside and outside of the lens with a mild detergent and wipe dry.
4. Wipe off the reflective base surrounding the bulb with a soft cloth.
5. Replace the bulb.
6. Install the case/lens assembly and tighten the nuts securely.

Turn Signal Light Replacement

1. Remove the screws (**Figure 83**) securing the lens and remove the lens.
2. Wash out the inside and outside of it with a mild detergent.
3. Replace the bulb.
4. Install the lens; do not overtighten the screws as that will crack the lens.

Speedometer and Tachometer Illumination Light Replacement (CB400T I, CB400T II, CB400A)

1. Unscrew the speedometer and tachometer cables from the backside of their respective meters.
2. Remove the screws (**Figure 84**) securing the top of the instrument cluster and remove the top.
3. Remove the nuts securing the lower portion of the instrument cluster. Pull the lower portion down to gain access to the bulb(s) at the bottom of each unit.
4. Pull the bulb holder out and replace the bulb(s).
5. Push the lower portion of the instrument cluster up and install the nuts.
6. Install the top of the instrument cluster and screws. Tighten the screws securely.
7. Screw the speedometer and tachometer cables into the backside of their respective meters.

Speedometer Illumination Light Replacement (Rebel 450)

> *NOTE*
> *The Rebel 450 is not equipped with a tachometer.*

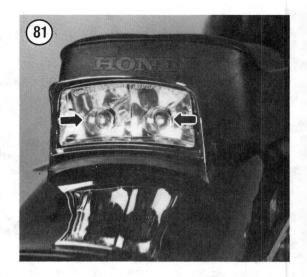

1. Unscrew the speedometer cable (A, **Figure 85**) from the backside of the meter.
2. Remove the screws (B, **Figure 85**) securing the speedometer to the case.
3. Pull the speedometer unit (C, **Figure 85**) up and out of the case (D, **Figure 85**) to gain access to the bulb(s) at the bottom of the unit.
4. Pull the bulb holder out and replace the bulb(s).
5. Push the speedometer unit into the case install the screws. Tighten the screws securely.
6. Screw the speedometer cable into the backside of the meter.

Speedometer and Tachometer Illumination Light Replacement (All Other Models)

1. Unscrew the speedometer and the tachometer cable from the backside of their respective meter.
2. Remove the nuts securing the meter to the meter base.
3. Pull the meter unit up and out of the meter base to gain access to the bulb(s) at the bottom of the unit.
4. Pull the bulb holder out and replace the bulb(s).
5. Push the meter back into the meter base and install the nuts. Tighten the nuts securely.
6. Screw the speedometer or the tachometer cable into the backside of their respective meter.

Indicator Light Replacement (CB400T I, CB400T II, CB400A)

1. Remove the screws (**Figure 84**) securing the top of the instrument cluster and remove the top.
2. Remove and replace the defective bulb(s).
3. Install the cluster top and screws. Tighten the screws securely.

Indicator Light Replacement (Rebel 450)

1. Remove the bolts (A, **Figure 86**) securing the speedometer housing and the indicator panel assembly.
2. Move the speedometer housing (B, **Figure 86**) slightly forward and out of the way.
3. Carefully pull the indicator panel assembly (C, **Figure 86**) up and away from the handlebars.
4. From the underside of the indicator panel, remove and replace the defective bulb(s).
5. Move the indicator panel back into position.
6. Move the speedometer housing back into position. Place the speedometer housing mounting plate on top of the indicator panel mounting tabs and install the bolts. Tighten the bolts securely.

8

Indicator Light Replacement
(All Other Models)

1. Remove the screws (**Figure 87**) securing the top
of the instrument cluster and remove the top.
2. Remove and replace the defective bulb(s).
3. Install the cluster top and screws. Tighten the
screws securely.

Front Brake Switch Replacement

1. Pull back on the rubber boot from the switch.
2. Pull the electrical wires from the connectors and
remove the switch. Refer to **Figure 88** for drum
type brakes or **Figure 89** for disc type brakes.
3. Remove the screw securing the switch and
remove the switch.
4. Install a new switch and reconnect the electrical
wires onto the switch connectors.

Rear Brake Light Switch
Replacement

1. On all models except Rebel 450, remove the
right-hand side cover.
2. Unhook the spring from the brake arm.
3. Unscrew the switch housing and locknut from
the bracket (**Figure 90**).
4. Pull up the rubber boot and remove the
electrical wires.
5. Replace the switch; reinstall and adjust the
switch as described under *Rear Brake Light Switch
Adjustment* in this chapter.

Rear Brake Light Switch
Adjustment

1. Turn the ignition switch to the ON position.
2. Depress the brake pedal. The light should come
on just as the brake begins to work.

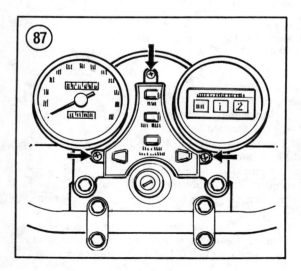

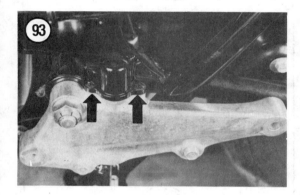

3. To make the light come on earlier, hold the switch body and turn adjusting locknut (**Figure 91**) clockwise as viewed from the top. Turn the nut counterclockwise to delay the light.

NOTE
Some riders prefer the light to come on a little early. This way they can tap the pedal without braking to warn drivers who follow too closely.

CLUTCH SWITCH

Replacement
(Models So Equipped)

1. Pull back on the rubber boot from the switch.
2. Pull the electrical wires from the connectors.
3. Remove the screw securing the switch and remove the switch.
4. Install a new switch and reconnect the electrical wires onto the switch connectors.

SIDESTAND SWITCH

Replacement
(Models So Equipped)

1. Raise the sidestand and remove the switch return spring (**Figure 92**) from the bottom of the switch.
2. Disconnect the electrical wires from the switch.
3. Remove the screws (**Figure 93**) securing the cap and remove the cap.
4. Remove the switch.
5. Attach the spring onto the switch.
6. Align switch lug with the step in the holder and insert the switch and spring.
7. Attach the electrical wires and hook the spring onto the sidestand.

HORN

Removal/Installation

NOTE
The horn location varies among the various models and years. This procedure is typical for all models.

1. Disconnect electrical connector (**Figure 94**) from the horn.
2. Remove the bolt securing horn to bracket (**Figure 95**).
3. Install the bolt and tighten securely.
4. Connect the electrical connector to the horn.

Horn Testing

1. Disconnect horn wires from harness.
2. Connect horn wires to 12-volt battery. If it is good, it will sound. If not, replace the horn.

8

INSTRUMENT CLUSTER

Removal/Installation
(All Models Except Rebel 450)

1. Remove the right-hand side cover.
2. Disconnect the negative lead from the battery.
3. Remove the speedometer drive cable (**Figure 96**) and tachometer drive cable on models so equipped.
4. Remove the headlight lens as described in this chapter.
5. Disconnect all terminal connectors leading to the instrument cluster.
6A. On CB400T I, CB400T II, CB400A, remove the bolts (**Figure 97**) securing the instrument cluster to the attachment bracket and remove the cluster assembly.
6B. On all other models except Rebel 450, remove the bolts (**Figure 98**) securing the instrument cluster to the attachment bracket and remove the cluster assembly.
7. Install by reversing these removal steps.

SPEEDOMETER AND INDICATOR PANEL

Removal/Installation (Rebel 450)

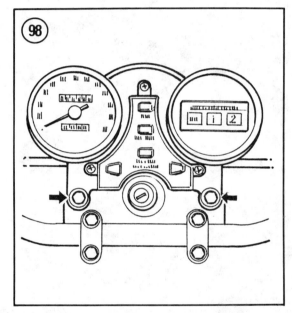

> *NOTE*
> *The Rebel 450 is not equipped with a tachometer. The indicator panel is removed at the same time along with the speedometer since the illumination light electrical harness is tied into both components.*

1. Unscrew the speedometer cable (A, **Figure 85**) from the backside of the meter.
2. Remove the screws securing the electrical connector junction box cover (**Figure 99**) and remove the cover.
3. Within the junction box, disconnect the electrical connectors (**Figure 100**) for the speedometer and the indicator light panel.

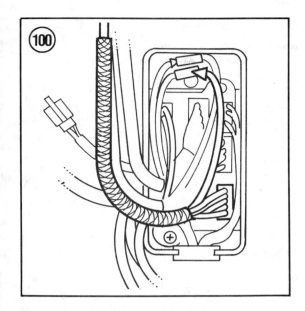

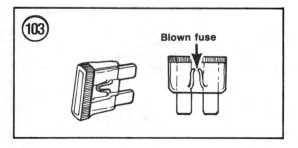

Blown fuse

4. Remove the bolts (A, **Figure 86**) securing the speedometer housing and the indicator panel assembly.

5. Move the speedometer housing (B, **Figure 86**) slightly forward and away from the handlebar.

6. Carefully pull the indicator panel assembly up and away from the handlebars.

7. Carefully pull the illumination light electrical wire harness for the speedometer and indicator panel out from the steering stem area. Note the path of the wire harness as it must be installed in the same location.

8. Remove the speedometer and the indicator panel.

9. Install by reversing these steps, noting the following.

10. Move the indicator panel back into position.

11. Move the speedometer housing back into position. Place the speedometer housing mounting plate on top of the indicator panel mounting tabs and install the bolts. Tighten the bolts securely.

12. Do not bind or catch any electrical wires when installing the electrical connector junction box cover. Install the cover and tighten the screws securely.

13. Screw the speedometer cable into the backside of the meter.

8

FUSES

The number of fuses varies from model to model. The fuses are located in a fuse panel next to the battery. Inside the fuse box cover are two spare fuses; always carry spares.

On 1986-on models the main fuse (**Figure 101**) is located at the top of the starter solenoid. There is a spare fuse (**Figure 102**) under the solenoid; always carry spares.

NOTE
*On 1986-on models, the fuses (**Figure 103**) are not the typical glass with metal ends as used on the previous years.*

Whenever a fuse blows, find out the reason for the failure before replacing the fuse. Usually, the trouble is a short circuit in the wiring. This may be caused by worn-through insulation or a disconnected wire shorting to ground.

CAUTION
Never substitute aluminum foil or wire for a fuse. Never use a higher amperage fuse that specified. An overload could result in fire and complete loss of the bike.

Table 1 ALTERNATOR STATOR RESISTANCE *

Terminals	Resistance value (ohms)
1978-1981 Manual transmission	
Green-White	
1980 CM400T	300-400
All other models	400-500
Blue-White	75-130
Green-Brown	75-130
Green-Blue	75-130
Green-Pink	120-180
1978-1981 Automatic transmission	
Blue-White	4-7
White-Green	200-500
Brown-Orange	100-200
Pink-Green	10-30
Yellow-Yellow	0.2-1
Yellow-Yellow	0.2-1
Yellow-Yellow	0.2-1
1982-1983 Manual transmission	
Green-White	315-385
Blue-White	77-95
Green-Brown	76-92
Green-Light blue	95-116
Green-Pink	126-154
1982-1983 Automatic transmission	
Green-White	200-500
Blue-White	4-7
Brown-orange	100-200
Green-Pink	10-30
* Honda does not provide specifications for all models.	

Table 2 CDI TROUBLESHOOTING

Symptoms	Probable Cause
Weak spark	Poor connections (clean and retighten)
	High voltage leak (replace defective wire)
	Defective coil (replace ignition coil)
No spark	Wiring broken (replace wire)
	Defective ignition (replace coil)
	Defective pulser coil in magneto (replace coil)

Table 3 STARTER TROUBLESHOOTING

Symptom	Probable Cause	Remedy

Starter does not work	Low battery
	Worn brushes
	Defective relay
	Defective switch
	Defective wiring
	  or connection
	Internal short circuit
		Recharge battery
		Replace brushes
		Repair or replace
		Repair or replace
		Repair wire or clean
		  component
		Repair or replace defective
		  component

Starter action
  is weak
	Low battery
	Pitted relay contacts
	Worn brushes
	Defective connection
	Short circuit in
	  commutator
		Recharge battery
		Clean or replace
		Replace brushes
		Clean and tighten
		Replace armature

Starter runs continuously	Stuck relay	Replace relay

Starter turns;
  does not
  turn engine
	Defective starter
	  clutch
		Replace starter
		  clutch

Table 4 REPLACEMENT BULBS

Item	Number
Headlight	
Rebel 450	12V 60/55W
All other models	12V 50/35W
Tail/brakelight	SAE 1157
Directional	
Front	
1978-1983	SAE 1034
1985-on	SAE 1073
Rear	SAE 1073
Instrument lights	SAE 57
Running light	SAE 1034
(models so equipped)	

8

CHAPTER NINE

FRONT SUSPENSION AND STEERING

This chapter describes procedures for repair and maintenance of the front wheel, front forks and steering components.

Tables 1-3 are located at the end of this chapter.

FRONT WHEEL
(1980-1983 DRUM BRAKE)

Removal

1. Place wood blocks under the crankcase to support the bike securely with the front wheel off the ground.
2. Remove the set screw securing the speedometer cable (A, **Figure 1**) and pull the cable out of the speedometer housing.
3. Remove the bolt and lockwasher (B, **Figure 1**) securing the torque link to the brake panel.
4. Remove cotter pin (C, **Figure 1**) securing the brake cable to the leading brake arm. Discard the cotter pin. Never reuse a cotter pin as it may break and fall out.
5. Unhook the brake cable from the receptacle (D, **Figure 1**) on the brake backing plate.
6. Remove the axle nut cotter pin and discard it. Never reuse a cotter pin as it may break and fall out.
7. Remove axle nut (E, **Figure 1**).
8. Remove the axle holder nuts (**Figure 2**), lockwashers and washers. Remove the front axle holder.

9. Push the axle out from the left-hand side. Use a drift or screwdriver and remove the axle.
10. Remove the front wheel.
11. Inspect the front wheel as described under *Front Wheel Inspection (All Models)* in this chapter.

Installation

1. Make sure the axle bearing surfaces of the fork sliders are free from burrs and nicks.
2. Clean the front axle in solvent and dry it thoroughly. Make sure all surfaces that the axle comes in contact with are clean and free from road dirt and old grease prior to installation.
3. Position the front wheel and insert the axle from the right-hand side. The speedometer gear box must be horizontal in order to accept the speedometer cable.
4. Install the front axle holder with the "F" mark and arrow facing forward. Install the washers, lockwashers and nuts. Tighten the nuts lightly.
5. Install the front axle nut. Hold onto the front axle with a wrench and tighten the axle nut to the torque specification listed in **Table 1**. Install a new cotter pin and bend the ends over completely.
6. Insert the brake cable through the receptacle (D, **Figure 1**) on the brake backing plate.
7. Attach the brake cable to the leading brake arm and install a new cotter pin. Never reuse a cotter pin as it may break and fall out.

8. Install the lockwasher and bolt (B, **Figure 1**) securing the torque link to the brake panel. Tighten the bolt to the torque specification listed in **Table 1**.

9. Spin the front wheel slowly and insert the speedometer cable into the speedometer gear box. Install and tighten the set screw securely.

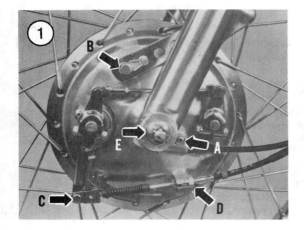

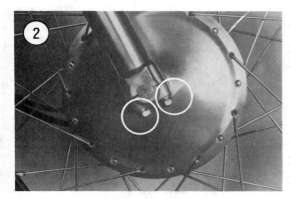

10. Remove the wood blocks from under the crankcase.

11. With the front brake applied, push down hard on the handlebars and pump the forks several times to seat the front axle within the front forks.

12. Tighten the front axle holder nuts. Tighten the front nut first and then the rear nut. Tighten the nuts to the torque specification listed in **Table 1**.

> *WARNING*
> *The axle holder nuts must be tightened in this manner and to this torque value. After installation is complete, there will be a slight gap at the rear, with no gap at the front. If done incorrectly, the studs may fail, resulting in the loss of control of the bike when riding.*

13. After the wheel is installed completely, rotate it. Apply and release the brake several times to make sure the wheel rotates freely and that the brake is operating properly.

14. Adjust the brake lever free play as described under *Front Brake (Drum Type) Adjustment* in Chapter Three.

FRONT WHEEL
(SINGLE PISTON CALIPER DISC BRAKE)

1. Place wood blocks under the crankcase to support the bike securely with the front wheel off the ground.

2. Remove the set screw securing the speedometer cable (A, **Figure 3**) and pull the cable out of the speedometer housing.

3. Remove the axle nut cotter pin and discard it. Never reuse a cotter pin as it may break and fall out.

4. Remove axle nut (B, **Figure 3**).

5. Remove the axle holder nuts, lockwashers and washers. Remove the front axle holder.

6. Push the axle out from the left-hand side. Use a drift or screwdriver and remove the axle.

7. Pull the front wheel forward to disengage the brake disc from the caliper assembly. Remove the front wheel.

> *CAUTION*
> *Do not set the wheel down on the disc surface as it may get scratched or warped. Set the wheel on 2 blocks of wood.*

> *NOTE*
> *Insert a piece of wood or vinyl tubing in the caliper in place of the disc. That way, if the brake lever is inadvertently squeezed, the piston will not be forced out of the cylinder. If this does happen,*

the caliper might have to be disassembled to reseat the piston and the system will have to be bled. By using the wood or vinyl tubing, bleeding the brake is not necessary when installing the wheel.

8. Inspect the front wheel as described under *Front Wheel Inspection (All Models)* in this chapter.

Installation

1. Make sure the axle bearing surfaces of the fork sliders are free from burrs and nicks.
2. Clean the front axle in solvent and dry it thoroughly. Make sure all surfaces that the axle comes in contact with are clean and free from road dirt and old grease prior to installation.
3. Remove the piece of wood or vinyl tubing from the brake caliper.
4. Position the front wheel, and carefully insert the disc between the brake pads.
5. Insert the axle from the right-hand side. The speedometer gear box must be horizontal in order to accept the speedometer cable.
6. Install the front axle holder with the "F" mark and arrow facing forward. Install the washers, lockwashers and nuts. Tighten the nuts only finger-tight at this time.
7. Install the front axle nut. Hold onto the front axle with a wrench and tighten the axle nut to the torque specification listed in **Table 1**. Install a new cotter pin and bend the ends over completely.
8. Spin the front wheel slowly and insert the speedometer cable into the speedometer gear box. Install and tighten the set screw securely.
9. Remove the wood blocks from under the crankcase.
10. With the front brake applied, push down hard on the handlebars and pump the forks several times to seat the front axle within the front forks.
11. Tighten the front axle holder nuts. Tighten the front nut first and then the rear nut. Tighten the nuts to the torque specification listed in **Table 1**.

> *WARNING*
> *The axle holder nuts must be tightened in this manner and to this torque value. After installation is complete, there will be a slight gap at the rear, with no gap at the front. If done incorrectly, the studs may fail, resulting in the loss of control of the bike when riding.*

12. After the wheel is installed completely, rotate it. Apply the brake several times to make sure it rotates freely and that the brake is operating properly.

13. Adjust the brake lever free play as described under *Front Brake (Drum Type) Adjustment* in Chapter Three.

FRONT WHEEL (DUAL-PISTON CALIPER MODELS EXCEPT REBEL 450)

Removal

1. Place wood blocks under the engine to support the bike securely with the front wheel off of the ground.
2. Remove the front brake caliper as described under *Front Brake Caliper Removal* in Chapter Eleven. Refer to A, **Figure 4** or A, **Figure 5**.
3. Tie the caliper up to the front fork to relieve strain on the brake line.
4. Unscrew the speedometer cable set screw and pull the speedometer cable free from the hub. Refer to B, **Figure 4** for CB450SC models or B, **Figure 5** for all other models.
5A. On models so equipped, remove the cotter pin and remove the axle nut. Discard the cotter pin.

5B. On all other models remove the self-locking nut (C, **Figure 4**).

6. Remove the front axle holder nuts, lockwashers and washers on the right-hand fork leg. Remove the front axle holder.

7. Withdraw the front axle from the right-hand side.

8. Pull the wheel down and forward being careful not to damage the studs on the right-hand fork leg. Remove the front wheel.

> *CAUTION*
> *Do not set the wheel down on the disc surface as it may get scratched or warped. Set the wheel on 2 blocks of wood.*

> *NOTE*
> *Insert a piece of wood or vinyl tubing in the caliper in place of the disc. That way, if the brake lever is inadvertently squeezed, the pistons will not be forced out of the cylinders. If this does happen, the caliper might have to be disassembled to reseat the pistons and the system would have to be bled. By using the wood, bleeding the brake is not necessary when installing the wheel.*

9. Inspect the wheel as described under *Front Wheel Inspection (All Models)* in this chapter.

Installation

1. Make sure the axle bearing surfaces of the fork sliders are free from burrs and nicks.

2. Clean the front axle in solvent and dry it thoroughly. Make sure all surfaces that the axle comes in contact with are clean and free from road dirt and old grease prior to installation.

3. Remove the piece of wood or vinyl tubing from the brake caliper.

4. Position the front wheel, and carefully insert the disc between the brake pads.

5. Install the front axle from the right-hand side.

6. Install the axle holder with the arrow facing forward. Install the washers, lockwashers and nuts. Tighten the nuts only finger-tight at this time.

7. Position the speedometer housing so that the cable inlet is at the 4 o'clock position. Also make sure the tang on the speedometer housing is located in back of the lug on the fork slider. This is necessary for proper speedometer operation.

8. Install the front axle nut. Hold onto the front axle with a wrench and tighten the axle nut to the torque specification listed in **Table 1**. Install a new cotter pin and bend the ends over completely.

9. Spin the front wheel slowly and insert the speedometer cable into the speedometer gear box. Install and tighten the set screw securely.

10. Install the front brake caliper as described under *Front Brake Caliper Installation* in chapter Eleven.

11. Remove the wood blocks from under the crankcase.

12. With the front brake applied, push down hard on the handlebars and pump the forks several times to seat the front axle within the front forks.

13. Tighten the front axle holder nuts. Tighten the front nut first and then the rear nut. Tighten the nuts to the torque specification listed in **Table 1**.

> *WARNING*
> *The axle holder nuts must be tightened in this manner and to this torque value. After installation is complete, there will be a slight gap at the rear, with no gap at the front. If done incorrectly, the studs may fail, resulting in the loss of control of the bike when riding.*

14. After the wheel is installed completely, rotate it. Apply and release the brake several times to make sure the wheel rotates freely and that the brake is operating properly.

FRONT WHEEL (REBEL 450)

Removal

1. Place wood blocks under the engine to support the bike securely with the front wheel off of the ground.

2. Unscrew the speedometer cable set screw (**Figure 6**) and pull the speedometer cable free from the hub.

3. Remove the front brake caliper as described under *Front Brake Caliper Removal* in Chapter Eleven.

4. Tie the caliper up to the front fork to relieve strain on the brake line.

5. Loosen the front axle holder nuts (**Figure 7**) on the right-hand fork leg. It is not necessary to remove the front axle holder, just loosen it enough to clear the front axle.

6. Loosen the front axle (**Figure 8**).

7. Withdraw the front axle from the right-hand side.

8. Pull the wheel down and forward and remove the front wheel.

> *CAUTION*
> *Do not set the wheel down on the disc surface as it may get scratched or warped. Set the wheel on 2 blocks of wood (**Figure 9**).*

> *NOTE*
> *Insert a piece of wood or vinyl tubing in the caliper in place of the disc. That way, if the brake lever is inadvertently squeezed, the pistons will not be forced out of the cylinders. If this does happen, the caliper might have to be disassembled to reseat the pistons and the system would have to be bled. By using the wood, bleeding the brake is not necessary when installing the wheel.*

9. Inspect the wheel as described under *Front Wheel Inspection (All Models)* in this chapter.

Installation

1. Make sure the axle bearing surfaces of the fork sliders are free from burrs and nicks.

2. Clean the front axle in solvent and dry it thoroughly. Make sure all surfaces that the axle comes in contact with are clean and free from road dirt and old grease prior to installation.

3. Remove the piece of wood or vinyl tubing from the brake caliper.

4. Position the front wheel, and carefully insert the disc between the brake pads.

5. Install the front axle from the right-hand side.

6. Tighten the front axle holder nuts only finger-tight at this time.

7. Position the speedometer housing so that the cable inlet is at the 4 o'clock position. Also make sure the tang on the speedometer housing is located in back of the lug on the fork slider. This is necessary for proper speedometer operation.

8. Tighten the axle to the torque specification listed in **Table 1**.

9. Spin the front wheel slowly and insert the speedometer cable into the speedometer gear box. Install and tighten the set screw securely.

10. Install the front brake caliper as described under *Front Brake Caliper Installation* in chapter Eleven.

11. Remove the wood blocks from under the crankcase.

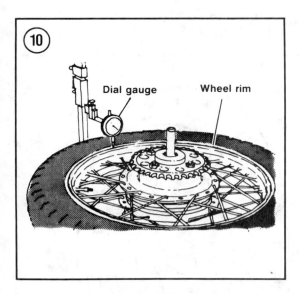

Dial gauge   Wheel rim

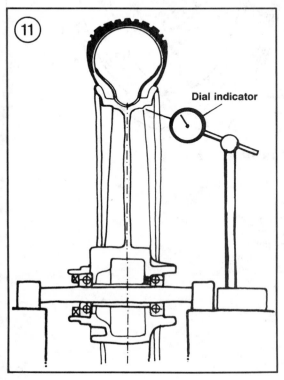

Dial indicator

12. With the front brake applied, push down hard on the handlebars and pump the forks several times to seat the front axle within the front forks.

13. Tighten the front axle holder nuts. Tighten the front nut first and then the rear nut. Tighten the nuts to the torque specification listed in **Table 1**.

> *WARNING*
> *The axle holder nuts must be tightened in this manner and to this torque value. After installation is complete, there will be a slight gap at the rear, with no gap at the front. If done incorrectly, the studs may fail, resulting in the loss of control of the bike when riding.*

14. After the wheel is installed completely, rotate it; apply the brake several times to make sure it rotates freely and that the brake is operating properly.

Front Wheel Inspection (All Models)

Measure the wobble and runout of the wheel rim with a dial indicator as shown in **Figure 10** or **Figure 11**. The standard value for both radial and axial runout is 0.5 mm (0.02 in.). The maximum permissible limit is 2.0 mm (0.08 in.).

On wire wheels, tighten or replace any bent or loose spokes. Refer to *Spoke Adjustment* in this chapter.

If the runout on a ComStar (stamped) or ComCast (cast alloy) wheel exceeds the limit, it will have to be replaced, as the wheel cannot be serviced. Inspect the wheel for cracks, fractures, dents or bends. If it is damaged in any way, it must be replaced.

FRONT HUB

Inspection

Inspect each wheel bearing prior to removing it from the wheel hub.

> *CAUTION*
> *Do not remove the wheel bearings for inspection purposes as they will be damaged during the removal process. Remove the wheel bearings only if they are to be replaced.*

1. Perform Steps 1-7 of *Disassembly* in this chapter.

2. Turn each bearing by hand. Make sure each bearing turns smoothly.

3. On non-sealed bearings, check the balls for evidence of wear, pitting, or excessive heat (bluish tint). Replace bearings if necessary; always replace as a complete set. When replacing the bearings, be

9

sure to take your old bearings along to ensure a perfect matchup.

NOTE
Fully sealed bearings are available from many bearing specialty shops. Fully sealed bearings provide better protection from moisture that may get into the hub.

4. Check the axle for wear and straightness. Use V-blocks and a dial indicator. If the runout is 0.2 mm (0.008 in.) or greater, the axle must be replaced.

Disassembly

Refer to the following illustrations for this procedure:

a. **Figure 12**: Drum brake models.
b. **Figure 13**: Rebel 450.
c. **Figure 14**: ComStar stamped steel wheel.
d. **Figure 15**: ComCast alloy wheel.

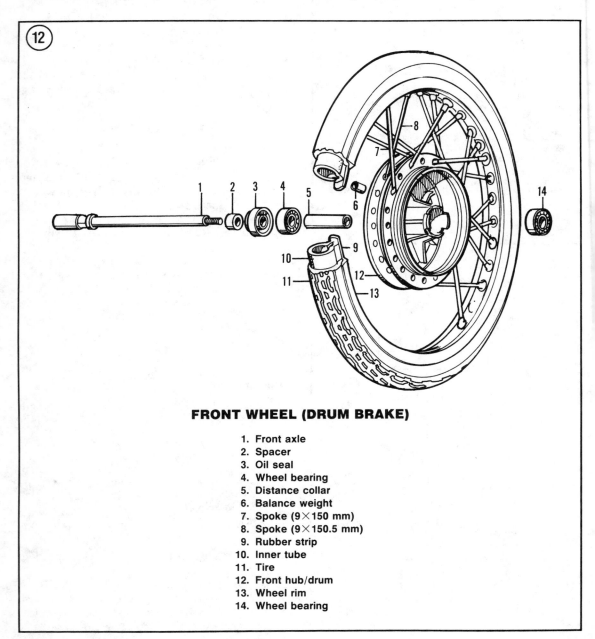

FRONT WHEEL (DRUM BRAKE)

1. Front axle
2. Spacer
3. Oil seal
4. Wheel bearing
5. Distance collar
6. Balance weight
7. Spoke (9×150 mm)
8. Spoke (9×150.5 mm)
9. Rubber strip
10. Inner tube
11. Tire
12. Front hub/drum
13. Wheel rim
14. Wheel bearing

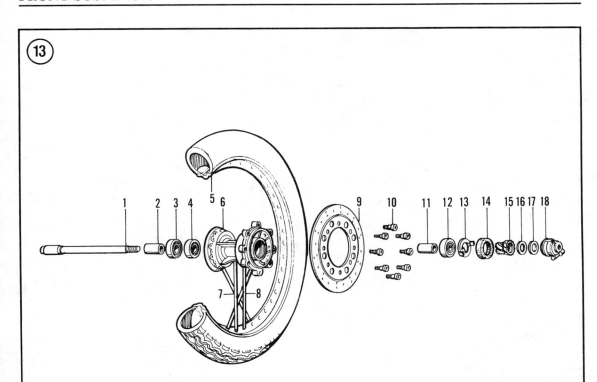

**FRONT WHEEL—
DISC BRAKE (REBEL 450)**

1. Front axle
2. Spacer
3. Oil seal
4. Wheel bearing
5. Wheel rim
6. Front hub
7. Spoke set "B"
8. Spoke set "A"
9. Brake disc
10. Disc bolt
11. Distance collar
12. Wheel bearing
13. Retainer
14. Oil seal
15. Speedometer gear
16. Washer
17. Washer
18. Speedometer housing

9

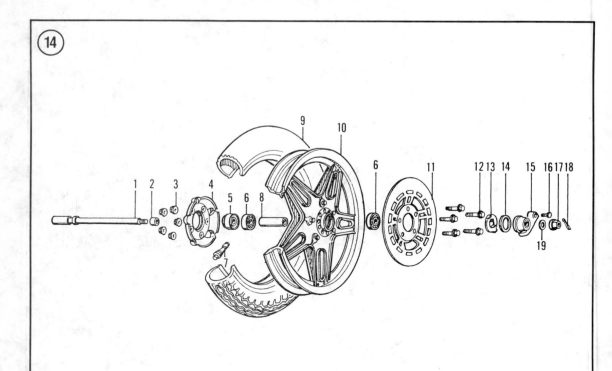

FRONT WHEEL—COMSTAR

1. Front axle
2. Spacer
3. Nut
4. Cover
5. Oil seal
6. Wheel bearing
7. Valve stem
8. Distance collar
9. Tire
10. Wheel
11. Brake disc
12. Disc bolt
13. Retainer
14. Oil seal
15. Speedometer housing
16. Bolt
17. Nut
18. Cotter pin
19. Washer

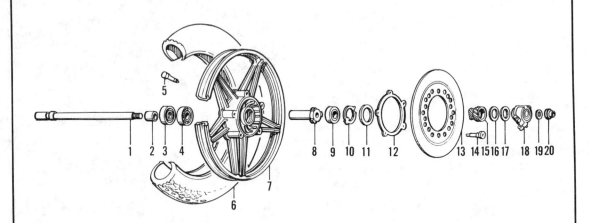

FRONT WHEEL—COMCAST

1. Front axle
2. Spacer
3. Oil seal
4. Wheel bearing
5. Valve stem
6. Tire
7. Wheel rim
8. Distance collar
9. Wheel bearing
10. Retainer
11. Oil seal
12. Damping shim
13. Brake disc
14. Brake disc bolts
15. Speedometer gear
16. Washer
17. Washer
18. Speedometer housing
19. Washer
20. Spacer

9

This procedure is shown on a Rebel 450 and represents a typical front hub disassembly and assembly procedure. Where differences occur among the various models they are identified.

1. Remove the front wheel as described under *Front Wheel Removal*, for your particular model, in this chapter.

> *CAUTION*
> *On disc brake models, do not set the wheel down on the disc surface as it may get scratched or warped. Set the wheel on 2 blocks of wood (**Figure 9**).*

2. On drum brake models, pull the brake panel assembly (**Figure 16**) straight up and out of the brake drum.

3. On CB450T models, remove the bolts and nuts securing the brake disc on the left-hand side and the cover on the right-hand side. Remove the brake disc and the cover.

4. Remove the front axle spacer (**Figure 17**) and the oil seal from the right-hand side.

5. Remove the speedometer gear box (**Figure 18**) from the left-hand side.

6. Remove the oil seal and the retainer (**Figure 19**) from the left-hand side.

7. On all models except CB400T, remove the bolts securing the brake disc (A, **Figure 20**) and remove the disc.

8. Before proceeding any further, inspect the wheel bearings as described under *Front Hub Inspection* in this chapter.

9. To remove the left- and right-hand bearings and the distance collar, perform the following:

    a. Insert a soft aluminum or brass drift into one side of the hub.

    b. Push the distance collar over to one side and place the drift onto the inner race of the opposite bearing.

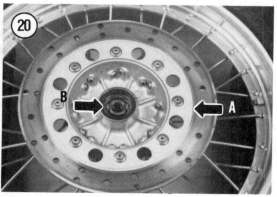

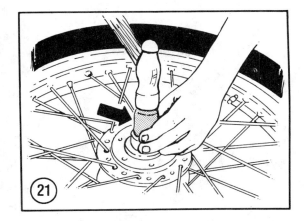

c. Using a hammer, tap around the perimeter of the inner race and tap the bearing out of the hub.

d. Remove the distance collar.

e. Remove the other bearing in the same manner.

Assembly

1. Pack the bearings thoroughly with multi-purpose grease. Work the grease in between the balls thoroughly. Turn the bearing by hand a couple of times to make sure the grease is distributed evenly inside the bearing.

2. Pack the wheel hub and axle spacer with multipurpose grease.

CAUTION
Install non-sealed bearings with the sealed side facing outward.

CAUTION
*Tap the bearings squarely into place and tap on the outer race only. Use a socket (**Figure 21**) that matches the outer race diameter. Do not tap on the inner race or the bearing might be damaged. Be sure that the bearings are completely seated.*

3. Install the right-hand bearing and distance collar.

4. Install the left-hand bearing.

5. On all models except CB400T, install the brake disc and the bolts. Tighten the bolts to the torque specification listed in **Table 1**.

6. Install the retainer and the oil seal (**Figure 19**) into the left-hand side.

7. On CB450T models, install brake disc on the left-hand side and the cover on the right-hand side. Install and tighten the bolts and nuts and tighten to the torque specification listed in **Table 1**.

8. Align the tangs of the retainer (B, **Figure 20**) with the notches in the speedometer gear box. Install the speedometer gear box (**Figure 18**) onto the left-hand side.

9. Install the oil seal (**Figure 22**) and the front axle spacer (**Figure 17**) onto the right-hand side.

NOTE
*Make sure that the lugs on the drum brake plate (**Figure 23**) align with the depressions in the bearing retainer (**Figure 24**).*

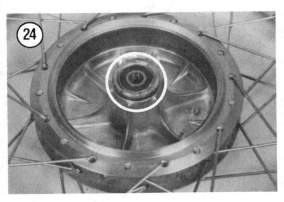

10. On the drum brake models, install the brake assembly into the brake drum.

WHEELS

Wheel Balance

An unbalanced wheel is unsafe to ride and hard on tires. The rider may experience anything from a mild vibration to a violent shimmy which may even result in loss of control.

NOTE
The wire wheel used on the Rebel 450 is different from those used on the other wire wheeled models. The Rebel 450 wheel uses a cast alloy rim with the spokes attached to a raised vertical boss. This design enables the Rebel 450 to be equipped with tubeless tires (previously not possible on a wire wheel).

On wire wheels (other than Rebel 450 models), the balance weights are applied to the spokes on the light side of the wheel.

On models equipped with the ComStar stamped steel wheels, ComCast alloy wheels, or the Rebel 450 wire wheel, the weights are attached to the rim. A kit of Tape-A-Weight, or equivalent may be purchased from most motorcycle supply stores. This kit contains test weights and strips of adhesive backed weights that can be cut to the desired weight and attached directly to the rim.

Before you attempt to balance the wheel, check to be sure that the wheel bearings are in good condition and properly lubricated and that the brakes do not drag. The wheel must rotate freely.

1. Remove the wheel as described under *Front Wheel Removal* in this chapter.
2. Mount the wheel on a fixture such as the one in **Figure 25** so it can rotate freely.
3. Give the wheel a spin and let it coast to a stop. Mark the tire at the lowest point.
4. Spin the wheel several more times. If the wheel keeps coming to rest at the same point, it is out of balance.
5. On wire wheels (except Rebel 450), attach a weight to the upper (or light) side of the wheel at the spoke (**Figure 26**). Weights come in four sizes: 5, 10, 15 and 20 grams. They are crimped onto the spoke with ordinary gas pliers.
6. On ComStar, ComCast and Rebel 450 models, tape a test weight to the upper (or light) side of the wheel.
7. Experiment with different weights until the wheel, when spun, comes to rest at a different position each time.
8. On ComStar, ComCast or Rebel 450 models, remove the test weight and install the correct size adhesive backed weight or clip in type weight.

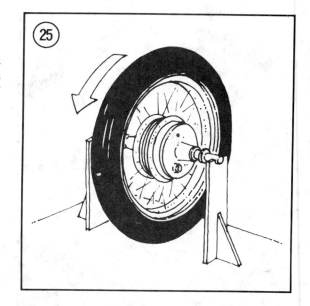

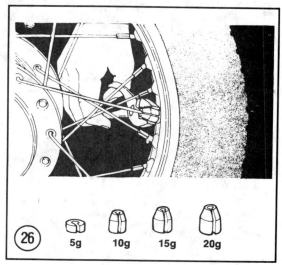

5g   10g   15g   20g

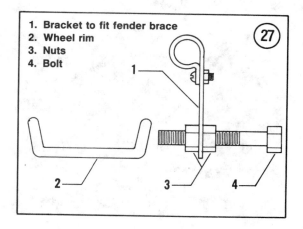

1. Bracket to fit fender brace
2. Wheel rim
3. Nuts
4. Bolt

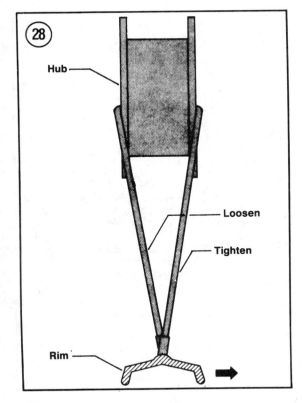

Spoke Adjustment

Spokes loosen with use and should be checked periodically. If all appear loose, tighten all spokes on one side of the hub, then tighten all the spokes on the other side. One-half to one turn should be sufficient; do not overtighten. If you have a torque spoke wrench, tighten the spokes to the torque specifications listed in **Table 1**.

On Rebel 450, the adjustment nipples are located at the hub center instead of at the rim end of the spoke as on all other models.

After tightening spokes, check rim runout to be sure you haven't pulled the rim out of shape.

One way to check rim runout is to mount a dial indicator on the front fork so that it bears on the rim. If you don't have a dial indicator, improvise as shown in **Figure 27**. Adjust position of both until it just clears rim. Rotate rim and note whether clearance increases or decreases. Mark the tire with chalk or crayon at areas that produce significantly large or small clearance. Clearance must not change by more than 2.0 mm (0.08 in.).

To pull the rim out, tighten spokes which terminate on opposite sides of the hub (**Figure 28**). In most cases, only slight adjustment is necessary to true rim. After adjustment, rotate the rim and make sure another area has not been pulled out of true. Continue adjustment and checking until runout does not exceed 2.0 mm (0.08 in.).

Wheel Alignment

1. Measure the width of the 2 tires at their widest points.
2. Subtract the smaller dimension from the larger.
3. Make an alignment tool out of wood, approximately 7 feet long, with an offset equal to one half of the dimension obtained in Step 2. See (D) in **Figure 29**.
4. If the wheels are not aligned as in (A) and (C), **Figure 29** the rear wheel must be shifted to correct the situation.
5. Adjust the rear wheel with the chain adjuster bolts or nuts until the wheels align.

NOTE
*After this procedure is completed, refer to **Drive Chain Adjustment** in Chapter Three to make sure drive chain slack is within tolerance.*

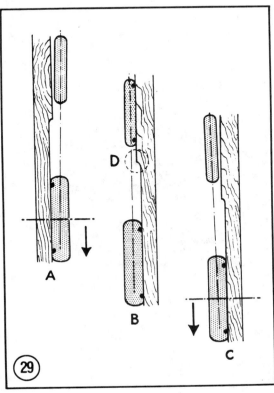

TIRE CHANGING

Removal

1. Remove the valve core to deflate the tire.

2. Press the entire bead on both sides of the tire into the center of the rim.

3. Lubricate the beads with soapy water.

4. Insert a tire iron under the bead next to the valve. Force the bead on the opposite side of the tire into the center of the rim and pry the bead over the rim with the tire iron (**Figure 30**).

5. Insert a second tire iron next to the first to hold the bead over the rim. Then work around the tire with the first tire iron, prying the bead over the rim (**Figure 31**). Be careful not to pinch the inner tube with the irons.

6. Remove the valve from the hole in the rim and remove the tube from the tire. Lift out and lay aside.

7. Stand the tire upright. Insert a tire iron between the second bead and the side of the rim that the first bead was pried over (**Figure 32**). Force the bead on the opposite side from the tire iron into the center of the rim. Pry the second bead off the rim, working around as with the first.

Installation

1. Carefully check the tire for any damage, especially inside.

2. A new tire may have balancing rubbers inside. These are not patches and should not be disturbed. A colored spot near the bead indicates a lighter

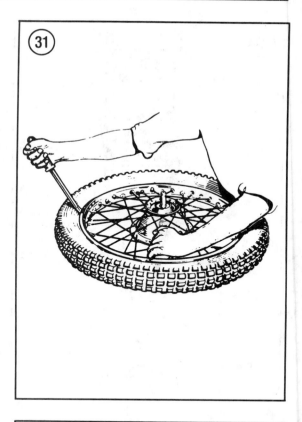

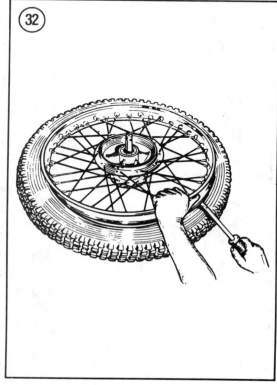

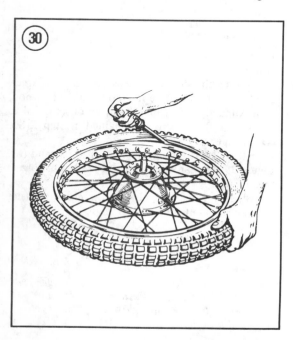

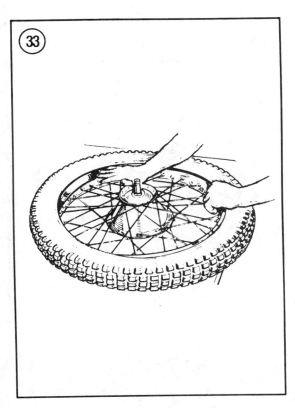

point on the tire. This should be placed next to the valve or on models so equipped, midway between 2 rim locks.

3. On wire wheel models (except Rebel 450), check that the spoke ends do not protrude through the nipples into the center of the rim to puncture the tube. File off any protruding spoke ends.

4. Be sure the rim rubber tape is in place with the rough side toward the rim.

5. Put the core in the tube valve. Put the tube in the tire and inflate just enough to round it out. Too much air will make installing the tire difficult, and too little will increase the chances of pinching the tube with the tire irons.

6. Lubricate the tire beads and rim with soapy water. Pull the tube partly out of the tire at the valve. Squeeze the beads together to hold the tube and insert the valve into the hole in the rim (**Figure 33**). The lower bead should go into the center of the rim with the upper bead outside it.

7. Press the lower bead into the rim center on each side of the valve, working around the tire in both directions. See **Figure 34**. Use a tire iron for the last few inches of bead (**Figure 35**).

8. Press the upper bead into the rim opposite the valve. Pry the bead into the rim on both sides of the initial point with a tire iron, working around the rim to the valve (**Figure 36**).

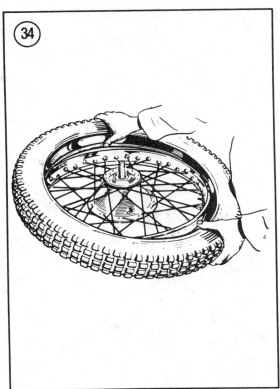

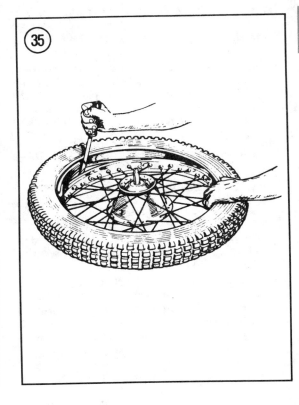

both sides of the initial point with a tire iron, working around the rim to the valve (**Figure 36**).

9. Wiggle the valve to be sure the tube is not trapped under the bead. Set the valve squarely in its hole before screwing on the valve nut to hold it against the rim.

10. Check the bead on both sides of the tire for even fit around the rim. Inflate the tire slowly to seat the beads in the rim. It may be necessary to bounce the tire to complete the seating. Inflate to the required pressure. Balance the wheel as described previously.

HANDLEBARS

Removal/Installation
(Drum Brake Models)

1. Remove the rear view mirror (A, **Figure 37**).

2. Remove the clamps (B, **Figure 37**) securing the electrical cables to the handlebar.

3A. On models with a manual transmission, perform the following:

    a. Loosen the locknut and turn the adjuster (C, **Figure 37**) in all the way to allow slack in the brake cable.

    b. Loosen the locknut and turn the adjuster (A, **Figure 38**) in all the way to allow slack in the clutch cable.

3B. On models with an automatic transmission, loosen the locknut and turn the adjuster (A, **Figure 39**) in all the way to allow slack in the brake and parking brake cable.

4. On the right-hand side, perform the following:

    a. Disconnect the electrical connectors from the front brake light switch on the brake lever assembly.

    b. Remove the screws securing the right-hand switch assembly together (D, **Figure 37**).

    c. Separate the 2 halves and remove the switch assembly from the handlebar.

    d. Disconnect the throttle cables from the throttle grip.

    e. Slide off the throttle grip assembly.

5. On the left-hand side, perform the following:

    a. Remove the rear view mirror (B, **Figure 38**).

    b. Remove the clamps (C, **Figure 38**) securing the electrical cables to the handlebar.

    c. Disconnect the electrical connectors from the clutch switch on the clutch lever assembly.

    d. Remove the screws securing the left-hand switch/clutch lever assembly together (D, **Figure 38**). Separate the 2 halves and remove the switch/clutch lever assembly from the handlebar.

6. If necessary, remove the hand grip.

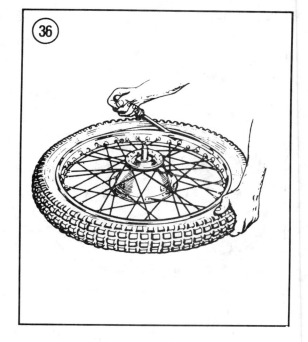

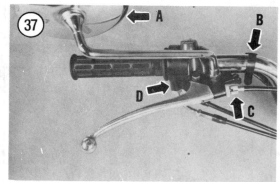

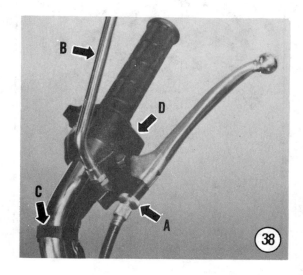

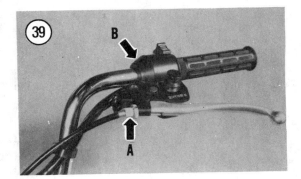

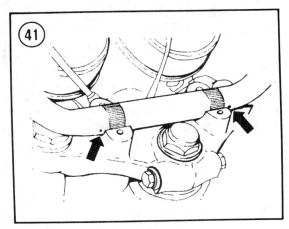

7. Remove the bolts (**Figure 40**) securing the handlebar upper holders and remove the holders.

8. Remove the handlebar.

9. Install by reversing the removal steps, noting the following.

10. Align the punch mark on the handlebar with the top surface of the lower holder (**Figure 41**).

11. Position the punch mark on the upper holders toward the front and install the holders.

12. Tighten the handlebar holder front bolts first then the rear bolts. Tighten to the torque specification listed in **Table 1**.

13. Apply a light coat of multipurpose grease to the right-hand end of the handlebar prior to installing the throttle grip assembly.

14. When installing the switch assemblies, align the punch mark on the handlebar with the split line on the switch assembly, then tighten the screws.

WARNING
After the grips (new or old) have been installed on the handlebar or throttle pipe assembly, do not ride the bike for at least one hour. This amount of time is required for the cement to set up and thoroughly dry. If ridden too soon, the grip(s) may slide off the handlebar which could result in a dangerous accident.

15. If the hand grips were removed, perform the following:

   a. Clean off all old cement residue from the left-hand end of the handlebar, the inside of the left-hand grip and the outside of the throttle pipe assembly.

   b. Apply Honda Grip Cement, or equivalent, to the inside surface of the new or old grips and to the outside surface of the left-hand handlebar and the throttle pipe assembly.

   c. Let the cement set for 3-5 minutes.

   d. Install and rotate the grips for even application of the cement. Push the grip all the way on until it bottoms out on the end of the handlebar or throttle pipe.

Removal
(Disc Brake Models)

1. On Rebel 450 models, remove the handlebar weights (**Figure 42**) at each end of the handlebar as follows:

   a. Wrap a shop cloth around the weight and secure the weight with a pair of gas pliers.

   b. Remove the Phillips screw securing the weight to the handlebar and remove each weight.

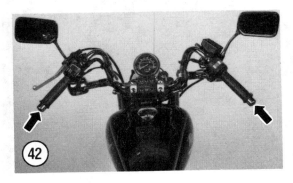

2. Remove the right-hand rear view mirror (A, **Figure 43**).

3. Remove the clamps (B, **Figure 43**) securing the electrical cables to the handlebar.

4. Disconnect the electrical connectors from the front brake light switch (C, **Figure 43**) on the master cylinder.

> *CAUTION*
> *Cover the fuel tank and front fender with a heavy cloth or plastic tarp to protect it from accidental spilling of brake fluid. Wash any brake fluid off of any painted or plated surface immediately, as it will destroy the finish. Use soapy water and rinse thoroughly.*

5. Remove the bolts and clamp securing the master cylinder (D, **Figure 43**) to the handlebar.

6. Remove the master cylinder and lay it on the fuel tank or tie it up to the frame. Keep the reservoir upright to minimize the loss of brake fluid and to keep air from entering into the brake system. It is not necessary to remove the hydraulic brake line from the master cylinder.

7. Remove the screws securing the right-hand switch assembly together (E, **Figure 43**). Separate the 2 halves and remove the switch assembly from the handlebar. Disconnect the throttle cables from the throttle grip.

8. Slide off the throttle grip assembly.

9. Remove the left-hand rear view mirror (A, **Figure 44**).

10. Remove the clamps (B, **Figure 44**) securing the electrical cables to the handlebar.

11. Disconnect the electrical connectors from the clutch switch on the clutch lever assembly.

12. Remove the bolts and clamp securing the clutch lever assembly (C, **Figure 44**) to the handlebar.

13. Remove the clutch lever assembly and lay the assembly and cable on the fuel tank over the front fender.

14A. On Rebel 450 models, perform the following:

  a. Remove the screws securing the left-hand switch assembly together (D, **Figure 44**).

  b. Separate the 2 halves and disconnect the choke cable from the choke lever.

  c. Remove the switch assembly from the handlebar.

  d. If necessary, remove the hand grip and slide off the choke lever.

14B. On all models except Rebel 450 models, perform the following:

  a. Remove the screws securing the left-hand switch assembly together.

  b. Separate the 2 halves and remove the switch assembly from the handlebar.

  c. If necessary, remove the hand grip.

15A. On CB450SC models, perform the following:

  a. Remove the caps from the bolt heads.

  b. Remove the Allen bolts securing the handlebar upper holder and remove the upper holder.

  c. Remove the handlebar.

15B. On Rebel 450 models, perform the following:

  a. Remove the bolts (A, **Figure 45**) securing the speedometer housing and the indicator panel assembly.

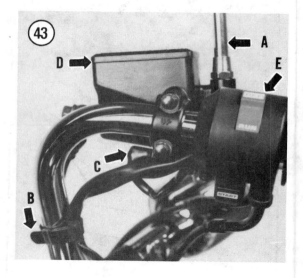

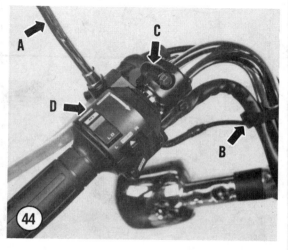

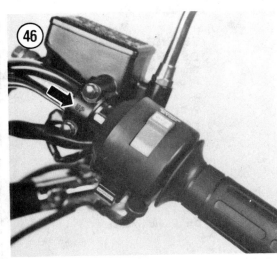

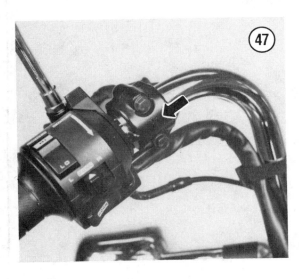

b. Move the speedometer housing (B, **Figure 45**) slightly forward and away from the handlebar.

c. Carefully pull the indicator panel assembly (C, **Figure 45**) up and away from the handlebars.

d. Remove the caps from the bolt heads.

e. Remove the Allen bolts securing the handlebar upper holders and remove the upper holders.

f. Remove the handlebar.

Installation
(Disc Brake Models)

1. Install by reversing the removal steps, noting the following.

2. Align the punch mark on the handlebar with the top surface of the lower holder (**Figure 41**).

3. On all models except CB450SC, position the punch mark on the upper holders toward the front and install the holders.

4. Tighten the handlebar holder front bolts first then the rear bolts. Tighten to the torque specification listed in **Table 1**.

5. On Rebel 450 models, perform the following:

a. Move the indicator panel back into position.

b. Move the speedometer housing back into position. Place the speedometer housing mounting plate on top of the indicator panel mounting tabs and install the bolts.

c. Tighten the Allen bolts securely and install the bolt head caps.

6A. On Rebel 450 models, when installing the switch assemblies, align the locating pin in the switch assembly with the hole in the handlebar, then tighten the screws.

6B. On all models except Rebel 450, when installing the switch assemblies, align the punch mark on the handlebar with the split line on the switch assembly, then tighten the screws.

7. When installing the master cylinder and the clutch lever assemblies, perform the following:

a. Position the Up mark on the clamp facing up. Refer to **Figure 46** for the brake master cylinder and **Figure 47** for the clutch lever assembly.

b. Install the clamp and the bolts. Tighten the upper bolt first then the lower bolt.

c. Tighten the master cylinder clamp bolts to the torque specification listed in **Table 1**.

d. Tighten the clutch lever assembly bolts

8. Apply a light coat of multipurpose grease to the right-hand end of the handlebar prior to installing the throttle grip assembly.

9

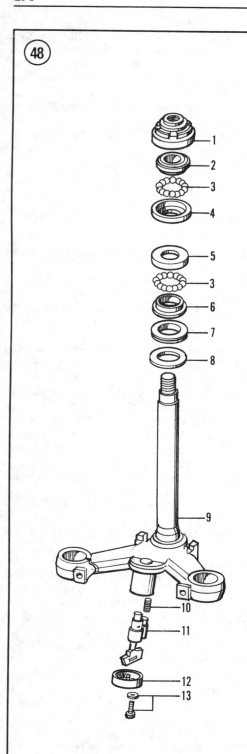

48

STEERING STEM—
LOOSE BALL BEARINGS

1. Steering stem adjust nut
2. Upper bearing upper race
3. Steel balls
4. Upper bearing lower race
5. Lower bearing upper race
6. Lower bearing lower race
7. Dust seal
8. Dust seal washer
9. Steering stem
10. Spring
11. Lock assembly
12. Cover
13. Screw and washer

WARNING
After the grips (new or old) have been installed on the handlebar or throttle pipe assembly, do not ride the bike for at least one hour. This amount of time is required for the cement to set up and thoroughly dry. If ridden too soon, the grip(s) may slide off the handlebar which could result in a dangerous accident.

9. If the hand grips were removed, perform the following:
   a. Clean off all old cement residue from the left-hand end of the handlebar, the inside of the left-hand grip and the outside of the throttle pipe assembly.
   b. Apply Honda Grip Cement, or equivalent, to the inside surface of the new or old grips and to the outside surface of the left-hand handlebar and the throttle pipe assembly.
   c. Let the cement set for 3-5 minutes.
   d. Install and rotate the grips for even application of the cement. Push the grip all the way on until it bottoms out on the end of the handlebar or throttle pipe.

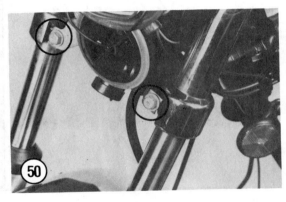

10. On Rebel 450 models, install the handlebar weights (**Figure 42**) at each end of the handlebar as follows:
   a. Install the weight into the end of the handlebar.
   b. Wrap a shop cloth around the weight and secure the weight with a pair of gas pliers.
   c. Install the Phillips screw securing the weight to the handlebar and tighten the screw securely.

STEERING HEAD AND STEM (LOOSE BALL BEARINGS)

Disassembly

Refer to **Figure 48** for this procedure.
1. Remove the front wheel as described under *Front Wheel Removal/Installation* in this chapter.
2. Remove the handlebar as described under *Handlebar Removal/Installation* in this chapter.
3. Remove the headlight as described under *Headlight Replacement* in Chapter Eight.
4. Remove the instrument cluster as described under *Instrument Cluster Removal/Installation* in Chapter Eight.
5. Remove the horn as described under *Horn Replacement* in Chapter Eight.
6. Remove the bolts securing the front fender and remove the front fender.
7. On models so equipped, remove the front brake caliper assembly as described under *Front Brake Caliper Removal/Installation* in Chapter Eleven.
8. On models so equipped, remove the center trim plate on the lower fork bridge.

NOTE
*All models with **non-air assist** front forks do not have a pinch-type bolt on the upper fork bridge. The fork cap bolt secures the fork tube to the upper fork bridge. The fork spring will **not** pop out when the fork cap bolt is removed. There is an internal Allen bolt in the fork tube that secures the internal fork components.*

9A. On models with *non-air assist* front forks, remove the fork cap bolt (A, **Figure 49**) and lower fork bridge bolt (**Figure 50**). Slide out both fork assemblies.
9B. On all other models, loosen the upper and lower (**Figure 50**) fork bridge bolts. Slide out both fork assemblies.
10. Remove the steering stem nut (B, **Figure 49**) and washer, then remove the upper fork bridge.

11. Loosen the steering stem adjust nut with the pin spanner provided in the factory tool kit or use a large drift and hammer or use the easily improvised tool shown in **Figure 51**.

12. Have an assistant hold a large pan under the steering stem to catch any loose balls that may fall out while you carefully lower the steering stem.

13. Lower the steering stem assembly down and out of the steering head.

14. Remove the upper bearing upper race from the steering head.

15. Remove the ball bearings from the upper and lower races. There are 37 ball bearings total (18 in the upper race and 19 in the lower race).

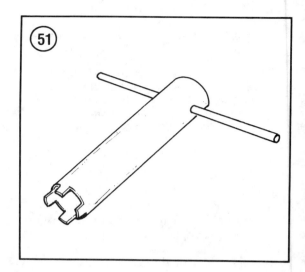

Inspection

1. Clean the bearing races in the steering head and the bearings with solvent.

2. Check the welds around the steering head for cracks and fractures. If any are found, have them repaired by a competent frame shop or welding service.

3. Check the balls for pitting, scratches or discoloration indicating wear or corrosion. Replace them in sets if any are bad.

4. Check the races for pitting, galling and corrosion. If any of these conditions exist, replace the races as described under *Steering Head Bearing Races (All Models)* in this chapter.

5. Check the steering stem for cracks and check its race for damage or wear. If this race or any race is damaged, the bearings should be replaced as a complete bearing set. Take the old races and bearings to your dealer to ensure accurate replacement.

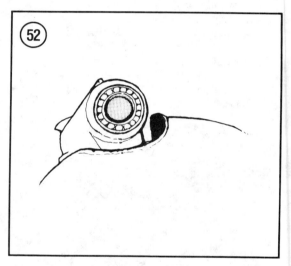

Steering Stem Assembly

Refer to **Figure 48** for this procedure.

1. Make sure the steering head and stem races are properly seated.

2. Apply a coat of cold grease to the upper bearing race cone and fit 18 ball bearings around it (**Figure 52**).

3. Apply a coat of cold grease to the lower bearing race cone on the steering stem and fit 19 ball bearings around it (**Figure 53**).

4. Install the steering stem into the head tube and hold it firmly in place.

5. Install the upper bearing upper race.

6A. On 1986 CB450SC models, install the steering stem adjust nut and tighten it (**Figure 54**) to the torque specification listed in **Table 1**.

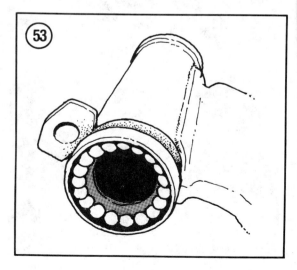

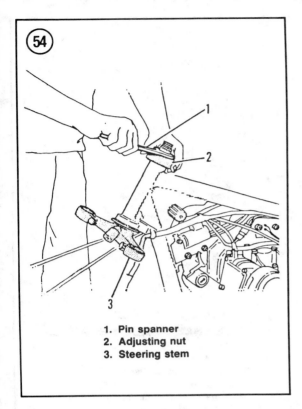

1. Pin spanner
2. Adjusting nut
3. Steering stem

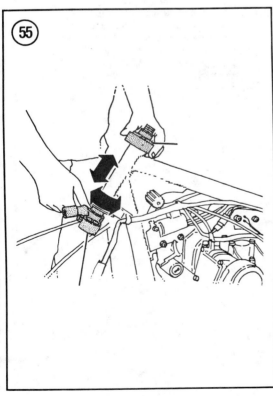

6B. On all models except 1986 CB450SC, install the steering stem adjust nut and tighten it (**Figure 54**) until it is snug against the upper race, then back it off 1/8 turn.

NOTE
*The adjusting nut should be just tight enough to remove both horizontal and vertical play (**Figure 55**), yet loose enough so that the assembly will turn to both lock positions under its own weight after an assist.*

7. Install the upper fork bridge and the steering stem nut.
    Do not tighten the steering stem nut at this time.

NOTE
Steps 8-10 must be performed in this order to assure proper upper and lower fork bridge to fork alignment.

8. Install the fork tubes and align them with the top surface of the upper fork bridge as described under *Front Fork Installation* in this chapter.
9. Tighten the *lower* fork bridge bolts to the torque specification listed in **Table 1**.
10. Tighten the steering stem nut to the torque specification listed in **Table 1**.

NOTE
*All models with **non-air assist** front forks do not have a pinch-type bolt on the upper fork bridge. The fork cap bolt secures the fork tube to the upper fork bridge.*

11A. On models with *non-air assist* forks, install the fork cap bolt (A, **Figure 49**) and tighten to the torque specification listed in **Table 1**.
11B. On all other models, tighten the *upper* fork bridge bolts to the torque specification listed in **Table 1**.
12. Install all items removed.

STEERING HEAD AND STEM (ASSEMBLED BALL BEARINGS)

Disassembly

Refer to **Figure 56** for this procedure.
1. Remove the front wheel as described under *Front Wheel Removal/Installation* in this chapter.
2. Remove the handlebar as described under *Handlebar Removal/Installation* in this chapter.

9

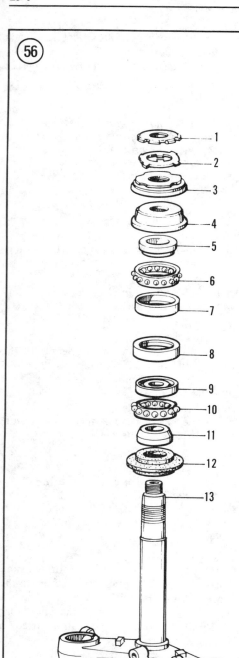

56

**STEERING STEM—
ASSEMBLED BALL BEARINGS**
1. Locknut
2. Lockwasher
3. Steering stem adjust nut
4. Dust seal
5. Upper bearing inner race
6. Assembled ball bearing
7. Upper bearing outer race
8. Lower bearing outer race
9. Grease retainer
10. Assembled ball bearing
11. Lower bearing inner race
12. Dust seal
13. Steering stem

3. Remove the headlight (A, **Figure 57**) as described under *Headlight Replacement* in Chapter Eight.

4. Remove the speedometer and indicator panel (B, **Figure 57**) as described under *Speedometer Removal/Installation* in Chapter Eight.

5. Remove the horn as described under *Horn Replacement* in Chapter Eight.

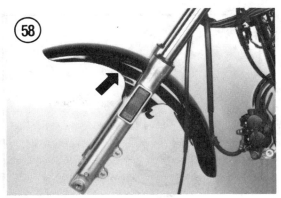

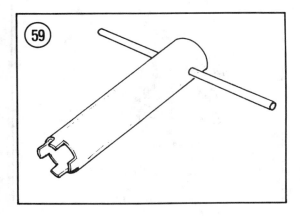

6. Remove the bolts securing the front fender (**Figure 58**) and remove the front fender.

7. Remove the front brake caliper assembly as described under *Front Brake Caliper Removal/ Installation* in Chapter Eleven.

8. Remove the center trim plate (D, **Figure 57**) on the lower fork bridge.

9. Loosen the upper and lower fork bridge bolts (C, **Figure 57**) and slide out both fork assemblies.

10. Remove the junction box assembly (E, **Figure 57**) and the ignition switch cover.

11. Remove the steering stem nut cover and the steering stem nut.

12. Remove the upper fork bridge (F, **Figure 57**).

13. Straighten the tab on the lockwasher and remove the locknut. Remove and discard the lockwasher as a new one must be installed during assembly.

14. Remove the steering stem adjust nut. To loosen the adjust nut, use a large drift and hammer or use the easily improvised tool shown in **Figure 59**.

15. Lower the steering stem assembly down and out of the steering head. Don't worry about catching any loose steel balls as the steering stem is equipped with assembled ball bearings.

16. Remove the dust seal from the top of the headset.

17. Remove the upper bearing inner race and upper bearing from the top of the headset.

18. Remove the grease retainer and lower bearing from the steering stem.

Inspection

1. Clean the bearing races in the steering head and the bearings with solvent.

2. Check the welds around the steering head for cracks and fractures. If any are found, have them repaired by a competent frame shop or welding service.

3. Check the balls for pitting, scratches or discoloration indicating wear or corrosion. Replace the bearing if any are bad.

4. Check the races for pitting, galling and corrosion. If any of these conditions exist, replace the races as described in this chapter.

5. Check the steering stem for cracks, damage or wear. If damaged in any way replace the steering stem.

Steering Stem Assembly

Refer to **Figure 56** for this procedure.

1. Make sure both bearing outer races are properly seated in the steering head tube.

2. Pack the bearing cavities of both ball bearings with bearing grease. Also apply bearing grease to the bearing outer races in the steering head tube and the lower bearing inner race on the steering stem.

3. Apply a coat of bearing grease to the threads of the steering stem and the steering stem adjust nut.

4. Install the lower bearing onto the steering stem.

5. Position the grease retainer with the cupped side facing up and install the grease retainer over the lower bearing on the steering stem.

6. Install the steering stem into the head tube and hold it firmly in place.

7. Install the upper bearing into the steering head tube.

8. Install the dust seal.

9. Install the steering stem adjust nut and tighten it to the torque specification listed in **Table 1**.

10. Turn the steering stem from lock-to-lock 4 or 5 times to seat the bearings.

11. Retighten the steering stem adjust nut to the torque specification listed in **Table 1**.

12. Repeat Step 10 and Step 11 twice. If during these steps the adjust nut will not tighten to the specified torque, remove the adjust nut and inspect both the adjust nut and the steering stem threads for dirt and/or burrs. Clean both parts and repeat Step 10 and Step 11. If necessary, replace the adjust nut.

13. Install a *new* lockwasher and bend 2 opposite tabs down into the notches in the steering stem adjust nut as shown in **Figure 60**. Never reinstall an old lockwasher as the tabs may break off, making the lockwasher ineffective.

14. Install the locknut finger-tight. Hold onto the steering stem adjusting nut and tighten the locknut to within 90° and align the grooves with the tabs of the lockwasher.

15. Bend up 2 tabs of the lockwasher into the grooves in the locknut.

16. Install the upper fork bridge and steering stem nut only finger-tight at this time.

NOTE
Steps 17-20 must be performed in this order to assure proper upper and lower fork bridge to fork alignment.

17. Slide the fork tubes into position so the top surface of the fork tube aligns with the top surface of the upper fork bridge.

18. Tighten the *lower* fork bridge bolts to the torque specification listed in **Table 1**.

19. Tighten the steering stem nut to the torque specification listed in **Table 1**.

20. Tighten the *upper* fork bridge bolts to the torque specification listed in **Table 1**.

21. Install all items removed.

STEERING HEAD BEARING RACES (ALL MODELS)

The headset and steering stem bearing races, on all models, are pressed into place. Because they are easily bent, do not remove them unless they are worn and require replacement.

Headset Bearing Race Removal/Installation

To remove the headset race, insert a hardwood stick or soft punch into the head tube (**Figure 61**) and carefully tap the race out from the inside. After it is started, tap around the race so that neither the race nor the head tube is damaged.

To install the headset race, tap it in slowly with a block of wood, a suitable size socket or piece of pipe (**Figure 62**). Make sure that the race is squarely seated in the headset race bore before tapping it into place. Tap the race in until it is flush with the steering head surface.

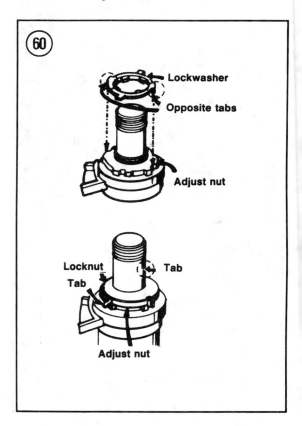

60

Lockwasher
Opposite tabs
Adjust nut

Locknut Tab
Tab
Adjust nut

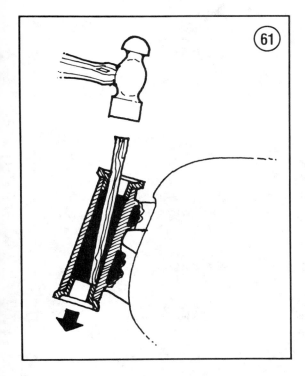

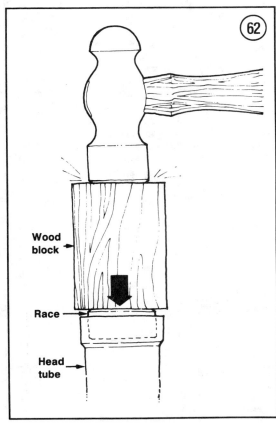

Steering Stem Bearing Race and Grease Seal Removal/Installation

1. To remove the steering stem race (bottom bearing lower race) try twisting and pulling it up by hand. If it will not come off, carefully pry it up with a screwdriver. Work around in a circle, prying a little at a time.

2A. On models with loose ball bearings, remove the bottom bearing lower race, the dust seal and the dust seal washer.

2B. On models with assembled ball bearings, remove the bottom bearing lower race and the dust seal.

3A. On models with loose ball bearings, install the dust seal washer and the dust seal. Slide the lower race over the steering stem with the bearing surface facing up.

3B. On models with assembled ball bearings install the dust seal. Slide the lower race over the steering stem with the bearing surface facing up.

4. Tap the lower race down with a piece of hardwood. Work around in a circle so the race will not be bent. Make sure it is seated squarely and is all the way down.

FRONT FORKS

The Honda front suspension consists of a spring-controlled, hydraulically damped telescopic fork. Some models have an air-assist feature that can change the damping effect of the front forks. Before suspecting major trouble, drain the fork oil and refill with the proper type and quantity as described in Chapter Three. If you still have trouble, such as poor damping, tendency to bottom out or top out, or leakage around rubber seals, then follow the service procedures in this section.

To simplify fork service and to prevent the mixing of parts, the legs should be removed, serviced and reinstalled individually.

NON-AIR ASSIST FRONT FORKS (REBEL 450)

Removal/Disassembly

Refer to **Figure 63** for this procedure.

1. Remove the front brake caliper assembly as described under *Front Brake Caliper Removal/Installation* in Chapter Eleven.

2. Remove the front wheel as described under *Front Wheel Removal/Installation* in this chapter.

3. Place a drain pan under the fork slider.

9

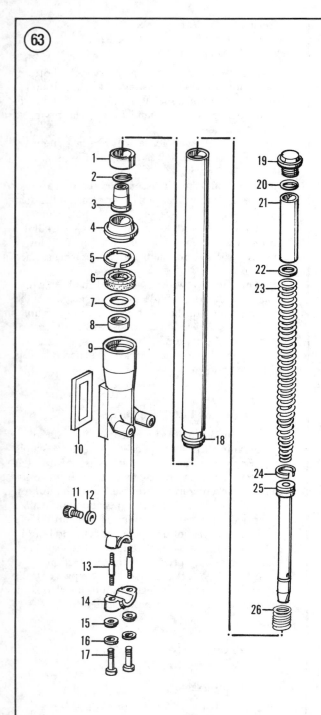

FRONT FORK (REBEL 450)

1. Fork tube bushing
2. Stop ring
3. Oil lock piece
4. Dust seal
5. Circlip
6. Oil seal
7. Backup ring
8. Slider bushing
9. Slider
10. Reflector
11. Drain bolt
12. Washer
13. Threaded stud
14. Axle holder
15. Washer
16. Lockwasher
17. Allen screw
18. Fork tube
19. Fork cap bolt
20. O-ring seal
21. Spacer
22. Spring seat
23. Fork spring
24. Piston ring
25. Damper rod
26. Rebound spring

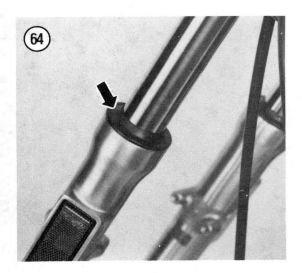

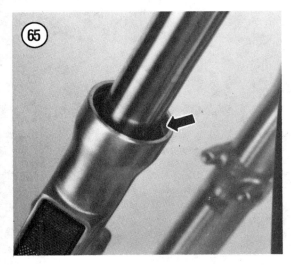

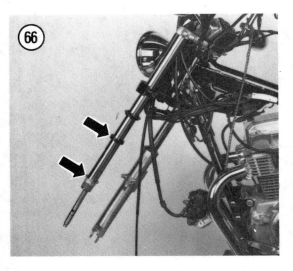

4. Remove the Allen head screw and gasket from the bottom of the slider. Let the fork oil drain out.

> *NOTE*
> *This screw has been secured with thread sealant and is often very difficult to remove because the damper rod will turn inside the slider. It sometimes can be removed with an air impact driver. If you are unable to remove it, take the fork tubes to a dealer and have the screws removed.*

5. Remove the dust seal (**Figure 64**) from the groove in the slider. Slide the dust seal up the fork tube.

6. Remove the circlip (**Figure 65**) from the slider.

> *NOTE*
> *On this type of fork, force is needed to remove the fork slider from the fork tube.*

> *NOTE*
> *It may be necessary to slightly heat the area on the slider around the oil seal prior to removal. Use a rag soaked in hot water; do not apply a flame directly to the fork slider.*

7. To remove the oil seal and slider bushing, perform the following:
   a. There is an interference fit between the bushing in the fork slider and the bushing on the fork tube. In order to remove the fork slider from the fork tube, pull hard on the fork slider using quick in and out strokes.
   b. Withdraw the fork slider from the fork tube.
   c. Doing this will withdraw the bushing, backup ring and oil seal (**Figure 66**) from the slider.

8. Remove the oil lock piece (**Figure 67**) from the damper rod.

9

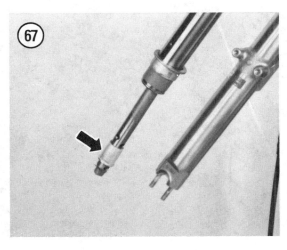

9. Loosen, but do not remove, the fork top cap bolt (**Figure 68**).

10. Loosen the upper and lower fork bridge bolts (**Figure 69**).

11. Remove the fork tube assembly. It may be necessary to slightly rotate the fork tube while pulling it down and out.

12. Take the fork tube assembly to your workbench for further disassembly.

13. Turn the fork tube upside down and slide off the oil seal, backup ring and slider bushing from the fork tube.

> *NOTE*
> *Do not discard the slider bushing at this time. It will be used during the installation procedure.*

14. Hold the upper fork tube in a vise with soft jaws and loosen the fork cap bolt (if it was not loosened in Step 9).

> *WARNING*
> *Be careful when removing the fork cap bolt as the spring is under pressure.*

15. Remove the fork cap bolt from the fork tube.

16. Remove the spacer and the fork spring.

17. Remove the fork from the vise, pour out any residual fork oil. Discard the fork oil—never reuse fork oil.

18. Remove the spring clip from the damper rod.

19. Remove the damper rod and rebound spring from the fork tube.

> *NOTE*
> *Do not remove the fork tube bushing unless it is going to be replaced.*

20. Inspect the fork as described under *Fork Inspection (All Models)* in this chapter.

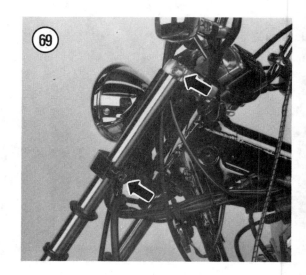

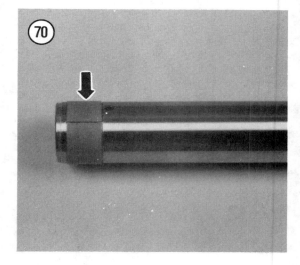

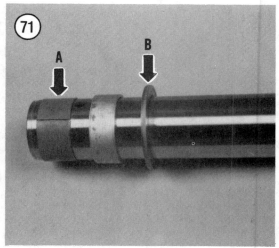

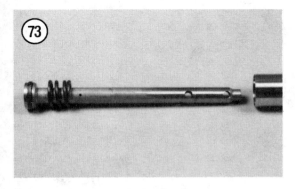

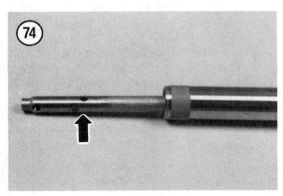

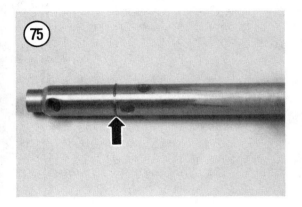

Assembly/Installation

Refer to **Figure 63** for this procedure.

1. Coat all parts with fresh Dexron automatic transmission fluid or fork oil prior to installation.

2. If removed, install a new fork tube bushing (**Figure 70**).

3. Slide the fork slider bushing (A, **Figure 71**) down the fork tube and rest it on the slider.

4. Slide the fork slider backup ring (flange side up) (B, **Figure 71**) down the fork tube and rest it on top of the fork slider bushing.

5. Position the seal with the marking facing upward (**Figure 72**) and slide it down onto the fork tube.

6. Slide the dust seal onto the fork tube.

7. Install the rebound spring onto the damper rod and slide this assembly into the fork tube (**Figure 73**).

8. Pull the damper rod down until it bottoms out (**Figure 74**) and install the spring clip (**Figure 75**).

9. Insert the fork tube up through the lower and upper fork bridges.

10. Position the fork tube so that the top of the fork tube aligns with the top surface of the upper fork bridge (**Figure 76**).

11. Tighten the upper and lower fork bridge bolts sufficiently to hold the fork tube in place.

12. Install the fork spring (**Figure 77**) with the closer wound coils toward the bottom.

9

13. Install the fork spring seat (**Figure 78**) into the fork tube. Check to make sure the spring seat is sitting flat on top of the fork spring. If it is sitting sideways, straighten it with a long screwdriver.

14. Install the spacer (**Figure 79**).

15. Install the fork cap bolt (**Figure 80**) while pushing down on the spacer and the spring. Start the bolt slowly, don't cross thread it.

16. Apply a light coat of grease to the oil lock piece and install the oil lock piece onto the damper rod (**Figure 81**).

17. Install the fork slider onto the fork tube assembly (**Figure 82**). Make sure the oil lock piece is still in place on the end of the damper rod. If the oil lock piece has fallen off, you will not be able to install the Allen head screw in Step 19.

18. Have an assistant hold the fork slider in position.

19. Apply Loctite Lock N' Seal to the threads of the Allen head screw prior to installation. Install it in the fork slider and tighten to the torque specifications listed in **Table 1**.

20A. To install an old fork slider bushing and oil seal, perform the following:

    a. Using a wide flat-bladed screwdriver and hammer, carefully tap the bushing and oil seal into the fork slider working around the *outer* perimeter of the oil seal.

    b. Continue to tap around the oil seal until it is seated and the circlip groove in the slider is visible.

    c. Install the circlip (**Figure 83**) and make sure it properly seated in the groove.

    d. Slide the dust seal down and into position (**Figure 84**).

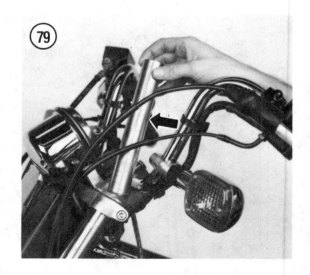

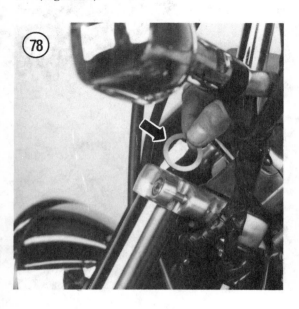

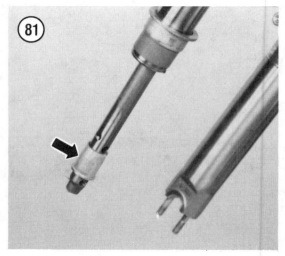

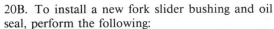

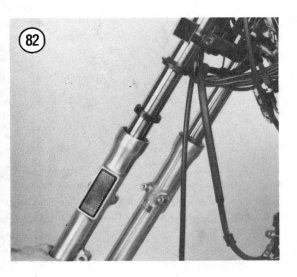

20B. To install a new fork slider bushing and oil seal, perform the following:

    a. Loosen the upper and lower fork bridge bolts and remove the fork assembly from the frame.

    b. Slide off the dust seal and the oil seal.

    c. Place the old slider bushing on top of the backup ring.

    d. Drive the bushing into the fork slider with Honda special tool Fork Seal Driver Body (part No. 07747-0010100) and Fork Seal Driver Attachment (part No. 07747-0010500); refer to **Figure 85**.

    e. Drive the bushing into place until it seats completely in the recess in the slider.

    f. Remove the installation tools and the old slider bushing.

    g. Coat the new seal with automatic transmission fluid.

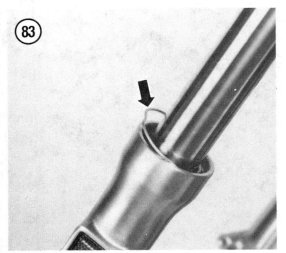

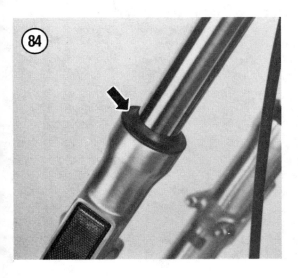

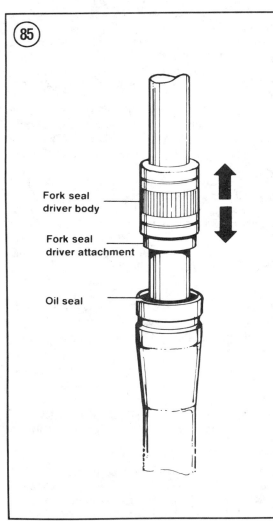

Fork seal driver body

Fork seal driver attachment

Oil seal

9

h. Position the seal with the marking facing upward (**Figure 86**) and slide it down onto the fork tube.

i. Drive the seal into the slider with Honda special tool Fork Seal Driver Body (part No. 07747-0010100) and Fork Seal Driver Attachment (part No. 07747-0010500); refer to **Figure 85**.

j. Drive the oil seal in until the groove in the slider can be seen above the top surface of the oil seal.

k. Remove the installation tools.

l. Install the circlip. Make sure the circlip is completely seated in the groove in the fork slider.

m. Slide on the dust seal.

n. Install the fork tube into the lower and upper fork bridge.

o. Position the fork tube so that the top of the fork tube aligns with the top surface of the upper fork bridge.

p. Tighten the upper and lower fork bridge bolts loosely at this time—just tight enough to hold the fork tube in place.

21. Remove the fork cap bolt and the spacer from the fork tube.

22. Refer to **Table 3** and fill the fork tube with the recommended quantity of DEXRON automatic transmission fluid or fork oil.

23. Tighten the lower bridge bolt to the torque specification listed in **Table 1**.

24. Inspect the O-ring seal (**Figure 87**) on the fork cap bolt; replace if necessary.

25. Install the fork cap bolt while pushing down on the spring. Start the bolt slowly, don't cross thread it.

26. Tighten the upper bridge bolt to the torque specification listed in **Table 1**.

27. Install the front fender and tighten the bolts securely.

28. Install the front wheel as described in this chapter.

29. Install the brake caliper assembly as described in Chapter Eleven.

NON-AIR ASSIST FRONT FORKS (ALL MODELS EXCEPT REBEL 450)

Removal/Installation

1. Remove the front wheel as described under *Front Wheel Removal/Installation* in this chapter.

2. Remove the bolts securing the front fender and remove the front fender.

3. On disc brake models, remove the brake caliper assembly as described under *Front Brake Caliper Removal/Installation* in Chapter Eleven.

CAUTION
The name badge is plastic, remove it carefully to avoid damage to the attachment pins.

4. On models so equipped, carefully pull straight out and remove the name badge from the lower fork bridge.

5. Loosen the lower fork bridge bolt (**Figure 88**).

6. Remove the fork cap bolt (**Figure 89**).

7. Remove the fork tube (**Figure 90**). It may be necessary to slightly rotate the tube while removing it.

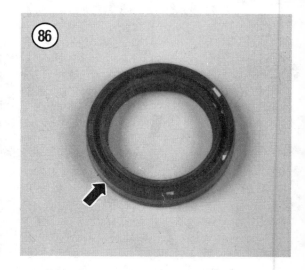

8. Install by reversing these removal steps, noting the following.

9. Tighten the fork cap bolts and the lower fork bridge bolts to the torque specifications listed in **Table 1**.

Disassembly

Refer to **Figure 91** for this procedure.

1. Clamp the slider in a vise with soft jaws.

> *NOTE*
> *In the next step the Allen screw has been secured with thread sealant and is often very difficult to remove because the damper rod will turn inside the slider. It sometimes can be removed with an air impact driver. If you are unable to remove it, take the fork tubes to a dealer and have the screws removed.*

2. Loosen the 6mm Allen screw (**Figure 92**) at the bottom of the slider. Remove the fork assembly from the vise.

3. Clamp the fork tube in a vise with soft jaws.

> *WARNING*
> *Be careful when removing the fork inner bolt as the fork spring is under pressure. Protect your eyes accordingly.*

4. Loosen the fork inner bolt in fork slider. Use a 14mm Allen wrench or insert the head of a 14mm bolt (**Figure 93**) into the socket of the fork inner bolt. Turn the 14mm bolt with Vise Grips.

5. Remove the fork inner bolt, the spring seat and the fork spring (**Figure 94**).

6. Remove the fork from the vise and pour out the fork oil. Discard the fork oil—never reuse fork oil. Pump the fork several times by hand to get most of the oil out.

7. Remove the dust seal (**Figure 95**) from the notch in the slider. Slide the dust seal off the fork tube.

8. Remove the 6mm Allen screw (**Figure 92**) at the bottom of the slider.

9. Pull the fork tube out of the slider.

10. Remove the oil lock piece (**Figure 96**).

11. Turn the fork tube upside down and slide out the damper rod (**Figure 97**) and the rebound spring.

12. Remove snap ring (**Figure 97**) from the slider.

13. Use a dull screwdriver blade and remove oil seal (**Figure 98**) from the slider (**Figure 99**). Do not damage the outer or inner surface of the slider.

14. Inspect the components as described under *Fork Inspection (All Models)* in this Chapter.

9

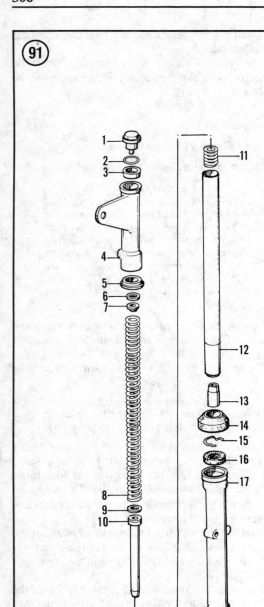

91

**FRONT FORK (NON-AIR ASSIST
EXCEPT REBEL 450)**

1. Fork cap bolt
2. O-ring seal
3. Cover upper cushion
4. Fork cover
5. Cover lower cushion
6. Inner bolt
7. Spring seat
8. Fork spring
9. Piston ring
10. Damper rod
11. Rebound spring
12. Fork tube
13. Oil lock piece
14. Dust seal
15. Snap ring
16. Oil seal
17. Slider
18. Threaded stud
19. Washer
20. Allen screw
21. Axle holder
22. Washer
23. Lockwasher
24. Allen screw

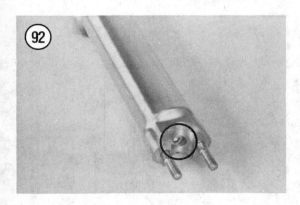

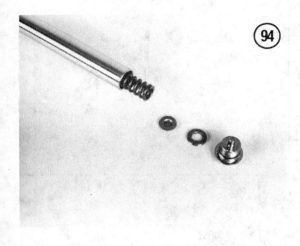

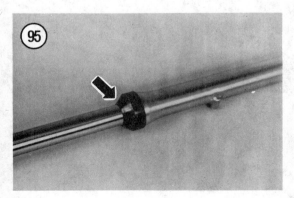

Assembly

1. Install the damper spring onto the damper rod and insert this assembly into fork tube (**Figure 97**).
2. Install oil lock piece (**Figure 96**) onto the end of the damper rod.
3. Apply a light coat of oil to the outside of the fork tube and install it into the slider.
4. Temporarily install the spring with the tapered end down. Install the spring seat and the inner bolt. Tighten the inner bolt using the same tool set-up used for removal. Tighten the bolt securely.
5. Apply Loctite Lock N' Seal to the threads of the Allen screw and install it (**Figure 92**). Tighten the Allen screw securely.
6. Coat the new seal with automatic transmission fluid or fork oil.

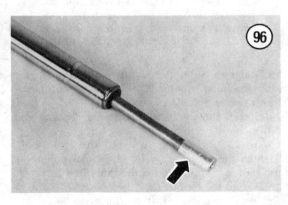

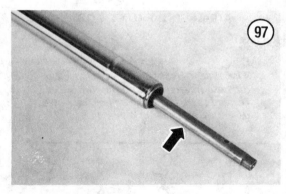

9

7. Position the fork seal with the marking facing upward and slide it down onto the fork tube.

8. Drive the new fork seal into the slider with Honda special tool Fork Seal Driver Body (part No. 07747-0010100) and Fork Seal Driver Attachment (part No. 07747-0010500) as shown in **Figure 100**.

9. Drive the oil seal in until the groove in the slider can be seen above the top surface of the oil seal. Remove the special tools from the fork tube.

10. Install the snap ring. Make sure the snap ring is completely seated in the groove in the fork slider.

11. Slide the dust seal (**Figure 95**) into place.

12. Remove the inner bolt, spring seat and the fork spring.

> *NOTE*
> *In order to measure the correct amount of fluid, use a plastic baby bottle. These have measurements in fluid ounces (oz.) and cubic centimeters (cc) on the side.*

13. Refer to **Table 3** and fill fork tube with the recommended quantity of Dexron automatic transmission fluid (ATF) or fork oil.

14. Install the fork spring with the tapered end down.

15. Install the spring seat and the inner bolt. Tighten the inner bolt using the same tool set-up used for removal. Tighten the inner bolt securely.

16. Install the fork as described under *Front Fork Removal/Installation* in this chapter.

AIR-ASSIST FRONT FORKS

Removal

> *NOTE*
> *The 1986 CB450SC does not have the air hose interconnecting the fork tubes. Instead there is a fork cap bolt/air valve assembly on each fork tube.*

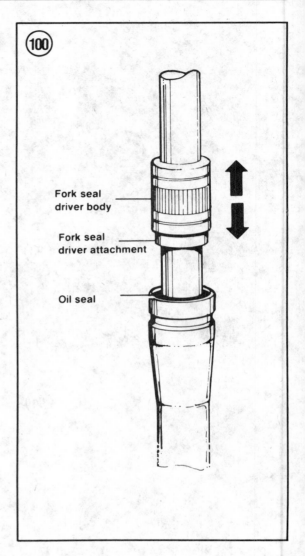

(100)

Fork seal driver body

Fork seal driver attachment

Oil seal

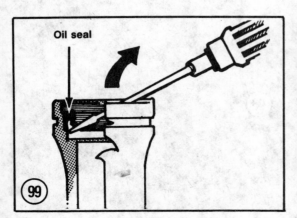

Oil seal

(99)

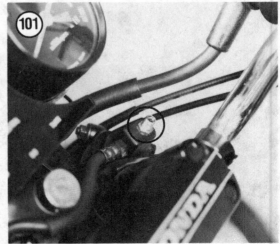

(101)

1. Remove the front brake caliper assembly as described under *Front Brake Caliper Removal/Installation* in Chapter Eleven.

2. Remove the front wheel as described under *Front Wheel Removal/Installation* in this chapter.

NOTE
On some models, it is easier to remove the handlebar assembly in order to gain additional room for removing the air hose fittings.

WARNING
Always bleed off all air pressure and do so gradually. If released too fast, fork oil will spurt out with the air. Protect your eyes and clothing accordingly.

3. Remove the air valve cap and *bleed off all air pressure* by depressing the valve stem (**Figure 101**).

4. On models so equipped, remove the trim panel above the air hose (**Figure 102**). The panel just snaps out of place, there are no fasteners.

5. On the left-hand fork, hold onto the connector (attached to the fork cap bolt) with a wrench and disconnect the air hose from the fork top cap bolt (**Figure 103**).

6. On the right-hand fork, disconnect the air hose from the fork top cap bolt.

7. On the left-hand fork, unscrew the connector (A, **Figure 104**) from the fork cap bolt.

8. Loosen, but do not remove, the fork top cap bolts (B, **Figure 104**).

9. Remove the bolts securing the front fender and remove the fender.

10. Loosen the upper and lower fork bridge bolts (**Figure 105**).

11. Remove the fork tube. It may be necessary to slightly rotate the fork tube while pulling it down and out.

9

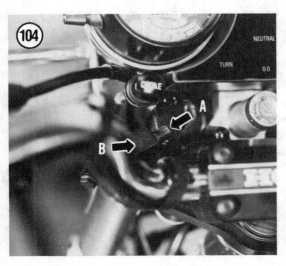

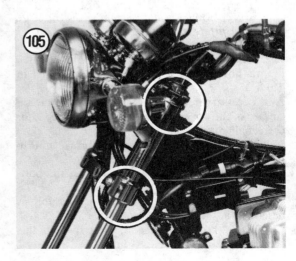

Installation

1. Insert the fork tube up through the lower and upper fork bridges.

2A. On CM400A, CM400C and CM400T models, position the fork tube so that the top of the fork tube is 3.0 mm (0.12 in.) above the top surface of the upper fork bridge (**Figure 106**).

2B. On all other models, position the fork tube so that the top of the fork tube aligns with the top surface of the upper fork bridge (**Figure 107**).

3. Tighten the upper and lower fork bridge bolts loosely at this time—just tight enough to hold them in place.

4. Apply a light coat of grease to the new O-ring seals (**Figure 108**) and install them onto the air hose fittings and to the connector.

> *NOTE*
> *The standard location for the connector is on the left-hand fork tube but the connector can be fitted to either the right- or left-hand fork tube.*

5. Install the connector into the left-hand fork cap bolt/air valve assembly and tighten to the torque specification listed in **Table 1**.

6. Install the air hose first onto the right-hand fork cap bolt (without the connector) and tighten to the torque specification listed in **Table 1**.

> *NOTE*
> *In the next step, if necessary, loosen the fork bridge bolts and rotate the fork tubes so the air hose will have a natural curve after installation.*

> *NOTE*
> *Hold onto the connector (attached to the fork cap bolt/air valve assembly) with a wrench while tightening the air hose fitting in the next step.*

7. Install the air hose to the connector and tighten the air hose to the torque specification listed in **Table 1**.

8. If necessary, realign the fork tube with the top surface of the upper fork bridge; refer to Step 2 for correct alignment.

9. Tighten the upper and lower fork bridge bolts to the torque specifications listed in **Table 1**.

10. Install the front fender and tighten the bolts securely.

11. If removed, install the handlebar assembly as described in this chapter.

12. Install the front wheel as described in this chapter.

13. Install the brake caliper assembly as described in Chapter Eleven.

> *WARNING*
> *Never use any type of compressed gas. Also never heat the fork assembly with a torch or place it near an open flame or extreme heat. Either could result in an explosion.*

14. With the front wheel off the ground, inflate the forks to the standard air pressure of 0.8 ± 0.2 kg/cm^2 (11 ± 3 psi). Do not use compressed air, only use a small hand-operated air pump as shown in **Figure 109**.

15. Take the bike off of the centerstand, apply the front brake and pump the forks several times. Recheck the air pressure and readjust if necessary.

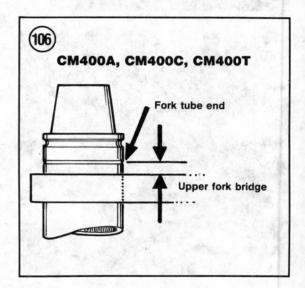

(106)

CM400A, CM400C, CM400T

Fork tube end

Upper fork bridge

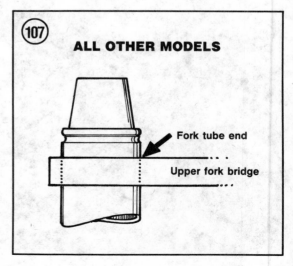

(107)

ALL OTHER MODELS

Fork tube end

Upper fork bridge

Disassembly

Refer to **Figure 110** during the disassembly and assembly procedures.

1. Clamp the slider in a vise with soft jaws.
2. Remove the Allen head screw and gasket from the bottom of the slider.

> *NOTE*
> *This screw has been secured with thread sealant and is often very difficult to remove because the damper rod will turn inside the slider. It sometimes can be removed with an air impact driver. If you are unable to remove it, take the fork tubes to a dealer and have the screws removed.*

3. Hold the upper fork tube in a vise with soft jaws and loosen the fork cap bolt/air valve assembly (if it was not loosened during the fork removal sequence).

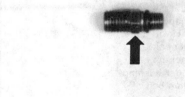

> *WARNING*
> *Be careful when removing the fork cap bolt/air valve assembly as the springs are under pressure.*

4. Remove the fork cap bolt/air valve assembly from the fork.
5. Remove the upper short spring A, spring seat and lower long spring B.
6. Remove the fork from the vise, pour the fork oil out and discard it. Pump the fork several times by hand to expel most of the remaining oil. Discard the fork oil—never reuse fork oil.
7. Remove the dust seal (**Figure 111**).
8. Remove the circlip (**Figure 112**) and the backup plate from the slider.

> *NOTE*
> *On this type of fork, force is needed to remove the fork tube from the slider.*

9. Install the fork slider in a vise with soft jaws.
10. There is an interference fit between the bushing in the fork slider and the bushing on the fork tube. In order to remove the fork tube from the slider, pull hard on the fork tube using quick in and out strokes (**Figure 113**). Doing this will withdraw the bushing, backup ring and oil seal from the slider.

> *NOTE*
> *It may be necessary to slightly heat the area on the slider around the oil seal prior to removal. Use a rag soaked in hot water; do not apply a flame directly to the fork slider.*

11. Withdraw the fork tube from the slider.

> *NOTE*
> *Do not remove the fork tube bushing unless it is going to be replaced. Inspect it as described under **Inspection** in this Chapter.*

12. Turn the fork tube upside down and slide off the oil seal, backup ring and slider bushing from the fork tube (**Figure 114**).

> *NOTE*
> *Do not discard the slider bushing at this time. It will be used during the installation procedure.*

13. Remove the oil lock piece, the damper rod and rebound spring.
14. Inspect the components as described under *Fork Inspection (All Models)* in this Chapter.

9

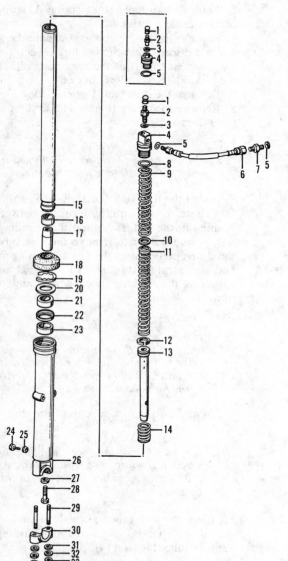

FRONT FORK—AIR ASSIST

1. Valve stem cap
2. Air valve
3. O-ring seal
4. Fork cap bolt
5. O-ring seal
6. Interconnecting air hose
7. Connector
8. O-ring
9. Upper fork spring "A"
10. Washer
11. Lower fork spring "B"
12. Piston ring
13. Damper rod
14. Rebound spring
15. Fork tube
16. Fork tube bushing
17. Oil lock piece
18. Dust seal
19. Snap ring
20. Back-up plate
21. Oil seal
22. Back-up ring
23. Slider bushing
24. Drain bolt
25. Washer
26. Fork slider
27. Gasket
28. Allen screw
29. Threaded stud
30. Axle holder
31. Washer
32. Lockwasher
33. Bolt

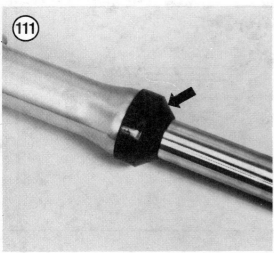

Assembly

1. Coat all parts with fresh Dexron automatic transmission fluid or fork oil prior to installation.
2. If removed, install a new fork tube bushing.
3. Install the rebound spring onto the damper rod and insert this assembly into the fork tube.
4. Temporarily install the fork spring(s) and fork cap bolt/air valve assembly to hold the damper rod in place.
5. Install the oil lock piece onto the damper rod (**Figure 115**).
6. Install the upper fork assembly into the slider (**Figure 116**).
7. Slide the fork slider bushing down the fork tube and rest it on the slider.
8. Slide the fork slider backup ring (flange side up) down the fork tube and rest it on top of the fork slider bushing.

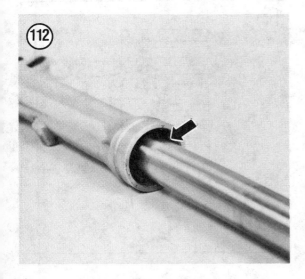

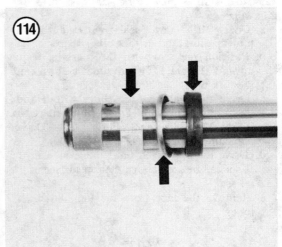

9

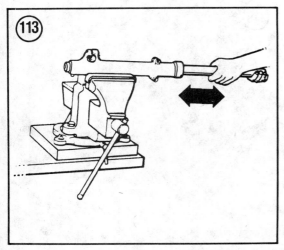

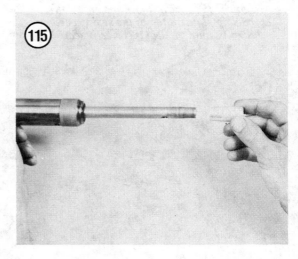

9. To install the fork slider bushing, perform the following:

   a. Place the old slider bushing on top of the backup ring.

   b. Drive the bushing into the fork slider with Honda special tool Fork Seal Driver Body (part No. 07747-0010100) and Fork Seal Driver Attachment (part No. 07747-0010500); refer to **Figure 100**.

   c. Drive the bushing into place until it seats completely in the recess in the slider.

   d. Remove the installation tools and the old slider bushing.

10. Install the backup ring.

11. To prevent damage to the inside of the new fork seal during installation, wrap the groove in the top of the fork tube with clear tape (something smooth and non-abrasive—do not use duct or masking tape).

12. To install a new fork seal, perform the following:

   a. Coat the new seal with automatic transmission fluid or fork oil.

   b. Position the seal with the marking facing upward (**Figure 117**) and slide it down onto the fork tube.

   c. Drive the seal into the slider with Honda special tool Fork Seal Driver Body (part No. 07747-0010100) and Fork Seal Driver Attachment (part No. 07747-0010500).

   d. Drive the oil seal in until the groove in the slider can be seen above the top surface of the oil seal.

   e. Remove the tape from the top of the fork tube.

NOTE
If the seal must be driven further down, remove the special tools and insert the backup plate on top of the seal. Repeat Step 12 until the seal is correctly seated.

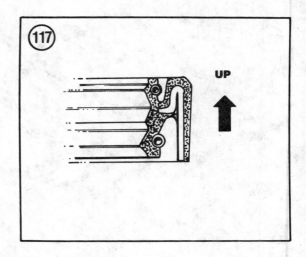

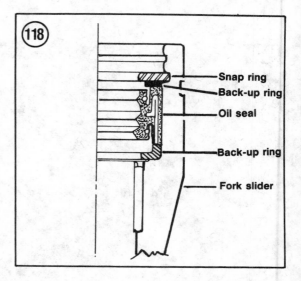

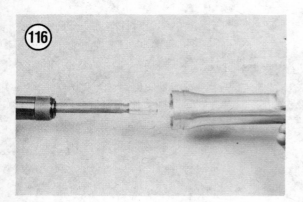

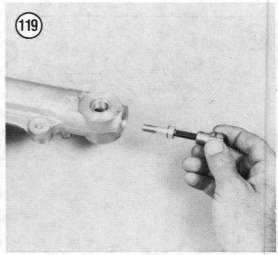

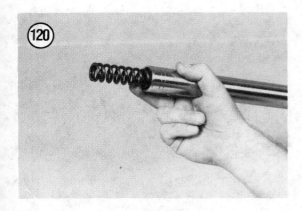

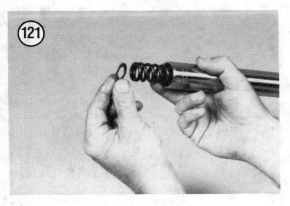

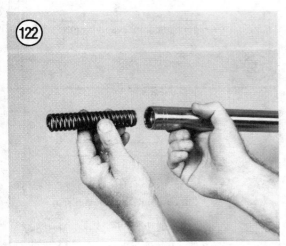

13. Install the backup plate and circlip. Make sure the circlip is completely seated in the groove in the fork slider.

NOTE
*All components should be installed as shown in **Figure 118**.*

14. Install the dust seal (**Figure 111**).

15. Make sure the gasket is on the Allen head screw.

16. Apply Loctite Lock N' Seal to the threads of the Allen head screw prior to installation. Install it in the fork slider (**Figure 119**) and tighten to the torque specifications listed in **Table 1**.

17. Remove the fork cap bolt/air valve assembly and both fork springs.

18. Refer to **Table 3** and fill the fork tube with the recommended quantity of DEXRON automatic transmission fluid or fork oil.

19. Install the lower long fork spring "B" (**Figure 120**), the spring seat (**Figure 121**) and the upper short fork spring A (**Figure 122**).

20. Inspect the O-ring seal (**Figure 123**) on the fork cap bolt/air valve assembly; replace if necessary.

21. Install the fork cap bolt/air valve assembly (**Figure 124**) while pushing down on the springs. Start the bolt slowly, don't cross thread it.

22. Place the slider in a vise with soft jaws and tighten the fork top cap bolt to the torque specification listed in **Table 1**.

23. Repeat for the other fork assembly.

24. Install the fork assembly as described in this chapter.

9

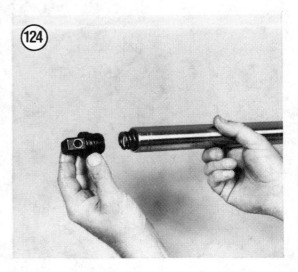

FORK INSPECTION (ALL MODELS)

1. Thoroughly clean all parts in solvent and dry them. Check the fork tube for signs of wear or scratches.

2. Check the damper rod for straightness. **Figure 125** shows one method. Use 1/2 of the total runout reading to determine the actual runout. The rod should be replaced if the runout is 0.2 mm (0.01 in.) or greater.

3. Check the damper rod and piston ring (**Figure 126**) for wear or damage. Make sure the oil holes (**Figure 127**) are clear.

4. Check the upper fork tube for straightness. If bent or severely scratched, it should be replaced.

5. Check the lower slider for dents or exterior damage that may cause the upper fork tube to hang up during riding. Replace if necessary.

6. Measure the uncompressed length of the fork springs (not rebound spring) as shown in **Figure 128**. If the spring has sagged to the service limit dimension listed in **Table 2** or less,it must be replaced.

7. Inspect the slider and fork tube bushings. If either is scratched or scored they must be replaced. If the Teflon coating is worn off so that the copper base material is showing on approximately 3/4 of the total surface, the bushing must be replaced. Also check for distortion on the check points of the backup ring; replace as necessary. Refer to **Figure 129**.

8. Any parts that are worn or damaged should be replaced. Simply cleaning and reinstalling unserviceable components will not improve performance of the front suspension.

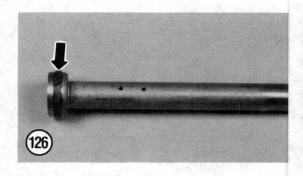

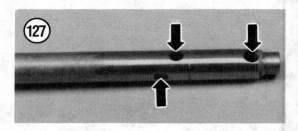

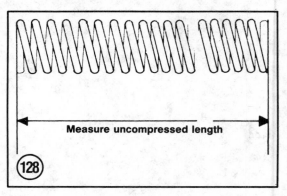

Measure uncompressed length

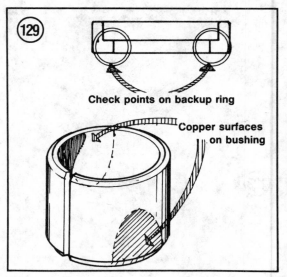

Check points on backup ring

Copper surfaces on bushing

Table 1 FRONT SUSPENSION TORQUE SPECIFICATIONS

Item	N•m	ft.-lb.
Front axle holder nuts	18-25	13-18
Front axle nut		
1978-1985	50-80	36-58
1986-on	55-65	40-47
Front drum brake		
torque link bolt	18-24	13-18
Brake disc mounting bolts		
1983-1986 CB450SC, Rebel 450	37-43	27-31
All other models	27-33	20-24
Wire spokes		
Rebel 450	7-11	5-8
All other models	2.5-3.5	1.4-2.5
Handlebar holder bolts		
Drum brake models	18-24	13-18
Disc brake models	NA	NA
Master cylinder clamp bolts	10-14	7-10
Steering stem adjust nut		
1985 CB450SC	14-16	10-12
Rebel 450	23-27	17-20
Steering stem nut		
1986 CB450SC	90-100	65-87
All other models	100-110	72-80
Upper fork bridge bolts		
1978-1980	*	*
1986 CB450SC	10-14	7-10
All other models	9-13	7-9
Lower fork bridge bolts		
1978-1980	18-30	13-22
1986 CB450SC	20-24	14-17
All other models	18-25	13-18
Front fork cap bolt		
1978-1980	70-90	51-65
1986 CB450SC	16-20	12-14
All other models	15-30	11-22
Air-assist front fork		
Connector	4-7	3-5
Air hose-to-fork cap bolt	4-7	3-5
Air hose-to-connector	15-20	11-14
Fork slider Allen bolt	15-25	11-18

NA= Information not available from Honda. Tighten these fasteners securely.
* 1978-1980 models are not equipped with upper fork bridge bolts.

9

Table 2 FRONT FORK SPRING SPECIFICATIONS

Model	Standard mm	in.	Service length mm	in.
1981 CB400T, CB450T				
Spring A	240.4	9.47	235	9.25
Spring B	341.9	13.46	335	13.19
1981 CM400A, CM400C, CM400T				
Spring A	237.4	9.35	232	9.13
Spring B	312.4	12.30	306	12.06
1981 CM450A, CM450C				
Spring A	237.4	9.35	232	9.13
Spring B	362.4	14.27	355	14
1982-1985 CM450SC	NA	NA	NA	NA
1986 CM450SC				
Spring A	240.4	9.47	235	9.25
Spring B	341.9	13.46	335	13.2
Rebel 450	356.8	14.05	350	13.8
All non-air assist				
(except Rebel 450)	490.9	19.33	480	18.9

NA = Information not available from Honda.

Table 3 FRONT FORK OIL CAPACITY *

Model	Standard capacity cc	fl. oz.
1981		
CB400T	187	6.3
CM400A, CM400C, CM400T	190	6.4
CM400E	135	4.6
1982-on		
CB450T	187	6.3
CM450A, CM450C	220	7.4
CM450E	135	4.6
CM450SC	651	22.0
1983-1985 CM450SC	187.5-192.5	6.3-6.5
1986 CM450SC	182.5-187.5	6.25-6.27
Rebel 450	363.5-368.5	12.3-12.5
Non air-assist (except Rebel 450)	137-143	4.8-5.0

* Capacity for each fork leg.

REAR SUSPENSION

This chapter includes procedures for repair and maintenance of the rear wheel, drive chain, driven sprocket assembly and the rear suspension.

Power from the engine is transmitted to the rear wheel by a drive sprocket, drive chain and the driven sprocket.

Tire changing, tire repair and wheel balancing are covered in Chapter Nine.

Table 1 and **Table 2** are located at the end of this chapter.

REAR WHEEL

Removal/Installation

1. Place wood blocks under the crankcase to support the bike securely with the rear wheel off the ground.
2. On 1978 models, the mufflers are long and extend past the rear axle area. It is not necessary, but it does allow additional work room if you remove the right-hand muffler as follows:
   a. Loosen the clamp (A, **Figure 1**) securing the right-hand muffler to the common collector.
   b. Remove the bolt securing the right-hand rear footpeg and right-hand muffler (B, **Figure 1**).
   c. Slide the muffler out of the collector and remove the muffler.
3A. On all models except Rebel 450, perform the following:

a. Remove the brake rod adjusting nut (A, **Figure 2**). Separate the rod from the brake arm.
b. Remove the cotter pin, backing plate, stop nut, washer, rubber grommet (B, **Figure 2**) and disconnect the torque arm from the backing plate.
c. Remove the cotter pin (models so equipped) and the axle nut (C, **Figure 2**). Discard the cotter pin.
3B. On Rebel 450 models, perform the following:
   a. Remove the brake rod adjusting nut. Separate the rod from the brake arm.
   b. Remove the cotter pin, nut, washer and rubber spacer. Withdraw the pivot bolt and disconnect the torque arm from the backing plate.
   c. Remove the rear axle nut (**Figure 3**).
4. Withdraw the rear axle from the left-hand side.
5. Let the wheel drop down. Push the wheel forward and disengage the drive chain from the driven sprocket.
6. Don't lose the wheel spacer on either the right-hand side (**Figure 4**) or left-hand side of the wheel.
7. Install by reversing the removal steps.
8. Be sure to install the wheel spacer on either the right-hand side or left-hand side of the wheel before installing the rear axle.

10

9. Torque the axle nut to the torque specification listed in **Table 1**.

10. On models so equipped, install a new cotter pin and bend the ends over completely.

11. Adjust the rear brake and the drive chain as described in Chapter Three.

Inspection

Measure the wobble and runout of the wheel rim with a dial indicator as shown in **Figure 5** or **Figure 6**. The standard value for both radial and axial runout is 0.5 mm (0.02 in.). The maximum permissible limit is 2.0 mm (0.08 in.).

On wire wheels, tighten or replace any bent or loose spokes. Refer to *Spoke Adjustment* in this chapter.

If the runout on a ComStar (stamped) or ComCast (cast alloy) wheel exceeds the limit, it will have to be replaced, as the wheel cannot be serviced. Inspect the wheel for cracks, fractures, dents or bends. If it is damaged in any way, it must be replaced.

REAR HUB

Inspection

Inspect each wheel bearing before removing it from the wheel hub.

> *CAUTION*
> *Do not remove the wheel bearings for inspection purposes as they will be damaged during the removal process. Remove the wheel bearings only if they are to be replaced.*

1. Perform Steps 1-3 or Steps 1-4, depending on model, of *Disassembly* in this chapter.

2. Turn each bearing by hand. Make sure each bearing turns smoothly.

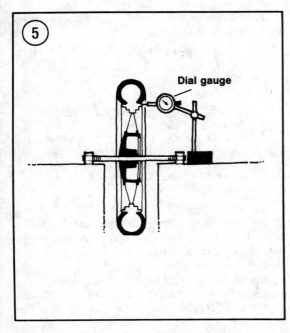

Dial gauge

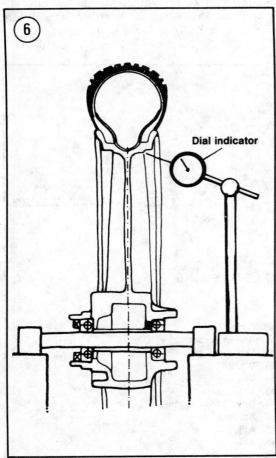

Dial indicator

3. On non-sealed bearings, check the balls for evidence of wear, pitting, or excessive heat (bluish tint). Replace bearings if necessary; always replace as a complete set. When replacing the bearings, be sure to take your old bearings along to ensure a perfect matchup.

NOTE
Fully sealed bearings are available from many bearing specialty shops. Fully sealed bearings provide better protection from moisture that may get into the hub.

4. Check the axle for wear and straightness. Use V-blocks and a dial indicator as shown in **Figure 7**. If the runout is 0.2 mm (0.008 in.) or greater, the axle must be replaced.

REAR HUB
(1978-1981 SPOKE WHEEL)

Disassembly

Refer to **Figure 8** for this procedure.

NOTE
It is not necessary to remove the final driven sprocket assembly from the rear wheel for this procedure.

1. Remove the rear wheel as described under *Rear Wheel Removal/Installation* in this chapter.
2. Pull the brake panel assembly straight up and out of the brake drum.
3. Remove the dust seal from the left-hand side.
4. Before proceeding any further, inspect the wheel bearings as described under *Rear Hub Inspection* in this chapter.

10

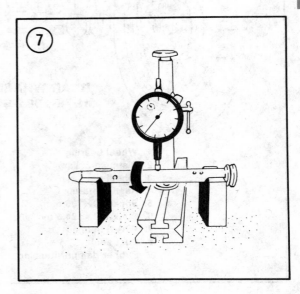

5. To remove the left- and right-hand bearings and the distance collar, perform the following:

   a. Insert a soft aluminum or brass drift into one side of the hub.

   b. Push the distance collar over to one side and place the drift onto the inner race of the opposite bearing.

   c. Using a hammer, tap around the perimeter of the inner race and tap the bearing out of the hub.

   d. Remove the distance collar.

   e. Remove the other bearing in the same manner.

6. Clean the inside and outside of the hub with solvent. Dry with compressed air.

Assembly

1. Pack the bearings thoroughly with multipurpose grease. Work the grease in between the balls thoroughly. Turn the bearing by hand a couple of times to make sure the grease is distributed evenly inside the bearing.

2. Blow any dirt or foreign matter out of the hub before installing the bearings.

3. Pack the wheel hub and axle distance collar with multipurpose grease.

> *CAUTION*
> *Install non-sealed the bearings with the sealed side facing outward.*

> *CAUTION*
> *Tap the bearings squarely into place and tap on the outer race only. Use a socket (**Figure 9**) that matches the outer race diameter. Do not tap on the inner race or the bearing might be damaged. Be sure that the bearings are completely seated.*

4. Install the right-hand bearing.

5. Position the distance collar with the flange side toward the left-hand side (driven sprocket side). Install the distance collar.

6. Install the left-hand bearing.

7. Install the dust seal on the left-hand side.

8. Using a soft-faced mallet, tap around the perimeter of the driven sprocket to make sure it is completely seated in the wheel hub.

9. Install the brake assembly into the drum.

10. Install the wheel as described under *Rear Wheel Removal/Installation* in this chapter.

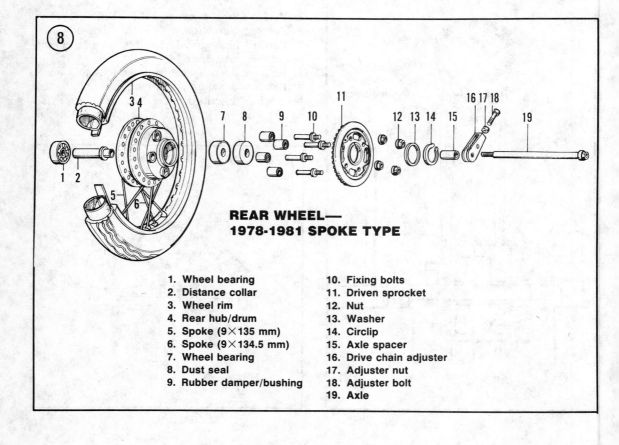

**REAR WHEEL—
1978-1981 SPOKE TYPE**

1. Wheel bearing
2. Distance collar
3. Wheel rim
4. Rear hub/drum
5. Spoke (9×135 mm)
6. Spoke (9×134.5 mm)
7. Wheel bearing
8. Dust seal
9. Rubber damper/bushing
10. Fixing bolts
11. Driven sprocket
12. Nut
13. Washer
14. Circlip
15. Axle spacer
16. Drive chain adjuster
17. Adjuster nut
18. Adjuster bolt
19. Axle

REAR HUB
(REBEL 450 SPOKE WHEEL,
COMSTAR AND COMCAST WHEEL)

Disassembly

Refer to the following illustrations for this procedure:

    a. **Figure 10**: Rebel 450 spoke wheel.

    b. **Figure 11**: ComStar (1982 CB450SC) stamped steel wheel.

    c. **Figure 12**: ComStar (all models except 1982 CB450SC) stamped steel wheel.

    d. **Figure 13**: ComCast alloy wheel.

This procedure is shown on a Rebel 450 and represents a typical rear hub disassembly and assembly procedure. Where differences occur among the various models they are identified.

1. Remove the rear wheel as described under *Rear Wheel Removal/Installation* in this chapter.

2. Pull the brake panel assembly straight up and out of the brake drum.

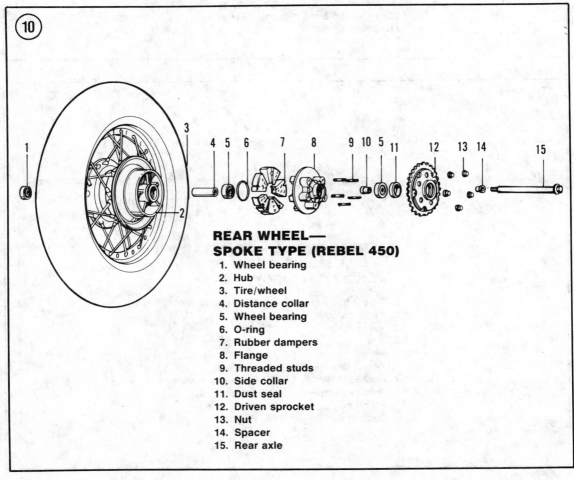

REAR WHEEL—
SPOKE TYPE (REBEL 450)

  1. Wheel bearing
  2. Hub
  3. Tire/wheel
  4. Distance collar
  5. Wheel bearing
  6. O-ring
  7. Rubber dampers
  8. Flange
  9. Threaded studs
10. Side collar
11. Dust seal
12. Driven sprocket
13. Nut
14. Spacer
15. Rear axle

10

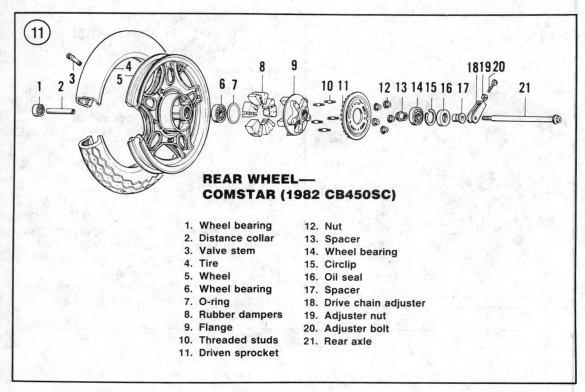

REAR WHEEL— COMSTAR (1982 CB450SC)

1. Wheel bearing
2. Distance collar
3. Valve stem
4. Tire
5. Wheel
6. Wheel bearing
7. O-ring
8. Rubber dampers
9. Flange
10. Threaded studs
11. Driven sprocket
12. Nut
13. Spacer
14. Wheel bearing
15. Circlip
16. Oil seal
17. Spacer
18. Drive chain adjuster
19. Adjuster nut
20. Adjuster bolt
21. Rear axle

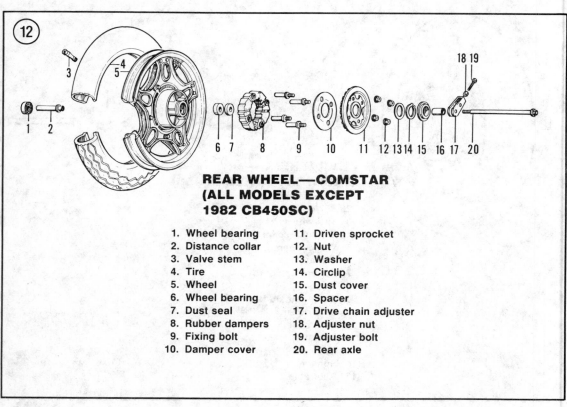

REAR WHEEL—COMSTAR (ALL MODELS EXCEPT 1982 CB450SC)

1. Wheel bearing
2. Distance collar
3. Valve stem
4. Tire
5. Wheel
6. Wheel bearing
7. Dust seal
8. Rubber dampers
9. Fixing bolt
10. Damper cover
11. Driven sprocket
12. Nut
13. Washer
14. Circlip
15. Dust cover
16. Spacer
17. Drive chain adjuster
18. Adjuster nut
19. Adjuster bolt
20. Rear axle

3. Remove the driven sprocket assembly from the hub as described under *Driven Sprocket Removal/Installation* in this chapter.

4. Remove the rubber dampers (**Figure 14**) from the hub.

5. Before proceeding any further, inspect the wheel bearings as described under *Rear Hub Inspection* in this chapter.

6. On models so equipped, remove the O-ring seal (A, **Figure 15**) from the left-hand side of the hub.

7. To remove the left- and right-hand bearings and the distance collar, perform the following:

a. Insert a soft aluminum or brass drift into one side of the hub.

b. Push the distance collar over to one side and place the drift onto the inner race of the opposite bearing.

c. Using a hammer, tap around the perimeter of the inner race and tap the bearing out of the hub.

d. Remove the distance collar.

e. Remove the other bearing in the same manner.

8. Clean the inside and outside of the hub with solvent. Dry with compressed air.

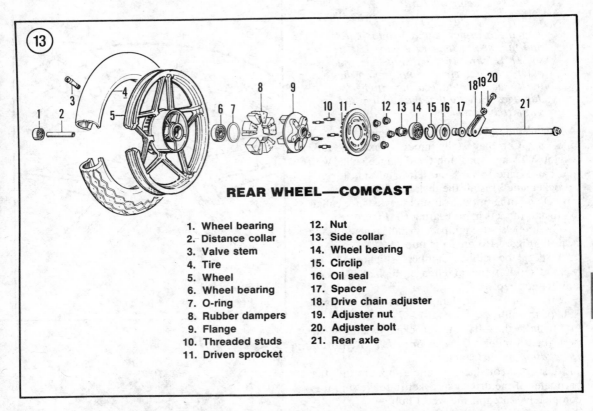

REAR WHEEL—COMCAST

1. Wheel bearing
2. Distance collar
3. Valve stem
4. Tire
5. Wheel
6. Wheel bearing
7. O-ring
8. Rubber dampers
9. Flange
10. Threaded studs
11. Driven sprocket
12. Nut
13. Side collar
14. Wheel bearing
15. Circlip
16. Oil seal
17. Spacer
18. Drive chain adjuster
19. Adjuster nut
20. Adjuster bolt
21. Rear axle

10

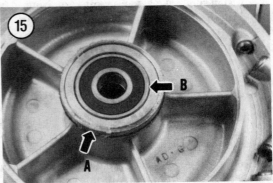

Assembly

1. Pack the bearings thoroughly with multipurpose grease. Work the grease in between the balls thoroughly. Turn the bearing by hand a couple of times to make sure the grease is distributed evenly inside the bearing.

2. Blow any dirt or foreign matter out of the hub before installing the bearings.

3. Pack the wheel hub and axle distance collar with multipurpose grease.

CAUTION
Install non-sealed the bearings with the sealed side facing outward.

CAUTION
Tap the bearings squarely into place and tap on the outer race only. Use a socket (Figure 16) that matches the outer race diameter. Do not tap on the inner race or the bearing might be damaged. Be sure that the bearings are completely seated.

4. Install the right-hand bearing (**Figure 17**).

5A. On ComStar (all models except 1982 CB450SC) wheel, position the distance collar with the flange side toward the left-hand side (driven sprocket side). Install the distance collar.

5B. On all other models, install the distance collar.

6. Install the left-hand bearing (B, **Figure 15**).

7. On models so equipped, install a new O-ring seal (A, **Figure 15**) onto the hub.

8. Inspect the rubber dampers (**Figure 18**) for wear, deterioration and damage. Replace as a set if any require replacing.

9. Install the rubber dampers into the left-hand side of the hub.

10. Install the driven sprocket assembly as described under *Driven Sprocket Removal/ Installation* in this chapter.

11. Using a soft-faced mallet, tap around the perimeter of the driven sprocket to make sure it is completely seated in the wheel hub.

12. Install the brake assembly into the drum.

13. Install the wheel as described under *Rear Wheel Removal/Installation* in this chapter.

DRIVEN SPROCKET ASSEMBLY

**Removal/Installation
(Rebel 450, ComStar 1982 CB450SC
and ComCast Wheels)**

1. Remove the rear wheel as described under *Rear Wheel Removal/Installation* in this chapter.

NOTE
If the driven sprocket assembly is difficult to remove, tap on the backside of the sprocket (from the opposite side through the spokes) with a wooden handle of a hammer. Tap evenly around the perimeter of the sprocket until the assembly is free.

2. Pull the driven sprocket assembly out of the hub.

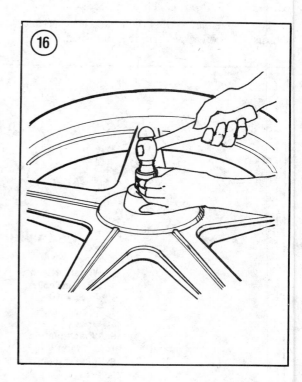

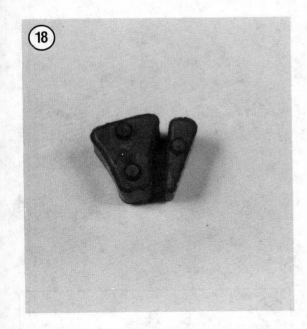

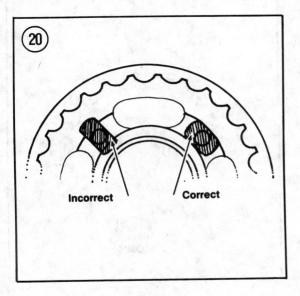

Incorrect   **Correct**

3. Inspect the driven sprocket as described under *Driven Sprocket Inspection* in this chapter.

4. If removed, install the rubber dampers into the left-hand side of the hub.

5. Install the driven sprocket assembly into the hub.

6. Using a soft-faced mallet, tap around the perimeter of the driven sprocket to make sure it is completely seated in the wheel hub.

7. Install the rear wheel as described under *Rear Wheel Removal/Installation* in this chapter.

**Removal/Installation
(All Other Models)**

1. Remove the rear wheel as described under *Rear Wheel Removal/Installation* in this chapter.

2. On ComStar wheels remove the dust seal (A, **Figure 19**) from the driven sprocket.

3. Remove the circlip and washer securing the driven sprocket to the hub.

4. If the driven sprocket is going to be disassembled, loosen, but do not remove, the nuts (B, **Figure 19**) securing the sprocket fixing bolts.

> *NOTE*
> *If the driven sprocket assembly is difficult to remove, tap on the backside of the sprocket (from the opposite side through the spokes) with a wooden handle of a hammer. Tap evenly around the perimeter of the sprocket until the assembly is free.*

5. Pull the driven sprocket assembly out of the hub.

6. Inspect the driven sprocket as described under *Driven Sprocket Inspection* in this chapter.

7. If the fixing bolts were removed, install them correctly into the groove in the backside of the sprocket as shown in **Figure 20**. Install the nuts and tighten only finger-tight at this time.

8. Install the driven sprocket assembly into the hub.

9. Using a soft-faced mallet, tap around the perimeter of the driven sprocket to make sure it is completely seated in the wheel hub.

10. Install the washer and the circlip securing the driven sprocket to the hub.

11. On ComStar wheels install the dust seal (A, **Figure 19**) into the driven sprocket.

12. If the driven sprocket was disassembled, securely tighten the nuts (B, **Figure 19**) securing the sprocket fixing bolts.

13. Install the rear wheel as described under *Rear Wheel Removal/Installation* in this chapter.

10

Inspection (All Models)

1. Inspect the sprocket teeth (A, **Figure 21**) for wear and distortion. Compare with **Figure 22**. If it is worn or distorted, it must be replaced.

2A. On 1978-1981 wire wheel models, inspect the rubber damper/bushing assemblies for wear, deterioration and damage. Replace as a set if any require replacing.

2B. On all models except 1978-1981 wire wheels, inspect the rubber dampers (**Figure 18**) for wear, deterioration and damage. Replace as a set if any require replacing.

3. On models so equipped, inspect the bosses on the backside of the flange (**Figure 23**) where they make contact with the rubber dampers. Check for cracks or damage to the bosses; replace if necessary.

Driven Sprocket Replacement (1978-1981 All Models and All ComStar Wheels Except 1982 CB450SC Models)

Refer to **Figure 8** and **Figure 12** for this procedure.

Only the driven sprocket and the fixing bolts attached to the sprocket can be replaced.

1. On all ComStar Wheels (except 1982 CB450SC models), remove the damper cover from behind the sprocket.

2. To remove the fixing bolts, remove the nuts securing the fixing bolts to the driven sprocket and remove the fixing bolts.

3. Install and position the fixing bolts correctly into the groove in the backside of the sprocket as shown in **Figure 20**. Install the nuts and tighten securely.

Driven Sprocket and Bearing Replacement (1982 CB450SC ComStar Wheels and All ComCast Wheels)

Refer to **Figure 11** and **Figure 13** for this procedure.

1. If not already removed, remove the side collar (**Figure 24**) from the backside of the bearing.

2. Remove the dust seal and the circlip from the flange.

3. Turn the driven sprocket assembly upside down.

4. Using a suitable size socket, drive the bearing out of the driven sprocket.

5. Remove the nuts securing the driven sprocket to the flange and remove the sprocket.

6. Pack the bearing thoroughly with multipurpose grease. Work the grease in between the balls

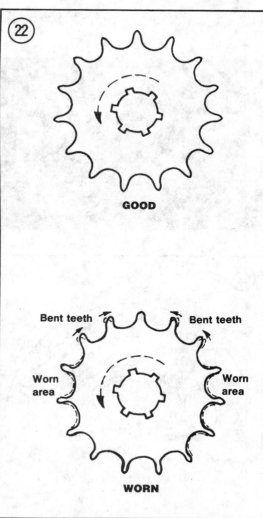

thoroughly. Turn the bearing by hand a couple of times to make sure the grease is distributed evenly inside the bearing.

7. Blow any dirt or foreign matter out of the flange before installing the bearing.

8. Install the bearing into the flange as follows:
   a. Tap the bearing squarely into place and tap on the outer race only. Do not tap on the inner race or the bearing might be damaged.
   b. Using a suitable size socket, drive the bearing into the driven sprocket.
   c. Drive the bearing in until it is completely seated.

9. Install the driven sprocket onto the flange and install the nuts. Do not tighten the nuts at this time.

10. Install the circlip and the dust seal into the flange.

11. Install the side collar (**Figure 24**) into the backside of the bearing.

12. Install the driven flange assembly into the rear wheel then tighten the driven sprocket nuts to the torque specification listed in **Table 1**.

Driven Sprocket and Bearing Replacement (Rebel 450)

Refer to **Figure 10** for this procedure.

1. If not already removed, remove the side collar (**Figure 24**) from the backside of the bearing.

2. Remove the dust seal (A, **Figure 25**) from the flange.

3. Turn the driven sprocket assembly upside down.

4. Using a suitable size socket, drive the bearing (B, **Figure 25**) out of the driven sprocket.

5. Remove the nuts (B, **Figure 21**) securing the driven sprocket to the flange and remove the sprocket.

6. Pack the bearing thoroughly with multipurpose grease. Work the grease in between the balls thoroughly. Turn the bearing by hand a couple of times to make sure the grease is distributed evenly inside the bearing.

7. Blow any dirt or foreign matter out of the flange before installing the bearing.

8. Install the bearing into the flange as follows:
   a. Tap the bearing squarely into place and tap on the outer race only. Do not tap on the inner race or the bearing might be damaged.
   b. Using a suitable size socket, drive the bearing into the driven sprocket.
   c. Drive the bearing in until it is completely seated.

10

9. Install the driven sprocket onto the flange and install the nuts. Do not tighten the nuts at this time.

10. Install the dust seal into the flange.

11. Install the side collar (**Figure 24**) into the backside of the bearing.

12. Install the driven flange assembly into the rear wheel then tighten the driven sprocket nuts to the torque specification listed in **Table 1**.

DRIVE CHAIN

For drive chain cleaning, lubrication and adjustment procedures, refer to *Drive Chain* in Chapter Three.

Drive chain replacement numbers are listed in **Table 2**.

Removal/Installation
(Modeis Equipped With a Master Link)

1. Place wood blocks under the crankcase to support the bike with the rear wheel off the ground.

2. To loosen the drive chain tension, perform the following:

   a. On models so equipped, remove the rear axle nut cotter pin.

   b. Loosen the rear axle nut (A, **Figure 26**).

   c. Loosen the drive chain adjuster locknut (B, **Figure 26**) on each side of the swing arm.

   d. Turn the drive chain adjuster bolt (C, **Figure 26**) on each of the swing arm ends until the tension is relieved on the drive chain.

3. Rotate the rear wheel until the master link is accessible.

4. Remove the master link clip (**Figure 27**), plate and link from the drive chain.

5. Remove the drive chain from the drive and driven sprockets.

6. Install by reversing these removal steps, noting the following.

7. Reinstall the master link and plate.

8. Install a master link clip so that the closed end is facing in the direction of travel (**Figure 28**).

9. Adjust the drive chain tension as described under *Drive Chain Adjustment* in Chapter Three.

Removal/Installation
(CB450SC and Rebel 450 Models
With No Master Link)

The factory equipped drive chain, on these models, is a closed-loop type with no master link. If your bike has the factory equipped drive chain, the swing arm must be removed in order to remove the drive chain. If the drive chain has been replaced with an after-market type with a master

link, refer to *Drive Chain Removal/Installation (Models Equipped With a Master Link)* in this chapter.

1. Place wood blocks under the crankcase to support the bike with the rear wheel off the ground.

2A. On CB450SC models, perform the following:

   a. Remove the bolt and nut clamping the shift lever to the shaft and remove the shift lever.

   b. Remove the bolts securing the left-hand engine cover and remove the cover and gasket.

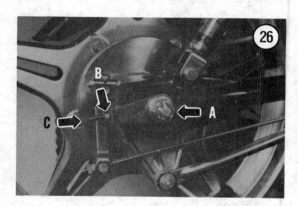

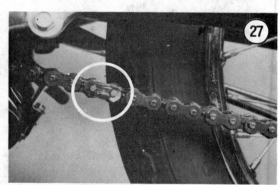

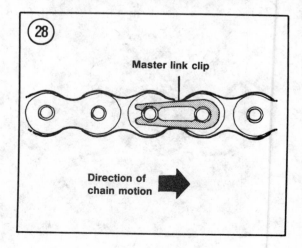

Master link clip

Direction of
chain motion

2B. On Rebel 450 models, perform the following:
  a. Remove the bolt and nut clamping the shift lever to the shaft and remove the shift lever (A, **Figure 29**).
  b. Remove the bolt securing the front left-hand footpeg and remove the footpeg (B, **Figure 29**).

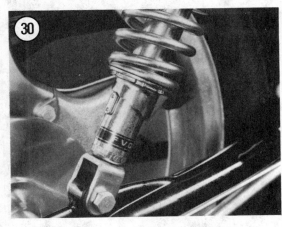

  c. Remove the bolts securing the left-hand engine cover and remove the cover and gasket (C, **Figure 29**).
3. Remove the swing arm as described under *Swing Arm Removal/Installation* in this chapter.
4. Remove the drive chain and install a new one.
5. Install the swing arm as described under *Swing Arm Removal/Installation* in this chapter.
6. Install the left-hand engine cover and gasket. Tighten the bolts securely.
7. Install the front footpeg and gearshift lever.

REAR SHOCK ABSORBERS

Spring Preload Adjustment

The rear shock absorbers on all models are spring controlled and hydraulically dampened. Spring preload can be adjusted by rotating the cam ring at the base of the spring (**Figure 30**). Rotate the cam ring *clockwise* to increase preload and *counterclockwise* to decrease it.

Both cams must be indexed on the same detent. The shock absorbers are sealed and cannot be rebuilt. Service is limited to removal and replacement of the hydraulic unit.

Removal/Installation
(CB400A, CB400T I, CB400T II, CB400T, CB450T)

Removal and installation of the rear shock absorbers is easier if they are done separately. The remaining unit will support the rear of the bike and maintain the correct relationship between the top and bottom mounts.

1. Place wood blocks under the crankcase so the bike is supported securely with the rear wheel off the ground.
2. Adjust both shock absorbers to their softest setting, completely *counterclockwise*.
3. Loosen the clamps securing the muffler (A, **Figure 31**) to the collector.
4. Remove the bolt (B, **Figure 31**) securing the rear footpeg and muffler.
5. Slide the muffler out of the collector and remove the muffler.
6. Remove upper and lower bolts (**Figure 32**) securing the shock absorber to the frame and to the swing arm.
7. Remove the shock absorber.
8. Install by reversing the removal steps.
9. Tighten the mounting bolts to the torque specifications listed in **Table 1**.
10. Repeat for the other side.

10

Removal/Installation
(Rebel 450)

Removal and installation of the rear shock absorbers is easier if they are done separately. The remaining unit will support the rear of the bike and maintain the correct relationship between the top and bottom mounts.

1. Place wood blocks under the crankcase so the bike is supported securely with the rear wheel off the ground.
2. Adjust both shock absorbers to their softest setting, completely *counterclockwise*.
3. Remove upper and lower bolts (A, **Figure 33**) securing the shock absorber to the frame and to the swing arm.
4. Remove the shock absorber (B, **Figure 33**).
5. Install by reversing the removal steps.
6. Tighten the mounting bolts to the torque specifications listed in **Table 1**.
7. Repeat for the other side.

Removal/Installation
(All Other Models)

Removal and installation of the rear shock absorbers is easier if they are done separately. The remaining unit will support the rear of the bike and maintain the correct relationship between the top and bottom mounts.

1. Place wood blocks under the crankcase so the bike is supported securely with the rear wheel off the ground.
2. Adjust both shock absorbers to their softest setting, completely *counterclockwise*.
3. Remove the rubber plug from the front of the grip bar.
4. Remove the bolt and washers (**Figure 34**) securing the upper portion of the shock absorber to the frame. Note the location of the washers.
5. Remove the rubber plug from the receptacle in the grip bar.
6. Remove the 8 mm Allen bolt (A, **Figure 35**) securing the grip bar to the frame.
7. Remove the bolt (B, **Figure 35**) securing the lower portion of the shock absorber to the swing arm.
8. Carefully pull out on the forward portion of the grip bar enough to remove the shock unit from the mounting stud on the frame.
9. Remove the shock absorber.

10. Install by reversing the removal steps.
11. Tighten the mounting bolts to the torque specifications listed in **Table 1**. Tighten the Allen bolt securing the grip bar securely.
12. Install the rubber plugs in the receptacles in the grip bar.
13. Repeat for the other side.

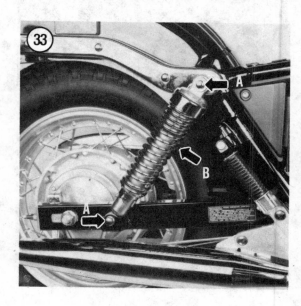

**Disassembly/Inspection/Assembly
(CB400A, CB400T I,
CB400T II, CB400T, CB450T)**

Refer to **Figure 36** for this procedure.

WARNING
*Without the proper tool, this procedure
can be dangerous. The spring can fly
loose, causing injury. For a small bench
fee, a dealer can do the job for you. In
fact the dealer who sells you the new
shock absorbers may swap the springs
over for free if you ask.*

1. Remove the locknut and washer (A, **Figure 37**)
from the upper joint.
2. Install the shock absorber in a compression
tool. This is a special tool and is available from a
Honda dealer. It is the Shock Absorber
Compressor Tool (part No. 07959-3290001).

CAUTION
*Be sure the compressor tool base is
properly adjusted to fit the shock spring
seat.*

3. Compress the shock spring enough to relieve
spring pressure on the upper joint.

NOTE
*The damper rod may be difficult to
break loose from the upper joint, as a
locking agent was applied during
assembly.*

4. Insert a screwdriver into the slot in the damper
rod (B, **Figure 37**). Unscrew the damper rod down
and completely out of the upper joint.
5. Release the spring tension and remove the
shock from the compression tool.
6. Remove the upper joint.
7. Remove the spring, spring seat and spring
adjuster.
8. Measure the spring free length (**Figure 38**). The
spring must be replaced if it has sagged to the
service limit listed in **Table 3** or less.
9. Inspect the rubber stopper. If it is worn or
deteriorated, slide off the rubber stopper and
replace with a new one.
10. Check the damper unit for leakage and make
sure the damper rod is straight.

NOTE
*The damper unit cannot be rebuilt; it
must be replaced as a unit.*

11. Inspect the rubber bushing in the upper joint;
replace if necessary.
12. Assembly is the reverse of these disassembly
steps, noting the following.
13. Install the spring with the tightly wound coils
toward the top.
14. Pull the damper rod out until it is fully
extended.
15. Assemble all parts onto the damper unit and
reinstall this assembly into the spring compression
tool.
16. Compress the spring until the damper rod end
is above the surface of the upper joint.

NOTE
*Apply Loctite Lock N' Seal to the
threads of the damper rod before
installing the upper joint.*

17. Install the upper joint. Thread the damper rod
back up and into the upper joint until it stops.
18. Install the washer and the locknut. Tighten the
locknut securely.

10

**Disassembly/Inspection/Assembly
(Rebel 450, CM400A, CM400C, CM400E,
CM400T, CM450A, CM450SC)**

Refer to the following illustrations for this
procedure:
  a. **Figure 39**: Rebel 450.
  b. **Figure 40**: CM400A, CM400C, CM400E,
     CM400T, CM450A, CM450C, CM450E,
     CM450SC.

WARNING
*Without the proper tool, this procedure
can be dangerous. The spring can fly
loose, causing injury. For a small bench
fee, a dealer can do the job for you. In
fact the dealer who sells your the new
shock absorbers may swap the springs
over for free if you ask.*

1. Install the shock absorber in a compression tool
as shown in **Figure 41**. This is a special tool and is

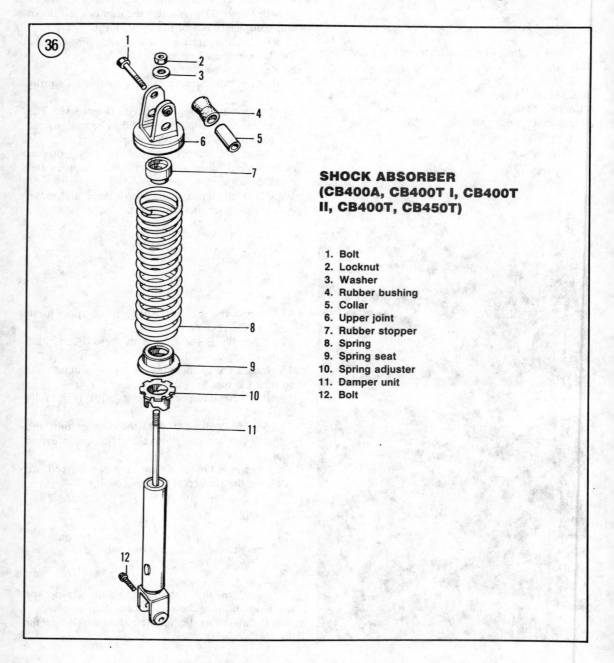

**SHOCK ABSORBER
(CB400A, CB400T I, CB400T
II, CB400T, CB450T)**

1. Bolt
2. Locknut
3. Washer
4. Rubber bushing
5. Collar
6. Upper joint
7. Rubber stopper
8. Spring
9. Spring seat
10. Spring adjuster
11. Damper unit
12. Bolt

available from a Honda dealer. It is the Shock Absorber Compressor Tool (part No. 07959-3290001). The Rebel 450 model also requires a compressor attachment (part No. 07959-MB1000) that fits into the upper portion of the standard compressor tool.

CAUTION
Be sure the compressor tool base is properly adjusted to fit the shock spring seat.

2. Compress the shock spring just enough to gain access to the spring seat. Remove the spring seat.

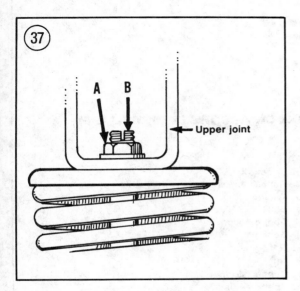

3. Place the upper joint in a vise with soft jaws and loosen the locknut.
4. Completely unscrew the upper joint. This part may be difficult to break loose as a locking agent was applied during assembly.
5. Release the spring tension and remove the shock from the compression tool.
6. Remove the spring cover, spring, spring seat and the spring adjuster from the damper unit.
7. Measure the spring free length (**Figure 38**). The spring must be replaced if it has sagged to the service limit listed in **Table 3** or less.
8. Check the damper unit for leakage and make sure the damper rod is straight.

NOTE
The damper unit cannot be rebuilt; it must be replaced as a unit.

9. Inspect the rubber bushings in the upper joint and on Rebel 450 models also the lower joint; replace if necessary.
10. Inspect the rubber stopper. If it is worn or deteriorated, remove the locknut and slide off the rubber stopper; replace with a new one.
11. Assembly is the reverse of these disassembly steps, noting the following.
12. Apply Loctite Lock N' Seal to the threads of the damper rod before installing the locknut. Temporarily screw the locknut all the way down and tight against the end of the threads.
13. Apply Loctite Lock N' Seal to the threads of the damper rod before installing the upper joint. Screw the upper joint on all the way. Secure the upper joint in a vise with soft jaws and tighten the locknut along with the damper rod against the lower joint.

NOTE
After the locknut is tightened completely the locknut must be against the bottom surface of the upper joint and against the end of the threads on the damper rod.

SWING ARM

In time, the bushings (or bearings) will wear and require replacement. The condition of the bushings (or bearings) can greatly affect handling performance. If worn parts are not replaced they can produce erratic and dangerous handling. Common symptoms are wheel hop, pulling to one side during acceleration and pulling to the other side during braking.

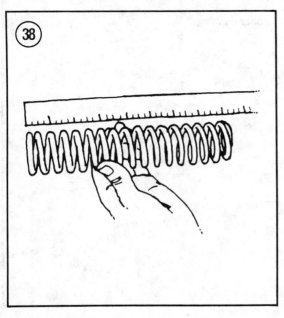

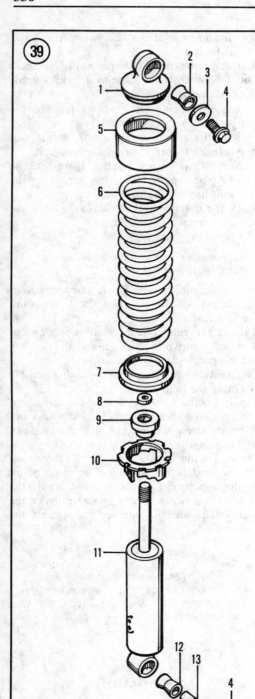

SHOCK ABSORBER (REBEL 450)

1. Upper joint
2. Rubber bushing
3. Washer
4. Bolt
5. Spring cover
6. Spring
7. Spring seat
8. Nut
9. Rubber stopper
10. Spring adjuster
11. Damper unit
12. Rubber bushing
13. Collar

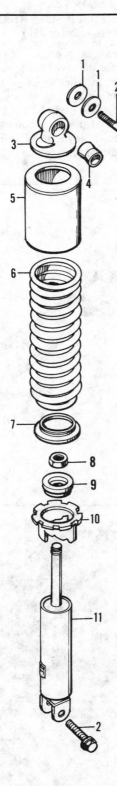

SHOCK ABSORBER (CM400A, CM400C, CM400E, CM400T, CM450A, CM450C, CM450E, CM450SC)

1. Washer
2. Bolt
3. Upper joint
4. Rubber bushing
5. Spring cover
6. Spring
7. Spring seat
8. Nut
9. Rubber stopper
10. Spring adjuster
11. Damper unit

10

Removal/Installation
(All Models)

1. Remove the rear wheel as described under *Rear Wheel Removal/Installation* in this chapter.
2. Remove the lower mounting bolt (A, **Figure 42**) on each shock absorber.

> *NOTE*
> *It is not necessary to remove the shock absorber units (B, Figure 42) just pivot the units up and out of the way.*

3. Grasp the rear end of the swing arm (C, **Figure 42**) and try to move it from side to side in a horizontal arc. There should be no noticeable side play. If play is evident, and the pivot bolt nut is tightened correctly, then the bushings (or bearings) or pivot collars are worn and require replacement.
4. Remove the bolts securing the drive chain cover and remove the cover.
5A. On Rebel 450 models, remove the pivot bolt self-locking nut (**Figure 43**) and withdraw the pivot bolt from the left-hand side.
5B. On all other models, remove the pivot bolt nut and withdraw the pivot bolt (**Figure 44**) from the right-hand side.
6. Pull back on the swing arm, free it from the frame and remove it from the frame.
7. On models with a closed loop drive chain, remove the drive chain from the left-hand side of the swing arm.

> *NOTE*
> *Don't lose the dust caps or oil seals on each side of the pivot points; they may fall off during removal.*

8. Install by reversing these removal steps, noting the following.
9. On models with a closed loop drive chain, hook the drive chain over the left-hand side of the swing arm before installing the swing arm into the frame.
10. Position the swing arm into the mounting area of the frame. Align the holes in the swing arm with the holes in the frame.
11. Apply a light coat of grease to the pivot bolt before installation.
12. Tighten the pivot bolt nut to the torque specification listed in **Table 1**.
13. Move the swing arm up and down several times to make sure all components are properly seated.
14. Adjust the drive chain and rear brake as described in Chapter Three.

Inspection and Pivot Bushing Replacement
(All Models Except Rebel 450)

Honda does not provide service dimension specifications for the pivot bolt, pivot collars or the pivot bushings for this series of bikes. You will have to determine if these parts require replacing strictly by feel. If the pivot bolt has noticeable play between itself and the pivot collars, replace either one or all parts. If the pivot collar feels too loose in the pivot bushings, replace one or all parts.

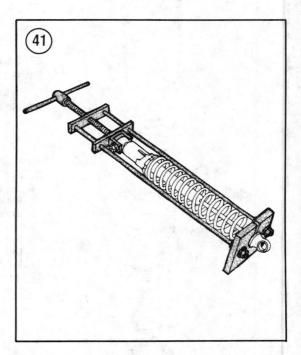

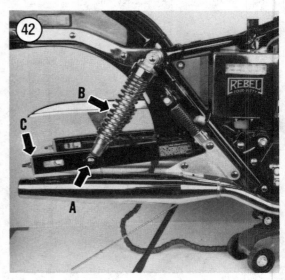

Refer to **Figure 45** and **Figure 46** for this procedure.

1. Remove the drive chain slider from the left-hand side.

2. Remove the cotter pin, nut, washer and lockwasher securing the brake torque link to the swing arm. Remove the pivot bolt and remove the brake torque link.

3. Remove the dust seal from each side of both pivot points on the swing arm. Discard the dust seals they are to be replaced.

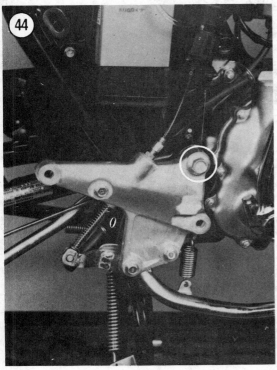

4. Withdraw the pivot collars from the swing arm.

5. Secure the swing arm in a vise with soft jaws.

6. Using a suitable size drift and hammer, tap the bushing out of each side of both pivot points of the swing arm.

7. Thoroughly clean out the inside of the swing arm with solvent and dry with compressed air.

8. Inspect the inside and outside surfaces of the pivot collars for wear or damage. Replace as a set even if only one collar shows sign of wear or damage.

9. Inspect the inside surfaces of the pivot bushings for wear or damage. Replace as a set of 4 even if only one collar shows sign of wear or damage.

10. Inspect the outside surfaces of the pivot bolt where the pivot bushings ride for wear or damage. Replace the pivot bolt if it shows signs of wear or damage.

11. Apply a light coat of oil to the inside and outside surfaces of the new pivot bushings before installation.

CAUTION
Never reinstall a pivot bushing that has been removed. During the removal procedure it becomes slightly damaged and is no longer true to alignment. If reinstalled, it will damage the pivot collar and create an unsafe riding condition.

12. Tap one pivot bushing into place slowly and squarely into the swing arm with a hammer and a block of wood. Make sure it completely seats and is not cocked in the bore of the swing arm.

13. Repeat Step 12 and install the remaining pivot bushings.

14. Apply a light coat of molybdenum disulfide grease to the pivot collars and the inside surface of all pivot bushings.

15. Install all new dust seals. Apply a light coat of grease to their lips before installation.

16. Inspect the drive chain slider for wear; replace if necessary.

Inspection (Rebel 450)

Honda does not provide service dimension specifications for the pivot bolt or the pivot collars for this series of bikes. You will have to determine if these parts require replacing strictly by feel. If the pivot bolt has a lot of play between itself and the pivot collars, replace either one or all parts.

The ball bearings and the needle bearing also do not have any wear specifications. If the bearings feel rough or do not rotate smoothly, replace them.

10

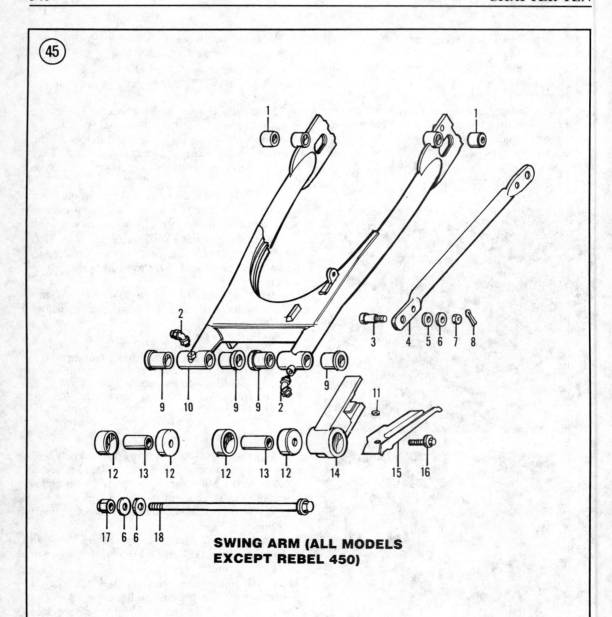

SWING ARM (ALL MODELS EXCEPT REBEL 450)

1. Rubber bushing
2. Grease fitting
3. Pivot bolt
4. Brake torque link
5. Lockwasher
6. Washer
7. Nut
8. Cotter pin
9. Pivot bushing
10. Swing arm
11. Plug
12. Dust seal
13. Pivot collar
14. Drive chain slider
15. Oil guide plate
16. Bolt
17. Nut
18. Pivot bolt

Refer to **Figure 47** for this procedure.

1. Remove the drive chain slider from the left-hand side.

2. Remove the cotter pin, nut, washer and lockwasher securing the brake torque link to the swing arm. Remove the pivot bolt and remove the brake torque link.

3. Remove the oil seal from each side of both pivot points on the swing arm. Discard the oil seals.

4. Withdraw the pivot collars. Note the location of the pivot collars as they are all different lengths as follows:

   a. The long one goes on the left-hand pivot point.
   b. The medium one goes on the outside of the right-hand side.
   c. The short one goes on the inside of the right-hand side.

5. Thoroughly clean all pivot collars in solvent and thoroughly dry.

6. Inspect the inside and outside surfaces of the pivot collars for wear or damage. Replace all 3 as a set even if only one collar shows sign of wear or damage.

NOTE
If the pivot collars are replaced, the needle bearing and ball bearings at each end must also be replaced at the same time.

7. Inspect the needle and ball bearings as follows:

   a. Wipe off any excess grease from the needle and ball bearings at each end of the swing arm.
   b. Turn each bearing with your fingers; make sure they rotate smoothly. The needle bearings wear very slowly and wear is very difficult to measure.
   c. Check the rollers, or balls, for evidence of wear, pitting or color change (bluish tint) indicating heat from lack of lubrication.

NOTE
Always replace the needle bearing and both ball bearings even though only one may be worn.

8. Before installing the pivot collars, coat the collar, both ball bearings and the needle bearings with molybdenum disulfide grease.

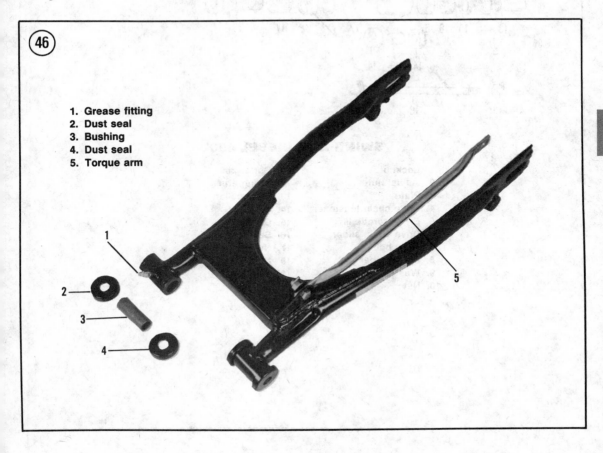

46

1. **Grease fitting**
2. **Dust seal**
3. **Bushing**
4. **Dust seal**
5. **Torque arm**

10

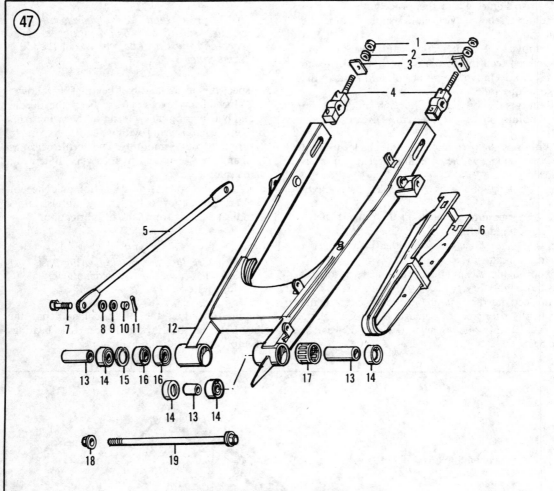

SWING ARM (REBEL 450)

1. Locknut
2. Adjust nut
3. Plate
4. Drive chain tensioner
5. Brake torque link
6. Drive chain slider
7. Pivot bolt
8. Lockwasher
9. Washer
10. Nut
11. Cotter pin
12. Swing arm
13. Pivot collar
14. Oil seal
15. Circlip
16. Ball bearing
17. Needle bearing
18. Nut
19. Pivot bolt

9. Insert the pivot collars in their correct location. The different lengths are as follows:
   a. The long one goes on the left-hand pivot point.
   b. The medium one goes on the outside of the right-hand.
   c. The short one goes on the inside of the right-hand side.
10. Coat the inside of all oil seals with molybdenum disulfide grease and install them onto the ends of both pivot points of the swing arm.
11. Inspect the drive chain slider for wear; replace if necessary.

Ball Bearing and Needle Bearing Replacement

The swing arm is equipped with a needle bearing on the left-hand side and 2 ball bearings on the right-hand side. The bearings are pressed in place and have to be removed with force. The bearings will get distorted when removed, so don't remove them unless they are to be replaced.

The bearings must be removed and installed with special tools that are available from a Honda dealer. Due to the number of special tools required, compare the price of the special tools against the price to have the bearings replaced by a dealer.

The special tools are as follows:
   a. Ball bearing and needle bearing remover/installer (part No. 07946-KA50000).
   b. Needle bearing installation tools: Driver (part No. 07749-0010000); Attachment, 28×30 mm (part No. 07946-1870100); Pilot 22 mm (07746-0041100).
   c. Ball bearing installation tools: Driver (part No. 07749-0010000); Attachment, 32×35 mm (part No. 07746-0010100); Pilot 15 mm (07746-0040300).

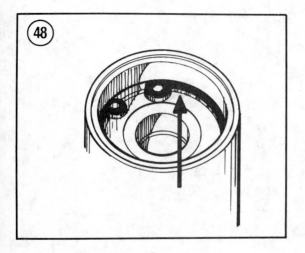

1. Remove the swing arm as described under *Swing Arm Removal/Installation* in this chapter.
2. Remove the oil seal from each side of both pivot points of the swing arm.
3. Secure the right-hand side of the swing arm in a vise with soft jaws.
4. Remove the circlip from the right-hand pivot point (**Figure 48**).
5. Install the bearing remover/installer special tool and drive out both ball bearings from the inside surface of the pivot point.
6. Turn the swing arm over.
7. Install the bearing remover/installer special tool and drive out the needle bearing from the inside surface of the pivot point.
8. Thoroughly clean the inside of the swing arm with solvent and dry with compressed air.
9. Apply a light coat of molybdenum disulfide grease to all parts before installation.

NOTE
Either the right- or left-hand bearing(s) can be installed first.

CAUTION
*For correct alignment the new needle bearings **should** be pressed into place by a Honda dealer with the use of special tools and a hydraulic press. The following procedure is provided if you choose to perform this operation yourself. If done incorrectly, the needle bearing and the pivot point of the swing arm can be damaged during installation and may not be aligned correctly.*

10

CAUTION
Never reinstall a ball bearing or needle bearing that has been removed. During removal it becomes slightly damaged and is no longer true to alignment. If installed, it will damage the pivot collar and create an unsafe riding condition.

10. Blow any dirt or foreign matter out of the pivot point before installing the needle bearing.
11. Position the new needle bearing onto the outside surface of the left-hand pivot point.
12. Use the following Honda special tools:
   a. Driver: part No. 07749-0010000.
   b. Attachment, 28×30 mm: part No. 07946-1870100.
   c. Pilot 22 mm: 07746-0041100.

13. Place the Honda special tools onto the needle bearing (**Figure 49**).

14. Using a hammer, slowly and carefully drive the needle bearing into place squarely until the driver attachment bottoms out on the swing arm. Make sure it is properly seated.

15. Remove the special tools.

16. Pack both ball bearings thoroughly with multipurpose grease. Work the grease in between the balls thoroughly. Turn the bearing by hand a couple of times to make sure the grease is distributed evenly inside the bearing.

17. Blow any dirt or foreign matter out of the pivot point before installing the ball bearings.

18. Position the new ball bearings onto the outside surface of the right-hand pivot point.

19. Use the following Honda special tools:

   a. Driver: part No. 07749-0010000.

   b. Attachment, 32×35 mm: part No. 07746-0010100.

   c. Pilot 15 mm: 07746-0040300.

20. Place the Honda special tools onto the needle bearing (**Figure 49**).

21. Using a hammer, slowly and carefully drive the ball bearings into place squarely until they are fully seated.

22. Remove the special tools.

23. Install the circlip (**Figure 48**).

24. Coat the inside of all oil seals with molybdenum disulfide grease and install them onto the ends of both pivot points of the swing arm.

25. Install the swing arm as described in this chapter.

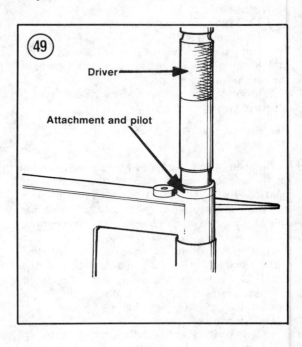

Driver

Attachment and pilot

Table 1 REAR SUSPENSION TORQUE SPECIFICATIONS

Item	N·m	ft.-lb.
Rear axle nut		
1978-1981	78-90	58-72
1982-on	90-100	65-72
Driven sprocket nuts *		
1982 CM450SC, ComStar, ComCast	60-70	43-51
Swing arm pivot bolt and nut		
All models except Rebel 450	55-70	40-51
Rebel 450	60-70	43-51
Shock absorbers mounting bolts		
All models except Rebel 450	30-40	22-29
Rebel 450		
Upper	24-30	17-22
Lower	30-40	22-29

* Specifications not available for models not listed.

Table 2 DRIVE CHAIN REPLACEMENT NUMBERS

Model	Number
CB400T, CB400A, CB450T, CM400E	DID 50DS-100L or RK 50KS-100L
CM400A, CM400C, CM400T	DID 50DS-102L or RK 50KS-102L
CM450A, CM450C, CM450E	DID 50DS-102L or RK 50KS-102L
CB450SC	DID 50H1-106LE or Takasago 520-106LE
Rebel 450	DID 525V or RK525 MO-21

Table 3 REAR SHOCK SPRING FREE LENGTH

Model	Standard mm	in.	Service length mm	in.
All models				
(except Rebel 450)	208.3	8.20	198	7.8
Rebel 450	238.8	9.40	234	9.2

11

CHAPTER ELEVEN

BRAKES

This chapter includes procedures for repair and maintenance of the front and rear brake system components. The brake system consists of either a drum or single disc up front with a drum brake at the back on all models.

Tables 1-3 are located at the end of this chapter.

FRONT DRUM BRAKE

WARNING
*When working on the brake system, do **not** inhale brake dust. It may contain asbestos, which can cause lung injury and cancer.*

Refer to **Figure 1** for this procedure.

Disassembly

1. Remove the front wheel as described under *Front Wheel Removal* in Chapter Nine.
2. Pull the brake panel assembly (**Figure 2**) straight up and out of the brake drum.

NOTE
*Before removing the brake shoes from the backing plate, measure them as described under **Inspection** in this chapter.*

3. Remove the cotter pins and washers (**Figure 3**) from the brake shoe pivot pins.

4. Place a clean shop cloth on the brake linings to protect them from oil and grease during removal.
5. Remove the brake shoes from the backing plate by pulling up on the center of each shoe as shown in **Figure 4**.
6. Remove the bolts and nuts (A, **Figure 5**) on both brake arms.
7. Loosen the locknut on the link rod (B, **Figure 5**) and remove the link rod (C, **Figure 5**).
8. Remove both brake arms from their camshafts.
9. Remove both camshafts from the backing plate.
10. Inspect the brake assembly as described under *Drum Brake Inspection—Front and Rear* in this chapter.

Assembly

1. Assemble the brake by reversing the disassembly steps.
2. Grease the camshafts and pivot post with a light coat of molybdenum disulfide grease; avoid getting any grease on the brake plate where the linings may come in contact with it.
3. When installing each brake arm onto their camshaft, be sure to align the dimples on the 2 parts (**Figure 6**).
4. Install the front wheel as described under *Front Wheel Installation* in Chapter Nine.

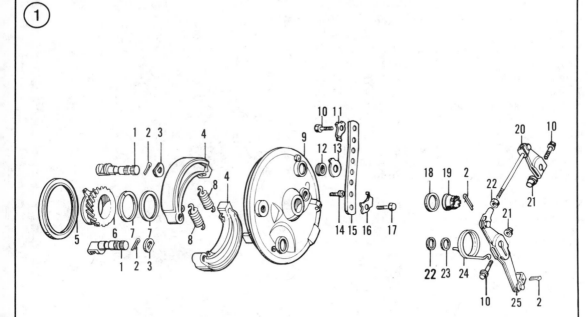

FRONT DRUM BRAKE

1. Camshaft
2. Cotter pin
3. Washer
4. Brake shoes
5. Oil seal
6. Speedometer gear
7. Washer
8. Return spring
9. Brake panel
10. Bolt
11. Lockwasher
12. Dust seal
13. Wear indicator plate
14. Screw
15. Torque link
16. Lockwasher
17. Bolt
18. Washer
19. Nut
20. Trailing brake arm
21. Nut
22. Nut
23. Washer
24. Return spring
25. Leading brake arm

11

Adjustment

1. Remove the clevis pin from the top brake arm (A, **Figure 7**).

2. Have an assistant pull both of the brake arms forward to bring the shoes in contact with the drum and hold them there.

3. Turn the link adjuster either in or out until the clevis pin can be installed with a light push fit. Install the clevis pin and tighten the locknut on the link (B, **Figure 7**).

4. Adjust the brake cable so that the brake is applied with a slight movement of the hand lever but the shoes do not drag in the drum when the lever is relaxed.

5. Hold the adjuster (A, **Figure 8**) to prevent it from turning, and tighten the locknut (B, **Figure 8**).

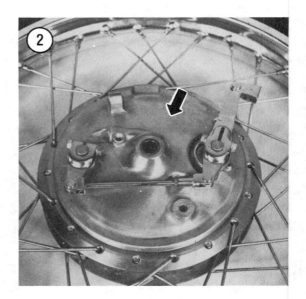

REAR DRUM BRAKE

WARNING
*When working on the brake system, do **not** inhale brake dust. It may contain asbestos, which can cause lung injury and cancer.*

Refer to the following illustrations for this procedure:
    a. **Figure 9**: all models except Rebel 450.
    b. **Figure 10**: Rebel 450.

Disassembly

1. Remove the rear wheel as described under *Rear Wheel Removal* in Chapter Ten.

2. Pull the brake assembly straight up and out of the brake drum.

3. Remove the cotter pin and washer from the brake shoe pivot pin (**Figure 11**).

4. Place a clean shop cloth on the brake linings to protect them from oil and grease during removal.

5. Remove the brake shoes from the backing plate by pulling up on the center of each shoe as shown in **Figure 4**.

6. Remove the bolt and nut (**Figure 12**) on the brake arm.

7. Remove the arm from the camshaft and pull the cam out of the backing plate.

8. Inspect the brake assembly as described under *Drum Brake Inspection—Front and Rear* in this chapter.

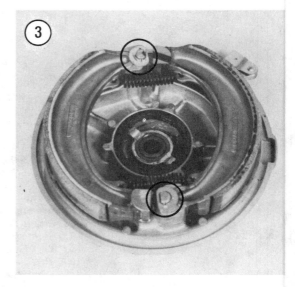

Assembly

1. Assemble the brake by reversing the disassembly steps.

2. Grease the camshaft and pivot post (**Figure 13**) with a light coat of molybdenum disulfide grease.

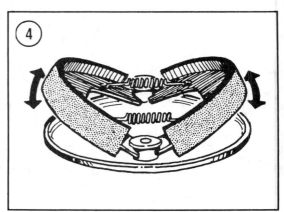

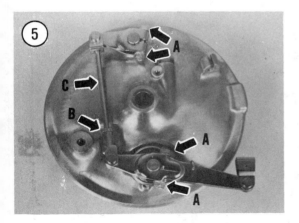

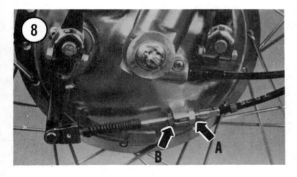

Avoid getting any grease on the brake plate where the linings may come in contact with it.

3. Make sure the brake linings are correctly seated against the pivot post and the camshaft (**Figure 14**).

4. When installing the brake arm onto the camshaft, be sure to align the dimples on the 2 parts.

5. Install the rear wheel as described under *Rear Wheel Installation* in Chapter Ten.

DRUM BRAKE INSPECTION FRONT AND REAR

WARNING
*When working on the brake system, do **not** inhale brake dust. It may contain asbestos, which can cause lung injury and cancer.*

1. Thoroughly clean all the parts except the linings in solvent.

2. Check the contact surface of the drum for scoring. Refer to **Figure 15** for the front drum and **Figure 16** for the rear drum. If there are deep grooves, deep enough to snag a fingernail, the drum should be reground.

3. Use a vernier caliper and measure the inside diameter of the brake drum for out-of-round or excessive wear (**Figure 17**). Replace the drum if worn to the service limit listed in **Table 1** or greater.

4. If the drum is turned, the linings will have to be replaced and the new ones arced to the new drum contour.

5. Measure the brake lining with a vernier caliper (**Figure 18**). They should be replaced if worn to the service limit listed in **Table 1** or less.

6. Inspect the linings for embedded foreign material. Dirt can be removed with a stiff wire brush. Check for any traces of oil or grease. If they are contaminated they must be replaced.

7. Inspect the cam lobe and the pivot pin area of the shaft for wear and corrosion. Minor roughness can be removed with fine emery cloth.

8. Inspect the brake shoe return springs for wear. If they are stretched, the brake shoes will not fully retract and wear out prematurely. Replace if necessary and always replace as a pair.

FRONT DISC BRAKE

The front disc brake is actuated by hydraulic fluid and is controlled by a hand lever. As the brake pads wear, the brake fluid level drops in the reservoir and automatically adjusts for wear.

When working on hydraulic brake systems, it is necessary that the work area and all tools be absolutely clean. Any tiny particle of foreign

11

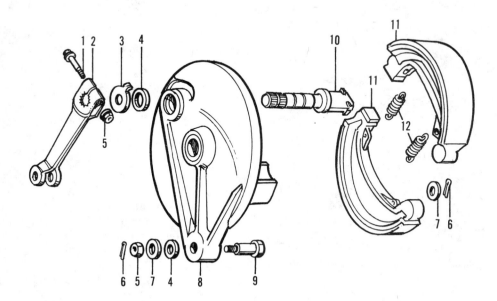

REAR DRUM BRAKE
(ALL MODELS EXCEPT REBEL 450)

1. Bolt
2. Brake arm
3. Wear indicator plate
4. Dust seal
5. Nut
6. Cotter pin
7. Washer
8. Brake panel
9. Bolt
10. Camshaft
11. Brake shoes
12. Return springs

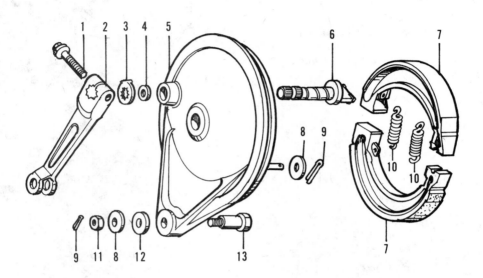

REAR DRUM BRAKE (REBEL 450)

1. Bolt
2. Brake arm
3. Wear indicator plate
4. Dust seal
5. Brake panel
6. Camshaft
7. Brake shoes
8. Washer
9. Cotter pin
10. Return springs
11. Nut
12. Rubber spacer
13. Bolt

11

matter and grit in the caliper assembly or the
master cylinder can damage the components. Also,
sharp tools must not be used inside the caliper or
on the piston. If there is any doubt about you
ability to correctly and safely carry out major
service on brake components, take the job to a
Honda dealer or brake specialist.

WARNING
When working on the brake system, do
not *inhale brake dust. It may contain*
asbestos, which can cause lung injury
and cancer.

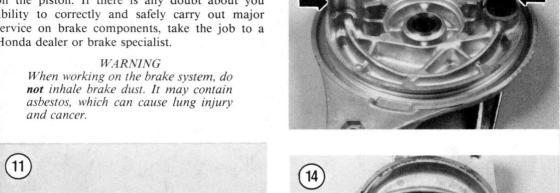

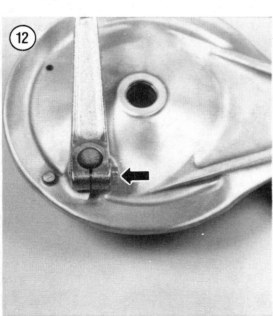

FRONT DISC BRAKE PAD REPLACEMENT

There is no recommended mileage interval for changing the friction pads in the disc brake. Pad wear depends greatly on riding habits and conditions. The disc pads should be checked for wear every 6 months and replaced when the red line on the pad reaches the edges of the brake disc. Refer to **Figure 19** or **Figure 20**. Always replace both pads at the same time.

> *CAUTION*
> *Watch the pads more closely when the red line approaches the disc. On some pads, the red line is very close to the pad's metal backing plate. If pad wear happens to be uneven for some reason the backing plate may come in contact with the disc and cause damage.*

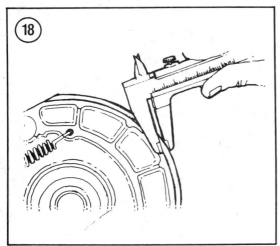

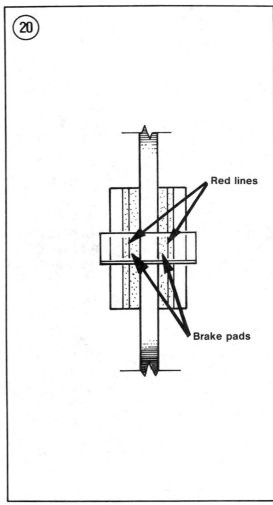

Red lines

Brake pads

**Brake Pad Replacement
(CB400A, CB400T II,
1980 CB400T, CM400A, CM400T)**

Refer to **Figure 21** for this procedure.

1. Remove the screw (**Figure 22**) securing the caliper cover and remove the cover.
2. Pull up and remove the pad pin clip (**Figure 23**).
3. Remove the pad pins securing the pads in place.
4. Remove the pads (**Figure 24**) and discard them.
5. Clean the pad recess and end of the piston with a soft brush. Do not use solvent, wire brush, or any hard tool which would damage the cylinder or the piston.
6. Carefully remove any rust or corrosion from the disc.

7. Lightly coat the end of the piston and the backs of the new pads (not the friction material) with disc brake lubricant.

NOTE
Check with your dealer to make sure the friction compound of the new pads is compatible with the disc material. Remove any roughness from the backs of the new pads with a fine cut file and blow them clean with compressed air.

8A. On 1978 models, unscrew the cap (**Figure 25**) from the master cylinder.
8B. On 1979-1980 models, remove the screws securing the cover and remove the cover, the diaphragm plate and the diaphragm.

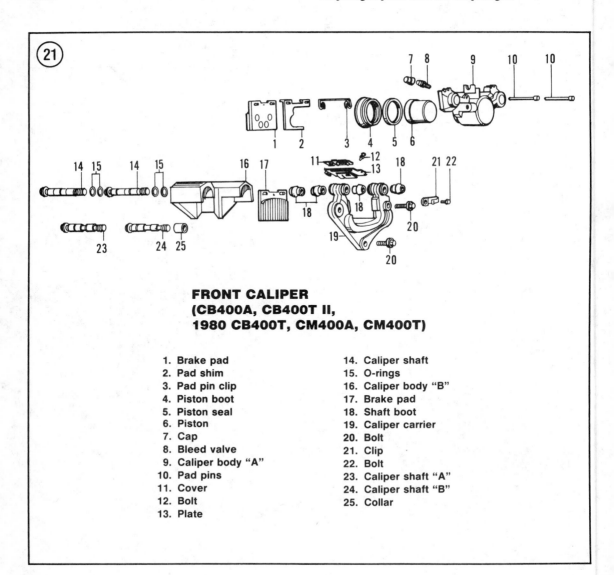

**FRONT CALIPER
(CB400A, CB400T II,
1980 CB400T, CM400A, CM400T)**

1. Brake pad
2. Pad shim
3. Pad pin clip
4. Piston boot
5. Piston seal
6. Piston
7. Cap
8. Bleed valve
9. Caliper body "A"
10. Pad pins
11. Cover
12. Bolt
13. Plate

14. Caliper shaft
15. O-rings
16. Caliper body "B"
17. Brake pad
18. Shaft boot
19. Caliper carrier
20. Bolt
21. Clip
22. Bolt
23. Caliper shaft "A"
24. Caliper shaft "B"
25. Collar

9. Slowly push the piston into the caliper to make sure the brake fluid does not overflow. Remove fluid if necessary before overflowing. The piston should move freely. If it does not and there is any evidence of it sticking in the cylinder, the caliper should be removed and serviced as described under *Caliper Rebuilding* in this chapter.

10. Install the new pads with the anti-rattle shim on the outboard pad next to the piston.

11. Insert the pad pins with the holes facing upward in order to accept the pad pin clip.

12. Install the pad pin clip (**Figure 23**) and push it all the way down. Make sure it is completely seated in both pad pins.

13. Install the caliper cover and screw (**Figure 22**). Tighten the screw securely.

14. If open, snap the inspection cover closed (**Figure 26**).

15. Carefully remove any rust or corrosion from the disc.

16. Place wood blocks under the crankcase to support the bike with the front wheel off the ground.

17. Spin the front wheel and activate the brake lever for as many times as it takes to refill the cylinder in the caliper and correctly locate the pads.

> *WARNING*
> *Use brake fluid from a sealed container marked DOT 3 or DOT 4 only (specified for disc brakes). Other types may vaporize and cause brake failure. Do not intermix different brands or types as they may not be compatible. Do not intermix a silicone based (DOT 5) brake fluid as it can cause brake component damage leading to brake system failure.*

11

18. Refill the fluid in the reservoir to correct the level. Refill to the upper level line. Refer to **Figure 27** for 1978 models or **Figure 28** for 1979-on models.

19. Screw on the top cap or install the cover and screws.

> *WARNING*
> *Do not ride the motorcycle until you are sure that the brake is operating correctly with full hydraulic advantage. If necessary, bleed the brakes as described under **Bleeding the System** in this chapter.*

20. Bed the pads in gradually for the first 800 km (500 miles) by using only light pressure as much as possible. Immediate hard application will glaze the new friction pads and greatly reduce the effectiveness of the brake.

Brake Pad Replacement (1981-on CM400C, CB400T, CM450A, CM450C)

Refer to the following illustrations for this procedure.

    a. **Figure 29**: CM400C, 1981 CB400T.
    b. **Figure 30**: 1982 CB400T, CM450A, CM450C.

1. Remove the bolts securing the caliper assembly to the caliper bracket (**Figure 31**). Remove the caliper assembly from the disc.

2. Remove the bolt (**Figure 32**) securing the pad pin retainer to the caliper assembly and remove the pad pin retainer.

3. Remove the 2 pad pins (**Figure 33**) securing the brake pads in place.

4. Remove both brake pads.

5. Clean the pad recess and the end of the pistons with a soft brush. Do not use solvent, a wire brush or any hard tool which would damage the cylinders or pistons.

6. Carefully remove any rust or corrosion from the disc.

7. Lightly coat the ends of the pistons and the backs of the new pads, *not the friction material* with disc brake lubricant.

> *NOTE*
> *When purchasing new pads, check with your dealer to make sure the friction compound of the new pads is compatible with the disc material. Remove any roughness from the backs of the new pads with a fine-cut file; blow them clean with compressed air.*

8. When new pads are installed in the caliper the master cylinder brake fluid level will rise as the caliper pistons are repositioned. Clean the top of the master cylinder of all dirt and foreign matter. Remove the cap and diaphragm from the master cylinder.

9. Slowly push the caliper pistons into the caliper. Constantly check the reservoir to make sure brake fluid does not overflow. Remove fluid, if necessary, before it overflows. The pistons should move freely. If they don't, and there is evidence of a piston sticking in the cylinder, the caliper should be removed and serviced as described under *Caliper Rebuilding* in this chapter.

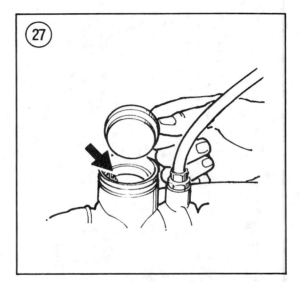

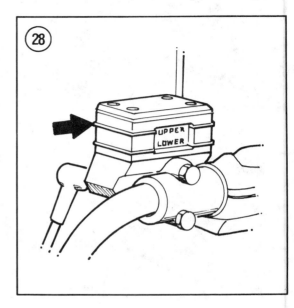

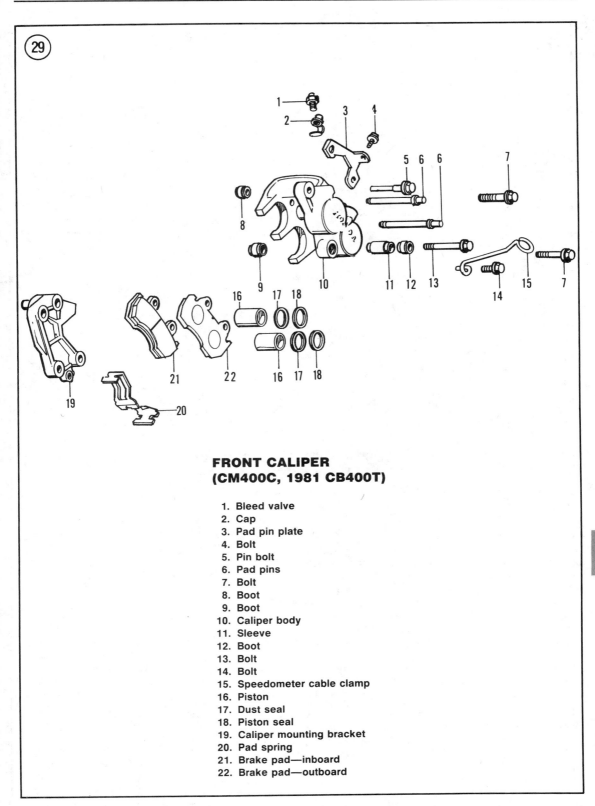

**FRONT CALIPER
(CM400C, 1981 CB400T)**

1. Bleed valve
2. Cap
3. Pad pin plate
4. Bolt
5. Pin bolt
6. Pad pins
7. Bolt
8. Boot
9. Boot
10. Caliper body
11. Sleeve
12. Boot
13. Bolt
14. Bolt
15. Speedometer cable clamp
16. Piston
17. Dust seal
18. Piston seal
19. Caliper mounting bracket
20. Pad spring
21. Brake pad—inboard
22. Brake pad—outboard

11

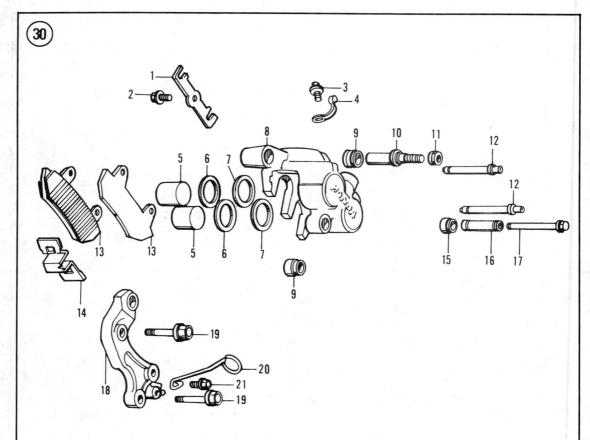

FRONT CALIPER (1982 CB400T, CM450A, CM450C)

1. Pad pin retainer
2. Bolt
3. Bleed valve
4. Cap
5. Piston
6. Dust seal
7. Piston seal
8. Caliper body
9. Pin bolt boot
10. Pin bolt
11. Nut
12. Pad pins
13. Brake pads
14. Pad spring
15. Boot
16. Sleeve
17. Bolt
18. Caliper mounting bracket
19. Bolt
20. Speedometer cable clamp
21. Bolt

10. Push the caliper pistons in all the way (**Figure 34**) to allow room for the new pads.

11. Install the anti-rattle spring as shown in **Figure 35**.

12. Install the outboard pad (**Figure 36**) and partially install one pad pin through that pad.

13. Install the inboard pad and push the pad pin all the way through.

14. Push both pads against the anti-rattle spring, then insert the other pad pin. Push this pad pin all the way through both pads.

15. Install the pad pin retainer onto the ends of the pad pins. Push the pad pin retainer down and make sure it seats completely on the groove in each pad pin.

16. Install the pad pin retaining bolt and tighten to the torque specification listed in **Table 2**.

17. Carefully install the caliper assembly onto the disc. Be careful not to damage the leading edge of the pads during installation.

18. Lubricate the caliper upper pivot bolt with silicone grease.

11

19. Install the caliper upper pivot bolt and tighten to the torque specification listed in **Table 2**.
20. Install the caliper lower mounting bolt and tighten to the torque specification listed in **Table 2**.
21. Place wood blocks under the engine to support the bike securely with the front wheel off the ground.
22. Spin the front wheel and activate the brake lever as many times as it takes to refill the cylinder in the caliper and correctly locate the pads.
23. Refill the master cylinder reservoir, if necessary, to maintain the correct fluid level. Install the diaphragm and top cap.

> *WARNING*
> *Use brake fluid from a sealed container marked DOT 3 or DOT 4 only (specified for disc brakes). Other types may vaporize and cause brake failure. Do not intermix different brands or types as they may not be compatible. Do not intermix a silicone based (DOT 5) brake fluid as it can cause brake component damage leading to brake system failure.*

> *WARNING*
> *Do not ride the motorcycle until you are sure the brake is operating correctly with full hydraulic advantage. If necessary, bleed the brake as described under* ***Bleeding the System*** *in this chapter.*

24. Bed the pads in gradually for the first 800 km (500 miles) by using only light pressure as much as possible. Immediate hard application will glaze the new friction pads and greatly reduce the effectiveness of the brake.

Brake Pad Replacement
(CB450SC)

Refer to **Figure 37** for this procedure.
1. Remove the lower bolt (A, **Figure 38**) and the upper nut (B, **Figure 38**) securing the caliper assembly to the caliper bracket on the fork. Remove the caliper assembly from the brake disc.
2. Remove the bolt (A, **Figure 39**) securing the pad pin retainer to the caliper assembly and remove the pad pin retainer (B, **Figure 39**).
3. Remove the 2 pins (C, **Figure 39**) securing the brake pads in place.
4. Remove both brake pads.
5. Clean the pad recess and the end of the pistons with a soft brush. Do not use solvent, wire brush or any hard tool which would damage the cylinders or pistons.

6. Carefully remove any rust or corrosion from the disc.
7. Lightly coat the end of the pistons and the backs of the new pads, *not the friction material*, with disc brake lubricant.

> *NOTE*
> *When purchasing new pads, check with your dealer to make sure the friction compound of the new pad is compatible with the disc material. Remove any roughness from the backs of the new pads with a fine-cut file; blow them clean with compressed air.*

8. When new pads are installed in the caliper, the master cylinder brake fluid level will rise as the caliper pistons are repositioned. Clean the top of the master cylinder of all dirt and foreign matter.

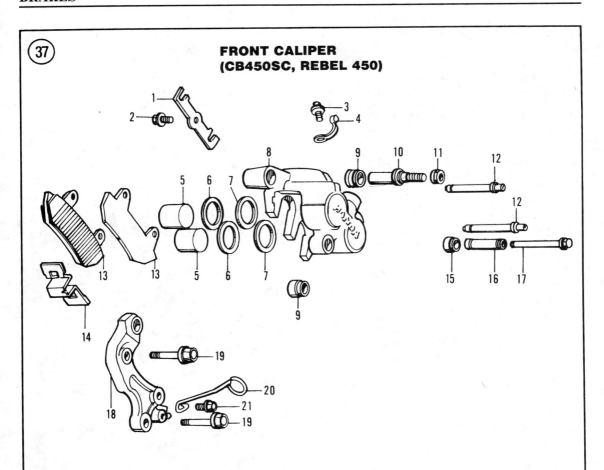

FRONT CALIPER
(CB450SC, REBEL 450)

1. Pad pin retainer
2. Bolt
3. Bleed valve
4. Cap
5. Piston
6. Dust seal
7. Piston seal
8. Caliper body
9. Pin bolt boot
10. Pin bolt
11. Nut
12. Pad pins
13. Brake pads
14. Pad spring
15. Boot
16. Sleeve
17. Bolt
18. Caliper mounting bracket
19. Bolt
20. Speedometer cable clamp
21. Bolt

11

9. Remove the screws securing the cover. Remove the cover and the diaphragm from the master cylinder.

10. Slowly push the caliper pistons into the caliper. Constantly check the reservoir to make sure brake fluid does not overflow. Remove fluid, if necessary, before it overflows. The pistons should move freely. If they don't and there is evidence of a piston sticking in the cylinder, the caliper should be removed and serviced as described under *Caliper Rebuilding* in this Chapter.

11. Push the caliper pistons in all the way to allow room for the new pads.

12. Install the anti-rattle spring with the flat portion of the spring (**Figure 40**) in the area of the lower piston.

13. Install the outboard pad (**Figure 41**) and partially install the pad pins through that pad.

14. Install the inboard pad (**Figure 42**) and push the pad pins all the way through both pads.

15. Install the pad pin retainer onto the ends of the pins. Push the pad pin retainer down and make sure it seats completely on the groove in each pad pin.

16. Install the pad pin retaining bolt (A, **Figure 39**) and tighten to the torque specification listed in **Table 2**.

17. Carefully install the caliper assembly onto the disc. Be careful not to damage the leading edge of the pads during installation.

18. Lubricate the caliper upper pivot bolt with silicone grease.

19. Install the caliper assembly onto the upper pivot bolt and pivot the caliper assembly down onto the brake disc.

20. Install the caliper upper mounting nut and tighten to the torque specification listed in **Table 2**.

21. Install the caliper lower mounting bolt and tighten to the torque specification listed in **Table 2**.

22. Place wood blocks under the engine to support the bike securely with the front wheel off the ground.

23. Spin the front wheel and activate the brake lever as many times as it takes to refill the cylinder in the caliper and correctly locate the pads.

24. Refill the master cylinder reservoir, if necessary, to maintain the correct fluid level. Install the diaphragm and cover.

WARNING
Use brake fluid from a sealed container marked DOT 3 or DOT 4 only (specified for disc brakes). Other types may vaporize and cause brake failure. Do not intermix different brands or

types as they may not be compatible. Do not intermix a silicone based (DOT 5) brake fluid as it can cause brake component damage leading to brake system failure.

WARNING
Do not ride the motorcycle until you are sure the brake is operating correctly with full hydraulic advantage. If necessary, bleed the brake as described under **Bleeding the System** *in this chapter.*

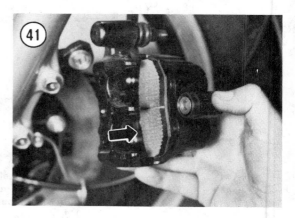

25. Bed the pads in gradually for the first 800 km (500 miles) by using only light pressure as much as possible. Immediate hard application will glaze the new friction pads and greatly reduce the effectiveness of the brake.

**Brake Pad Replacement
(Rebel 450)**

Refer to **Figure 37** for this procedure.

1. Remove the caliper mounting bolt (**Figure 43**) securing the caliper assembly to the caliper bracket on the fork.

2. Remove the bolt (**Figure 44**) securing the pin retainer to the caliper assembly.

3. Pivot the lower portion of the caliper assembly up (**Figure 45**) on the caliper pin bolt and off of the brake disc. Withdraw the caliper assembly from the caliper mounting bracket and remove the caliper assembly.

4. Remove the pin retainer (A, **Figure 46**) from the caliper.

5. Remove the 2 pins (B, **Figure 46**) securing the brake pads in place.

6. Remove both brake pads.

7. Clean the pad recess and the end of the pistons with a soft brush. Do not use solvent, wire brush or any hard tool which would damage the cylinders or pistons.

8. Carefully remove any rust or corrosion from the disc.

9. Lightly coat the end of the pistons and the backs of the new pads, *not the friction material*, with disc brake lubricant.

> *NOTE*
> *When purchasing new pads, check with your dealer to make sure the friction compound of the new pad is compatible with the disc material. Remove any roughness from the backs of the new pads with a fine-cut file; blow them clean with compressed air.*

10. When new pads are installed in the caliper, the master cylinder brake fluid level will rise as the caliper pistons are repositioned. Clean the top of the master cylinder of all dirt and foreign matter.

11. Remove the screws securing the cover (**Figure 47**). Remove the cover and the diaphragm from the master cylinder.

12. Slowly push the caliper pistons into the caliper. Constantly check the reservoir to make sure brake fluid does not overflow. Remove fluid, if necessary, before it overflows. The pistons should move freely. If they don't and there is

11

evidence of a piston sticking in the cylinder, the caliper should be removed and serviced as described under *Caliper Rebuilding* in this Chapter.

13. Push the caliper pistons in all the way to allow room for the new pads.

14. Install the anti-rattle spring (**Figure 48**) into the caliper.

15. Install the outboard pad (A, **Figure 49**) and partially install one of the pad pins (B, **Figure 49**) through that pad.

16. Install the inboard pad (**Figure 50**) and push the pad pin all the way through both pads.

17. Install the remaining pad pin and push the pad pin all the way through both pads.

18. Install the pad pin retainer onto the ends of the pad pins. Push the pin retainer down and make sure it seats completely on the groove in each pad pin (B, **Figure 46**).

19. Install the pad pin retaining bolt only finger-tight at this time.

20. Apply a light coat of silicone grease to the caliper pin bolt boot (A, **Figure 51**) on the caliper mounting bracket.

21. Make sure the retainer clip (B, **Figure 51**) is in place on the caliper mounting bracket.

22. Install the pin bolt on the caliper assembly into the pin bolt boot on the caliper mounting bracket and push the caliper assembly all the way onto the mounting bracket.

23. Pivot the lower portion of the caliper assembly down onto the brake disc. Be careful not to damage the leading edge of the pads during installation.

24. Install the caliper mounting bolt (**Figure 43**) and tighten to the torque specification listed in **Table 2**.

25. Tighten the pad pin retainer bolt (**Figure 44**) to the torque specification listed in **Table 2**.

26. Place wood blocks under the engine to support the bike securely with the front wheel off the ground.

27. Spin the front wheel and activate the brake lever as many times as it takes to refill the cylinder in the caliper and correctly locate the pads.

28. Refill the master cylinder reservoir, if necessary, to maintain the correct fluid level. Install the diaphragm and top cap.

WARNING
Use brake fluid from a sealed container marked DOT 3 or DOT 4 only (specified for disc brakes). Other types may vaporize and cause brake failure. Do not intermix different brands or types as they may not be compatible. Do not intermix a silicone based (DOT

5) brake fluid as it can cause brake component damage leading to brake system failure.

WARNING
*Do not ride the motorcycle until you are sure the brake is operating correctly with full hydraulic advantage. If necessary, bleed the brake as described under **Bleeding the System** in this chapter.*

50

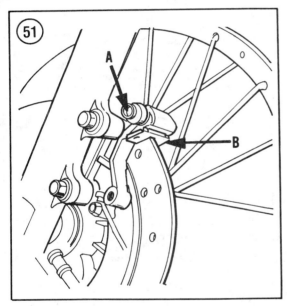

51

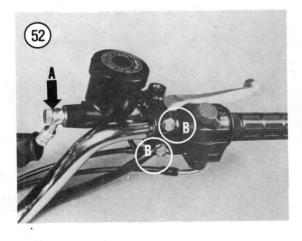

52

29. Bed the pads in gradually for the first 800 km (500 miles) by using only light pressure as much as possible. Immediate hard application will glaze the new friction pads and greatly reduce the effectiveness of the brake.

FRONT MASTER CYLINDER
(1978-1983)

Removal/Installation
(1978-1980)

1. Remove the rear view mirror.

> *CAUTION*
> *Cover the fuel tank and instrument cluster with a heavy cloth or plastic tarp to protect it from accidental spilling of brake fluid. Wash any brake fluid off of any painted or plated surface immediately, as it will destroy the finish. Use soapy water and rinse completely.*

2A. On 1978 models, perform the following:

   a. Remove the union bolt (A, **Figure 52**) securing the brake hose to the master cylinder. Remove the brake hose and both sealing washers. Tie the brake hose up and cover the end to prevent the entry of dirt and foreign matter.

   b. Disconnect the electrical leads from the brake light switch (A, **Figure 53**).

   c. Remove the bolt and nut (B, **Figure 53**) securing the brake lever and remove the lever.

   d. Remove the bolts (B, **Figure 52**) securing the master cylinder to the handlebar. Remove the clamp and the master cylinder.

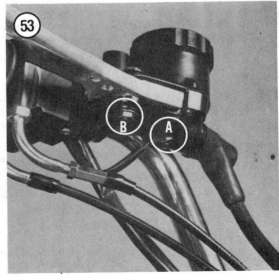

53

11

2B. On 1979-1980 models, perform the following:

a. Remove the union bolt (A, **Figure 54**) securing the brake hose to the master cylinder. Remove the brake hose and both sealing washers. Tie the brake hose up and cover the end to prevent the entry of dirt and foreign matter.

b. Remove the electrical leads from the brake light switch.

c. Remove the bolt and nut securing the brake lever and remove the lever.

d. Remove the bolts (B, **Figure 54**) securing the master cylinder to the handlebar. Remove the clamp and the master cylinder.

3. Install by reversing the removal steps, noting the following.

4. Tighten the clamping bolts securely. Tighten the union bolt to the torque specifications listed in **Table 2**.

5. Bleed the brake as described under *Bleeding the System* in this chapter.

Removal/Installation (1981-1983)

1. Remove the rear view mirror (A, **Figure 55**).

> *CAUTION*
> *Cover the fuel tank and instrument cluster with a heavy cloth or plastic tarp to protect it from accidental spilling of brake fluid. Wash any brake fluid off of any painted or plated surface immediately, as it will destroy the finish. Use soapy water and rinse completely.*

2. Slide back the rubber boot (B, **Figure 55**).

3. Remove the union bolt securing the brake hose to the master cylinder. Remove the brake hose and the 2 sealing washers. Tie the brake hose up and cover the end to prevent the entry of foreign matter.

4. Disconnect the electrical wires to the brake light switch (C, **Figure 55**).

5. Remove the clamping bolts (D, **Figure 55**) and clamp securing the master cylinder to the handlebar and remove the master cylinder.

6. Install by reversing these removal steps, noting the following.

7. Install the clamp with the UP arrow facing up. Align the lug with the punch mark on the handlebar and tighten the upper bolt first, then the lower. Tighten both bolts securely.

8. Install the brake hose onto the master cylinder. Be sure to place a sealing washer on each side of the fitting and install the union bolt. Tighten the

union bolt to the torque specifications listed in **Table 2**.

9. Bleed the brake as described under *Bleeding the System* in this chapter.

Master Cylinder Disassembly

Refer to the following illustrations for this procedure.

a. **Figure 56**: CB400A, 1978 CB400T II.

b. **Figure 57**: 1979 CB400T II, CB400T.

c. **Figure 58**: 1979-1980 CM400A, 1979-1980 CM400T.

d. **Figure 59**: 1981 CB400T, 1981 CM400A, 1981 CM400C, 1981 CM400T, CM450A, CM450C.

e. **Figure 60**: CB450T, 1982-1983 CB450SC.

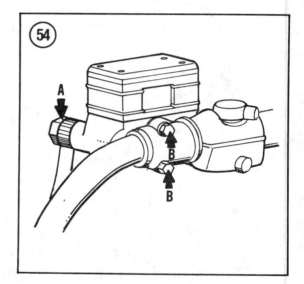

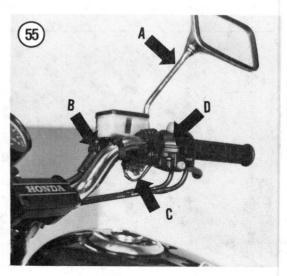

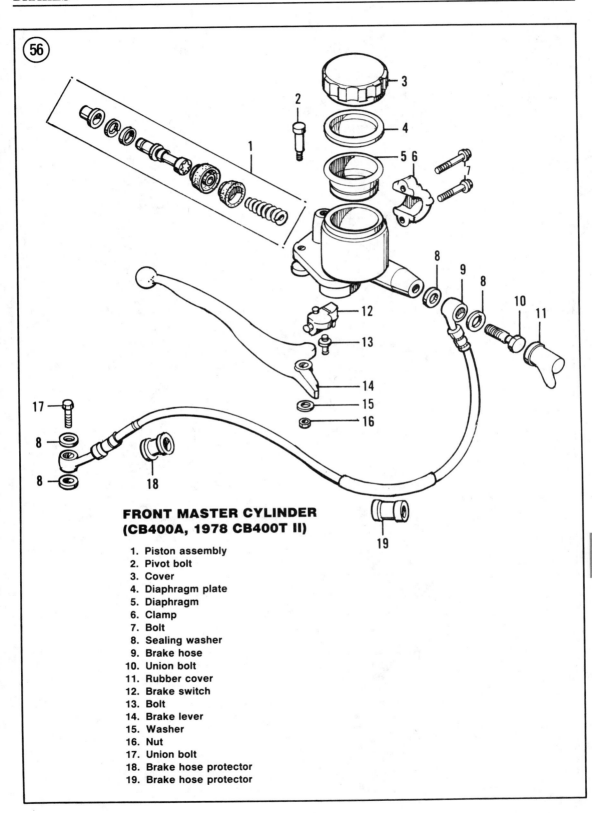

**FRONT MASTER CYLINDER
(CB400A, 1978 CB400T II)**

1. Piston assembly
2. Pivot bolt
3. Cover
4. Diaphragm plate
5. Diaphragm
6. Clamp
7. Bolt
8. Sealing washer
9. Brake hose
10. Union bolt
11. Rubber cover
12. Brake switch
13. Bolt
14. Brake lever
15. Washer
16. Nut
17. Union bolt
18. Brake hose protector
19. Brake hose protector

11

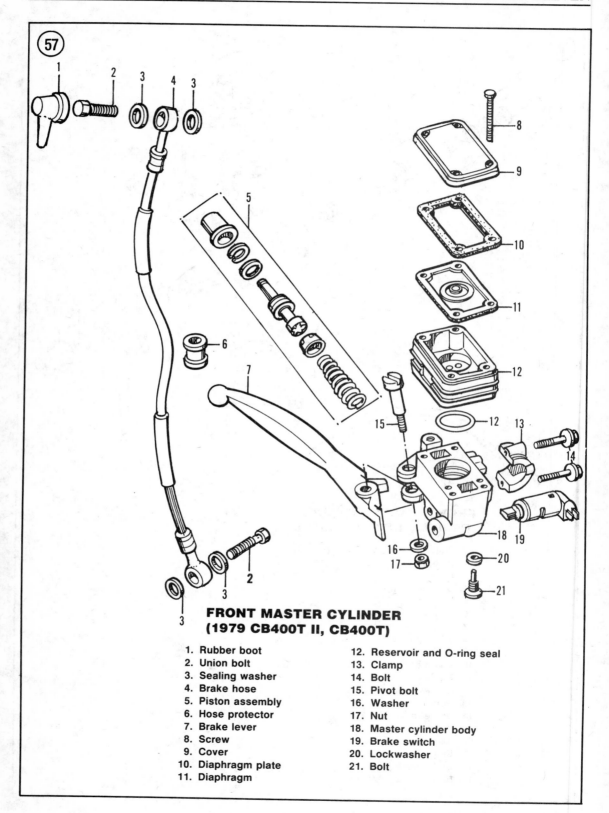

**FRONT MASTER CYLINDER
(1979 CB400T II, CB400T)**

1. Rubber boot
2. Union bolt
3. Sealing washer
4. Brake hose
5. Piston assembly
6. Hose protector
7. Brake lever
8. Screw
9. Cover
10. Diaphragm plate
11. Diaphragm
12. Reservoir and O-ring seal
13. Clamp
14. Bolt
15. Pivot bolt
16. Washer
17. Nut
18. Master cylinder body
19. Brake switch
20. Lockwasher
21. Bolt

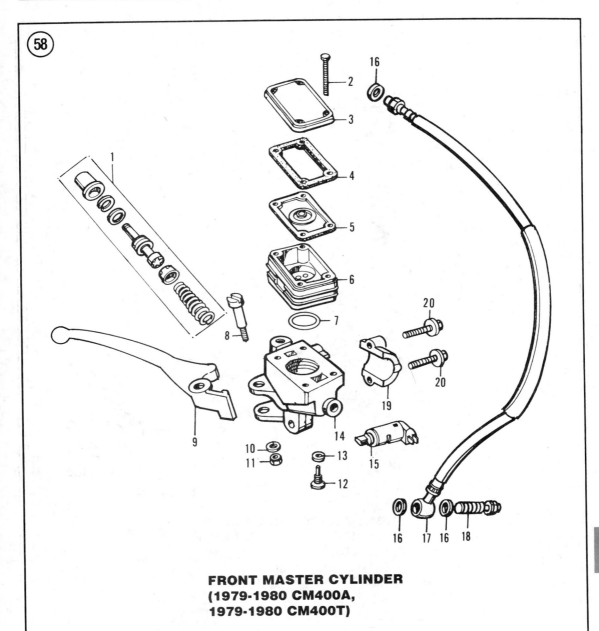

FRONT MASTER CYLINDER
(1979-1980 CM400A,
1979-1980 CM400T)

1. Piston assembly
2. Screw
3. Cover
4. Diaphragm plate
5. Diaphragm
6. Reservoir
7. O-ring seal
8. Pivot bolt
9. Brake lever
10. Washer

11. Nut
12. Bolt
13. Lockwasher
14. Master cylinder body
15. Brake switch
16. Sealing washer
17. Brake hose
18. Union bolt
19. Clamp
20. Bolt

11

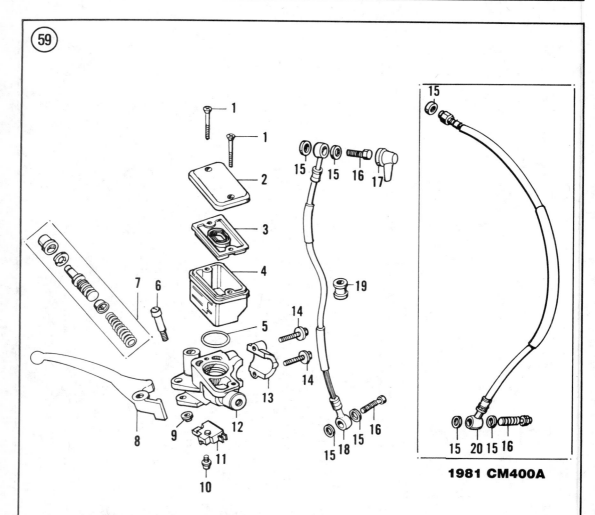

1981 CM400A

**FRONT MASTER CYLINDER
(1981 CB400T, 1981 CM400A,
1981 CM400C, 1981 CM400T,
CM450A, CM450C)**

1. Screw
2. Cover
3. Diaphragm
4. Reservoir
5. O-ring seal
6. Pivot bolt
7. Piston assembly
8. Brake lever
9. Nut
10. Screw
11. Brake switch
12. Master cylinder body
13. Clamp
14. Bolt
15. Sealing washer
16. Union bolt
17. Rubber boot
18. Brake hose
19. Hose protector
20. Brake hose

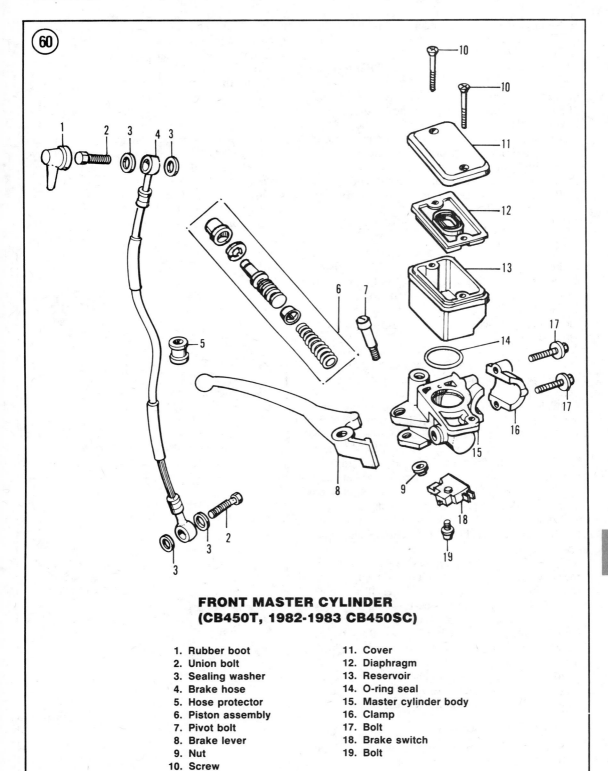

**FRONT MASTER CYLINDER
(CB450T, 1982-1983 CB450SC)**

1. Rubber boot
2. Union bolt
3. Sealing washer
4. Brake hose
5. Hose protector
6. Piston assembly
7. Pivot bolt
8. Brake lever
9. Nut
10. Screw
11. Cover
12. Diaphragm
13. Reservoir
14. O-ring seal
15. Master cylinder body
16. Clamp
17. Bolt
18. Brake switch
19. Bolt

11

1. Remove the master cylinder as described under *Master Cylinder Removal/Installation* in this chapter.

2A. On CB400A and 1978 CB400T models, unscrew the cover, pour out the brake fluid and discard it. *Never* reuse brake fluid.

2B. On all other models, remove the screws securing the cover and remove the cover, diaphragm plate (models so equipped) and diaphragm. Pour out the brake fluid and discard it. *Never* reuse brake fluid.

3. Remove the rubber boot and the circlip.

4. Remove the washer, piston, secondary and primary caps and the spring.

Master Cylinder Inspection

1. Clean all parts in denatured alcohol or fresh brake fluid. Inspect the cylinder bore and piston contact surfaces for signs of wear and damage. If either part is less than perfect, replace it.

2. Check the end of the piston for wear caused by the lever and check the pivot bore in the lever. Discard the caps.

3. Make sure the brake fluid passage(s) in the bottom of the brake fluid reservoir are clear. Check the reservoir cap and diaphragm for damage and deterioration and replace as necessary.

4. Inspect the condition of the threads in the bores for the brake line and the switch.

5. Check the hand lever pivot lug for cracks.

6. On all models except 1978 CB400A and CB400T II, if the fluid reservoir was removed from the master cylinder body, replace the O-ring seal between the 2 parts. The O-ring must be replaced every time these 2 parts are separated.

7. Remove the primary and secondary cups from the piston assembly. Discard the cups as they must be replaced.

8A. On CB400A and 1978 CB400T models, measure the cylinder bore (**Figure 61**) with a bore gauge. Replace the master cylinder if the bore exceeds the service limit listed in **Table 3**.

8B. On all other models, measure the cylinder bore (**Figure 62**) with a bore gauge. Replace the master cylinder if the bore exceeds the service limit listed in **Table 3** or greater.

9. Measure the outside diameter of the piston (**Figure 63**). Replace the piston if it is worn to the service limit listed in **Table 3** or less.

Master Cylinder Assembly

1. Soak the new caps in fresh brake fluid for at least 15 minutes to make them pliable.

2. Coat the inside of the master cylinder bore with fresh brake fluid before the assembly of parts.

3. Install the spring with the tapered end facing toward the primary cup.

4. Install the primary and secondary cups into the cylinder.

5. Install the piston and washer.

6. Install the circlip and the boot.

7A. On CB400A and 1978 CB400T models, screw on the cover.

7B. On all other models, install the diaphragm, diaphragm plate (models so equipped) and cover. Do not tighten the cover screws at this time as brake fluid will have to be added later.

8. Install the master cylinder on the handlebar as described under *Master Cylinder Removal/Installation* in this chapter.

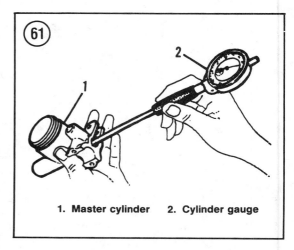

1. Master cylinder   2. Cylinder gauge

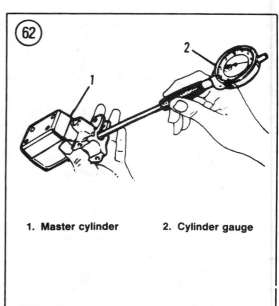

1. Master cylinder   2. Cylinder gauge

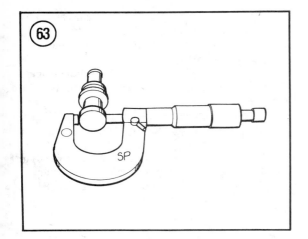

63

FRONT MASTER CYLINDER
(1985-ON)

Removal/Installation
(CB450SC)

1. Remove the rear view mirror (A, **Figure 64**) from the master cylinder.

CAUTION
Cover the fuel tank and instrument cluster with a heavy cloth or plastic tarp to protect them from accidental brake fluid spills. Wash any brake fluid off any painted or plated surfaces immediately, as it will destroy the finish. Use soapy water and rinse completely.

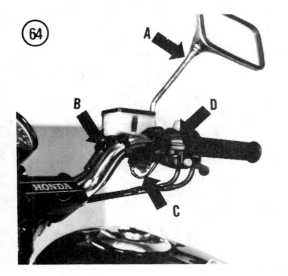

64

2. Pull back the rubber boot (B, **Figure 64**) and remove the union bolt securing the brake hose to the master cylinder. Remove the brake hose. Tie the brake hose up and cover the end to prevent the entry of foreign matter.
3. Disconnect the electrical wires to the brake light switch (C, **Figure 64**).
4. Remove the clamping bolts (D, **Figure 64**) and clamp securing the master cylinder to the handlebar and remove the master cylinder.
5. Install by reversing these removal steps, noting the following.
6. Install the clamp with the UP arrow facing up. Align the lug with the punch mark on the handlebar and tighten the upper bolt first, then the lower. Tighten both bolts securely.
7. Install the brake hose onto the master cylinder. Be sure to place a sealing washer on each side of the fitting and install the union bolt. Tighten the union bolt to the torque specification listed in **Table 2**.
8. Bleed the brake as described under *Bleeding the System* in this chapter.

11

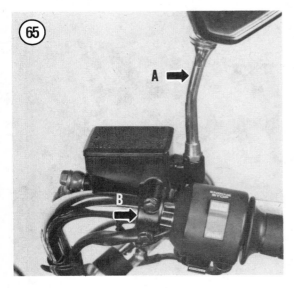

65

Removal/Installation
(Rebel 450)

1. Remove the rear view mirror (A, **Figure 65**) from the master cylinder.

CAUTION
Cover the fuel tank and speedometer with a heavy cloth or plastic tarp to protect them from accidental brake fluid spills. Wash any brake fluid off any painted or plated surfaces immediately, as it will destroy the finish. Use soapy water and rinse completely.

2. Remove the union bolt (A, **Figure 66**) securing the brake hose to the master cylinder. Remove the brake hose and 2 sealing washers. Tie the brake hose up and cover the end to prevent the entry of foreign matter.

3. Disconnect the electrical wires to the brake light switch (B, **Figure 66**).

4. Remove the clamping bolts (B, **Figure 65**) and clamp securing the master cylinder to the handlebar and remove the master cylinder.

5. Install by reversing these removal steps, noting the following.

6. Install the clamp with the UP mark facing up (**Figure 67**). Align the lug with the punch mark on the handlebar and tighten the upper bolt first, then the lower. Tighten both bolts securely.

7. Install the brake hose onto the master cylinder. Be sure to place a sealing washer on each side of the fitting and install the union bolt. Tighten the union bolt to the torque specification listed in **Table 2**.

8. Bleed the brake as described under *Bleeding the System* in this chapter.

Master Cylinder Disassembly

Refer to the following illustrations for this procedure.

   a. **Figure 68**: CB450SC.
   b. **Figure 69**: Rebel 450.

1. Remove the master cylinder as described under *Master Cylinder Removal/Installation* in this chapter.

2. Remove the bolt and nut (**Figure 70**) securing the brake hand lever and remove the hand lever.

3. Remove the screw securing the brake light switch and remove the switch (**Figure 71**).

4. Remove the screws (**Figure 72**) securing the cover.

5. Remove the cover, diaphragm plate (**Figure 73**) and diaphragm (**Figure 74**); pour out the brake fluid and discard it. *Never* reuse brake fluid.

6. Remove the rubber boot (**Figure 75**) from the area where the hand lever actuates the internal piston.

7. Using circlip pliers, remove the internal circlip (**Figure 76**) from the body.

8. Remove the piston assembly (**Figure 77**) and spring from the body.

Master Cylinder Inspection

1. Clean all parts in denatured alcohol or fresh brake fluid. Inspect the cylinder bore and piston contact surfaces for signs of wear and damage. If either part is less than perfect, replace it.

2. Check the end of the piston for wear caused by the hand lever and check the pivot bore in the hand lever. Replace the piston if the secondary cup requires replacement.

3. Inspect the brake hand lever pivot hole (**Figure 78**) in the master cylinder. If worn or elongated the cylinder must be replaced.

4. Inspect the brake hand lever pivot hole (**Figure 79**). If worn or elongated the hand lever must be replaced.

5. Make sure the brake fluid opening (**Figure 80**) in the bottom of the brake fluid reservoir is clear.

6. Make sure the brake fluid opening (**Figure 81**) in the union bolt is clear.

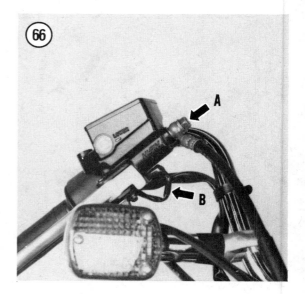

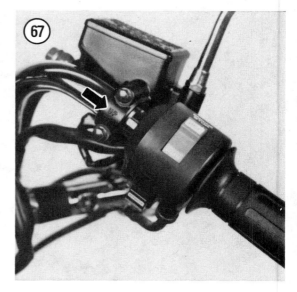

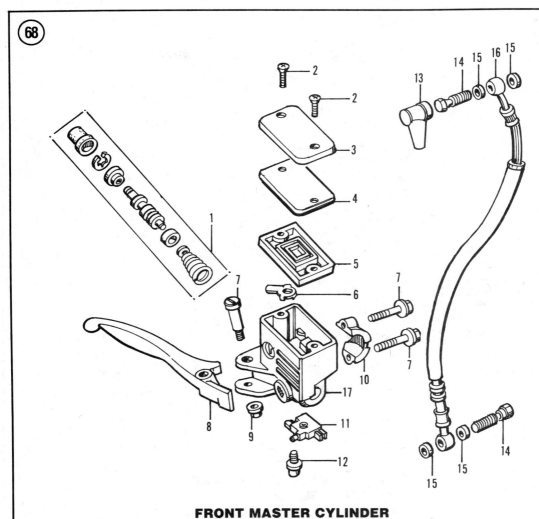

**FRONT MASTER CYLINDER
(CB450SC)**

1. Piston assembly
2. Screw
3. Cover
4. Diaphragm plate
5. Diaphragm
6. Lockwasher
7. Pivot bolt
8. Brake lever
9. Nut
10. Clamp
11. Brake switch
12. Screw
13. Rubber boot
14. Union bolt
15. Sealing washer
16. Brake hose
17. Master cylinder body

11

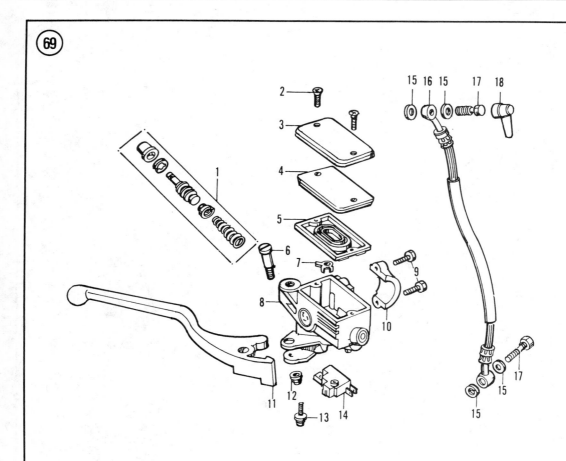

**FRONT MASTER CYLINDER
(REBEL 450)**

1. Piston assembly
2. Screw
3. Cover
4. Diaphragm plate
5. Diaphragm
6. Pivot bolt
7. Lockwasher
8. Master cylinder body
9. Bolt
10. Clamp
11. Brake lever
12. Nut
13. Screw
14. Brake switch
15. Sealing washer
16. Brake hose
17. Union bolt
18. Rubber boot

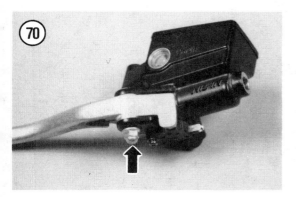

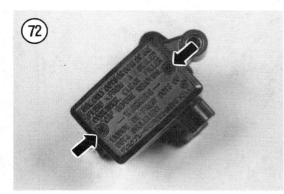

7. Check the reservoir cap, diaphragm (**Figure 82**) and diaphragm plate for damage and deterioration and replace as necessary.

8. Inspect the threads in the bore for the brake line.

9. Remove the primary and secondary cups (**Figure 83**) from the piston assembly. Discard the cups as they must be replaced.

11

10. Measure the cylinder bore (**Figure 84**). Replace the master cylinder if the bore is worn to the service limit dimension listed in **Table 3** or greater.

11. Measure the outside diameter of the piston as shown in **Figure 85** with a micrometer. Replace the piston assembly if it is worn to the service limit dimension listed in **Table 3** or less.

Master Cylinder Assembly

NOTE
Be sure to install the primary cup with the open end in first, toward the spring.

1. Soak the new cups in fresh brake fluid for at least 15 minutes to make them pliable. Install the primary and secondary cups (**Figure 83**) onto the piston assembly.

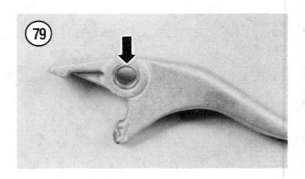

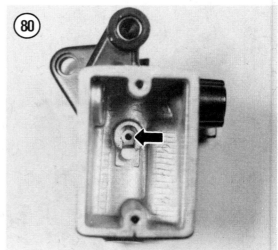

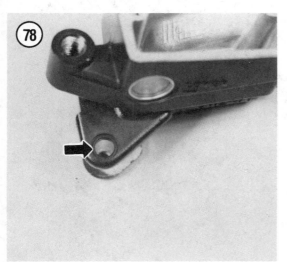

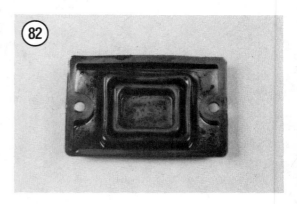

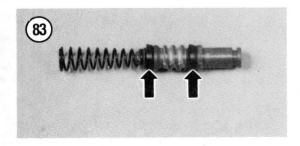

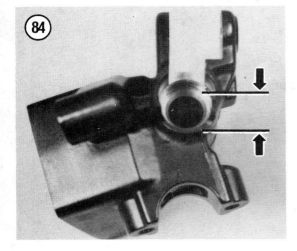

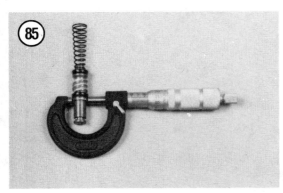

2. Coat the inside of the master cylinder bore with fresh brake fluid before the assembly of parts.

CAUTION
When installing the piston assembly, do not allow the cups to turn inside out as they will be damaged and allow brake fluid leakage within the cylinder bore.

3. Position the spring with the tapered end facing toward the piston assembly (**Figure 86**).

4. Install the spring and piston assembly into the cylinder together.

5. Install the circlip (**Figure 87**). Make sure it is correctly seated in the groove in the master cylinder body.

6. Slide in the rubber boot (**Figure 76**).

7. Install the diaphragm, diaphragm plate and cover. Do not tighten the cover screws at this time as fluid will have to be added later.

8. Install the brake lever onto the master cylinder body.

9. Install the brake light switch and tighten the screw securely.

10. Install the master cylinder as described under *Master Cylinder Removal/Installation* in this chapter.

FRONT CALIPER

Single Piston Caliper
Removal/Installation
(CB400A, CB400T II,
1980 CB400T, CM400A, CM400T)

Refer to **Figure 88** for this procedure.

It is not necessary to remove the front wheel in order to remove the caliper assembly.

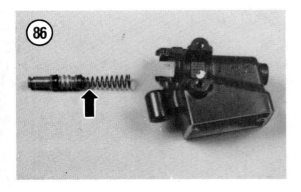

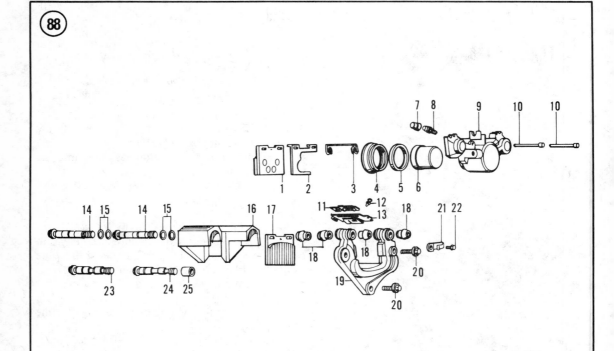

**FRONT CALIPER
(CB400A, CB400T II,
1980 CB400T, CM400A, CM400T)**

1. Brake pad
2. Pad shim
3. Pad pin clip
4. Piston boot
5. Piston seal
6. Piston
7. Cap
8. Bleed valve
9. Caliper body "A"
10. Pad pins
11. Cover
12. Bolt
13. Plate
14. Caliper shaft
15. O-rings
16. Caliper body "B"
17. Brake pad
18. Shaft boot
19. Caliper carrier
20. Bolt
21. Clip
22. Bolt
23. Caliper shaft "A"
24. Caliper shaft "B"
25. Collar

1. Disconnect the speedometer cable clip (A, **Figure 89**).

> *CAUTION*
> *Do not spill any brake fluid on the painted portion of the ComStar wheel. Wash off any spilled brake fluid immediately, as it will destroy the finish. Use soapy water and rinse completely.*

2. Place a container under the brake hose at the caliper. Remove the union bolt (**Figure 90**) and sealing washers securing the brake hose to the caliper assembly.

3. Remove the brake hose and let the brake fluid drain out into the container. Dispose of this brake fluid—*never* reuse brake fluid. To prevent the entry of moisture and dirt, cap the end of the brake hose and tie the loose end up to the forks.

4. Loosen the caliper mounting bolts (B, **Figure 89**) gradually in several steps. Push on the caliper while loosening the bolts to push the piston back into the caliper.

5. Remove the caliper mounting bolts and remove the caliper assembly from the brake disc.

6. Install the caliper by reversing the removal steps, noting the following.

7. Carefully install the caliper assembly onto the disc. Be careful not to damage the leading edge of the pads during installation.

8. Tighten the caliper mounting bolts to the torque specification listed in **Table 2**.

9. Install the brake hose, with a sealing washer on each side of the fitting, onto the caliper. Install the union bolt and tighten it to the torque specification listed in **Table 2**.

10. Bleed the brake as described under *Bleeding the System* in this chapter.

> *WARNING*
> *Do not ride the motorcycle until you are sure that the brakes are operating properly.*

Dual-piston Caliper
Removal/Installation
(CM400C, 1981-1982 CB400T,
CM450A, CM450C)

Refer to the following illustrations for this procedure.
  a. **Figure 91**: CM400C, 1981 CB400T.
  b. **Figure 92**: 1982 CB400T, CM450A, CM450C.

It is not necessary to remove the front wheel in order to remove the caliper assembly.

> *CAUTION*
> *Do not spill any brake fluid on the painted portion of the ComStar wheel. Wash off any spilled brake fluid immediately, as it will destroy the finish. Use soapy water and rinse completely.*

1. Place a container under the brake hose at the caliper. Remove the union bolt (A, **Figure 93**) and sealing washers securing the brake hose to the caliper assembly.

2. Remove the brake hose and let the brake fluid drain out into the container. Dispose of this brake fluid—*never* reuse brake fluid. To prevent the entry of moisture and dirt, cap the end of the brake hose and tie the loose end up to the forks.

11

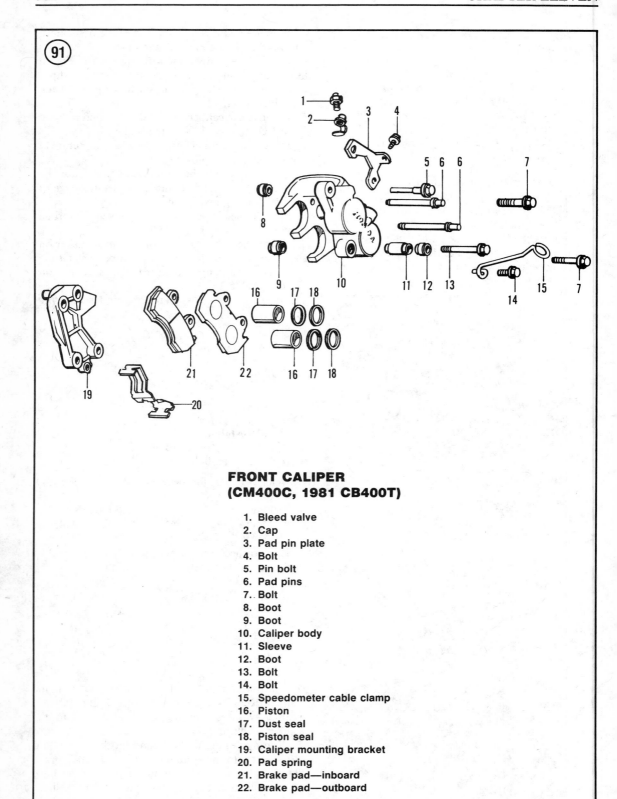

**FRONT CALIPER
(CM400C, 1981 CB400T)**

1. Bleed valve
2. Cap
3. Pad pin plate
4. Bolt
5. Pin bolt
6. Pad pins
7. Bolt
8. Boot
9. Boot
10. Caliper body
11. Sleeve
12. Boot
13. Bolt
14. Bolt
15. Speedometer cable clamp
16. Piston
17. Dust seal
18. Piston seal
19. Caliper mounting bracket
20. Pad spring
21. Brake pad—inboard
22. Brake pad—outboard

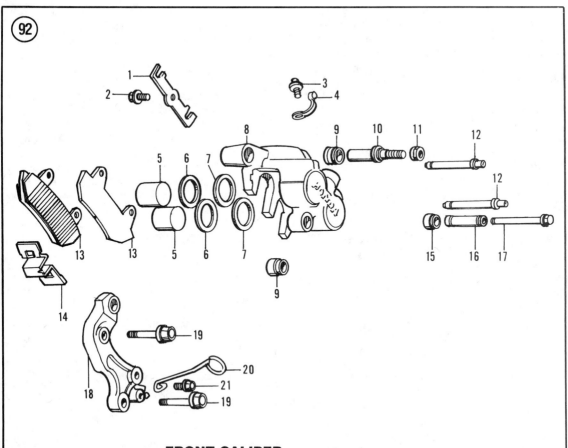

FRONT CALIPER
(1982 CB400T, CM450A, CM450C)

1. Pad pin retainer
2. Bolt
3. Bleed valve
4. Cap
5. Piston
6. Dust seal
7. Piston seal
8. Caliper body
9. Pin bolt boot
10. Pin bolt
11. Nut
12. Pad pins
13. Brake pads
14. Pad spring
15. Boot
16. Sleeve
17. Bolt
18. Caliper mounting bracket
19. Bolt
20. Speedometer cable clamp
21. Bolt

11

3. Loosen the caliper upper pivot bolt and caliper lower mounting bolt (B, **Figure 93**) gradually in several steps. Push on the caliper while loosening the bolts to push the pistons back into the caliper.

4. Remove the caliper bracket mounting bolts and remove the caliper assembly.

5. Lubricate the caliper upper pivot bolt with silicone grease.

6. Install by reversing these removal steps, noting the following.

7. Carefully install the caliper assembly onto the disc. Be careful not to damage the leading edge of the pads during installation.

8. Tighten the caliper mounting bolts to the torque specifications listed in **Table 2**.

9. Install the brake hose, with a sealing washer on each side of the fitting, onto the caliper. Install the union bolt and tighten it to the torque specification listed in **Table 2**.

10. Bleed the brake as described under *Bleeding the System* in this chapter.

> *WARNING*
> *Do not ride the motorcycle until you are sure that the brakes are operating properly.*

Dual-piston Caliper
Removal/Installation
(CB450SC)

Refer to **Figure 94** for this procedure.

It is not necessary to remove the front wheel in order to remove the caliper assembly.

> *CAUTION*
> *Do not spill any brake fluid on the painted portion of the ComStar or ComCast wheel. Wash off any spilled brake fluid immediately, as it will destroy the finish. Use soapy water and rinse completely.*

1. Place a container under the brake hose at the caliper. Remove the union bolt and sealing washers (A, **Figure 95**) securing the brake hose to the caliper assembly.

2. Remove the brake hose and let the brake fluid drain out into the container. Dispose of this brake fluid—*never* reuse brake fluid. To prevent the entry of moisture and dirt, cap the end of the brake hose and tie the loose end up to the forks.

3. Loosen the lower bolt (B, **Figure 95**) and the upper nut (C, **Figure 95**) gradually in several steps. Push on the caliper while loosening the bolts to push the pistons back into the caliper.

4. Remove the lower bolt (B, **Figure 95**) and the upper nut (C, **Figure 95**) securing the caliper

assembly to the caliper bracket on the fork. Remove the caliper assembly from the brake disc.

5. Install by reversing these removal steps, noting the following.

6. Lubricate the caliper upper pivot bolt with silicone grease.

7. Carefully install the caliper assembly onto the disc. Be careful not to damage the leading edge of the pads during installation.

8. Tighten the caliper mounting bolts to the torque specifications listed in **Table 2**.

9. Install the brake hose, with a sealing washer on each side of the fitting, onto the caliper. Install the union bolt and tighten it to the torque specification listed in **Table 2**.

10. Bleed the brake as described under *Bleeding the System* in this chapter.

> *WARNING*
> *Do not ride the motorcycle until you are sure that the brakes are operating properly.*

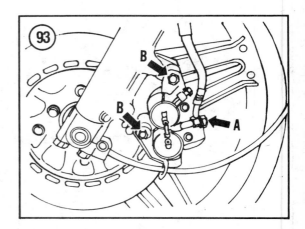

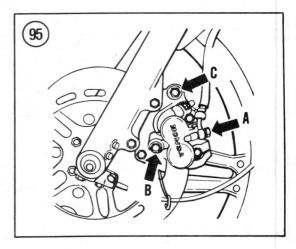

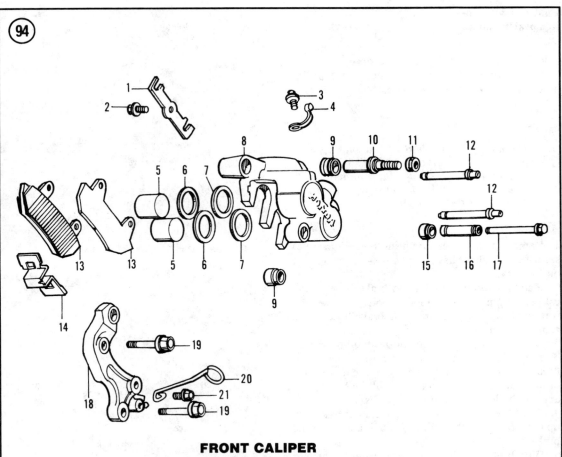

**FRONT CALIPER
(CB450SC, REBEL 450)**

1. Pad pin retainer
2. Bolt
3. Bleed valve
4. Cap
5. Piston
6. Dust seal
7. Piston seal
8. Caliper body
9. Pin bolt boot
10. Pin bolt
11. Nut
12. Pad pins
13. Brake pads
14. Pad spring
15. Boot
16. Sleeve
17. Bolt
18. Caliper mounting bracket
19. Bolt
20. Speedometer cable clamp
21. Bolt

11

Dual-piston Caliper
Removal/Installation
(Rebel 450)

Refer to **Figure 94** for this procedure.

It is not necessary to remove the front wheel in order to remove the caliper assembly.

> *CAUTION*
> *Do not spill any brake fluid on the plated portion of the wire wheel. Wash off any spilled brake fluid immediately, as it will destroy the finish. Use soapy water and rinse completely.*

1. Remove the caliper mounting bolt (**Figure 96**) securing the caliper assembly to the caliper bracket on the fork.

2. Place a container under the brake hose at the caliper. Remove the union bolt and sealing washers (**Figure 97**) securing the brake hose to the caliper assembly.

3. Remove the brake hose and let the brake fluid drain out into the container. Dispose of this brake fluid—*never* reuse brake fluid. To prevent the entry of moisture and dirt, cap the end of the brake hose and tie the loose end up to the forks.

4. Pivot the lower portion of the caliper assembly up (**Figure 98**) on the caliper pin bolt and off of the brake disc.

5. Withdraw the caliper assembly from the caliper mounting bracket and remove the caliper assembly.

6. Install by reversing these removal steps, noting the following.

7. Apply a light coat of silicone grease to the caliper pin bolt boot (A, **Figure 99**) on the caliper mounting bracket.

8. Make sure the retainer clip (B, **Figure 99**) is in place on the caliper mounting bracket.

9. Install the pin bolt on the caliper assembly into the pin bolt boot on the caliper mounting bracket and push the caliper assembly all the way onto the mounting bracket.

10. Pivot the lower portion of the caliper assembly down onto the brake disc. Be careful not to damage the leading edge of the pads during installation.

11. Install the caliper mounting bolt (**Figure 96**) and tighten to the torque specification listed in **Table 2**.

12. Install the brake hose, with a sealing washer on each side of the fitting, onto the caliper. Install the union bolt and tighten it to the torque specification listed in **Table 2**.

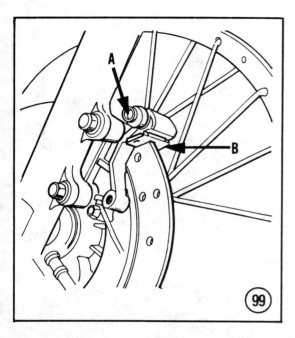

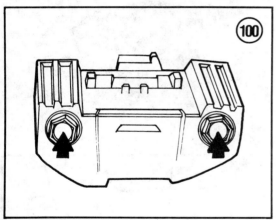

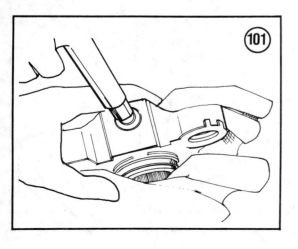

13. Bleed the brake as described under *Bleeding the System* in this chapter.

WARNING
Do not ride the motorcycle until you are sure that the brakes are operating properly.

FRONT CALIPER REBUILDING

Caliper Disassembly/Rebuilding/Assembly (CB400A, CB400T II, 1980 CB400T, CM400A, CM400T)

Refer to **Figure 88** for this procedure.
1. Remove the caliper and brake pads as described in this chapter.
2. Separate caliper "A" from caliper "B" as follows:

CAUTION
In the following sub-step, loosen the caliper shafts in stages. To prevent binding during separation, loosen one shaft 2-3 turns and then the other shaft 2-3 turns. Continue this until caliper "A" is free.

    a. Loosen the caliper shafts (**Figure 100**) securing caliper "A" to caliper "B".
    b. Separate caliper "A" from caliper "B".
3. Remove the piston boot from caliper "A." Discard the boot as it must be replaced.
4. Place caliper "A" assembly on the workbench with the piston facing down. Place a shop cloth or piece of soft wood under the piston.

WARNING
*In the next step, the piston may shoot out of the caliper body like a bullet. Keep your fingers out of the way. Wear safety glasses and shop gloves. Apply air pressure gradually. Do **not** use high pressure air or place the air hose nozzle directly against the hydraulic hose fitting inlet in the caliper body. Hold the air nozzle away from the inlet, allowing some of the air to escape.*

5. Apply the air pressure in short spurts to the hydraulic hose fitting inlet (**Figure 101**) and force the piston out. Use a service station air hose if you don't have a compressor.

11

CAUTION
In the following step, do not use a sharp tool to remove the piston seal from the caliper cylinder. Do not damage the cylinder surface.

6. Use a piece of plastic or wood and carefully push the piston seal in toward the caliper cylinder and out of its groove (**Figure 102**). Remove the piston seal from the cylinder and discard the seal.

7. Inspect the caliper body for damage. Replace the caliper body if necessary.

8. Inspect the cylinder and the piston for scratches, scoring or other damage. Light dirt may be removed with a cloth dipped in rubbing alcohol or clean brake fluid. If rust is present, replace the caliper assembly.

9. If serviceable, clean the caliper body with rubbing alcohol and rinse with clean brake fluid.

10. Measure the inside diameter of the caliper cylinder with an inside micrometer. If worn to the service limit dimension listed in **Table 3**, or greater, replace the caliper assembly.

11. Measure the outside diameter of the piston with a micrometer. If worn to the service limit dimension listed in **Table 3**, or less, replace the piston.

NOTE
Never reuse the old piston seal. Very minor damage or age deterioration can make the seal useless.

12. Coat the new piston seal with fresh DOT 3 or DOT 4 brake fluid.

13. Carefully install the new piston seal in the groove in the caliper cylinder. Make sure the seal is properly seated in the groove.

14. Coat the piston and caliper cylinder with fresh DOT 3 or DOT 4 brake fluid.

15. Position the piston with the groove side facing out toward the brake pads and install the piston into the caliper cylinder. Push the piston in until it bottoms out.

16. Install a new piston boot.

17. Assemble caliper "A" onto caliper "B" as follows:

   a. Position caliper "A" against caliper "B".

CAUTION
In the next step, tighten the caliper shafts in stages. Tighten one shaft 2-3 turns and then the other shaft 2-3 turns. Continue this until caliper "A" is up against caliper "B." This will prevent the binding of caliper "A".

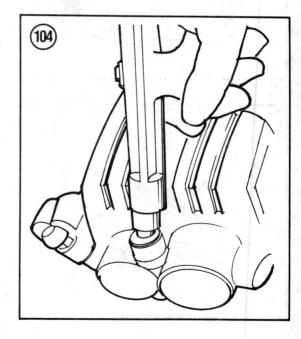

b. Tighten the caliper shafts (**Figure 100**) securing caliper "A" to caliper "B," while gently pushing caliper "A" against caliper "B".

c. Make sure that the mating surface of caliper "A" is evenly against the mating surface of caliper "B".

d. Tighten the caliper shafts securely.

18. Install the brake pads and the caliper as described in this chapter.

Caliper Rebuilding
(All Other Models)

Refer to the following illustrations for this procedure.

   a. **Figure 91**: CM400C, 1981 CB400T.

   b. **Figure 92**: 1982 CB400T, CM450A, CM450C.

   c. **Figure 94**: CB450SC, Rebel 450.

1. Remove the caliper and brake pads as described in this chapter.

2. If not already removed, remove the brake pad spring (**Figure 103**).

3. Place a shop cloth or piece of soft wood in the area normally occupied by the brake pads.

4. Place the caliper assembly on the workbench with the pistons facing down.

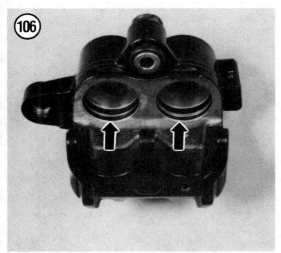

> *WARNING*
> *In the next step, the pistons may shoot out of the caliper body like a bullet. Keep your fingers out of the way. Wear safety glasses and shop gloves. Apply air pressure gradually. Do **not** use high pressure air or place the air hose nozzle directly against the hydraulic hose fitting inlet in the caliper body. Hold the air nozzle away from the inlet, allowing some of the air to escape.*

5. Apply the air pressure in short spurts to the hydraulic hose fitting inlet (**Figure 104**) and force the pistons out. Use a service station air hose if you don't have a compressor. Remove both pistons (**Figure 105**).

> *CAUTION*
> *In the following step, do not use a sharp tool to remove the dust and piston seals from the caliper cylinders. Do not damage the cylinder surface.*

6. Use a piece of plastic or wood and carefully push the dust and piston seals (**Figure 106**) in toward the caliper cylinder and out of their grooves. Remove the dust seal and piston seal from the cylinder and discard the seals (**Figure 107**).

11

7. Inspect the caliper body for damage. Replace the caliper body if necessary.

8. Inspect the cylinder and the piston for scratches, scoring or other damage. Light dirt may be removed with a cloth dipped in rubbing alcohol or clean brake fluid. If rust is present, replace the caliper assembly.

9. If serviceable, clean the caliper body with rubbing alcohol and rinse with clean brake fluid.

10. Measure the inside diameter of each caliper cylinder (**Figure 108**) with an inside micrometer. If either cylinder is worn to the service limit dimension listed in **Table 3**, or greater, replace the caliper assembly.

11. Measure the outside diameter of each piston with a micrometer as shown in **Figure 109**. If worn to the service limit dimension listed in **Table 3**, or less, replace the piston.

> *NOTE*
> *Never reuse the old dust seals and piston seals. Very minor damage or age deterioration can make the seals useless.*

12. Coat the new dust seals and piston seals with fresh DOT 3 or DOT 4 brake fluid.

13. Position the new dust seal and piston seal with the smaller diameter end *facing in* toward the caliper.

14. Carefully install the new dust seal and piston seal (**Figure 106**) in the grooves in the caliper cylinder. Make sure the seals are properly seated in their respective grooves.

15. Coat each piston and caliper cylinders with fresh DOT 3 or DOT 4 brake fluid.

16. Position the piston with the open side facing out toward the brake pads and install the piston into the caliper cylinder (**Figure 110**). Push the piston in until it bottoms out.

17. Remove the pivot collar and pivot boots from the caliper. Apply silicone grease to the caliper rubber pivot boots. Install the boots and the pivot collar (**Figure 111**) into the caliper body.

18. Install the brake pads and the caliper as described in this chapter.

BRAKE DISC

Removal/Installation

1. Remove the front wheel as described under *Front Wheel Removal* in Chapter Nine.

2A. On CB450T models, remove the bolts and nuts securing the brake disc on the left-hand side and the cover on the right-hand side. Remove the brake disc and the cover.

2B. On all other models, remove the bolts securing the disc to the wheel and remove the disc.

3. Install by reversing the removal steps, noting the following.

4A. On CB450T models, install brake disc on the left-hand side and the cover on the right-hand side.

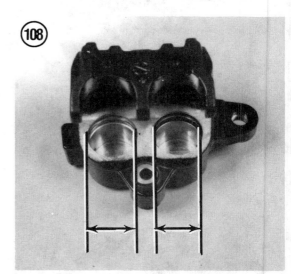

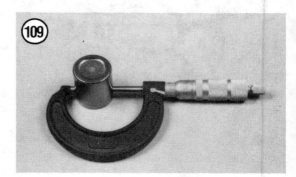

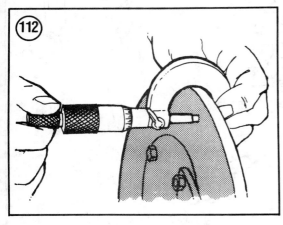

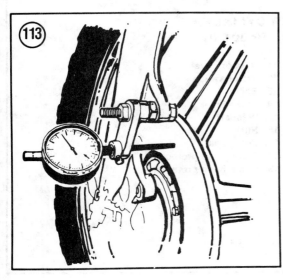

Install and tighten the bolts and nuts and tighten to the torque specifications listed in **Table 2**.

4B. On all other models, install the brake disc and tighten the bolts to the torque specifications listed in **Table 2**.

Brake Disc Inspection

It is not necessary to remove the disc from the wheel to inspect it. Small marks on the disc are not important, but deep radial scratches reduce braking effectiveness and increase pad wear. The disc should be replaced.

1. Measure the thickness at several points around the disc with a vernier caliper or micrometer (**Figure 112**). Replace the disc if worn to the service limit listed in **Table 3** or less at any point around the disc surface.

2. Make sure the disc mounting bolts are tight before running this check. Check the disc runout with a dial indicator as shown in **Figure 113**. Slowly rotate the wheel and watch the dial indicator. Replace the disc if the runout is to the service limit listed in **Table 3** or greater.

3. Clean the disc of any rust or corrosion and wipe clean with lacquer thinner. *Never* use an oil-based solvent that may leave an oil residue on the disc.

FRONT BRAKE HOSE REPLACEMENT

There is no factory-recommended replacement interval but it is a good idea to replace the brake hose every four years or when it shows signs of cracking or damage.

This procedure is shown on a Rebel 450 and represents a typical replacement procedure. Where differences occur, they are identified.

Removal/Installation

Refer to the following illustrations for this procedure.

- a. **Figure 114**: CB400A, 1978 CB400T II.
- b. **Figure 115**: 1979 CB400T II, CB400T.
- c. **Figure 116**: 1979-1980 CM400A, 1979-1980 CM400T.
- d. **Figure 117**: 1981 CB400T, 1981 CM400A, 1981 CM400C, 1981 CM400T, CM450A, CM450C.
- e. **Figure 118A**: CB450T, 1982-1983 CB450SC.
- f. **Figure 118B**: 1985-1986 CB450SC.
- g. **Figure 119**: Rebel 450.

11

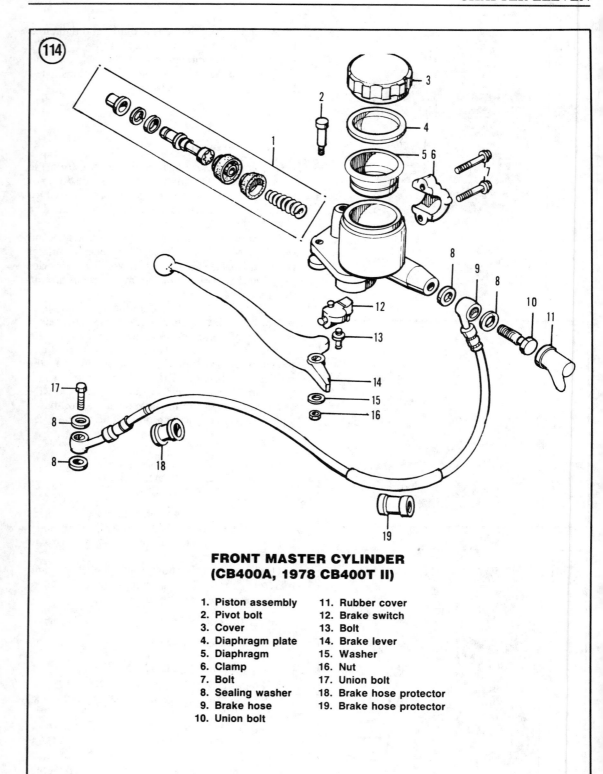

**FRONT MASTER CYLINDER
(CB400A, 1978 CB400T II)**

1. Piston assembly
2. Pivot bolt
3. Cover
4. Diaphragm plate
5. Diaphragm
6. Clamp
7. Bolt
8. Sealing washer
9. Brake hose
10. Union bolt
11. Rubber cover
12. Brake switch
13. Bolt
14. Brake lever
15. Washer
16. Nut
17. Union bolt
18. Brake hose protector
19. Brake hose protector

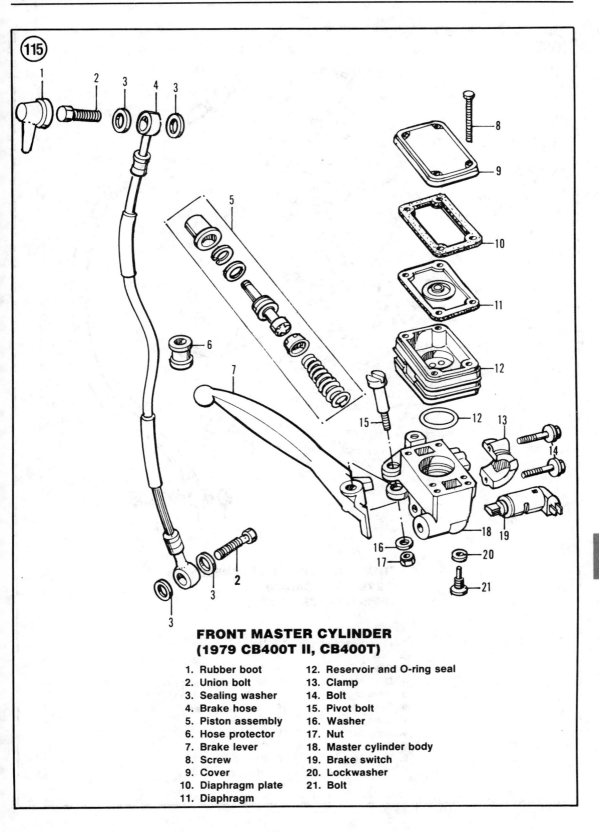

**FRONT MASTER CYLINDER
(1979 CB400T II, CB400T)**

1. Rubber boot
2. Union bolt
3. Sealing washer
4. Brake hose
5. Piston assembly
6. Hose protector
7. Brake lever
8. Screw
9. Cover
10. Diaphragm plate
11. Diaphragm
12. Reservoir and O-ring seal
13. Clamp
14. Bolt
15. Pivot bolt
16. Washer
17. Nut
18. Master cylinder body
19. Brake switch
20. Lockwasher
21. Bolt

11

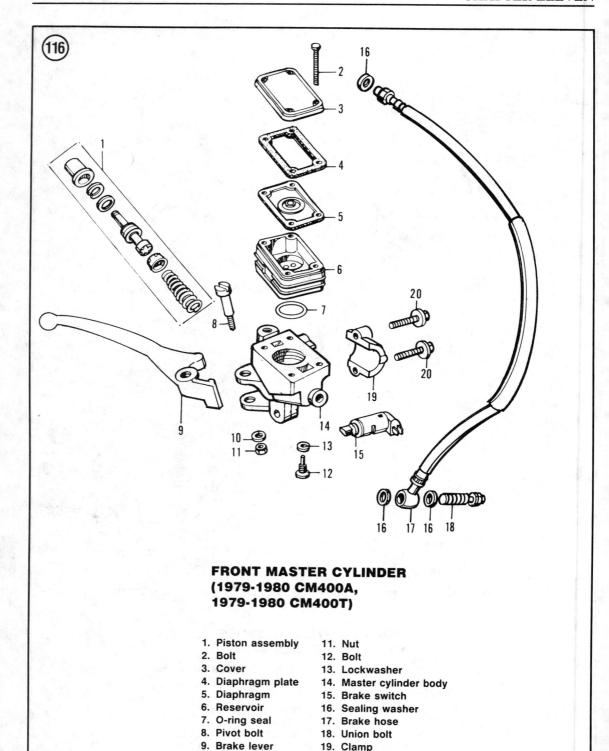

**FRONT MASTER CYLINDER
(1979-1980 CM400A,
1979-1980 CM400T)**

1. Piston assembly
2. Bolt
3. Cover
4. Diaphragm plate
5. Diaphragm
6. Reservoir
7. O-ring seal
8. Pivot bolt
9. Brake lever
10. Washer
11. Nut
12. Bolt
13. Lockwasher
14. Master cylinder body
15. Brake switch
16. Sealing washer
17. Brake hose
18. Union bolt
19. Clamp
20. Bolt

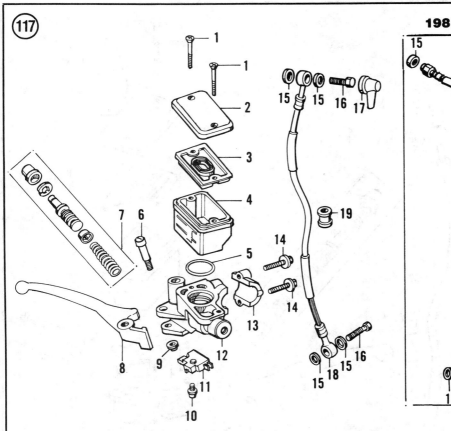

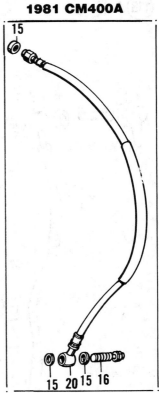

1981 CM400A

FRONT MASTER CYLINDER
(1981 CB400T, 1981 CM400A, 1981 CM400C, 1981 CM400T, CM450A, CM450C)

1. Screw
2. Cover
3. Diaphragm
4. Reservoir
5. O-ring seal
6. Pivot bolt
7. Piston assembly
8. Brake lever
9. Nut
10. Screw
11. Brake switch
12. Master cylinder body
13. Clamp
14. Bolt
15. Sealing washer
16. Union bolt
17. Rubber boot
18. Brake hose
19. Hose protector
20. Brake hose

11

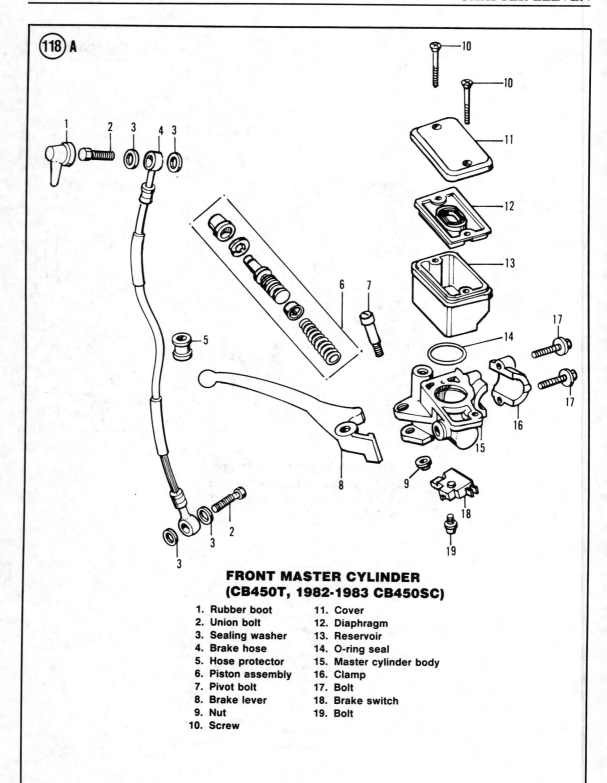

**FRONT MASTER CYLINDER
(CB450T, 1982-1983 CB450SC)**

1. Rubber boot
2. Union bolt
3. Sealing washer
4. Brake hose
5. Hose protector
6. Piston assembly
7. Pivot bolt
8. Brake lever
9. Nut
10. Screw
11. Cover
12. Diaphragm
13. Reservoir
14. O-ring seal
15. Master cylinder body
16. Clamp
17. Bolt
18. Brake switch
19. Bolt

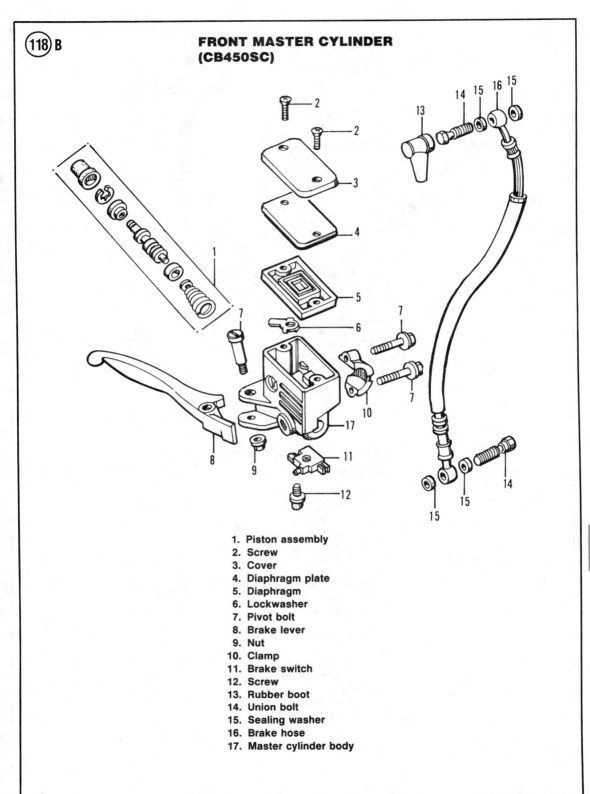

FRONT MASTER CYLINDER (CB450SC)

1. Piston assembly
2. Screw
3. Cover
4. Diaphragm plate
5. Diaphragm
6. Lockwasher
7. Pivot bolt
8. Brake lever
9. Nut
10. Clamp
11. Brake switch
12. Screw
13. Rubber boot
14. Union bolt
15. Sealing washer
16. Brake hose
17. Master cylinder body

11

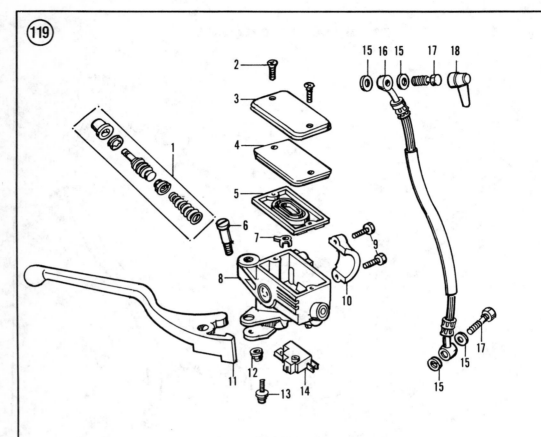

**FRONT MASTER CYLINDER
(REBEL 450)**

1. Piston assembly
2. Screw
3. Cover
4. Diaphragm plate
5. Diaphragm
6. Pivot bolt
7. Lockwasher
8. Master cylinder body
9. Bolt
10. Clamp
11. Brake lever
12. Nut
13. Screw
14. Brake switch
15. Sealing washer
16. Brake hose
17. Union bolt
18. Rubber boot

CAUTION
Cover the front wheel, fender and fuel tank with a heavy cloth or plastic tarp to protect it from accidental spilling of brake fluid. Wash any brake fluid off of any plastic, painted or plated surface immediately, as it will destroy the finish. Use soapy water and rinse completely.

1. Place wood blocks under the engine with the front wheel off the ground.
2. On models so equipped, disconnect the brake hose from the clamp (**Figure 120**) on the right-hand fork slider.
3. Place a container under the brake hose at the caliper.
4. Remove the union bolt and sealing washers (**Figure 121**) securing the brake hose to the caliper assembly.
5. Remove the brake hose from the caliper and let the brake fluid drain out into the container.

WARNING
Dispose of this brake fluid. Never reuse brake fluid. Contaminated brake fluid can cause brake failure.

6. To prevent the entry of moisture and dirt, cap the caliper assembly where the brake hose attaches.
7. On models so equipped. disconnect the brake hose from any clamps (**Figure 122**) on the lower fork bridge.
8. Remove the union bolt and sealing washers securing the brake hose to the master cylinder and remove the hose.
9. Install a new flexible brake hose, sealing washers and union bolts in the reverse order of removal.
10. Be sure to install a new sealing washer on each side of the brake hose fittings at the master cylinder and the front brake caliper.
11. Tighten the union bolts to the torque specification listed in **Table 2**.

WARNING
Use brake fluid from a sealed container marked DOT 3 or DOT 4 only (specified for disc brakes). Other types may vaporize and cause brake failure. Do not intermix different brands or types as they may not be compatible. Do not intermix a silicone based (DOT 5) brake fluid as it can cause brake component damage leading to brake system failure.

12. Refill the master cylinder with fresh brake fluid marked DOT 3 or DOT 4 only. Bleed the brake as described under *Bleeding the System* in this chapter.

WARNING
Do not ride the bike until you are sure that the brake is operating properly.

DRAINING THE SYSTEM

Every time the reservoir cap is removed, a small amount of dirt and moisture enters the brake fluid system. The same thing happens if a leak occurs or any part of the hydraulic brake system is loosened or disconnected. Dirt can clog the system and cause unnecessary wear. Water in the brake fluid vaporizes at high temperature, impairing the hydraulic action and reducing the brake's stopping ability.

To maintain peak braking efficiency, change the brake fluid every year. To change brake fluid, follow the *Bleeding the System* procedure in this chapter. Continue adding new brake fluid to the master cylinder and bleed the fluid out at the caliper until the brake fluid leaving the caliper is clean and free of contaminants.

> *WARNING*
> *Use brake fluid marked DOT 3 or DOT 4 (specified for disc brakes). Others may vaporize and cause brake failure. Do not intermix different brands or types of brake fluid as they may not be compatible. Do not intermix silicone based (DOT 5) brake fluid as it can cause brake component damage leading to brake system failure.*

BLEEDING THE SYSTEM

This procedure is not necessary unless the brakes feel spongy, there has been a leak in the system, a component has been replaced or the brake fluid has been replaced.

This procedure is shown on a Rebel 450 and represents a typical replacement procedure. Where differences occur, they are identified.

Brake Bleeder Process

This procedure uses a brake bleeder that is available from motorcycle or automotive supply stores or from mail order outlets.

1. Remove the dust cap from the bleed valve (**Figure 123**) on the caliper assembly.
2. Connect the bleed hose of the brake bleeder to the bleed valve on the caliper assembly (**Figure 124**).

> *CAUTION*
> *Cover the front wheel with a heavy cloth or plastic tarp to protect it from the accidental spilling of brake fluid. Wash any brake fluid off of any plastic, painted or plated surface immediately as it will destroy the finish. Use soapy water and rinse completely.*

3. Clean the top of the master cylinder of all dirt and foreign matter.
4A. On CB400A and 1978 CB400T models, perform the following:
  a. Unscrew the cover.
  b. Fill the reservoir almost to the top lip and screw on the cover loosely. Leave the cover in place during this procedure to prevent the entry of dirt.
4B. On all other models, perform the following:
  a. Remove the screws securing the cover (**Figure 125**) and remove the cover, diaphragm plate (models so equipped) and diaphragm.
  b. Fill the reservoir almost to the top lip. Insert the diaphragm plate (models so equipped), diaphragm and the cover loosely. Leave the

cover in place during this procedure to prevent the entry of dirt.

> *WARNING*
> *Use brake fluid from a sealed container marked DOT 3 or DOT 4 only (specified for disc brakes). Other types may vaporize and cause brake failure. Do not intermix different brands or types as they may not be compatible. Do not intermix a silicone based (DOT 5) brake fluid as it can cause brake component damage leading to brake system failure.*

5. Open the bleed valve about one-half turn and pump the brake bleeder lever.

> *NOTE*
> *If air is entering the brake bleeder hose from around the bleed valve, apply several layers of Teflon tape to the bleed valve. This should make a good seal between the bleed valve and the brake bleeder hose.*

6. As the fluid enters the system and exits into the brake bleeder the level will drop in the reservoir. Maintain the level at about 3/8 inch from the top of the reservoir to prevent air from being drawn into the system.

7. Continue to pump the lever on the brake bleeder until the fluid emerging from the hose is completely free of bubbles. At this point, tighten the bleed valve.

NOTE
Do not allow the reservoir to empty during the bleeding operation or more air will enter the system. If this occurs, the entire procedure must be repeated.

8. When the brake fluid is free of bubbles, tighten the bleed valve, remove the brake bleeder tube and install the bleed valve dust cap.

9. If necessary, add fluid to correct the level in the reservoir. It should be to the upper level line.

10A. On CB400A and 1978 CB400T models, screw the cover on tightly.

10B. On all other models, install the diaphragm plate (models so equipped), diaphragm and the cover. Tighten the screws securely.

11. Test the feel of the brake lever. It should be firm and should offer the same resistance each time it's operated. If it feels spongy, it is likely that there is still air in the system and it must be bled again. When all air has been bled from the system and the fluid level is correct in the reservoir, double-check for leaks and tighten all fittings.

12. Test ride the bike slowly at first to make sure that the brakes are operating properly.

Without a Brake Bleeder

1. Remove the dust cap from the bleed valve (**Figure 123**) on the caliper assembly.

2. Connect a length of clear tubing to the bleed valve on the caliper assembly (**Figure 126**).

CAUTION
Cover the front wheel with a heavy cloth or plastic tarp to protect it from the accidental spilling of brake fluid. Wash any brake fluid off of any plastic, painted or plated surface immediately; as it will destroy the finish. Use soapy water and rinse completely.

3. Place the other end of the tube into a clean container. Fill the container with enough fresh brake fluid to keep the end submerged. The tube should be long enough so that a loop can be made higher than the bleed valve to prevent air from being drawn into the caliper during bleeding.

4. Clean the top of the master cylinder of all dirt and foreign matter.

5A. On CB400A and 1978 CB400T models, perform the following:
  a. Unscrew the cover.
  b. Fill the reservoir almost to the top lip and screw on the cover loosely. Leave the cover in place during this procedure to prevent the entry of dirt.

5B. On all other models, perform the following:
  a. Remove the screws securing the cover (**Figure 125**) and remove the cover, diaphragm plate (models so equipped) and diaphragm.
  b. Fill the reservoir almost to the top lip. Insert the diaphragm plate (models so equipped), diaphragm and the cover loosely. Leave the cover in place during this procedure to prevent the entry of dirt.

WARNING
Use brake fluid from a sealed container marked DOT 3 or DOT 4 only (specified for disc brakes). Other types may vaporize and cause brake failure. Do not intermix different brands or types as they may not be compatible. Do not intermix a silicone based (DOT 5) brake fluid as it can cause brake component damage leading to brake system failure.

6. Slowly apply the brake lever several times as follows:
  a. Pull the lever in. Hold the lever or pedal in the applied position.
  b. Open the bleed valve about one-half turn. Allow the lever to travel to its limit.

11

c. When this limit is reached, tighten the bleed screw.

7. As the fluid enters the system, the level will drop in the reservoir. Maintain the level at about 3/8 inch from the top of the reservoir to prevent air from being drawn into the system.

8. Continue to pump the lever and fill the reservoir until the fluid emerging from the hose is completely free of bubbles.

NOTE
Do not allow the reservoir to empty during the bleeding operation or more air will enter the system. If this occurs, the entire procedure must be repeated.

9. Hold the lever in, tighten the bleed valve, remove the bleed tube and install the bleed valve dust cap.

10. If necessary, add fluid to correct the level in the reservoir. It should be to the upper level line.

11A. On CB400A and 1978 CB400T models, screw the cover on tightly.

11B. On all other models, install the diaphragm plate (models so equipped), diaphragm and the cover. Tighten the screws securely.

12. Test the feel of the brake lever. It should be firm and should offer the same resistance each time it's operated. If it feels spongy, it is likely that there is still air in the system and it must be bled again. When all air has been bled from the system and the fluid level is correct in the reservoir, double-check for leaks and tighten all fittings.

13. Test ride the bike slowly at first to make sure that the brakes are operating properly.

Table 1 DRUM BRAKE SPECIFICATIONS

Model	Standard		Service limit	
	mm	in.	mm	in.
Front brake drum I.D.	180.1	7.09	181.0	7.13
Rear brake drum I.D.	140.1	5.52	141.0	5.55
Brake shoe thickness	4.9	0.19	2.0	0.08

Table 2 BRAKE TORQUE SPECIFICATIONS

Item	N•m	ft.-lb.
Drum brakes		
Brake cam and arm		
bolts and nuts	6-9	8-12
Caliper mounting bolts		
CB400TI, CB400TII, 1980 CB400T,		
CM400A, CM400T	29-39	22-29
Caliper mounting bolts		
CM400C, 1981 CM400T, 1982 CB400T,		
CM450A, CM450C		
Mounting bolt	30-40	22-29
Pivot bolt	25-30	18-22
Caliper mounting bolts and nuts		
1981 CM400C, 1981 CB400T, CM450A,		
CM450T, CB450T		
Upper pivot bolt	25-30	18-22
Lower mounting bolt	20-25	14-18
CB450SC		
Upper mounting nut	25-33	18-24
Lower mounting bolt	20-25	14-18

(continued)

Table 2 BRAKE TORQUE SPECIFICATIONS (continued)

Item	N•m	ft.-lb.
Rebel 450		
Lower mounting bolt	20-25	14-18
Pad retaining bolts	8-13	6-9
Caliper and master		
cylinder union bolt	22-29	30-40
Master cylinder clamp bolts	10-14	7-10
Brake disc mounting bolts		
1983-1986 CB450SC, Rebel 450	37-43	27-31
All other models	27-33	20-24

Table 3 DISC BRAKE SPECIFICATIONS*

Model	Standard	Service limit
Master cylinder		
CB400A, CB400T		
Bore I.D.	14.0-14.043 mm (0.5512-0.5529 in.)	14.055 (0.5533 in.)
Piston O.D.	13.957-13.984 mm (0.5495-0.5506 in.)	13.940 (0.5488 in.)
All CB450 and CM450 models		
Bore I.D.	14.0-14.043 mm (0.5512-0.5529 in.)	14.055 (0.5533 in.)
Piston O.D.	13.057-13.084 mm (0.5141-0.5151 in.)	13.945 (0.5490 in.)
Rebel 450		
Bore I.D.	12.7-12.743 mm (0.5000-0.5017 in.)	12.76 (0.502 in.)
Piston O.D.	12.657-12.684 mm (0.4983-0.4994 in.)	12.76 (0.502 in.)
Caliper		
CB400A, CB400T		
Cylinder I.D.	38.180-38.200 mm (1.5031-1.5039 in.)	38.212 (1.5045 in.)
Piston O.D.	38.115-38.180 mm (1.5006-1.5031 in.)	38.105 (1.5002 in.)
All CB450 and CM450 models		
Cylinder I.D.	30.230-30.306 mm (1.1902-1.1931 in.)	30.136 (1.1865 in.)
Piston O.D.	30.150-30.200 mm (1.1870-1.1890 in.)	30.142 (1.5002 in.)
Rebel 450		
Cylinder I.D.	30.230-30.280 mm (1.1902-1.1921 in.)	30.29 (1.193 in.)
Piston O.D.	30.148-30.198 mm (1.1869-1.1889 in.)	30.14 (1.187 in.)
Brake disc		
Thickness		
CB400A, CM400T	4.9-5.1 mm (0.19-0.20 in.)	4.0 mm (0.16 in.)
All CB450 and CM450 models, Rebel 450	4.8-5.2 mm (0.19-0.20 in.)	4.0 mm (0.16 in.)
Runout	0-0.1 mm (0-0.004 in.)	0.30 mm (0.01 in.)

*Honda does not provide specifications for all models.

11

CHAPTER TWELVE

FRAME AND REPAINTING

The frame does not require routine maintenance. However, it should be inspected immediately after any accident or spill.

This chapter describes procedures for completely stripping the frame. In addition, recommendations are provided for repainting the stripped frame.

This chapter also includes procedures for the center stand and sidestand.

Table 1 is at the end of this chapter.

CENTERSTAND

Removal/Installation

1. Block up the engine or support the bike on the kickstand.
2. Loosen the clamps securing the mufflers (A, **Figure 1**) to the collector and remove the bolts securing the rear footpegs and mufflers (B, **Figure 1**). Slide the mufflers out of the collector and remove them.
3. Remove rear wheel as described under *Rear Wheel Removal/Installation* in Chapter Ten.
4. Remove the front right-hand footpeg as described in this chapter.
5. Place the center stand in the raised position and disconnect the return spring and the C-shaped retaining ring from the frame.

6. Loosen the bolt and nut on the clamp holding the carburetor drain tubes and the battery breather tube (**Figure 2**).
7. Disconnect the brake rod (A, **Figure 3**) and the torque link (B, **Figure 3**) at the rear wheel.
8. On automatic transmission models, remove the parking brake cable (A, **Figure 4**) from the brake lever.
9. Remove the brake lever return spring (B, **Figure 4**).
10. Remove the bolt (C, **Figure 4**) and brake lever pivot bolt (D, **Figure 4**).
11. Loosen, but do not remove, the rear swing arm pivot bolt (E, **Figure 4**), pivot the cast bracket up and remove the brake lever and center stand.
12. Install by reversing the removal steps. Tighten the pivot bolt and nut to the torque specification listed in **Table 1**.

KICKSTAND

Removal/Installation

1. Block up the engine or support the bike on the center stand.
2. Disconnect the kickstand return spring (A, **Figure 5**) from the frame with Vise Grips. On models with automatic transmission, remove the safety switch spring (**Figure 6**).

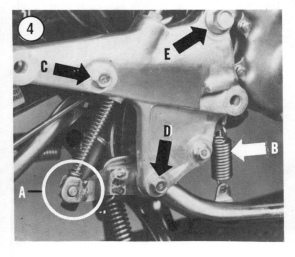

3. Remove the bolt (B, **Figure 5**) securing the kickstand to the frame tab. Remove the kickstand.

4. Install by reversing the removal steps. Apply a light coat of multipurpose grease to the pivot surfaces of the frame tab and the kickstand yoke before installation.

5. Tighten the bolt securely.

FOOTPEGS

Front Footpeg Replacement (Rebel 450)

1. To remove the right-hand footpeg, perform the following:

    a. Remove the bolt (A, **Figure 7**) securing the brake lever to the brake shaft.

    b. Remove the Allen bolts (B, **Figure 7**) securing the front footpegs to the frame.

    c. Remove the footpeg assembly.

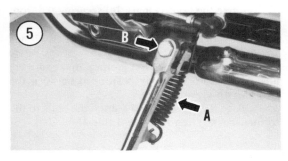

2. To remove the left-hand footpeg, perform the following:
   a. Remove the bolt (A, **Figure 8**) securing the shift lever to the shift shaft.
   b. Remove the Allen bolts (B, **Figure 8**) securing the front footpegs to the frame.
   c. Remove the footpeg assembly.
3. Tighten all bolts securely.

Rear Footpeg Replacement (Rebel 450)

Remove the Allen bolts securing the rear footpeg assembly (**Figure 9**) to the frame and remove the assembly.

Install the assembly and tighten all bolts securely.

Footpegs—Front and Rear (All Models Except Rebel 450)

1. Remove the bolts (**Figure 10**) securing the front and/or rear footpeg to the frame.
2. Remove the footpeg(s). The rear bolt also holds the muffler in place.
3. When installing the front footpeg, make sure the alignment tab is correctly positioned between the two lugs on the side plate.
4. Replace the footpegs and tighten the bolts to the torque specification listed in **Table 1**.

FRAME

The frame does not require periodic maintenance. However, all welds should be examined immediately after any accident, even a slight one.

Component Removal/Installation

1. Disconnect the negative battery cable. Remove the fuel tank, seat and battery.
2. Remove the engine as described in Chapter Four.
3. Remove the front wheel, steering and suspension components as described in Chapter Nine.
4. Remove the rear wheel and suspension components. See Chapter Ten.
5. Remove the lighting and other electrical equipment. Remove the wiring harness. See Chapter Eight and the wiring diagrams at the end of the book.
6. Remove the kickstand and center stand as described in this chapter.
7. Remove the bearing races from the steering head tube as described in Chapter Nine.

8. Check the frame for bends, cracks or other damage, especially around welded joints and areas which are rusted.
9. Assemble by reversing the removal steps.

Stripping and Painting

Remove all components from the frame. Thoroughly strip off all old paint. The best way is to have it sandblasted down to bare metal. If this is not possible, you can use a liquid paint remover like Strypeeze, or equivalent, and steel wool and a fine hard wire brush.

> *NOTE*
> *The side panels and chain guard (some models) are plastic. If you wish to change the color of these parts, consult an automotive paint supplier for the proper procedure.*

> *CAUTION*
> *Do not use any liquid paint remover on plastic components as it will damage the surface. The color is an integral part of the component, in most cases, and cannot be removed.*

When the frame is down to bare metal, have it inspected for hairline and internal cracks. Magnafluxing is the most common process.

Make sure that the paint primer is compatible with the type of paint you are going to use for the final coat. Spray one or two coats of primer as smoothly as possible. Let it dry thoroughly and use a fine grade of wet sandpaper (400-600 grit) to remove any flaws. Carefully wipe the surface clean with a dry, lint-free cloth and then spray the final coat. Use either lacquer or enamel and follow the manufacturer's instructions.

A shop specializing in painting will probably do the best job. However, you can do a surprisingly

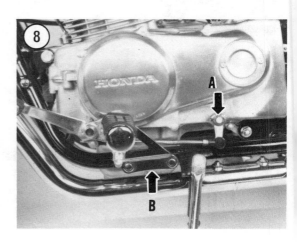

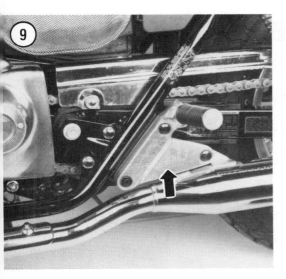

good job with a good grade of spray paint. Spend a few extra bucks and get a good grade of paint as it will make a difference in how well it looks and how long it will stand up. One trick in using spray paints is to first shake the can thoroughly. When purchasing the spray paint, make sure the ball inside the can is loose. Don't buy the can if the ball is not loose. The ball is necessary to mix up the paint inside the can. Shake the can as long as is stated on the can. Then immerse the can upright in a pot or bucket of warm water (not hot—not over 100° F).

WARNING
Higher temperatures could cause the can to burst. Do not place the can in direct contact with any flame or heat source.

Leave the can in for several minutes. When thoroughly warmed, shake the can again and spray the frame. Several light mist coats are better than one heavy coat. Spray painting is best done in temperatures of 21-26° C (70-80° F); any temperature above or below this will give you problems.

After the final coat has dried completely, at least 48 hours, any overspray or orange peel may be removed with a light application of rubbing compound and finished with polishing compound. Be careful not to rub too hard as you may go through the finish.

Finish off with a couple of good coats of wax before reassembling all the components.

Table 1 FRAME TORQUE SPECIFICATIONS

Item	N·m	ft.-lb.
Centerstand pivot bolt	54-69	40-51
Footpeg bolts		
All models except Rebel 450	45-64	33-47
Gearshift pedal arm bolt		
Rebel 450	10-14	7-10

12

INDEX

A

Alternator 107-112, 236-237

B

Battery 27-29
Brakes
  bleeding the system 400-402
  brake disc 390-391
  draining the system 399-400
  drum brake inspection,
    front and rear 349
  front brake hose
    replacement 391-399
  front caliper 379-390
  front disc brake 349-352
  front disc brake pad
    replacement 353-365
  front drum brake 346-348
  front master cylinder 365-379
  maintenance 43-45
  rear drum brake 348-349
  troubleshooting 24

C

Capacitor discharge ignition
  (CDI) system 239-243
Carburetor
  adjustments 212-214
  disassembly/assembly 201-212
  idle adjustment 63
  operation 198
  removal/installation 199-201
  service 198-199
Centerstand 404
Choke cable replacement 215-216
Clutch
  assembly/installation 153-155
  cable 155
  removal/disassembly 147-153
Charging system 233-236

E

Electrical system
  alternator 236-237
  charging system 233-236
  clutch switch 265
  fuses 267
  horn 265
  ignition coil 244-245
  ignition system (CDI) 239-243
  instrument cluster 266
  lighting system 257-265
  sidestand switch 265
  speedometer and indicator
    panel 266-267
  starter solenoid 254-257
  starting system 246-254
  voltage regulator/
    rectifier 237-239
Engine
  alternator 107-112
  break-in 140
  camshaft chain tensioner 98-99
  crankcase and balancer
    system 120-128
  crankshaft and connecting
    rods 128-133
  cylinder 99-102
  cylinder head, camshaft and rocker
    arm assemblies
    (1978-1981) 74-81
  cylinder head, camshaft and rocker
    arm assemblies (1982-on) 81-90
  electric starter gears 133-134
  kickstarter, automatic
    transmission 136-140
  kickstarter, manual
    transmission 134-135
  noises 23
  oil cooler (1982-on except
    Rebel 450) 118-119
  oil pressure relief
    valve 119-120
  oil pump 112-118

performance 22-23
piston, piston pins and piston
    rings 102-107
removal/installation 72-74
servicing engine in frame 68
starting 21-22
troubleshooting 21-24
valves and valve
    components 90-98
vibration 23
Evaporative emission control system
(1985-on California
models only) 223-226
Exhaust emission control system
(1986 CB450SC California
models only) 226
Exhaust system
    except Rebel 450 226-228
    Rebel 450 228-230

F

Fasteners 5-7
Footpegs 405-406
Frame 406-407
Fuel system
    carburetor 198-214
    crankcase breather system
        (1986-on U.S. only) 220-222
    fuel filter 220
    fuel shutoff valve 216-218
    fuel tank 218-220
    gasoline/alcohol blend test 220
Fuses 267

G

Gasoline/alcohol blend test 220
Gearshift drum and fork 193-195
Gearshift mechanism, external 155-159

H

Horn 265
Hub, front 275-281
Hub, rear
    inspection 320-321
    1978-1981 spoke wheel 321-323
    Rebel 450 spoke wheel, ComStar
        and ComCast wheel 323-326

I

Ignition coil 244-245
Ignition system 239-243
Instrument cluster 266

K

Kickstand 404-405
Kickstarter
    automatic transmission 136-140
    manual transmission 134-135

L

Lighting system 257-265
Lubricants 8
Lubrication 23-24, 29-38

M

Maintenance
    battery 27-29
    checks, routine 25-26
    periodic 38-54
    pre-checks 25
    service intervals 26
    tires and wheels 26-27
Master cylinder, front brake
    1978-1983 365-372
    1985-on 373-379

O

Oil cooler 118-119, 195
Oil pressure relief valve 119-120
Oil pump 112-118
Operating requirements 19-20

S

Safety 2, 15-16
Serial numbers 9
Service hints 2-4
Service intervals 26
Shift mechanism, internal
    automatic transmission 190-193
    manual transmission 160, 172-177
Spark plugs 57-60
Speedometer and indicator
    panel 266-267
Starter solenoid 254-257
Starting system 246-254

13

Steering
    handlebars 286-291
    steering head and stem 290-296
    steering head bearing races
       (all models) 296-297
    troubleshooting 24
Suspension, front
    air-assist front forks 308-315
    fork inspection (all models) 316
    front forks 297
    front hub 275-281
    front wheel 270-275
    non-air assist
       front forks 297-308
    tire changing 284-286
    troubleshooting 24
    wheels 282-284
Suspension, rear
    drive chain 330-331
    driven sprocket assembly 326-330
    rear hub 320-326
    rear shock absorbers 331-335
    rear wheel 319-320
    swing arm 335-344

T

Throttle cable replacement 214-215
Tire changing 284-286
Tires and wheels 26-27,
Tools 9-14
Torque converter 180-183
Torque specifications 4-5
Transmission, automatic
    countershaft 186-190
    gearshift drum and fork 193-195

installation 184-185
mainshaft and statorshaft 186
removal 183-184
shift mechanism,
    internal 190-193
troubleshooting 24
Transmission, manual
    installation 161-164
    5-Speed 164-167
    removal 160
    shift mechanism, internal 160, 172-177
    6-Speed 167-172
    troubleshooting 24
Troubleshooting
    brake problems 24
    emergency 20-21
    front suspension and steering 24
    lubrication troubles 23-24
    transmission, automatic
       and manual 24
Tune-up 54-63
    carburetor idle adjustment 63
    compression test 56-57
    spark plugs 57-59

V

Valves and valve components 90-98
Voltage regulator/
    rectifier 237-239

W

Wheels 282-284

NOTES

NOTES

1978 CB400 T1 Hawk Type I

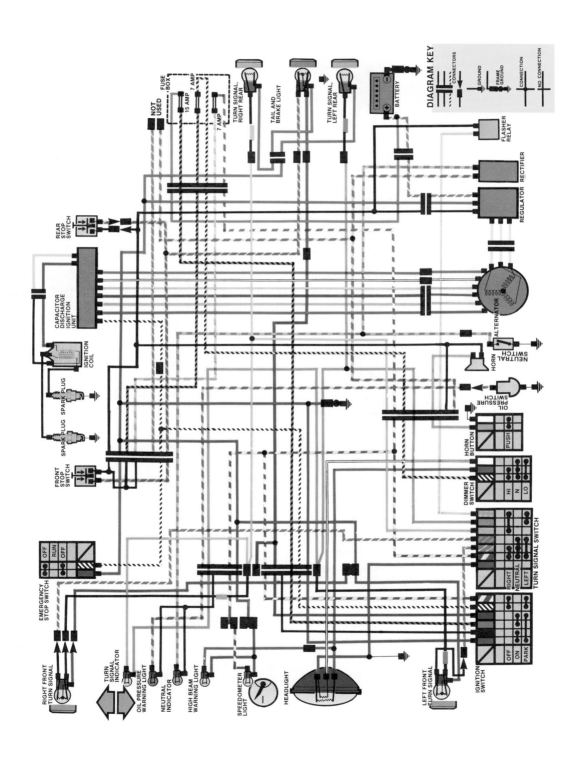

1

1978-1979 CB400T2 Hawk Type II

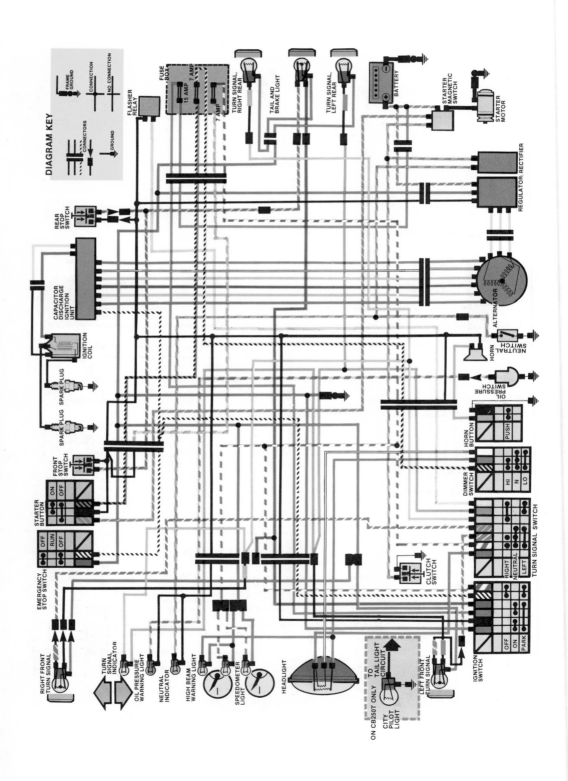

1978 CB400A

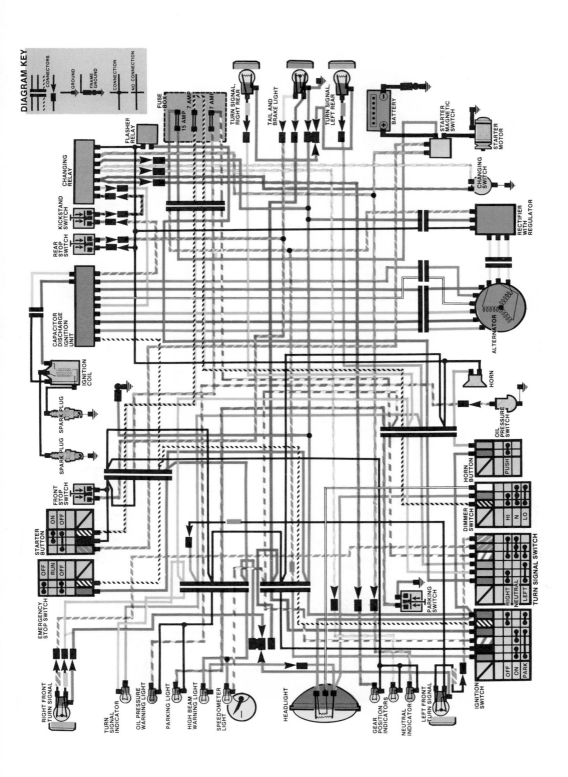

1980 CB400T

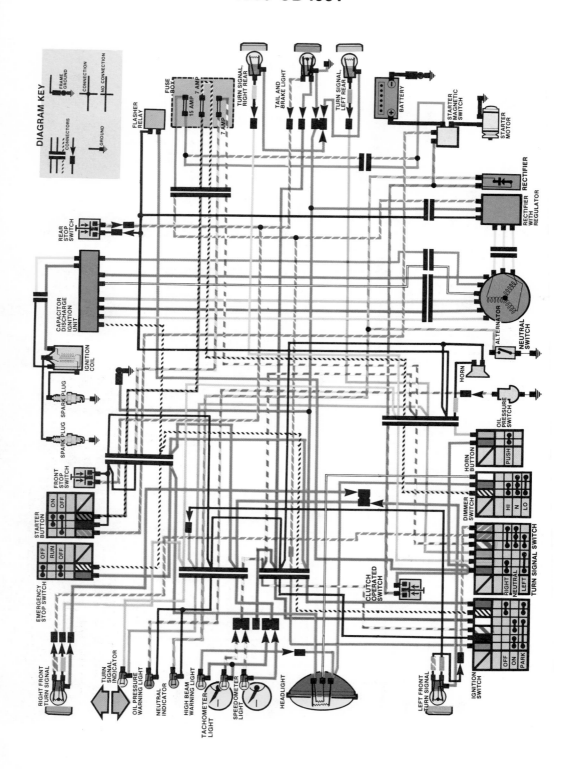

1979-1981 CM400A

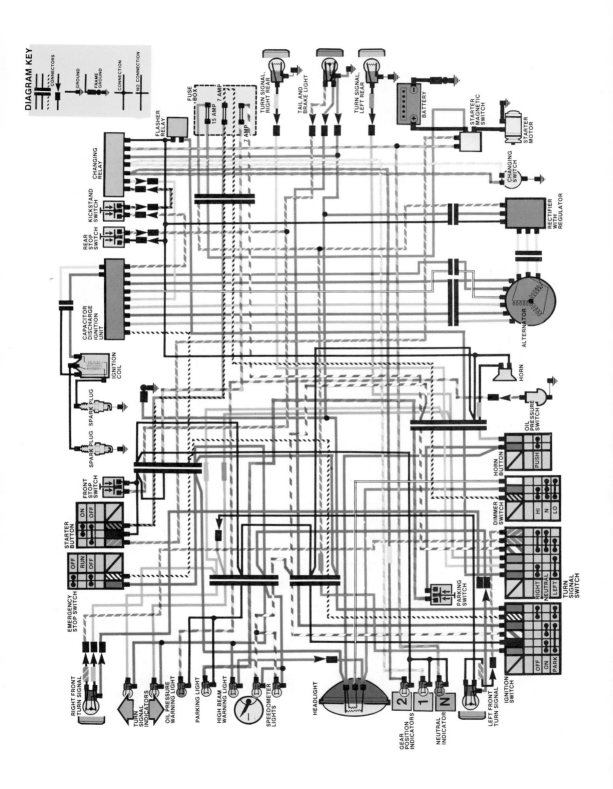

1979-1980 CM400T & 1980-1981 CM400E

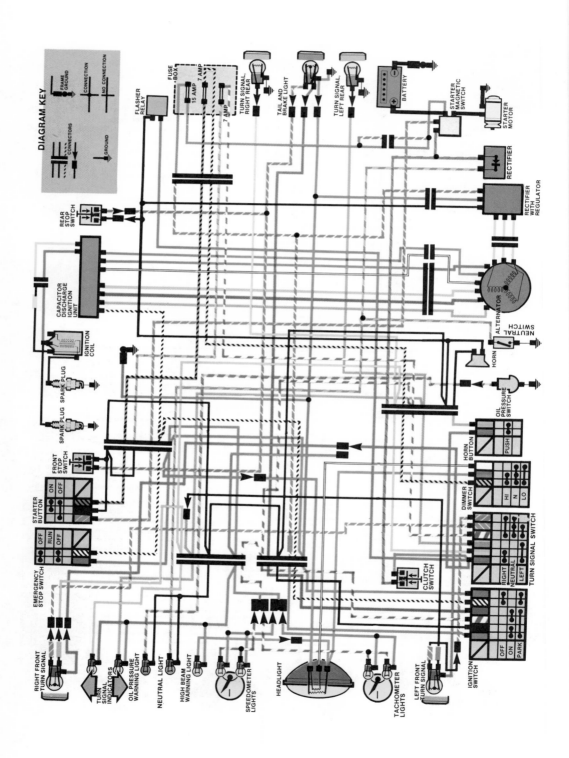

1981 CM400C & CM400T

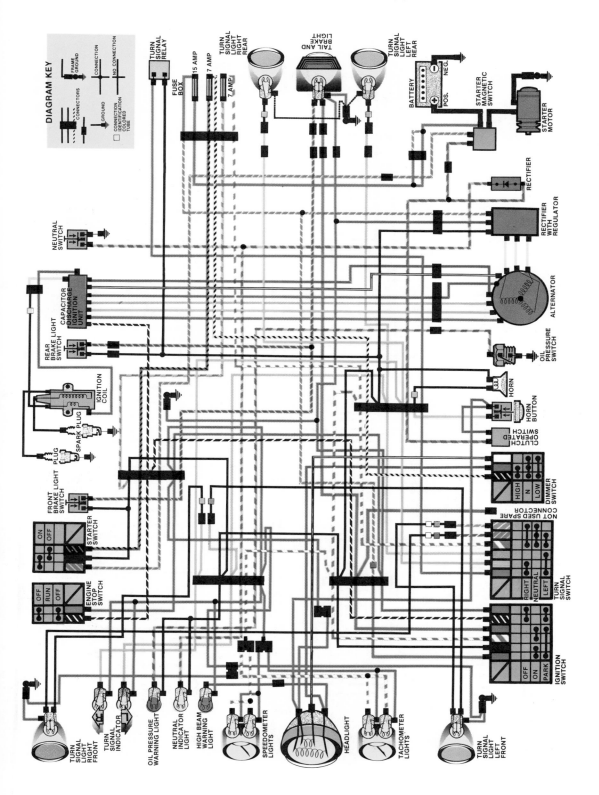

1982 CB450T

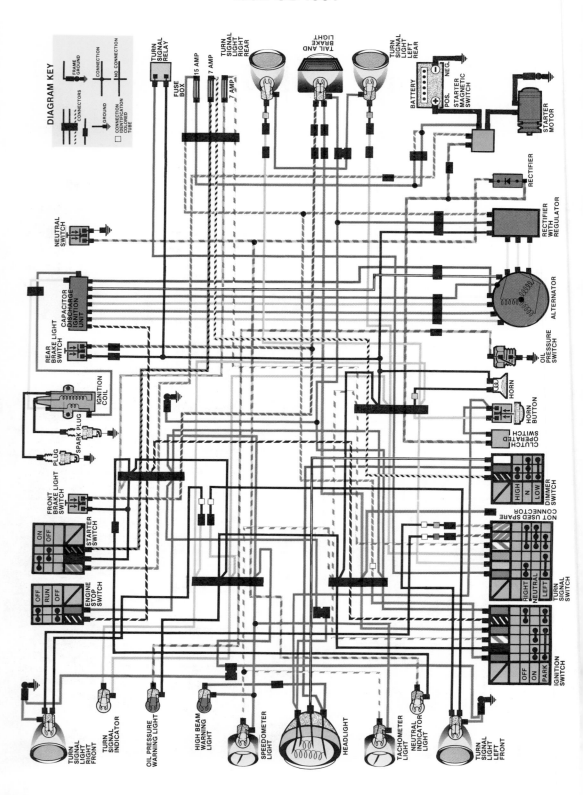

1982-1983 CB450SC Nighthawk
1985 CB450SC

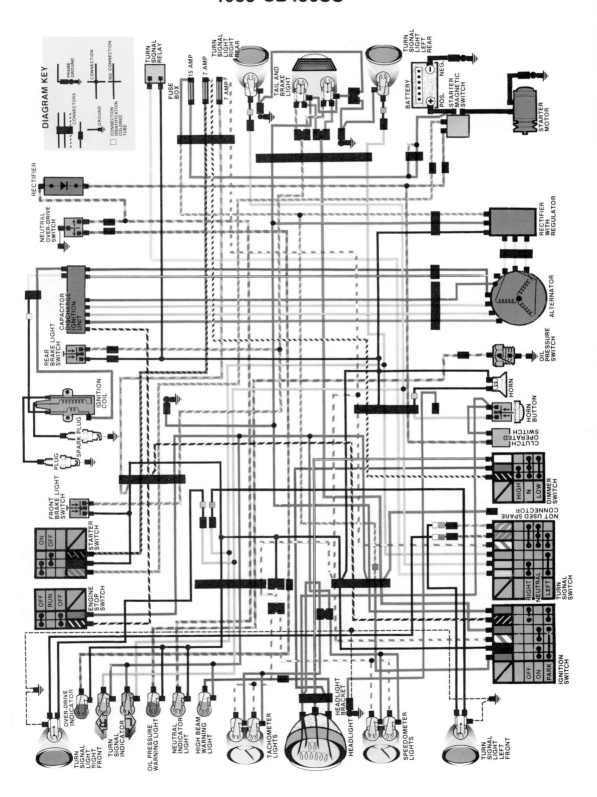

9

1982-1983 CM450A

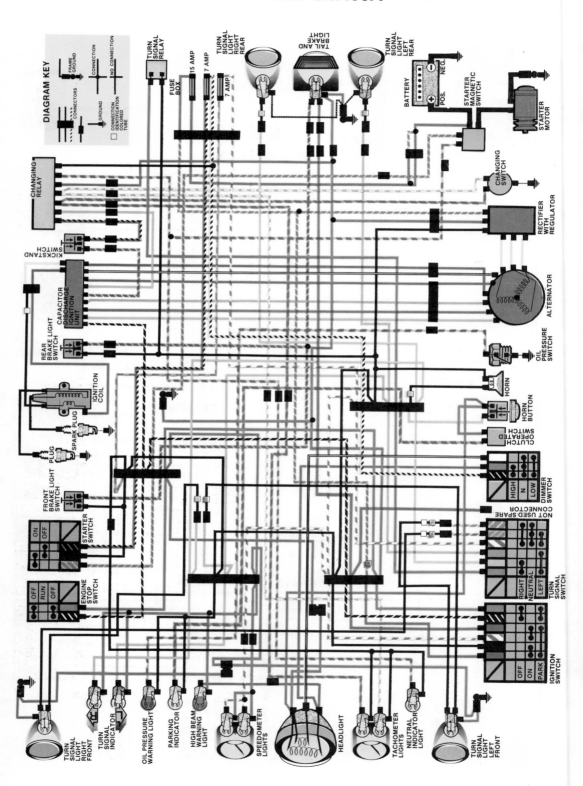

1982 CM450C

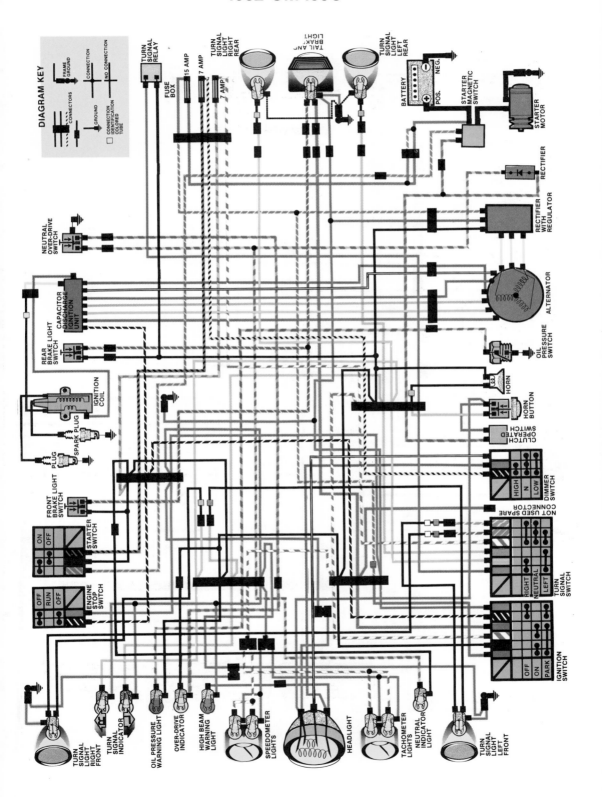

1986 CB450SC

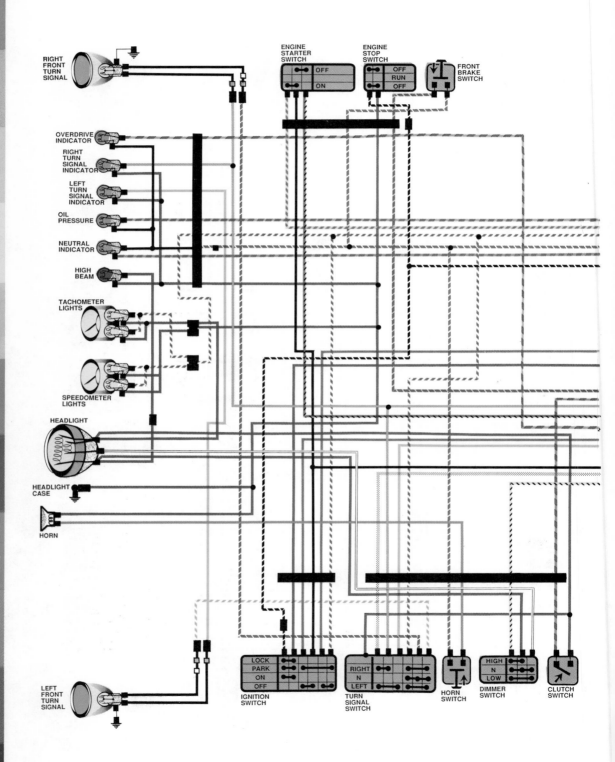

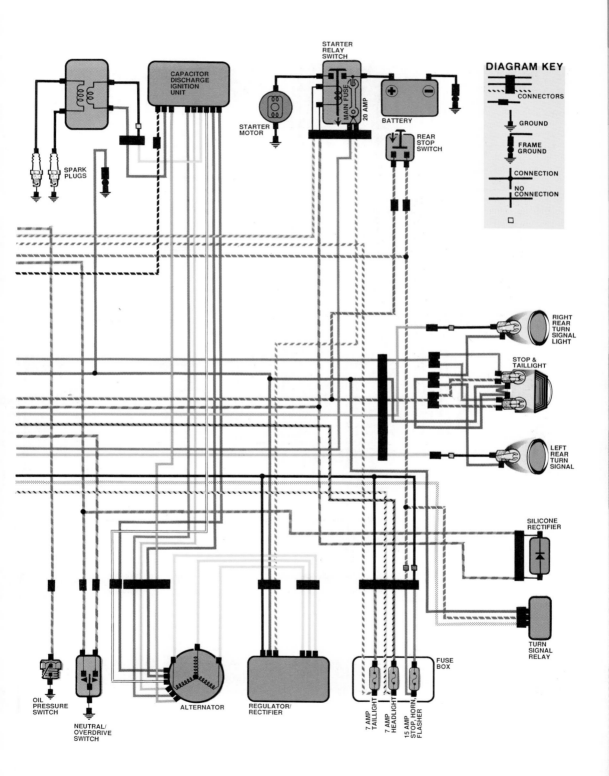

STARTER
RELAY
SWITCH

CAPACITOR
DISCHARGE
IGNITION
UNIT

STARTER
MOTOR

MAIN FUSE
20 AMP

BATTERY

REAR
STOP
SWITCH

SPARK
PLUGS

DIAGRAM KEY

CONNECTORS

GROUND

FRAME
GROUND

CONNECTION

NO
CONNECTION

RIGHT
REAR
TURN
SIGNAL
LIGHT

STOP &
TAILLIGHT

LEFT
REAR
TURN
SIGNAL

SILICONE
RECTIFIER

TURN
SIGNAL
RELAY

OIL
PRESSURE
SWITCH

NEUTRAL/
OVERDRIVE
SWITCH

ALTERNATOR

REGULATOR/
RECTIFIER

7 AMP
TAILLIGHT

7 AMP
HEADLIGHT

15 AMP
STOP, HORN,
FLASHER

FUSE
BOX

1986-1987 CMX450C

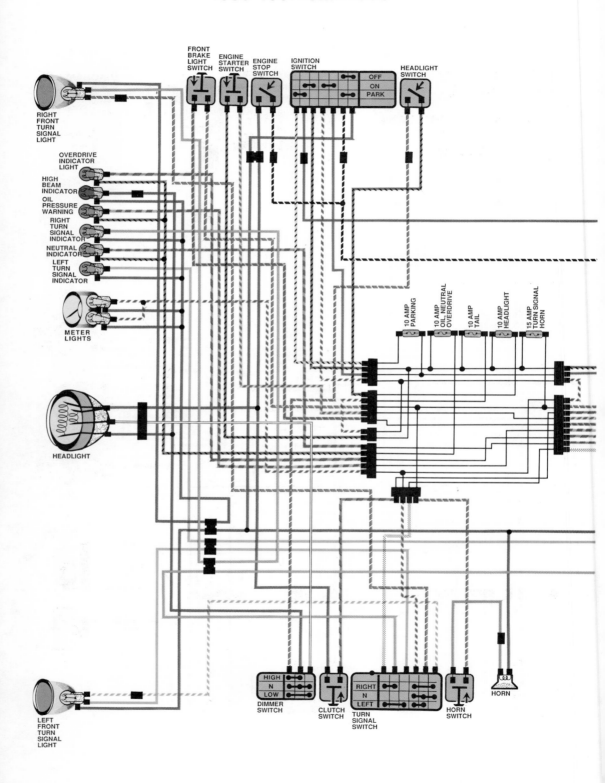

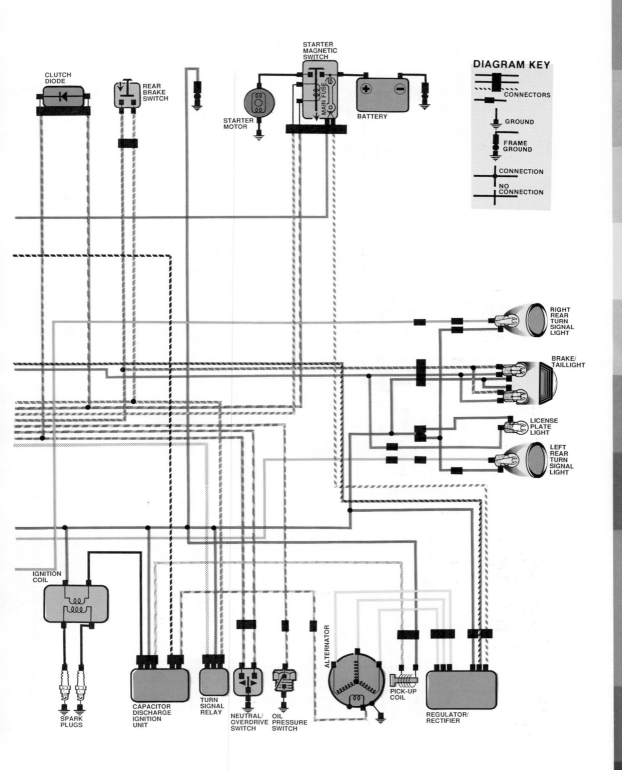

DIAGRAM KEY

CONNECTORS

GROUND

FRAME GROUND

CONNECTION

NO CONNECTION

CLUTCH DIODE

REAR BRAKE SWITCH

STARTER MAGNETIC SWITCH

STARTER MOTOR

MAIN FUSE

BATTERY

RIGHT REAR TURN SIGNAL LIGHT

BRAKE/ TAILLIGHT

LICENSE PLATE LIGHT

LEFT REAR TURN SIGNAL LIGHT

IGNITION COIL

SPARK PLUGS

CAPACITOR DISCHARGE IGNITION UNIT

TURN SIGNAL RELAY

NEUTRAL/ OVERDRIVE SWITCH

OIL PRESSURE SWITCH

ALTERNATOR

PICK-UP COIL

REGULATOR/ RECTIFIER

15

1982-1983 CM450E

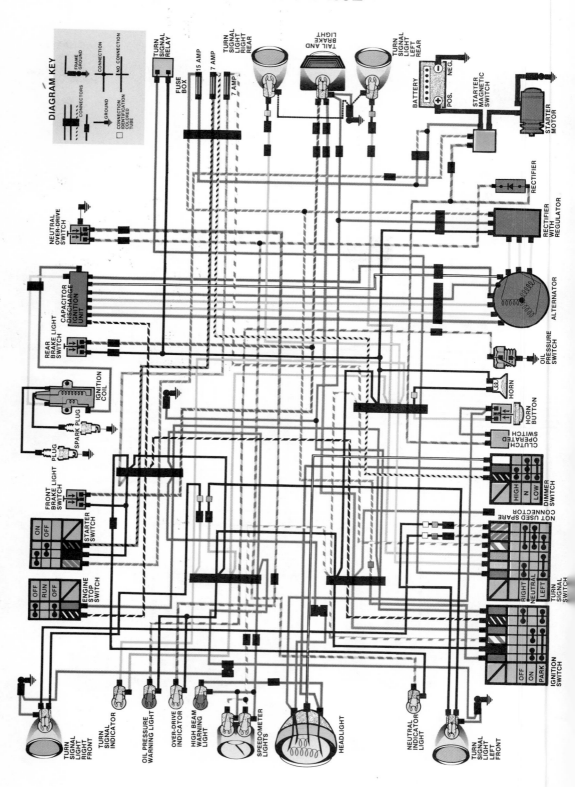